CHINA AND THE ASIA PA Y

CHINA AND THE ASIA PACIFIC ECONOMY

Edited by

Joseph C.H. Chai
Y.Y. Kueh
Clement A. Tisdell

NOVA SCIENCE PUBLISHERS, INC.
Commack, NY

Editorial Production: Susan Boriotti
Assistant Vice President/Art Director: Maria Ester Hawrys
Office Manager: Annette Hellinger
Graphics: Frank Grucci
Acquisitions Editor: Tatiana Shohov
Book Production: Ludmila Kwartiroff, Christine Mathosian,
Joanne Metal and Tammy Sauter
Circulation: Iyatunde Abdullah, Cathy DeGregory, and Maryanne Schmidt

Library of Congress Cataloging-in-Publication Data
available upon request

ISBN 1-56072-523-0

6080 Jericho Turnpike, Suite 207
Commack, New York 11725
Tele. 516-499-3103 Fax 516-499-3146
E-Mail: Novascience@earthlink.net
Web Site: http://www.nexusworld.com/nova

Printed in the United States of America

CONTENTS

LIST OF FIGURES

LIST OF TABLES

PREFACE

This volume draws together a number of papers specifically prepared for an international conference on China and the Asian Pacific Economy which was jointly organised by the Economics Department of the University of Queensland, the Chinese Economic Studies Association (Australia) and the Centre for Asian Pacific Studies at Lingnan College, Hong Kong and held in Brisbane, Australia, 14-17 June 1996. All papers have been revised and updated during 1996/97 in the light of comments made at the conference and by the referees as well as to take account of recent developments in China's economic relationships with the other Asian Pacific economies. We believe that the volume provides a timely and insightful examination of the key issues involved and sheds light on the possible directions of change in the years to come in the economic role China plays within the broader Asia Pacific region.

We would like to thank the various sponsors who have given valuable financial and organisational support to the original conference:

AusAID
Australia-China Council
Centre for Pacific Law and Business, Victoria University of Wellington, New Zealand
Lingnan College, Hong Kong
Commonwealth Bank
Embassy of the People's Republic of China (Australia)
Hong Kong Society of Asia Pacific 21
Queensland Chamber of Commerce and Industry
TEMTAC Pty Ltd (Economic Consultants, PO Box 79, Corinda, Qld 4075)
The National Centre for Development Studies, Australian National University, and
The Economic Society of Australia (Queensland) Inc

We would like to extend our deepest appreciation to Miss Margaret Cowan for her valuable assistance through out the entire project; to Mrs Robyn McDonald and Mrs Barbara Dempsey for typesetting the manuscript and to all the conference participants , without whose sharp insights and diligent efforts this volume would not have been possible.

Our special gratitude goes to Dr. Brian Bridges who has graciously helped to make many of the chapters much more readable and skilfully summarised the major findings of each chapter for the Introduction Chapter. We are also grateful to Dr. Raymond C.W.

Ng, of the Centre for Asian Pacific Studies at Lingnan College, for all his painstaking organisational work in bringing together the various Lingnan contributions for both the original conference and this book project.

Joseph C.H. Chai, Y.Y. Kueh, Clem Tisdell

LIST OF CONTRIBUTORS

Hans Blomqvist
Stockholm School of Economics
University of Helsinki
Helsinki, Finland

Katherine Braun
College of Commerce
University of Saskatchewan
Saskatchewan, Canada

Colin Brown
Department of Agriculture
University of Queensland
Brisbane, Australia

Brian Bridges
Department of Politics and Sociology
Lingnan College
Tuen Mun, Hong Kong

Joseph C.H. Chai
Department of Economics
University of Queensland
Brisbane, Australia

Yuk-shing Cheng
Department of Economics
Hong Kong Baptist University
Kowloon, Hong Kong

Kui-yin Cheung
Department of Economics
Lingnan College
Tuen Mun, Hong Kong

Harley Dale
Department of Economics
Research School of Pacific and Asian Studies
Australian National University
Canberra, Australia

Shengliang Deng
College of Commerce
University of Saskatchewan
Saskatchewan, Canada

Steve Harrison
Department of Economics
University of Queensland
Brisbane, Australia

C. Simon Fan
Department of Economics
Lingnan College
Tuen Mun, Hong Kong

Y.C. Jao
School of Economics and Finance
University of Hong Kong
Hong Kong

Neil D. Karunaratne
Department of Economics
University of Queensland
Brisbane, Australia

Noor Aini Khalifah
Faculty of Economics
National University of Malaysia
Kuala Lumpur, Malaysia

Y.Y. Kueh
Faculty of Social Sciences
Lingnan College
Tuen Mun, Hong Kong

Kai-cheong Lei
Department of Economics
Lingnan College
Tuen Mun, Hong Kong

Mohammad Haflah Piei
Faculty of Economics
National University of Malaysia
Kuala Lumpur, Malaysia

Bala Ramasamy
School of Applied and International Economics
Massey University
Palmerston North, New Zealand

Paul Riethmuller
Department of Economics
University of Queensland
Brisbane, Australia

Kartik C. Roy
Department of Economics
University of Queensland
Brisbane, Australia

Elspeth Thomson
Department of Economics
Lingnan College
Tuen Mun, Hong Kong

Clem A. Tisdell
Department of Economics
University of Queensland
Brisbane, Australia

Shu-ki Tsang
Department of Economics
Lingnan College
Tuen Mun, Hong Kong

Thomas Voon
Department of Economics
Lingnan College
Tuen Mun, Hong Kong

Xiangdong Wei
Department of Economics
Lingnan College
Tuen Mun, Hong Kong

Yushan Zhai
Academy of Sciences
Beijing, China

INTRODUCTION

INTRODUCTION

Y.Y. Kueh

The Asia Pacific region's enviable economic record, which saw it become the world's fastest growing region since 1965, is certain to be repeated again by the time this decade, the 1990s, ends. This dynamic economic activity, centering around flows of trade, aid, investment and technology, has in turn encouraged ideas of greater regional economic cooperation and integration. While slower off the mark than the Europeans in developing these kinds of concepts and institutions, during the 1990s the countries of the Asia Pacific region has been showing increasing interest in such regional cooperation. A number of organisations and concepts have been advocated and established, but the most prominent and the most comprehensive is the Asia Pacific Economic Cooperation (APEC) process, launched on an Australian initiative in 1989. Membership has grown from the initial 12 to currently 18 countries on both sides of the Pacific; a long waiting list of applicants now exists. It has also steadily moved from a loose consultative forum to an organisation with regular ministerial and summit-level meetings, a secretariat and an ambitious set of targets for economic liberalisation and cooperation.

APEC is of course marked by great diversity amongst its members in terms of economic weight and structure, geographical size, population, political systems, cultural and ethnic backgrounds. It is clear that within APEC China, by virtue of its sheer size and rapid economic growth in recent years, has become a major player. When China first joined APEC in 1991, together with Taiwan and Hong Kong, it kept a rather low profile, but its enhanced economic standing has made it an increasingly important factor in the future development of intra-regional trade and investment and of APEC itself as an institution. This book draws on expertise from around the Asia Pacific region to analyse the crucial role that China is now playing within APEC and with individual member economies.

The first part of this book contains two broad overview chapters, setting the Chinese economy within the context of the region's economic situation and APEC's development. Bala Ramasamy introduces the history and evolution of APEC itself over the last decade, showing how it has moved to regularise its meetings and adopt the 'Action Agenda' with targets for free and open trade and investment within the region by the years 2010 and 2020. He then goes on to demonstrate how important this process is for China, whose economic interdependence with the region is growing, particularly while China's application to join the World Trade Organisation (WTO) is still stalled. Y.Y. Kueh also examines the overall role of China within APEC, but more specifically in terms of stimulating trade and related investment flows with the Asian members of APEC. He argues that the rapidly developing economic integration amongst the 'Greater China' economies (China, Hong Kong and Taiwan) and China's still strong economic ties with Japan and the United States (and to a lesser extent Western Europe) has meant a Chinese emphasis on what he describes as the 'northern' part of APEC rather than on the 'southern' APEC members (the countries of the Association of Southeast Asian Nations - ASEAN - and Australasia). However, he holds out the prospect that as China joins Japan as the critical economic core of the region, the southern APEC members will be drawn in and the dream of an APEC free trade bloc could become a reality.

The second part of the book examines in detail some of the aspects of the 'Greater China' concept raised by Y.Y. Kueh. As most of the chapters emphasise, Hong Kong has played a crucial role in the evolution of the 'Greater China' phenomenon. Shu-ki Tsang and Yuk-shing Cheng discuss the nature of the extensive integration between the economies of Hong Kong and southern China, especially Guangdong province, where huge numbers of Hong Kong enterprises have now invested, resulting in the popularly-used phrase of 'shop at the front (Hong Kong), factory at the back (Guangdong)'. While paying tribute to the market-driven nature of this transfer and to the commercial benefits accrued to both sides, they also carefully consider some of the negative side-effects and argue that a more balanced development, which ideally might include even a certain distancing of the two economies, may actually be more beneficial to both economies in the longer term. Two chapters analyse further the nature of this trade and industrial integration between Hong Kong and Guangdong through examining the outward processing trade. Harley Dale shows not only that the majority of Hong Kong-Guangdong trade is indeed taken up by outward processing trade but also that a significant proportion of total outward processing trade is also intra-industry trade, particularly for products such as electronics, textile and clothing, and toys. He finds empirical evidence which suggests that there is indeed a market integration process going on. Kui-yin Cheung's chapter specifically examines how this outward processing trade and investment has affected Hong Kong's own industrial structure. He notes the declining contribution of manufacturing to Hong Kong's gross domestic product (GDP) and argues that, although the outward investment and cross-border production have helped to prolong the life-cycle of labour-intensive production, they have contributed little, if anything, to the upgrading of manufacturing industries within Hong Kong.

One of Hong Kong's key roles has been to act as a financial centre for China and the region. Indeed, as Y.C. Jao argues, Hong Kong has become par excellence the international financial centre for 'Greater China' because of its economic freedom, political neutrality, and unrivalled record of national treatment and reciprocity - it has in effect become a financial entrepot. Provided that China carries out its promises after the July 1997 handover, then he does not see any of the potential rivals (Shanghai, Taipei and Singapore) as being able to supplant Hong Kong's pre-eminent role as the financial centre for the 'Greater China' region.

In recent years China has attracted a massive amount of foreign investment and, although Hong Kong entrepreneurs have been the most active in investing there, they are not of course the only ones. Simon Fan adopts the transaction cost approach to examine the broader flows of investment into China not just from Hong Kong but also from Taiwan, overseas Chinese elsewhere in Asia, and from the West. He shows that, although western companies can reduce transaction costs through flexible contractual forms such as joint ventures, the overseas Chinese have a competitive advantage in investing in China through the commonality of language and culture and their experience of relationship-based trade systems. Whereas Kui-yin Cheung had examined the role of economic links with China in Hong Kong's structural transformation, the chapter by Kai-cheong Lei looks at the way in which increasing trade with and investment in China has affected the Taiwanese economy. He is particularly concerned with the impact of investments and exports to mainland China; in 1993, he calculates, about 2% of Taiwan's GDP could be attributed to that activity. Wage income and non-wage income was positively affected across all major sectors of the economy.

China's economic modernisation since the late 1970s has been founded on the open door policy. This means opening doors not just to the immediate neighbours of Hong Kong and Taiwan, but also to other parts of the Asia Pacific region. Part three examines China's relations with Northeast Asia, namely Japan and the two Koreas. Elspeth Thomson examines trends in Japanese exports, investment and technology transfer since the early 1980s. She argues that over this period although the trends in Japanese exports and investment to China were erratic, mainly due to political factors within China, generally speaking the growth rates of exports have been slowing down but the investment growth rates have been increasing; she notes that investment does not appear to have been an influencing factor on manufacturing exports. Although Japan has been criticised for not transferring the most 'modern' technology to China, She argues that the increase in Japanese-supervised production, using Japanese technology and expertise, within China does benefit China. Brian Bridges examines the changing nature of China's economic relations with the troubled Korean peninsula in the 1990s, as China has shifted from an exclusive relationship with its ailing socialist ally North Korea, whose stumbling economy requires Chinese aid, to a new more balanced one including South Korea, which is becoming and increasingly important trading and investment partner for China. He also discusses the Tumen River development plan, which is still far from achieving anything like the economic linkages found in the Pearl River delta region.

Part four discusses China's economic relations with the countries of Southeast Asia, in particular the main economies of the ASEAN grouping. The key question examined by both chapters is how far China and ASEAN are in direct competition with each other, both in attracting inward investment and in exporting to third markets. Noor Aini Khalifah and Mohammad Haflah Piei show that the developed country markets of the United States, Japan and Western Europe are important for both China and ASEAN and that there is indeed competition in certain manufactured product exports, but they argue that as intra-industry trade develops within the region (in part stimulated by investment flows) their economies should become more complementary than competing. Thomas Voon and Xiangdong Wei focus directly on the US market as a case study. Using market share models, they show a comparatively strong level of competition for exports to the US market amongst China, Singapore and Malaysia. Due to its low wage rates and lowered exchange rate, China was gaining export share in the US market at the expense of all the ASEAN economies studied.

The final part of the book examines China's relations with other, non-Asian, members of APEC. Five chapters deal with Australia's trade relations with China. H.C. Blomqvist and K.C. Roy show that Australia's trade with China has grown since the early 1980s, but the export growth has been modest and the trade balance has actually shifted to a deficit. Their aggregate analysis suggests there is not any unutilised export potential in the merchandise trade, but they argue that Australia could well have a comparative advantage in the service sectors which could be exploited. Joseph C.H. Chai and Paul Riethmuller cover in more detail the record of Australian exporting of processed food to China. After suggesting that the 'westernisation' of Chinese tastes in food may be a myth, they do show that Australia has been losing market share in China to competing US companies, whose relative price competitiveness and greater investment inside China seem to have given them the edge.

Colin Brown analyses the potential and tensions that arise in Sino-Australian wool trade. He demonstrates that it is essential for the Australian to have a thorough understanding of the socio-political factors of China's wool industry and a grasp of the nuances of Chinese decision making in order to formulate strategies that maximise the opportunities of Sino-Australian wool trade.

Increased import penetration by China in Australia has rekindled neo-protectionist policy sentiments recently in Australia. Neil Karunaratne 's chapter analyses the income distribution and employment impact of China's increased import penetration in Australia. His study finds that contrary to conventional wisdom Australia's increased imports of labour-intensive manufactures from China has neither led to a widening wage gap between the skilled and unskilled workers nor been a significant factor behind the high level of unemployment among its unskilled labour.

While the first four chapters in part five examine the trade relation between China and Australia, the chapter by Steve Harrison and Yushan Zhai looks at Australia's economic aid to China under the Development Import Finance Facility (DIFF) scheme administered by AusAID. They shows that the scheme has provided significant economic and environmental benefits for both countries.

APEC as a organisation for regional economic cooperation contains within it one long-standing sub-regional economic organisation - ASEAN - and one comparatively new structure, NAFTA, the North America Free Trade Area, consisting of the United States, Canada and Mexico. The chapter by Shengliang Deng and Katherine Braun examines, against the background of the lively debate about the pros and cons of regional economic arrangements, the nature of China's economic relations with the NAFTA group. They note the growing penetration of Chinese exports into the NAFTA markets, especially the United States, and argue that any move towards more protectionist sentiments within NAFTA will certainly impact adversely on China. The implications of their caveats on NAFTA's development - that open regionalism is to be preferred - can certainly be applied to the case of APEC as a whole.

Taken together, the chapters of this book address China's developing economic relationships with the individual Asia Pacific economies and the APEC bloc as a whole. The wide range of issues raised clearly points to the enormous complexity and volatility in both bilateral and multilateral trade and investment relations within the region. The situation poses indeed, for both international economic and political analysts, an overwhelming intellectual challenge in observing and coming to grips with the possible direction and pattern of changes in intra-regional relations, leading up to, say, the APEC target of a fully-fledged trade and investment liberalisation by the year 2020.

Several important points should be made in relation to the changing context of China's economic interaction with the other Asia Pacific economies. The first point relates to the dynamic economic growth triangle comprising the Chinese Trio of Mainland China, Hong Kong, and Taiwan, which has, as a matter of fact, taken up the major portion of this study. With the return of Hong Kong to China on 1 July 1997, the legitimate question to be raised is whether the present pattern of economic integration will be altered, say, to the benefit of either or both of the two economic entities? And in what way might it change? This issue is certainly far more than a matter of academic curiosity. The expected convertibility of the renminbi (the Chinese currency), in terms of both current and capital accounts, for example, may throw serious doubt on the long-run viability of the "one-country two currencies" premises enshrined in the "one-country two systems" model for Hong Kong.[1] The situation with Taiwan is even more volatile and fundamental. Despite increased political tension, direct navigational and commercial links with the Chinese Mainland (banned on the part of Taiwan over past decades) were reestablished in early 1997. Modest as the initial scale of breakthrough may appear to be, there is no doubt that it will eventually bear most crucially on trade and investment flows across the Taiwan Straits.[2]

Secondly, China's economic relations with the United States and with Japan are equally in a state of flux. The former has increasingly been obsessed with mounting trade deficits with China and the latter has seen its trade surpluses of the past two or three decades

1 For a good discussion in this respect see S.K. Tsang (1997)

2 This is clearly implied in a wide ranging discussion in Y.W. Sung (1997)

dwindling rapidly in recent years, as a result of both the enormous Chinese export drive and a still highly protective Chinese import regime. Nonetheless, one may be able to count on a drastic reversal in the years to come, given the likely resolution of the long-standing Chinese bid to regain its membership of the World Trade Organisation, as this will oblige China to significantly open up its domestic market for foreign imports and direct investment, as well as for banking and financial services, on the basis of "national treatment".[3] Obviously, such a breakthrough can only help to further enhance China's economic linkages with APEC, but in particular with the entire northern APEC sphere.

The third issue deals with China's economic relations with Southeast Asia. The two relevant chapters of this book raise the issues of the ASEAN countries being possibly "crowded out" by China in the competitive North American export market. With or without WTO pressures, it is a bygone conclusion that the Chinese system of state control will inevitably give way to a full-scale marketisation of the Chinese economy in the new future. Coupled with an extensive decontrol of the large-scale state industrial enterprises, especially with respect to external trade decision-making, the day may not be too far away when China will emerge as a major industrial supplier to its Southeast Asian neighbours, while the latter may at the same time be drawn into the huge Chinese market to diversify their export outlets. Such a mutually reinforcing and complementing process of industrialisation does not appear to be at all a remote prospect, given the accumulated industrial strengths of the export-oriented small Asian dragons and the historical experience of European industrialisation.

Fourthly, will Australia and New Zealand be drawn onto the bandwagon of Asian dynamism as well? Or rather will they be marginalised as an Asian "output post" with their role confined to that of a peripheral mineral and foodstuffs supplier? The situation obviously remains a unsettled one.

The various chapters in this study represent a stock-taking exercise of the current pattern of China's economic interactions with other Asia Pacific economies. However, diverse as the perspectives and approaches adopted may be among the different chapters, they have all naturally touched upon, if only implicitly, the future implications of the changing overall context within which regional realignments of economic power are taking place. As such this book is not only meant to be a baseline study for gauging the possible extent of marginal changes in terms of trade, investment, and financial flows across the countries in the years to come. But more importantly, we hope to shed some light on the basic patterns and directions of intra-regional resource movements within the Asia Pacific context or even the broader global power constellation, as highlighted above.

A final note on politics is in order to render yet another real dimension to our intellectual discourse. While in the long- term positive economic fundamentals may well overwhelm short-run political intervention or even military conflict, there is little doubt that

3 See Y.Y. Kueh (1995) for a more detail discussion on the possible economic consequences in China of the country's admission to GATT/WTO.

such interrupting factors may sometimes significantly distort the desirable direction of change for a prolonged duration. Practical examples abound within the postwar context. The prolonged political and economic isolation of China from the West until its opening up in 1978/1979 is a good case in point. But it is obviously beyond the scope of this study to examine such possible complications.

REFERENCES

Y.Y. Kueh (1995), "GATT and its Consequences for the Transformation Process in the People's Republic of China", Dieter Cassel and Carsten Herrmaun-Pillath (eds). *The East, the West, and China's Growth: Challenge and Response*. Baden-Baden: Nomos Verlagsgesellschaft, pp. 309-334.

Y.W. Sung (1997), "The Implications of China's Admission to the WTO for Greater China", Y.Y. Kueh, *The Political Economy of Sino-American Relations: A Greater China Perspective*, Hong Kong: The University of Hong Kong Press, forthcoming.

Shu-ki Tsang (1997), "Towards the Full Convertibility of Renminbi?" Maurice Brosseau, Kuan Hsin-chi, Y.Y. Kueh, (eds.) *China Review 1997*, Hong Kong: The Chinese University Press, pp. 235-250.

PART I CHINA AND APEC

1. THE IMPORTANCE OF APEC TO CHINA

Bala Ramasamy

1. INTRODUCTION

The Asia Pacific Economic Co-operation (APEC) started out as an economic forum for nations around the Pacific Rim in 1989, through the efforts of the Australian Prime Minister Bob Hawke and academics, mainly from Japan and Australia. Since then, APEC has evolved into a powerful economic entity especially with the institutionalisation of the summit of leaders of member nations, this time through the efforts of US President Bill Clinton. APEC came to the limelight when the Uruguay Round was close to collapse. This instigated many like-minded nations to bond together to further the idea of free trade at a regional level. The North American Free Trade Area (NAFTA) and the ASEAN Free Trade Area (AFTA) were seriously considered during this time period. Similarly, APEC was considered, at that time, to be an avenue through which softer negotiations could take place. The impressive economic growth of Asian economies encouraged this consultation process since these economies had trade and investment as their engine for growth and liberalisation in these areas were paying off. For the US, Japan, Australia, Canada and New Zealand, any form of link with these high performing Asian economies will at the very least cause a spill-over effect on their own economies.

The sheer size of APEC warrants attention. Table 1.1 shows that APEC comprises 18 economies which controls 60 per cent of total world GDP in 1993 and nearly 40 per cent of the world population. Put together, these economies export 46 per cent of the world total and are responsible for 47 per cent of world imports. A large portion (between 70 and 80 per cent) of this trade occurs between these economies. They are also responsible for 46 to 47 per cent of total world foreign direct investment (FDI). Another important fact is that APEC includes China, the world's largest non-market economy. In this sense, APEC is probably one of the few trade organisation to include both market and non-market economies[1].

There is a symbiotic relationship between APEC and China. The membership of China means APEC has within its fold the three largest economies of the world. While it would take some time before China can challenge the economic might of Japan or the US, the market size of China will certainly be attractive to APEC members. The massive expansion of the Chinese economy provides other members of APEC with economic opportunities. For China, APEC is a means to return the fold of the world economy. China has had difficulties with other international forums like the GATT and even at times in the United Nations. APEC, however, has welcomed her with open arms. While this is so, China has so far remain a rather dormant member of APEC. It is the view of this chapter that China should be more active in APEC as this would facilitate China's easy entry into other international organisation, especially the World Trade Organisation (WTO)[2].

The chapter is set out in the following format. The evolution of APEC specifically from 1989 to 1995 is discussed in the next section. Key areas that stand in the way of China from becoming a member of the WTO is discussed in section three. In section four, the advantages and the need for active membership in APEC is provided. Finally a conclusion is extended.

2. THE EVOLUTION OF APEC, 1989 - 1995

The idea of economic co-operation among the Asia Pacific countries goes as far back as Kojima's (1971) proposal for a Pacific Free Trade Area (PAFTA). Soesastro (1994) calls Kojima's proposal as one of a reactionary one following integration in Europe. The idea of PAFTA was further modified by Kojima (1977) and Drysdale and Patrick (1979) following the OECD type of organisation i.e. a consultative forum rather than a full blown free trade area. A similar proposal was made in the form of the Pacific Basin Co-operation concept in 1980 by a Japanese Study Group which re-considers the various objections placed on Kojima's and Drysdale-Patrick's proposals. The suggestions of the Japanese Study Group were further discussed in a non-governmental seminar in Canberra in 1980. A Standing Committee called the Pacific Co-operation Committee was established. However, no government in the region volunteered to endorse it. The seminar at Canberra was followed by another seminar in Bangkok in 1982. To ensure that discussions on fostering greater consultation on the subject of economic co-operation continued, the seminar series were institutionalised into the Pacific Economic Co-operation Conference (PECC) which composed of a standing committee and four other study task forces. The establishment of

1 The other is ASEAN with the inclusion of Vietnam in 1995.

2 In fact, at the time of writing this paper, the China Trade News reported that China is shifting its lobbying efforts from membership in the WTO to gaining more recognition in APEC (The Evening Standard, 15 April 1996).

Table 1.1: APEC: Selected Economic Indicators, 1993

Country	GDP (US$ billion)	Population (million)	GDP per capita (US$)	GDP Growth (%)	Exports (US$ million)	Imports (US$ million)	Inward FDI (US$ million)	Outward FDI (US$ million)
Australia	310.0	17.66	17510	3.9	47572	53425	79709	29250
Brunei D.	4.0	2.68	15479	3.6	2140	1460	21	
Canada	512.4	27.30	17821	4.5	165376	155072	121665	87250
Chile	37.1	13.81	3070	4.3	11575	11825		
China	503.1	1198.50	490	11.8	121038	115693	29657	7401
Hong Kong	130.7	5.90	21800	5.5	151479	165894	15869	14015
Indonesia	126.4	179.19	650	6.3	40054	31983	42139	
Japan	4207.5	124.32	33764	-0.2	397005	275235	38720	250430
South Korea	328.7	44.06	7466	5.6	96013	102348	7095	4576
Malaysia	62.4	18.60	3275	8.0	58756	59581	22584	1469
Mexico	360.5	81.25	3893	0.4	60799	81472	37984	
New Zealand	44.7	3.59	12900	4.8	12181	11914	5749	4323
PNG	4.6	4.06	1120	1.1	2491	1299	2378	7
Philippines	66.3	65.78	961	5.1	13342	22531	2870	154
Singapore	68.7	2.93	20415	10.1	96826	102670	42073	6565
Taiwan	246.1	21.00	11604	6.5	92851	85519	11885	16443
Thailand	123.2	59.10	2300	8.4	45310	54520	12110	701
US	6738.4	248.71	27093	4.1	512521	689215	419526	488767
APEC	13875.1	2118.44	6550		1927329	2021656	892034	911563
World	23112.6	5501.50	4420		4215000	4333000	1948104	1932300
APEC/World	60 %	39 %			46 %	47 %	46 %	47 %

Source: UNCTAD, *World Investment Report 1994*; APEC Website: http://apec.tokio.co.jp

PECC and the principles that it advocated were crucial for APEC as PECC is considered the pre-cursor of APEC (Aggarwal, 1993).

While PECC was discussions primarily among businesses and academics, governments had on the main kept away from committing themselves to any output of the conferences. It was Australian Prime Minister Bob Hawke who first proposed the creation of a forum to promote greater economic co-operation in the Asia Pacific region at the governmental level, in 1989. The first APEC ministerial meeting was called for in the same year with twelve countries participating. Since 1989, annual ministerial meetings have taken place. In 1993, by invitation of US President Bill Clinton, APEC Informal Leaders' Meeting was initiated to add to the seriousness of co-operation and commitment to the APEC agenda. Since then, the leaders of member countries have continued the annual meeting, the last one being held in Osaka[3]. The main resolutions and important changes that took place at every meeting is briefly listed below:

First APEC Ministerial Meeting (November 1989 in Canberra)

- The basic principles of APEC was adopted. These are very similar to those suggested by PECC in 1982. The principles are:

    1. That APEC's objective is to sustain growth and development in the region and the world economy.
    2. That APEC favours an open multilateral trading system rather than a regional trading bloc.
    3. That APEC is an economic consultative body that encourages the free flow of goods, services, capital and technology.

Second APEC Ministerial Meeting (July 1990 in Singapore)

- Working groups on improving regional trade and investment data; enhancing technology transfer; development of human resources; promoting co-operation in energy, marine resources, telecommunication, transportation, tourism and fisheries were established.
- With the threat of failure in the Uruguay Round, the meeting endorsed the commitment of the region to a successful completion of the negotiations.
- The commitment for an open trading principle was re-emphasised but a non-discriminatory regional trade liberalisation was considered.

---

3 It is interesting to note that APEC's evolution is similar to that of ASEAN. In the case of ASEAN, the annual ministerial meeting was attended by foreign ministers. It was only in 1992 that the meetings of the heads of government were institutionalised.

Third APEC Ministerial Meeting (November 1991 in Seoul)

- China, Hong Kong and Taiwan were admitted into the organisation.
- An additional objective making it clear that APEC stands for reducing impediments to a freer flow of goods, services and investment in line with the principles of GATT was included.
- The scope of activity of APEC was re-emphasised.
- The mode of operation of APEC was clarified taking into account the different stages of economic development of member countries and their socio-political systems.
- The organisational structure of APEC consisting of an annual ministerial meeting, regular meetings of senior officials (SOM) and the various working groups were formally established.

Fourth APEC Ministerial Meeting (September 1992 in Bangkok)

- A permanent secretariat was agreed to be set up in Singapore (in January 1993) with the purpose of co-ordinating and assisting APEC's work projects, to facilitate communication between APEC members and to serve a public relations role.
- The APEC Central Fund was established.
- The Eminent Persons Group (EPG) was set up to identify the vision and constraints for APEC's regional trade liberalisation.
- Specific proposals to benefit businesses like the establishment of an electronic tariff database of APEC members, the harmonisation of customs procedures, an examination of administrative aspects of market access and the preparation of a guidebook on investment procedures in member countries were agreed on.

Fifth APEC Ministerial Meeting (November 1993 in Seattle)

- Mexico and Papua New Guinea were admitted into the organisation. Chile's membership was deferred to the following year and a three year moratorium for further membership was imposed.
- The report of the EPG was tabled and generally agreed. The SOM was asked to "develop pragmatic programmes" based on the recommendations of the EPG.
- A declaration on APEC Trade and Investment Framework was adopted. This framework established the APEC Committee on Trade and Investment whose objective was to "create a coherent APEC perspective and voice on global trade and investment" and to pursue and develop specific initiatives to facilitate a freer movement of goods, services, capital and technology.

First APEC Leaders Informal Meeting (November 1993 in Seattle)

- An Economic Vision Statement was issued which reaffirms APEC's support for a speedy conclusion of the Uruguay Round. It admits the diversity of APEC but promises to actively work together for the betterment of its people.
- The APEC Finance Ministers meeting was established to consult on macroeconomic development and capital flows.
- A Pacific Business Forum was established comprising of business leaders to identify issues that APEC should work on to increase regional trade and investment.
- The APEC Education Program and APEC Business Volunteer Programme were also established.

Sixth APEC Ministerial Meeting (November 1994 in Jakarta)

- A Declaration on Human Resource Development was endorsed.
- Infrastructure issues were highlighted.

Second APEC Leaders Informal Meeting (November 1994 in Bogor)

- The Declaration of Common Resolve was adopted.
- It agrees to spearhead economic co-operation in Asia Pacific by strengthening, enhancing and intensifying development co-operation especially in trade and investment.
- It adopts the long term goal of a free and open trade and investment in Asia-Pacific. This will be achieved by no later the 2010 for developed economies and 2020 for developing economies.
- The Declaration reiterates the co-operation which is required in the development of human resource, infrastructure, small and medium size enterprise and co-operation in the business sector.

Seventh APEC Ministerial Meeting (November 1995 in Osaka)

- The Action Agenda was agreed on.
- Structural issues of the agenda was consulted including the appointment of a Business Advisory Council (ABAC).
- The EPG was formally disbanded.
- The Partner for Progress scheme was introduced to promote economic and technical co-operation within APEC.

Third APEC Leaders Informal Meeting (November 1995 in Osaka)

- The Declaration of Common Resolve as adopted in Bogor entered the action phase. The Osaka Action Agenda was adopted.
- It identifies specific areas that will be pursued to enhance greater co-operation. The areas include the liberalisation and facilitation of trade and investment and economic and technical co-operation.
- The Agenda sets a list of principles which will guide the liberalisation process. It includes comprehensiveness; WTO consistency; comparability; non-discrimination; transparency; standstill; simultaneous start, continuous process and differentiated time tables; flexibility and co-operation. Concrete proposals based on these principles will be consulted in the Philippines in 1996 while the overall implementation will begin in January 1997.

Although the progress made by APEC is evident from the above, some skeptics still view APEC with caution. This is mainly due to the open-regionalism concept which is viewed as redundant (Watanabe, 1992; Inouchi and Terada, 1993) and the fear that APEC will move towards a trading bloc (Ariff, 1995).

3. MAJOR OBSTACLES TOWARDS CHINA'S ADMISSION IN THE WTO

The reluctance of a few members of the GATT to accept China into the organisation stems from a few unresolved issues. One major issue was due to the fact that China is not a market economy. Under such a situation other members of the organisation would need to compete on an unfair playing field with Chinese goods. The rationale here is that prices in a non-market economy would be artificially low compared to world prices. China's position on this issue is that since the implementation of its economic reforms and its position on a market economy based on socialistic principles, it has increasingly allowed market forces to determine prices. In fact, China claims that there is no economy in the world which is devoid of government intervention to reduce market failures (Feng and Chen, 1992). Even the World Bank (1993) admits that the high performing Asian economies have intervened into specific areas to stimulate growth. It must be noted further that admitting non-market economies like China into the WTO will make such organisations truly global especially with the emergence of China as the third largest economy in the world.

The second obstacle relates to the status of membership i.e. whether China should be admitted as a developing nation. China's position is clear: China should not be judged by the size of the economy but rather by the level of its economic development. With a per capita GDP of US$490 in 1993, China is still one of the poorer countries of the world. If China is accepted as a developed economy, certain trade practises need to be changed. For example, GATT forbids developed members to subsidise the export of manufactured products. This will immediately disadvantage China as it is at an early stage of the export promotion phase. It is the view of the Chinese officials that the export subsidies are to "compensate for an overvalued exchange rate and high domestic prices" (US Congress, March 1989). With the elimination of the dual foreign exchange rate system and the move to a swap market rate mechanism, subsidising exports will have to be gradually decreased[4].

Another obstacle that China faces is the issue of market access. First, concerns the extent of import tariffs. China's simple average tariff on all imports stands at 37.8 per cent while the weighted average is 16.7 per cent (Feng and Chen, 1992). Other reports like the Canadian Embassy (1995) put the average tariff at 40.1 per cent and the weighted average at 20 per cent. This is marginally below what is required by GATT at 13 - 14 per cent. The reform measures on foreign trade implemented by China has the reduction of tariffs in its agenda. In 1993 for example, China reduced tariff on 3371 items of which 202 were items on machinery (Scherer, 1994). Furthermore, the current level of tariff is below some of the Asian economies like Thailand whose average tariff was 44 per cent. However, while average tariffs may be relatively low, impediments to trade maybe in the form of non-tariff barriers. This is especially so for planned economies which use direct controls like quotas, licenses and other administrative instruments to protect domestic industries. The marketisation of state enterprises, a key feature in China's economic reforms, shows China's willingness to make import controls more transparent. Furthermore, import subsidies were abolished in 1994. Import license requirements were reduced to two thirds of imports in 1993/94. This goes to show that China has made great strides in giving market access to foreign firms in the 1990s.

The second area of market access concerns the commercial and economic practises in China. The main issue here is the arbitrariness of the government in dealing with foreign interest in China. Unless there are a set of rules and regulation which are clearly laid down, the uneasiness of foreign interest will be at stake. Under current conditions, Asians, notable investors from Hong Kong and Southeast Asia who are used to similar conditions in their own respective countries are able to manoeuvre through the ambiguous regulations[5]. However, investors with large scale investments, from the West for example, become uneasy with these regulations. Nevertheless, efforts are being made to clarify and standardise laws relating to trade and investment. The elimination of the dual currency and the official exchange rate in 1994, and the implementation of the Company Law of the PRC also in 1994 are two good examples of raising economic and commercial practises to international standards.

---

4 In 1989, for example, export subsidies accounted for 15 percent of China's export earnings (Central Intelligence Agency, 1989)

5 See Perkins (1994), pp. 31-35.

A third obstacle is the investment climate that need to be opened up for membership in the GATT/WTO. No doubt, China's openness to foreign investment has improved markedly since the 1978 reforms. There was an extensive reform programme in 1992 which relaxed a number of key restrictions on foreign investment including the opening of the services sector like finance, insurance, shipping and air transportation to foreign investors. While the method of foreign investment is still the joint venture (JV) mode, the life span of the JVs were increased from 10 - 20 years to 30 years. The amount of FDI increased from less than a billion US dollars in 1984 to close to US$26 billion in 1993 (Lardy, 1994). Although some sinologist consider China to be one of the most liberal foreign investment environments in the developing world (for example, Lardy, 1994), others like the PECC notes that China's impediments to FDI ranks among the highest in APEC (PECC, 1995). Again, WTO members tend to look at the existing impediments rather than the rate at which those impediments have been reduced by the Chinese government. The existing impediments are to protect the domestic market and industries and is another reason why China wants its membership in the WTO as a developing member.

4. APEC: THE SECOND BEST ALTERNATIVE

Both APEC and the GATT/WTO are trade organisations. Their objectives are similar i.e. to encourage free trade amongst its members and to allow the freedom of movement of capital and resources. APEC, at this point, cannot be branded as a trading bloc due to its open regionalism concept. However, APEC is an Asian style organisation while the WTO works on western principles and ethics. A major difference between these cultures is that while western initiatives emphasise deadlines and fixed schedules, Asians tend to be more flexible and emphasise unanimity in decision making[6]. Negotiations in the GATT are threatened by trade wars and retaliation whereas at the APEC level, sensitive issues are removed from the agenda, until such time when an agreement can be reached[7]. Both approaches do have merits and set backs, but there are indications that some kind of convergence seem to be taking place between the two styles of decision making (Naya and Imada, 1994).

While the objectives are basically the same, APEC allows greater flexibility in the fulfilment of the free trade objective. Member countries abide by the Action Agenda voluntarily. The Action Agenda covers main areas of trade and investment liberalisation and economic and technical co-operation. These areas of liberalisation are also WTO-consistent. The Action Agenda also covers specific areas of action including tariffs, non tariff measures, services, investment, standards and conformance, customs procedures, intellectual property rights,

---

6 See *The Economist*, November 11, 1995, pp. 31-32.

7 APEC seem to work similar to the ASEAN approach in this case.

competition policy, government procurement, deregulation, rules of origin, dispute mediation, mobility of business people, implementation of the Uruguay Round outcomes and information gathering analysis[8]. In fact, these areas of action covers nearly every trade barrier which the US has listed in its compilation on foreign trade barriers in China (Office of the US Trade Representative, 1994)[9]

APEC in the Action Agenda also acknowledges the general level of liberalisation and facilitation already achieved by each APEC economy. This favours China since the WTO seem to ignore the great strides that China has already made since the implementation of the Open Door Policy. In APEC, since China is accepted as a developing nation, it not only has an additional ten years to free up trade, APEC also allows a differential time-table towards achieving the goal of free trade.

Probably one of the few areas that concerns WTO but not APEC is China being a non-market economy. APEC does not make this distinction, and rightly so. APEC will probably be the first regional organisation which has both market and non-market economies. The ability of China adapting to the regional environment will also assist other non-market economies like Vietnam and Laos in the membership application into APEC.

There are several economic reasons why China should be in a trade organisation such as APEC or the WTO. In fact, it is crucial for China to be in a pro-free trade organisation with the US and Japan, at this stage of its economic development. Table 1.2 shows the trade and investment links between China and other APEC members in 1994. It is obvious here that nearly 61 per cent of China's imports and 74 per cent of its exports are with other APEC members. FDI too is mainly (91 per cent) from the APEC members. When the members are categorised, data shows that nearly 40 per cent of total trade is with the five developed economies of the APEC. The US and Japan are main partners of China. The NICs are more important export markets, mainly due to Hong Kong's entrepot nature. Hong Kong alone absorbs more than a quarter of China's total exports. From China's perspective, ASEAN and other Latin American economies are small trading partners. As for investment, the bulk of FDI for 1993 and 1994 (averaged) are from Hong Kong (60 per cent) and Taiwan (11 per cent). However, the US and Japan are also important sources. These figures indicate that as long as China belongs to a trade organisation which includes Japan, the US and the NICs, most of China's international economic needs will be satisfied.

Since the implementation of the Open Door Policy, the dependence of China on Japan and the US has increased markedly, both in terms of trade and investment. This is evident when we examine the degree of bilateral interdependence between China and these two economic powers. See Table 1.3. An interdependence coefficient is determined by adding bilateral trade data (imports and exports) and dividing by the sum of the two relevant nations' GDP (Takenaka, 1991). The coefficient expressed in percentage terms shows the

8 See website http://apec.tokio.co.jp/agenda/dec. for details of the action agenda.

9 It is also interesting to note that the same compilation admits the extent to which China is decreasing trade barriers to allow greater US imports. Yet, the US opposes China's application into the WTO.

Table 1.2: China's Economic Relationship with APEC

	Imports, 1994			Exports, 1994			FDI, 1993/94		
	Value (US$10,000)	% of APEC	% of World	Value (US$10,000)	% of APEC	% of World	Value (US$10,000)	% of APEC	% of World
Developed Countries	44890240	64.09	38.80	46107500	51.29	38.09	433797	15.49	14.06
United States	13970420	19.95	12.08	21461480	23.87	17.73	227933	8.14	7.39
Japan	26320770	37.58	22.75	21573120	24.00	17.82	172377	6.16	5.59
Australia	2451810	3.50	2.12	1487870	1.65	1.23	14930	0.53	0.48
New Zealand	316490	0.45	0.27	188090	0.21	0.16	910	0.03	0.03
Canada	1830750	2.61	1.58	1396940	1.55	1.15	17649	0.63	0.57
NICs	20550097	29.34	17.76	39471449	43.90	32.61	2306182	82.35	74.73
South Korea	7318340	10.45	6.33	4402310	4.90	3.64	55381	1.98	1.79
Hong Kong	9456620	13.50	8.17	32364540	36.00	26.74	1863381	66.54	60.38
Singapore	2482020	3.54	2.15	2558420	2.85	2.11	60896	2.17	0.97
Taiwan	1293117	1.85	1.12	146179	0.16	0.12	326524	11.66	10.58
ASEAN	4347820	3.76	3.76	3820590	4.25	3.16	60299	2.15	1.95
Malaysia	1622660	1.40	1.40	1117660	1.24	0.92	14621	0.52	0.47
Thailand	864390	0.75	0.75	1159280	1.29	0.96	23462	0.84	0.76
Philippines	272400	0.24	0.24	475690	0.53	0.39	13145	0.47	0.43
Indonesia	1588370	1.37	1.37	1051700	1.17	0.87	9071	0.32	0.29
Brunei	0	0.00	0.00	16260	0.02	0.01	0	0.00	0.00
Others	253530	0.22	0.22	502990	0.56	0.42	166	0.01	0.01
Chile	18310	0.02	0.02	285330	0.32	0.24	98	0.00	0.00
Mexico	93860	0.08	0.08	201470	0.22	0.17	0	0.00	0.00
PNG	141360	0.12	0.12	16190	0.02	0.01	68	0.00	0.00
Total APEC	70041687	100.00	60.54	89902529	100.00	74.28	2800444	100.00	90.75
Total World	115692800		100.0	121038480		100.0	3085835		100.0

Source: *China Statistical Yearbook 1995*

Table 1.3: Interdependency Coefficients for China and Selected Economies (%)

China's Interdependency Ratio with	1978	1988	1993
United States	0.07	0.42	1.01
Japan	0.90	1.16	1.71
Australia	0.36	0.44	0.72
New Zealand	n.a.	0.19	0.14
S. Korea	n.a.	n.a.	1.89
Hong Kong	1.73	13.46	18.79
Singapore	0.25	1.15	1.45
Malaysia	0.21	0.37	0.64
Thailand	n.a.	0.46	0.43
Philippines	n.a.	0.15	0.14
Indonesia	n.a.	0.35	0.61
European Union	0.26	0.54	0.55

Table 1.4: Net Exports of China's Manufactured Goods (US$ billion)

Year Manufactured Goods		1992	1993	1994
Consumer Goods	With Japan	6.32	8.48	11.69
	With the US	18.26	22.7	26.37
	With HKG	17.88	21.4	24.03
Intermediate Goods	With Japan	-1.66	-2.88	-2.03
	With the US	0.49	1.29	1.39
	With HKG	-4.78	-6.22	-7.71
Capital Goods	With Japan	-5.36	-7.98	-8.22
	With the US	0.65	0.54	4.33
	With HKG	-2.39	-5.64	-3.83
Total Net Exports	With Japan	-0.71	-2.38	1.45
	With the US	19.42	24.53	32.08
	With HKG	10.72	9.54	12.49

extent to which bilateral trade plays in the national economy. Comparing through time, it would also indicate the growing interdependency between the two economies.

The interdependency between the US and China is the most obvious case, increasing from 0.07 per cent in 1978 to 1.01 per cent in 1993. Marked increase in the ratio is also seen for Japan and the NICs. These five economies record a ratio of more than one. This would imply that, when we refer to China's increasing trade with the world, we are basically referring to China's trade with these five economies. This goes to show that as long as these five economies are within the trade organisation (for example, APEC), most of China's trade needs will be met. As a comparison, while the interdependency ratio with the European Union has doubled between 1978 and 1988, it has stagnated since. The importance of the European Union has probably reached a saturation point at about 0.5 per cent. The interdependency ratio with the ASEAN economies is less than one per cent but the ratio has nearly doubled for China's trade with Malaysia and Indonesia. Also, as a group, the interdependency between ASEAN and China is more important that the European Union. The trade relationship between China and the US and Japan can be characterised as follows: Japan as the supplier, China as the producer and the US as the absorber. Similar relationship existed and probably still does for the NICs and ASEAN (Takenaka, 1991). In such a relationship Japan acts as the supplier of capital and intermediate goods to China. These inputs are then utilised by China in the production process. The output then makes its way to the US. This can be seen in Table 1.4. Trade deficit was recorded with Japan for total net exports of manufactured goods until 1993. A surplus was recorded in 1994. With Hong Kong and the US, a huge trade surplus is evident.

When the components of the manufactured goods are considered, it is clear that Japan acts as the supplier of capital and intermediate goods (shown by the trade deficit in both categories for Japan). While Hong Kong also records a negative figure, the entrepot nature of Hong Kong does not allow us to make a concrete suggestion as to its role. With the US, on the other hand, a trade surplus is recorded for all components but consumer goods account for the largest portion. While net exports of consumer goods with Japan is also positive, the US is clearly a more important market. The crucial relationship that China has with Japan (as the supplier of capital) and the US (as the demander of output) would create further surpluses with the US leading to greater trade friction between the two countries (Park, 1993). This again indicates the need for China to be in some form of trade organisation with the two economic powerhouses as to reduce the likely friction that may occur between US and Asia.

5. CONCLUSION

APEC, since its establishment in 1989, has evolved into a powerful economic organisation. If the goal of an open free trade region is adhered to, APEC will spearhead towards a world with no impediments to a free flow of goods, services and capital. China is the third largest economy in the world and in APEC. However, until recently, China has played a low key in APEC. The failure in obtaining membership in the WTO in 1995 meant that China will not be considered as one of the founding members of the world body. The obstacles that stand in China's way from membership stems from opposition by some industrialised economies, namely the US. The chapter has shown that China has made great efforts towards dismantling some of these obstacles, especially in reducing tariff and non-tariff barriers and providing a sound economic and commercial environment. However, this has been insufficient to some WTO members. APEC, on the other hand, have been more accommodating. China has been considered a developing economy and being a non-market economy has never been an issue. APEC contains China's most important trading partners i.e. the US, Japan, Hong Kong, Taiwan and South Korea. The interdependency ratio and net exports between China and the US and between China and Japan further indicates the importance of these two economies to China. It is possible then to conclude that active membership in APEC would be in China's best interest. APEC, being an Asian style organisation, has an organisational culture that is easier for China to adhere to. Further, membership in APEC could be used as a stepping stone towards a place in the WTO. China's profile in APEC can be raised by:

- Hosting the annual informal meeting of the heads of government.
- Tabling proposals and background study on specific areas of co-operation. At the moment, China is the "lead shepherd" of the Industrial Science and Technology Working Group.
- Leading the developing nations of APEC to ensure that APEC is not hijacked by Japan and the US.This could be done by playing a key role in the East Asian Economic Caucus (EAEC) which meets in June 1996 in Kuala Lumpur[10].

REFERENCES

Aggarwal, V.K. (1993) "Building International Institutions in Asia-Pacific", *Asian Survey*, 33(11): 1029-42.

Arif M. (1995) "APEC Needs a Paradigm Shift", *The Star* 11 August, Kuala Lumpur, Malaysia.

Canadian Embassy (1995) *China Trade and Economic Development: Looking Ahead in 1995*, Beijing.

Central Intelligence Agency (1989) *The Chinese Economy in 1988 and 1989*, Washington.

Drysdale, P. and Patrick H. (1979) *An Asian-Pacific Regional Economic Organisation: An Exploratory Concept Paper*, Congressional Research Service, Washington.

Feng Yushu and Chen Dezhao (1992) "China Joins the Multilateral Trade System: Impact on Trade and Economic Co-operation between China and the ASEAN Countries", in Chia, S.Y. and Cheng, B. (eds.), *ASEAN-China Economic Relations In the Context of Pacific Economic Development and Co-operation*, Institute of World Economics and Politics and ISEAS, Singapore: 126-149.

---

10 The EAEC is now a possibility since the US and Australia have withdrawn their opposition to such an organisation. See *The Star*, 15 May, 1996.

Inouchi M. and Terada T. (1993) "Asia pacific Economic Co-operation and Australia-Japan Relations: A Japanese Perspective", *Pacific Economic Papers*, No. 224, Australia-Japan Research Centre, Canberra.

Kojima, K. (1971) *Japan and a Pacific Free Trade Area*, Macmillan, London.

Kojima, K. (1977) *Japan and a New World Order*, Carlos Tuttle and Co., Tokyo.

Lardy N. (1994) *China in the World Economy*, Institute for International Economics, Washington.

Naya S. and Imada-Iboshi P. (1994) "A Post-Uruguay Round Agenda for APEC: Promoting Convergence of North American and Asian Views", in Chia, S.Y. (ed.), *APEC Challenges and Opportunities*, ISEAS, Singapore: 54-93.

Office of the US Trade Representative (1994) *National Trade Estimate, Report on Foreign Trade Barriers*, Washington.

Park J.H. (1993) Impact of China's Open-Door Policy on Pacific Rim Trade and Investment, *Business Economics*, 28: 51-56.

PECC (1995) *Milestones in APEC Liberalisation: A Map of Market Opening Measures by APEC Economies*, Pacific Economies Cooperation Council, Singapore.

Perkins D. (1994) Completing China's Move to the Market, *Journal of Economic Perspectives*, 8(2).

Scherer J.L. (1994) *China Facts & Figures*, Academic International Press, Florida.

Soesastro H. (1994) The Institutional Framework for APEC: An ASEAN Perspective in Chia, S.Y. (ed.), *APEC Challenges and Opportunities*, ISEAS, Singapore: 36-53.

Takenaka H. (1991) The Macroeconomic Management of the Asia-Pacific Region: The Growing Significance of Japan's Role, *Pacific Macroeconomic Research Group Final Report*, Committee for Asia-Pacific Economic Research, Foundation for Advanced Information and Research, Japan.

The Evening Standard, 15 April 1996, Palmerston North, New Zealand.

The Economist, 11 November 1995.

The Star, 15 May 1996, Kuala Lumpur, Malaysia.

US Congress (1989) *Country Reports on Economic Policy and Trade Practises*, Washington.

Watanabe A. (1992) *Japan's Diplomacy and International Relations in the Asia-Pacific Region* (in Japanese), University of Tokyo Press, Tokyo.

World Bank (1993) *The East Asian Miracle*, Oxford University Press, Washington.

2. CHINA AND THE PROSPECTS FOR ECONOMIC INTEGRATION WITHIN APEC

Y. Y. Kueh

In the last few years it has been widely argued that the world's centre of gravity for economic activities will inevitably shift from the Atlantic to the Asian Pacific region in the 21st century. This popular perception has clearly been prompted by the spectacular economic growth of China in the past 15 years, following accelerated domestic reforms and, in particular, her "opening-up" to the outside world. There is no doubt that the 'China factor' has greatly assisted in sustaining the growth dynamism of the newly industrialised economies in Asia, (notably Taiwan and Hong Kong, but also - and increasingly - South Korea). The strength and global importance of the Japanese economy lends further weight to the emerging scenario for the 21st century.

There are two dimensions to the rising expectation of the emergence of an "Asian Pacific era". The first, reflecting a broader consideration relates to the involvement of the countries of the East Pacific, (above all the United States). The second - a narrower consideration - embraces the likelihood that self-sustaining development by the Asian-Pacific economies into a fully integrated regional economic entity, with China and Japan as the critical core by virtue of their industrial status and the market size.

In some questions, it has become a foregone conclusion that the perspective of the "Asian Pacific era" is already imminent. After all, "intra-regional" trade among number countries of the Asian Pacific Economic Cooperation (APEC), including the US and other North and South American economies facing the Pacific Ocean already accounted for 47 percent of total world trade in 1993. In addition, the APEC economies are responsible for the overwhelming share of global GNP, with the United States and Japan ranking first and second, and Mainland China approximating (after Germany) fourth in terms of purchasing power parity (PPP) estimates of GNP made recently by the World Bank.

Against this background, we propose to confine our analysis to the "APEC proper", by excluding countries on the American side of the Pacific. We do not, however, follow Premier Mahathir of Malaysia, whose radical concept of the East Asian Economic Caucus (EAEC) excludes Australia and New Zealand, as well as Taiwan and Hong Kong.

Several major issues follow in respect to the economic potential of the "narrower" APEC or "APEC proper", as just defined. It is as well to emphasise that it is not this chapter's intention to examine the domestic growth prospects of individual member countries. Our major task is to address the overall potential for intra-regional trade, as opposed to trade with outside world.

The main focus is, then, on trade and related investment issues. It is clear that China holds the key to many of these issues: after all, while "APEC proper" constitutes countries with economies which are already open and market-orientated - and whose potential for growth is marginal - , the Chinese economy remains in a state of flux. Any relaxation in market access restrictions, in terms adjustments to of tariffs and non-tariff barriers and the removal of impediments to foreign investment, promises substantially to alter the patterns of trade, service, and capital flows within the APEC region, in accordance with fundamental patterns of regional comparative advantage.

We shall therefore focus on China in order to show how, as an emerging economic power, it may help to promote economic integration in the Asia Pacific. In what follows, we first give a brief review of the relative strength in terms of GNP size, output structure, degree of industrialisation, and trade volume of the Chinese economy relative to that of the various APEC economies . This provides a background for assessing possible future patterns of economic interaction between China and other APEC economies.

In the second section, we examine the changing trends in China's trade within APEC, vis-a-vis trade with countries outside the region since the early 1980s. This serves to reveal the impact of China's economic and trade reforms in the past 15 years on regional trade, as well as indicating the potential for economic cooperation within APEC in the future.

Section three attempts to identify the major obstacles and constraints inherent in the present Chinese economic system and policies for further economic integration within APEC and with the outside world in general. This provides the necessary basis for assessing the prospects of China as a member of an APEC trading bloc.

Against this background the concluding section discusses the basic implications for China of the APEC tariff agenda established under the Bogor Declaration of November 1994, under which the long-term goal of free and open trade and investment in the Asia Pacific region is to be achieved no later than 2020, or by 2010 for the industrialised economies of APEC.

Underlying the analysis are overlapping, multifaceted and enormously complex problems. For almost every issue raised, in-depth careful research is needed before any firm statement can be made. To that extent the goals of this chapter are limited: that is, we seek to illustrate the broad contours of the fundamental issues and point to possible outcomes, rather than put forward firm conclusions and proposals. In short, the exercise generates more hypotheses and questions than it does answers.

THE RELATIVE STRENGTH OF CHINA AND THE APEC ECONOMIES

The Chinese economy assumes a leading position within the APEC context, whether defined as the broader APEC (including the American side of the Pacific) or the narrower APEC (merely embracing the Asian Pacific Rim (APR) economies). There are several aspects to this. The first is the sheer size of China's population and economic power. Adjusted by the PPP-estimate (which gives a multiple of around 6.6 over the official Chinese figure in terms of US Dollars, based on the depreciated official Renminbi rate), China's absolute GNP has already surpassed that of Japan, and is 11 times larger than that of South Korea - the next largest APR economy. It is also nearly 15 times the size of Australia's GNP in 1993/1994, as revealed in Table 2.1.

Second, with around 48 percent of her national gross output generated from manufacturing and construction, China is clearly also an industrial giant, standing alongside Japan within APEC. It is evident too that after four decades of forced-draft industrialisation under a highly protective trade regime, the country has built up an independent, comprehensive, and largely self-sufficient industrial system characterised by considerable technological sophistication. This is unmatched by any other APR economy except Japan.

Third, by the same PPP measure, per capita GDP in China (USD 2401) was as of 1993 already substantially higher than that of Indonesia, the Philippines and Thailand and only 30 percent below that of Malaysia. Note that the original, unadjusted Chinese per capita GDP (USD 360 in 1993) conveys no economic logic. The figure is indeed almost the same as that of the early 1980s, which was obtained by simply converting the official Renminbi value into US Dollar according to the prevailing official exchange rate. The accelerated Renminbi devaluation against the US Dollar since the mid 1980s has undoubtedly greatly distorted the comparative Chinese income strength. The reality is, however, that per capita GDP in China has grown, in real terms, by an average of 8.4 percent per year from 1980 to 1994, based on consistent Renminbi reckoning.[1]

In any case, the readjusted figure of USD 2401 for China clearly suggests a per capita GDP level which is substantially above the threshold of subsistence - implying indeed rising consumerism and increased potential for external trade. But it is also clear that substantial income disparity has emerged between coastal and interior Chinese provinces. In Guangdong province, for example, per capita GDP was probably around USD 4100 in 1994 (by the same PPP-measure), thus trailing behind South Korea by less than half of its level.[2] From this perspective, the prosperous Chinese coastal belt already constitutes a powerful base for economic cooperation with member APEC economies.

---

1 As reported by the State Statistical Bureau (SSB) (1995, p. 21), China's GNP/GDP grew at an annual average rate of 9.8 percent and population 1.4 percent from 1980-1994.

2 The figure is obtained by applying the GDP growth rates of the province for 1992-1994 (SSB, 1995, p. 33) to the estimated 1992 GDP of US$2806 as given in Kueh and Ash (1996, p. 151).

Table 2.1: Major Economic Indicators for China in Comparison with Other Major APEC Economies, 1993/1994

	Population (1994)		GNP (1993)		Per Capita GDP (1993)	Output Structure (1993)			Export (1994)		Import (1994)		Trade/GNP Ratio
	Millions	Per cent	US$ million	Per cent	US$	Per cent			US$ million	Per cent	US$ million	Per cent	Per cent
	(1)	(2)	(3)	(4)	(5)	(6) A	I	S	(7)	(8)	(9)	(10)	(11)
China	1191.8	68.11	581110 (3864382)	11.75 (46.97)	361 (2401)	20	48	33	104672	9.43	114564	11.12	37.73 (5.67)
Japan	124.0	7.09	2996052	60.59 (36.41)	31558	3	32	65	360705	32.49	238716	23.18	20.01
Hong Kong	6.3	0.36	104730	2.12 (1.27)	19600	0	17	83	151399	13.64	161841	15.71	299.09
S. Korea	44.5	2.54	338060	6.84 (4.11)	7496	7	43	50	96013	8.65	102349	9.94	58.68
Taiwan	21.0	1.20	226240	4.58 (2.75)	10703	4	37	59	92833	8.36	85489	8.30	78.82
Singapore	2.9	0.17	55370	1.12 (0.67)	18458	0	37	63	96457	8.69	102400	9.94	359.14
Malaysia	19.5	1.11	60060	1.21 (0.73)	3384	16	44	40	58147	5.24	59414	5.77	195.74
Indonesia	190.7	10.90	136990	2.77 (1.66)	773	19	39	42	39487	3.56	35132	3.41	54.47
Philippines	68.6	3.92	54610	1.10 (0.66)	747	22	33	45	12124	1.09	22638	2.20	63.66
Thailand	59.4	3.39	120240	2.43 (1.46)	1892	10	39	51	45061	4.06	54365	5.28	82.69
Australia	17.5	1.00	233109	4.71 (2.83)	14485	3	29	67	42723	3.85	43476	4.22	36.98
New Zealand	3.5	0.20	37956	0.77 (0.46)	10809	8	25	67	10430	0.94	9649	0.94	52.90
AP total	1749.7	100.00	4944527 (8227799)	100.00	3298 (4690)	5	34	60	1100511	100.00	1030033	100.00	43.28 (26.01)

Notes:

(1) The two bracketed GNP/GDP figures for China are derived by applying to the given official figures the ratio (6.65) of the World Bank's 1992 GDP figure for China (US$2,460 per capita) based on the "purchasing power parity" (PPP) estimates to the corresponding official Chinese figure (US$370 per capita) obtained by conversion at the official exchange rate. The International Monetary Fund (IMF) has made a similar PPP estimate for China, also for 1992, and come up with a lower per capita GDP of US$1,700 compared with the Bank s figure cited above. The IMF estimate would give a lower multiple of 4.59 (i.e. US$1,700/US$370), and therefore a lower total GNP of US$2,667,295 million and per capita GDP of US$1,657, but a higher trade/GNP ratio of 8.22.

(2) Output figures for the A (agriculture), I (industry) and S (service) sectors are all in gross value rather than in value-added term.

(3) The statistics for population, export and import for Japan, Australia and New Zealand are all 1993 figures.

Sources:

(1) All population, GNP/GDP, and trade statistics are from Asian Development Bank, *Key Indicators of Developing Asian and Pacific Countries, 1995*; except those for Japan, Australia and New Zealand which are given in World Bank, *World Tables 1995* and United Nations, *International Trade Statistics Yearbook 1994*; and the Hong Kong population figure which is form Hong Kong Government. *Hong Kong Yearbook 1995.*

(2) All gross output figures are from World Bank, *World Tables 1995*; except those for Taiwan which are taken from Council For Economic Planning and Development (Taipei). *Taiwan Statistical Data Book 1995.*

(3) The PPP-estimates are reported in *The Economist*, 15 May 1993 exports (for World Bank's) and *Dagongbao* (Hong Kong), 18 May 1993 (for IMF's).

Consider next the relative "openness" of the Chinese economy in terms of her external trade volume relative to GNP size. Surprisingly, the trade/GNP ratio given in Table 2.2.1 suggests that China is currently even more "open" than Japan and is comparable with Australia, even if it still lags far behind such entirely trade-dependent APEC economies as of Hong Kong and Singapore. If Guangdong province and Greater Shanghai municipality (another provincial-level unit) are taken as the basis for comparison[3], their ratios are certainly comparable with those of South Korea, Taiwan and Thailand, which are all heavily export-oriented.

Here again the real Chinese picture seems to have been highly distorted as a result of the statistical bias associated with the official Renminbi exchange rate used for the estimates. The reason is simple. While export and import statistics are normally based on the original US dollar quotation, Chinese GNP figures in US dollar are derived from straight-forward conversions from officially reported Renminbi values according to the highly depreciated yuan rate against the US dollar. This has helped grossly to understate Chinese GNP in Renminbi denomination.

Thus, if we were instead to apply the PPP-estimates of the World Bank in order to estimate China's GNP, the trade/GNP ratio would probably be reduced from 37.7 percent to no more than 6 percent (1993/94). Or, if the similar, but more conservative IMF estimate were used, the estimated trade ratio would be only around 8.2 percent in 1993 (see notes to

3 Cf. Kueh and Ash, ibid.

Table 2.1). Ultimately, no unambiguously precise estimate is possible. But it is safe to propose that the relative openness of the Chinese economy is substantially less than the "official" trade/GNP ratio would suggest.[4] The implication is that there still is considerable potential for enhancing trade and investment flows between China and other APEC members.

To sum up, given the size of the Chinese economy, which accounts for nearly 50 percent of the total GNP of APEC proper by the PPP-estimate, (or 12 percent by the nominal official statistics), there is a prima facie case for believing that China will join Japan to become one of the two preeminent forces in the economic integration of the Asian Pacific region, and, in the context of APEC, play a much more significant role than that of the United States in the global economy. Against this background, we now consider China's trade relations with member APEC economies since the early 1980s.

TRENDS IN CHINA'S TRADE WITH APEC ECONOMIES

The basic question here is whether, as a result of China's domestic reforms and accelerated opening up to the outside world, her trade flows with other APEC economies have been enhanced to any significant extent, vis-a-vis those with other countries outside of the Asian Pacific region. The widely-held view is that trade among APR countries has increased substantially in the past 15 years, highlighting strengthened economic integration within APEC proper. This view is further strengthened by the general perception that in addition to the benefits of geographical proximity, the APEC proper economies are complementary to each other, by virtue of their great diversity, (in terms of GNP size, factor endowment, stage of development, and technological levels).

However, the picture which emerges from the statistical trends shown in Table 2.2 is at best a mixed one. The figures there offer evidence of the changing magnitude of China's trade flows with various APEC proper economies relative to North American (NA) and selected western European countries (E) for the benchmark years 1980, 1985, 1990 and 1994. A number of points may be made.

First, in support of the general perception, China's merchandise trade (exports plus imports) with APEC countries as a whole did indeed increase from 46 percent (1980) to 57 percent (1994) of its global trade. However, such increases seem to have taken place at the expense of ROW (rest of the world) countries, (the share falling from 27 to 16.2 percent

---

4 An alternative estimate was made by Lardy (1992, pp. 150-155) for the trade ratio for 1988. He made use of the comparative indices of growth of GNP and trade (in real terms) for 1978 to 1988 (which are made available in official sources), and related the growing discrepancy to two different western PPP-based estimates of China's GNP for 1980, respectively by Herbert Block and Summers and Heston. The first estimate gives a trade/GNP ratio of 5.8 percent (in 1978) and 9.4 percent by (1988), while the second generated corresponding figures of 2.1 percent (1978) and 3.4 percent (1988). Lardy regards the higher estimate as more acceptable. However, it seems quite curious, in our view, that China's trade ratio could already stand at as high as 5.4 percent in 1978, after decades of self-imposed trade autarky.

Table 2.2: China's Trade with APEC Proper (AP), North America (NA) and Major European Countries (E), and with Rest of the World (ROW), 1980-1994

	Export								Import							
	1980		1985		1990		1994		1980		1985		1990		1994	
	US$ m	%	US$m	%	US$m	%	US$m	%	US$m	%	US$m	%	US$m	%	US$m	%
World	1813	100.0	27329	100.0	62876	100.0	120822	100.0	19505	100.0	42534	100.0	53915	100.0	115629	100.0
AP	9	54.2	16257	59.5	41492	66.0	68517	56.7	7613	39.0	22354	52.6	29226	54.2	66803	57.8
NA & E	9831	17.0	4195	15.3	10010	15.9	33012	27.3	7084	36.3	11171	26.3	15199	28.2	29722	25.7
ROW	3087	28.8	6877	25.2	11374	18.1	19293	16.0	4808	24.7	9009	21.2	9490	17.6	19104	16.5
	5221															
Japan	4032	22.2	6091	22.3	9210	14.6	21490	17.8	5169	26.5	15178	35.7	7656	14.2	26319	22.8
S. Korea					433	0.7	4376	3.6					236	0.4	7318	6.3
Taiwan					320	0.5	2242	1.9					2254	4.2	14084	12.2
Hong Kong	4353	24.0	7148	26.2	27163	43.2	32365	26.8	570	2.9	4762	11.2	14565	27.0	9488	8.2
Singapore	421	2.3	2063	7.5	2016	3.2	2563	2.1	190	1.0	241	0.6	849	1.6	2481	2.1
Malaysia	180	1.0	186	0.7	370	0.6	1118	0.9	240	1.2	198	0.5	852	1.6	1623	1.4
Thailand	312	1.7	116	0.4	854	1.4	1159	1.0	140	0.7	263	0.6	386	0.7	864	0.7
Indonesia	21	0.1	124	0.5	401	0.6	1052	0.9	14	0.1	330	0.8	849	1.6	1589	1.4
Philippines	258	1.4	314	1.1	205	0.3	476	0.4	70	0.4	97	0.2	90	0.2	272	0.2
Australia	224	1.2	183	0.7	468	0.7	1488	1.2	1063	5.4	1124	2.6	1361	2.5	2448	2.1
New Zealand	30	0.2	32	0.1	52	0.1	188	0.2	157	0.8	161	0.4	128	0.2	317	0.3
4 DRAGONS	4774	26.3	9211	33.7	29932	47.6	41546	34.4	760.0	3.9	5003	11.8	17904	33.2	33371	28.9
SK & TWN	0	0.0	0	0.0	753	1.2	6618	5.5	0	0.0	0	0.0	2490	4.6	21402	18.5
HK & SING	4774	26.3	9211	33.7	29179	46.4	34928	28.9	760.0	3.9	5003	11.8	15414	28.6	11969	10.4
ASEAN (expt SING)	771	4.3	740	2.7	1830	2.9	3805	3.1	464.0	2.4	888	2.1	2177	4.0	4348	3.8
AUS & NZ	254	1.4	215	0.8	520	0.8	1676	1.4	1220.0	6.3	1285	3.0	1489	2.8	2765	2.4

Table 2.2: China's Trade with APEC Proper (AP), North America (NA) and Major European Countries (E), and with Rest of the World (ROW), 1980-1994 (cont'd)

	Export + Import			
	1980	1985	1990	1994
	%	%	%	%
World	100.0	100.0	100.0	100.0
AP	46.3	55.3	60.6	57.2
NA & E	27.0	22.0	21.6	26.5
ROW	26.6	22.7	17.9	16.2
Japan	24.4	30.4	14.4	20.2
S. Korea			0.6	4.9
Taiwan			2.2	6.9
Hong Kong	13.1	17.0	35.7	17.7
Singapore	1.6	3.3	2.5	2.1
Malaysia	1.1	0.5	1.0	1.2
Thailand	1.2	0.5	1.1	0.9
Indonesia	0.1	0.6	1.1	1.1
Philippines	0.9	0.6	0.3	0.3
Australia	3.4	1.9	1.6	1.7
New Zealand	0.5	0.3	0.2	0.2
4 DRAGONS	14.7	20.3	41.0	31.7
SK & TWN			2.8	11.9
HK & SING	14.7	20.3	38.2	19.8
ASEAN (expt SING)	3.3	2.3	3.4	3.4
AUS & NZ	3.9	2.1	1.7	1.9

Notes: AP covers the individual countries as listed, NA United States and Canada, and E United Kingdom, Germany, France and Italy.

Source: International Monetary Fund, *Direction of Trade Statistics Yearbook*, various years.

between 1980 and 1994), rather than "NA + E" countries (share remaining at 27 percent from 1980 to 1994, despite a marginal decline to 22 percent in both 1985 and 1990). To the extent that the ROW share consistently declined after 1980 through the interval benchmarks 1985 and 1990 to 1994, it would appear that a realignment of China's trade links with APEC countries, away from such remote ROW trade partners as Africa, Latin America, and the Middle East countries, has taken place.

Second, however, China's increased trade share with the APEC countries seems to have essentially, if not exclusively, derived from the remarkable increases with Hong Kong and

Taiwan - and latterly South Korea. Such trends helped to boost China's combined trade share vis-a-vis the "four little dragons" (including Singapore) from 15 percent (1980) to 32 percent (1994).

Third, it is striking that the Chinese trade share with ASEAN (with or without Singapore), has remained virtually the same - a little more than 3 percent - during the past one and a half decades. It is interesting that this should be so, given the strategic aspiration voiced both by China and Malaysia in the context of APEC negotiations in Bogor with respect to the tariff agenda for the years 2010 and 2020,[5] as well as the continued improvement in political relations between China and ASEAN (whose exports and imports were 25 and 45 percent larger than those of China in 1994, excluding Singapore). Fourth and most remarkably, the combined share of Australia and New Zealand in China's external trade falls quite consistently from 3.9 percent (1980) to a mere 1.9 percent (1994). This decline took place despite massive efforts by the governments of both countries to boost their trade with China from the early 1980s. Moreover, Australia consistently enjoyed trade surpluses with China after the establishment of diplomatic relations, and was for many years a net recipient of Chinese capital, intended to develop iron ore and aluminum smelting for export back to China. Amongst China's major trading partners, Australia has also had fewest bilateral trade policy disputes with China.

The Australian and the New Zealand markets are of course too limited in size to exploit any scale economies in trading with China merely in order to sustain their share against the United States, Germany, Britain, France or Japan - all of whom can offer China much more advanced technology exports, as well as providing a larger export market.

These broad contours of change in China's trade relations clearly suggest that if economic integration within APEC is to be the main reference point, such integration has essentially taken place within what is popularly known as the "Greater China economic growth triangle", comprising the Chinese Mainland, Taiwan, Hong Kong and Macau. But in this context too, the nature of economic integration, as shown by the statistical evidence in Table 2.2 and discussed above should be interpreted with care.

Indeed, careful examination of the export and import statistics in Table 2.2 reveals that the increases in China's trade share with Hong Kong reflect changes in both exports and imports, with the latter perhaps assuming greater weight in the long-run. This apparent paradox is easily resolved.

Increases in China's exports and imports vis-a-vis Hong Kong derive from two different sources. The first is trade related to so-called "outward-processing" (OP) activities, commissioned by Hong Kong-based manufacturers from enterprises based in China. The latter include both the tens of thousands of joint ventures of Hong Kong origin, as well as a large number set up by local Chinese producers. While OP has become a familiar

5 China and Indonesia reestablished normal diplomatic relations in 1990 after a long break and the normalisation was then expected to give a great boost to bilateral trade.

phenomenon in South China, it may still be a surprise to anyone unfamiliar with the scale and intensity of the economic synergy that the magnitude of associated Hong Kong exports (of raw materials, semi-manufactures, and machine and equipment) to and imports (essentially processed goods) from China should have reached such spectacular levels. According to official estimates by the Hong Kong government, in 1994 OP related goods flowing from China accounted for 76 percent of Hong Kong's total imports from China, while goods outward bound for China within the same OP context constituted 69 percent of Hong Kong's domestic exports and 43 percent of total re-exports to China.[6]

Since 1987, Taiwan's trade relations with Mainland China have followed the same pattern as Hong Kong's, except that most of the island's exports to and imports from the Mainland have, for well-known political reasons, had to be channelled through Hong Kong. Figure 2.1 shows that, after the adoption of a new political reorientation towards Mainland China in 1987 (allowing "indirect" personal and business contacts with the Mainland counterparts through third parties), Taiwan's trade with Hong Kong soared dramatically. There is no doubt that the overwhelming proportion of Taiwan's exports to and imports from Hong Kong during this period, as may be measured by the discrepancy between the actual and predicted values shown in Figure 2.1, have been bound for or have originated from the Mainland. To the extent that these flows officially constitute trade with Hong Kong, the estimated Taiwanese shares of exports to and imports from the Mainland may already have been subsumed in Hong Kong's trade statistics with China.[7]

The share of South Korea in China's export and import trade also increased sharply following the establishment of diplomatic relations in 1992, (see Table 2.2). The major difference between Taiwan and South Korea in this respect is that the latter engages in direct trade with China and possesses no major political leverage for restricting imports from China, compared with Taiwan's. As a result, its positive trade balance appears to be less impressive than that of Taiwan.

Given the preeminence of outward-processing-related trade, it is a matter of debate whether increased trade flows between China and Hong Kong/Taiwan/South Korea really do indicate enhanced economic integration within Greater China or, more generally Northeast Asia.

---

6 See Kueh and Voon (1996) for more details in this respect.

7 As shown in Table 2, the IMF statistics give a separate entry for Taiwan's trade with Mainland China, as part of the catch-all category of "Asia not specified" in the original IMF compilation. It is not known, however, how the statistics are exactly obtained. Perhaps they are derived from the given statistics on Taiwan's trade with Hong Kong as shown in Figure 1. This would imply the possibility of double counting in the context of Table 2. However, it seems nonetheless inappropriate to assume that IMF should engage in such a double counting.

Figure 2.1: Taiwan's Trade with Hong Kong and the Chinese Mainland, 1975-1994 (USD million)

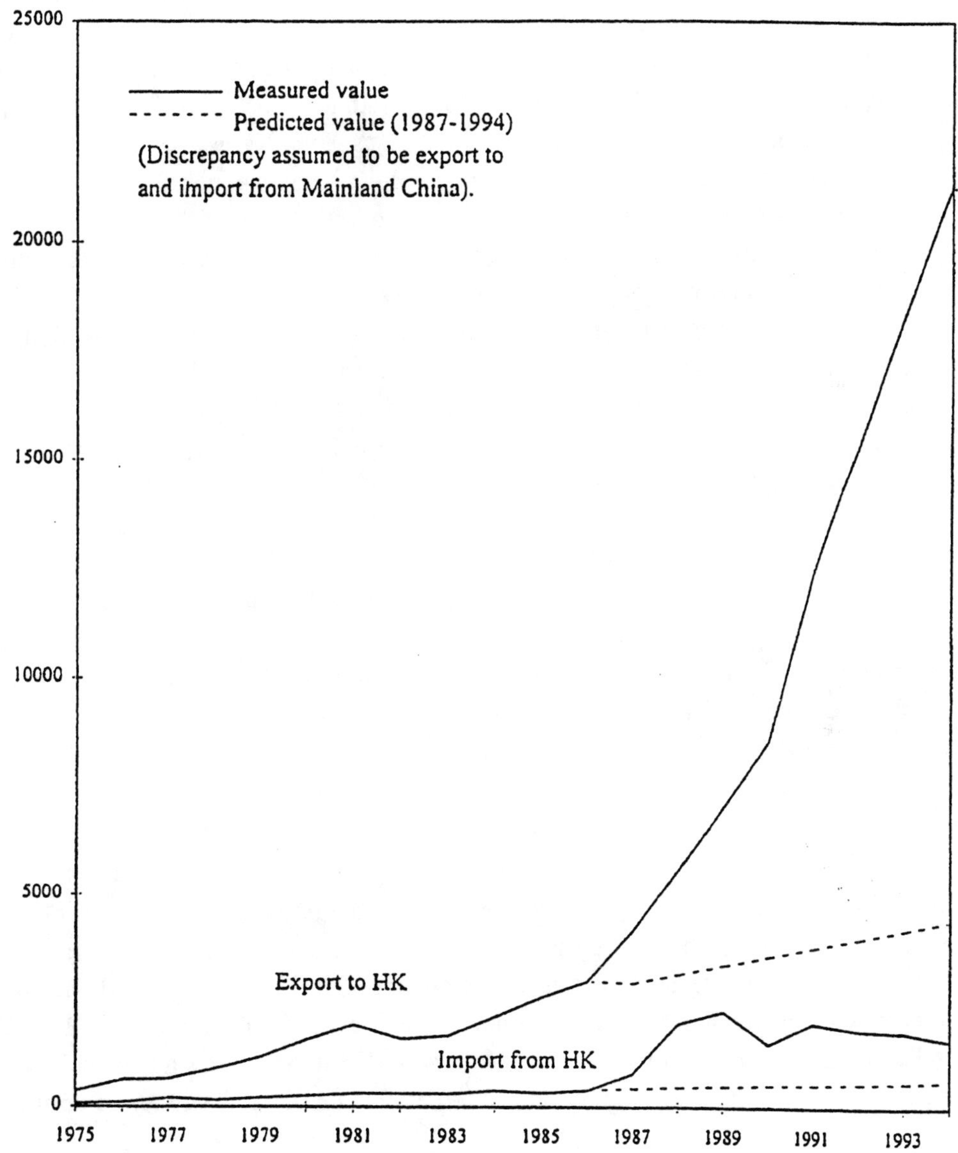

Note: The predicted values are derived from a linear time trend fitted with the 1975-86 data.
Source: *Taiwan Statistical Data Book*, 1995.

Before we consider this further, let us look at the second source of the increases of Hong Kong's share in China's external trade. This involves the accelerated increases in re-exports, both to and from China (in the latter case, especially to the United States).

According to our recent estimates made in a different context, the share of Hong Kong's total imports from China subsequently re-exported to the United States increased from 4.86 percent (1979) to 41.6 percent (1994), - an average growth of 12.8 percent p.a., in absolute terms. While the re-export value comprises a substantial proportion of OP-related imports from China - and should therefore be counted more as Hong Kong's than China's exports to the United States - it remains astonishing that Hong Kong's exports to China comprise goods of US origin which accounted for an average of 51 percent of the total during 1990-1994, (and which, as a share of total US exports to China increased from a negligible 1.6 percent in 1980 to a remarkable 29.6 percent in 1994).[8]

In other words, nearly one-third of total US exports to China are now channelled through Hong Kong. Nor is there any reason why European exports to China should not have followed the same pattern in the last 15 years in order to take advantage of the trading facilities offered by Hong Kong in respect to sourcing, marketing, telecommunication, shipping, banking, financing, insurance, etc.

But in accordance with the United States' statistical reporting convention that, indirect exports to China count as exports to the immediate importing destination (in this case Hong Kong), the figures in Table 2.2 clearly understate China's trade shares with the "NA+E" countries. If the Hong Kong connection, as described above, is taken into account, the corresponding AP share must be substantially readjusted downwards in favour of the "NA+E" share. That is, since the mid-1980s China's trade with "NA+E" may have grown even more rapidly than with the AP countries as a whole, at the expense of ROW countries.

IMPLICATIONS FOR ECONOMIC INTEGRATION WITH APEC PROPER

The foregoing discussion suggests that the most visible process of economic integration among APEC countries has taken place within the "Greater China" growth triangle. The accelerated increases in trade flows between Mainland China, Hong Kong, and Taiwan have also been accompanied or preceded by impressive direct investment made by Hong Kong and Taiwanese investors in the Chinese Mainland.[9] While this bears all the hallmarks of increased economic interaction among the three "Greater China" economic entities, the

8 For a detailed study and interpretation of the significance of the role played by Hong Kong in Sino-American economic relations see Kueh and Voon (1996). Consult also Ho and Kueh (1995) for the increasing magnitude of Hong Kong's re-export business in general.

9 For a more comprehensive study of FDI in China and the importance of Hong Kong and Taiwan as FDI supplier in Guangdong province and in China as a whole, see Kueh (1996) and Kueh and Ash (1996).

nature and intensity of the perceived integration demands careful interpretation. Several points may be made in respect to these findings:

The first is that massive OP-related trade flows have been associated with direct investment from Hong Kong and Taiwan in Mainland China, which has reflected no more than the massive relocation of Hong Kong and Taiwanese manufacturing activities to the vast Chinese hinterland. Such relocation has indeed resulted in a radical restructuring of the Hong Kong economy - and increasingly that of Taiwan - with significant implications for their output, employment, income and income redistribution.[10] The manner in which the Hong Kong and Taiwan economies have readjusted through increased economic interaction with the Chinese Mainland is a clear case of economic integration. The impact on both of these small open economies has also predictably been much more effective and intensive than the impact of such integration on the vast Mainland economy.

Second, however, by virtue of China's policy towards foreign direct investment (FDI) in China, the effect of the relocation of both Hong Kong and Taiwanese manufacturing activities onto the Chinese hinterland has inevitably been quite limited. It is well known that unlike the experience of many industrialising Asian countries, the Chinese government's FDI policy has leap-frogged from import-substitution to export-orientated foreign investment. This inherently denies "national treatment" to foreign investment, while requiring foreign investors (of Chinese policy practices) to "balance their own foreign exchange requirements" by generating as much foreign currency earning as possible from their joint venture exports to the outside world.

The upshot has been the emergence of a "one-country, two economies" system, under which a highly protective industrial system has received high priority in the national development and investment strategy, but has co-existed with a widely open sector catering for foreign investment and export drives.[11] Moreover, the chief mission of the latter has mainly been to use joint ventures with foreign investors to help generate sufficient foreign exchange earnings to finance investment in the forced-draft industrialisation programme. Viewed this way, the "two-economy" dichotomy implies an absolute denial of a strategy of full integration with outside economies.

Third, the China's "open-door" strategy for courting foreign investment has nonetheless helped - in a most impressive manner - to establish a new, *sui generis* economic system along the Chinese coastal belt, which has become increasingly and comprehensively integrated with the outside world and which has simultaneously assumed great economic importance in the national context. This is reflected not only in the growing importance of

10 See Ash and Kueh (1995), and especially the paper by K. C. Lei (1996), for a more systematic input-output analysis of the impact on the Taiwanese economy of increased FDI outflows to the Chinese Mainland.

11 For an elaboration on this point see Kueh (1990)

the "outward-processing" trade flows involving Hong Kong and Taiwan, but who - and more importantly - in the fact that FDI in China now constitutes about 20 percent of annual domestic fixed capital formation, with Sino-foreign joint venture exports accounting for around 40 percent of the national exports. In this respect, therefore, the "open-economy" sector of China has become fully integrated with the outside world.

The fourth point relates more specifically to the role of the "Greater China" growth triangle as a source of foreign exchange for the Chinese Mainland. The interaction with Hong Kong and Taiwan, both of whom have traditionally enjoyed huge trade surpluses with the United States, has decisively helped to transfer the surplus to Mainland China by way of investment and export-processing. In other words, economic synergies have enabled both Hong Kong and Taiwan to export their bilateral trade deficits with the US to the Mainland. Put differently, Mainland China has been able increasingly to resort to the traditional export markets of Hong Kong (latterly, Taiwan's too) to finance its trade deficits with the United States, Western Europe, and Japan.

Table 2.3 sets out China's balance of payments vis-a-vis Hong Kong and the outside world. Between 1979 and 1993, in every year except one China incurred a bilateral trade deficit with the United States. The combined total of US$23 billion for the period was however easily offset by its accumulated trade surplus of US$142 billion with Hong Kong. Indeed, that same surplus was more than 2 times greater than Chins's combined deficit with the United States and Japan.

In short, China's total export earnings from Hong Kong alone, net of the corresponding import expenditure, have been more than sufficient to finance China's net import bills incurred with the United States and Japan, or even the world at large, for the entire period 1979-1993. Even if the outward-processing (*sanlai yibu*) component is omitted from China's exports to Hong Kong, its trade surplus with Hong Kong has still been more than sufficient to offset the country's combined deficits with the United States and Japan for the period 1989-93 taken as whole. This unequivocally highlights the pivotal importance of Hong Kong in both Sino-American and Sino-Japanese trade relations, or indeed in the entire Chinese foreign trade system.[12]

This specific dimension of "economic integration" explains the accelerated growth of China's trade relations with APEC proper and with our aggregate category of "NA and E" countries, at the expense of ASEAN, and Australia and New Zealand.

Ignoring the economies of Australia and New Zealand, which are both small and remote, the ASEAN countries would appear to assume a competitive not complementary, position vis-a-vis the Chinese economy, in terms of its export drive. This would explain ASEAN's stagnating or shrinking relative trade volume with China, with economic integration with their northern neighbour remaining a distant prospect. The reality is that individual ASEAN

12 See Kueh and Voon (1996) for details.

Table 2.3: China's Trade Balance with Major Trading Partners, 1979-1994 (in USD 100 million)

Year	All Countries	USA	Japan	Hong Kong		Ratio 1	Ratio 2	Ratio 3
				Gross of Sanlai yibu	Net of Sanlai yibu			
	(1)	(2)	(3)	(4)	(5)	(4)/(1)	(4)/(2)	(4)/[(2)+(3)]
1979	-20.10	-12.62	-11.80	33.33	-	1.66	2.64	1.36
1980	-19.00	-28.48	-11.37	40.34	-	2.12	1.42	1.01
1981	-0.10	-31.49	-13.95	40.33	-	403.30	1.28	0.89
1982	30.30	-25.23	9.07	38.67	-	-	1.53	2.39
1983	8.40	-10.45	-9.83	41.05	-	-	3.93	2.02
1984	-12.70	-16.05	-30.86	39.60	-	3.12	2.47	0.84
1985	-149.00	-27.51	-89.26	24.07	-	0.16	0.87	0.21
1986	-119.60	-20.85	-76.59	41.75	-	0.35	2.00	0.43
1987	-37.80	-17.94	-36.76	53.41	-	1.41	2.98	0.98
1988	-77.60	-32.86	-31.41	62.93	-	0.81	1.92	0.98
1989	-66.00	-34.54	-21.39	93.76	46.69	1.42	2.71	1.68
1990	87.40	-14.09	14.23	123.96	55.67	-	8.80	-
1991	80.50	-18.49	1.88	146.74	39.36	-	7.94	8.83
1992	43.50	-3.07	-20.04	169.79	24.61	-	55.31	7.35
1993	-121.90	-12.13	-74.74	241.95	115.91	1.98	19.95	2.79
1994	53.46	74.91	-47.48	229.08	-	-	-	-8.35
Total	-320.24	-230.89	-450.30	1420.76	282.24	4.44	6.15	2.09
Average								
1979-85	-23.17	-21.69	-22.57	36.77	-	1.59	1.70	0.83
1986-94	-17.56	-8.78	-32.48	129.26	56.45	7.36	14.72	3.13
1979-94	-20.02	-14.43	-28.14	88.80	56.45	4.44	6.15	2.09

Table 2.3: continued

Note: Figures for 1981-1983 are converted from RMB yuan to US dollar by using the official annual average exchange rates.

The two 1993 figures for trade balance with HK are tentative estimates, and could be very problematic. The reasons are as follow: The year 1993 saw curiously both Chinese export (USD 22.1 billion) to and import (USD 10.5 billion) from HK being drastically curtailed from the previous year's high of USD 37.5 billion and 20.5 billion respectively. A likely explanation for the precipitous drop is that the 1993 figures do not include the sanlai yibu components with HK. This is because HK Government's statistics show that both outward-processing (sanlai yibu) consignments (USD 20.7 billion) to China and sanlia yibu imports (USD 38.2 billion) from China in 1993 (as given in Table 2.1 Panels A and B) are themselves even very substantially larger than the given Chinese total exports to and imports from HK. Thus, barring any other better explanation, we simply regard the original Chinese export and import figures as net of the sanlai yibu component. This results therefore in the trade balance with HK of USD 11.6 billion for 1993 as given for the net series. This figure is of course not directly comparable to those for 1989-92 (which are derived from HK Government statistics) and seems to be biased upward. For the 1993 trade balance (with HK) figure, we have in turn added Hong Kong's "outward processing"-related exports and imports to the original Chinese figures to derive the trade balance gross of the sanlai yibu components. In the estimates, HK's sanlai yibu import figure of USD 38.2 billion is adjusted downward by 10% and the comparable export figure adjusted upward by 5% to account for the possible f.o.b./c.i.f. discrepancy. This gives therefore the trade balance figure of USD 241.95 for 1993.

Source: State Statistical Bureau, *Zhongguo Tongji Nianjian (Statistical Yearbook of China)*, various issues.

countries have increasingly felt the full weight of Chinese export competition in the past decade or so.[13]

A few words about the Sino-Japanese economic relations are in order in this respect. Unlike its ASEAN counterparts, Japan has played a role for China which has been very similar to that of the United States, first, as a supplier of industrial producer goods needed to feed China's massive industrialisation programme; second, as an increasingly important export market for China as well. A very substantial proportion of Japanese exports to China has been channelled through Hong Kong. However, unlike the models of Hong Kong and Taiwan, re-exports of Japanese origin seem to have been more closely related to Hong Kong and Taiwanese FDI in China (in the form of industrial inputs, transport equipment, and machinery) than to Japanese FDI itself.[14]

In this context, it is interesting that the Japanese have contributed a much smaller share of FDI in China than Hong Kong, and have lagged behind Taiwan since the early 1990s. This has been widely interpreted as signalling a lack of Japanese interest in effecting

---

13 Thomas Voon (1996) gives a detailed analysis in this respect.

14 Elspeth Thomson (1996) reveals that Japanese exports to China are barely related to their FDI in China.

technology transfer to China. No doubt there is an element of truth in this. However, a more potent consideration is, in our view, that the Japanese have simply not recognised an urgent need to expand their share in the Chinese FDI market, because of their involvement, albeit indirect, as suppliers to Hong Kong and Taiwan investors of the bulk of the necessary industrial inputs as a back-up to their FDI in China. We would argue that this indirect involvement represents a more rational economic strategy, given widespread Japanese concern that the FDI market in China is still full of uncertainties associated with an undeveloped legal framework, bureaucratic complications, inadequate patent protection and, above all, pervasive restrictions to domestic market access.

From the Japanese perspective, it may well be more worthwhile to pay the tens of thousands of small "rent-seeking" firms from Hong Kong and Taiwan to expand their commodity export share in the Chinese market, rather than to become personally involved in establishing small export-processing plants in China in pursuit of the last margins of earnings from "second-round" exports to the third countries.

CONCLUSION: PROSPECTS FOR THE APEC TARIFF AGENDA

The main issues arising from the Bogor Declaration (1994) address the tariff agenda for the year 2020 more than for 2010. There is no doubt that the advanced industrialised APEC member economies should be able to meet the 2010 free trade and investment requirements with relative ease. But for the developing APEC economies (with the notable exceptions of Hong Kong and Singapore) reconciliation of tariff concessions could still pose serious problems. China's unweighed average tariff level was 35.9 percent in 1995. Even following the massive reductions by around 33 percent following the voluntary offer made by President Jiang Zemin at the APEC Summit meeting (Osaka: November 1995), it remains at 22 to 23 percent. This is much higher than the average of 8-13 percent for other major developing APEC economies, let alone the 3-4 percent for advanced countries. Thailand is the only country within APEC which has a higher average tariff level than China (39.6 percent in 1993).[15]

It is difficult to predict when China will effect a further adjustment of tariff rates in line with those of other APEC countries. The target set in the 9th Five-Year Plan (1996-2000) is to reduce the average level to 13 percent by the year 2000. Even if fulfilled, this would still be higher than the average for major developing APEC economies. Whether in such circumstances it would then be possible for China to further accelerate the process of tariff-reduction in pursuit of the long-term Bogor target of zero tariffs by 2020 is a matter for

15 For an illustration of the comparative tariff and non-tariff trade barriers existing among the APEC countries, see the recent comprehensive survey made by Pacific Economic Cooperation Council (1995).

conjecture. Both China and Malaysia made it clear in Bogor that while they agreed, in principle, with the Declaration, they did not wish officially to be bound by it.

In any case, from the present perspective, any accelerated tariff reductions undertaken by China could prove to be detrimental to many key branches of her infant industries, including electronics, chemicals, pharmaceuticals and - above all - the car industry. This is what is at stake in the prolonged Chinese negotiations with the United States for an early entry into GATT/WTO.[16]

Malaysia's reservations over the Bogor Declaration for an entirely free trade and investment regime by 2020 clearly reflect similar aspirations and concerns. Nor is there any apparent reason why the policies of other major Asian APEC members, such as Indonesia and Thailand, should not be driven by similar considerations.

In a sense, the WTO predicament facing the Chinese is compounded by their ambitious pursuit of foreign capital inflows. Exemptions of import duties for imports of raw materials, semi-manufactures, machine and equipment, for joint venture investments are still widely applied. In the framework of "one country two economies" (see above), nominal import tariffs may have to be kept at a relatively high level to compensate for concessions made to foreign investors, and to protect sizeable import-substitution and inward-orientated priority sectors. This basic policy orientation may obviously continue to hinder the major dismantling of the Chinese tariff system.

Nonetheless, the more fundamental issue raised in the context of this proper is whether, in the light of the Bogor target of 2020 for APEC to become a free trade and investment region, the Chinese economy will become more closely integrated with the advanced APEC economies, (Japan, the United States) and Western Europe, or with ASEAN and Australia. This is clearly not a zero-sum game situation and it deserves careful consideration.

First, what is certain is that for many years to come, China will continue to trade with Japan and the highly industrialised western countries to a much greater extent, in terms of bilateral flows of goods, investment and services, than with the countries of APEC proper. This trend will intensify, as the huge Chinese industrial system becomes increasingly mature and diversified.

Second, the South China growth triangle (comprising Hong Kong, Taiwan, and Guangdong province) is likely for many years to remain the driving force behind Chinese re-export and export processing activities, generating the necessary foreign hard currencies for financing the country's industrialisation programme. Shanghai apart, this will also remain the "Greater China" window for attracting foreign capital and investment in China in the foreseeable future.

Third, early admission of China into the WTO is likely merely to further enhance China's integration with the advanced industrialised west, or with the northern APEC, than to affect its relations with countries of the southern APEC proper. It is self-evident that any

16 See Kueh (1995) for an elaboration on the Chinese predicament over joining WTO.

further concessions which China may make in order to facilitate GATT/WTO membership - whether in relation to tariff and non-tariff barriers, investment impediments, or market restrictions to such service sectors as banking, insurance, telecommunication, transportation - will attract more complementary goods and capital inflows from the North rather than from the South.

The southern APEC members, especially ASEAN countries are, by virtue of their factor endowments and the stage of development each has reached, in basic competition with China for a share in the export markets of major western countries as well as for foreign investment. It is likely that they will lose out, as China's influence expands further.

However, such arguments are not intended to imply that growing Chinese economic power will marginalise the importance of the southern APEC member economies. A more likely scenario is that as China gradually becomes an industrial powerhouse of Asia, it will fuel growth and industrialisation within APEC proper, joining Japan to become a crucial source of supplying the bulk of industrial producer goods to her Asian neighbours. Moreover, the huge and highly diversified Chinese economy promises to provide sufficient market niches for the highly export-orientated ASEAN countries to diversify their overseas markets. It is not too much to hope that such developments will eventually help to make the APEC agenda for a free trading bloc a reality.

In the context of the massive export drive of all export-orientated members of APEC proper, China currently represents the very tail of the "flying geese" formation by reason of its comparative advantage in labour-intensive manufactures exports. However, the Asia-Pacific region must anticipate the time when the emerging industrial giant will join Japan as the dragon head of economic growth in the region. With or without the creation of a trading bloc under APEC, the economic centre of gravity of the world will then have shifted to the Asian Pacific region.

PART II GREATER CHINA: TRILATERAL ECONOMIC RELATIONS AMONG CHINA, TAIWAN AND HONG KONG

3. THE ECONOMIC LINK-UP OF GUANGDONG AND HONG KONG: STRUCTURAL AND DEVELOPMENTAL PROBLEMS

Shu-ki Tsang and Yuk-shing Cheng

I. INTRODUCTION

The phenomenal link-up between the Hong Kong and Guangdong economies has been proceeding at a remarkable speed since the launching of the Chinese economic reform in late 1978. The process has largely been market-driven and seems to suit the short-run comparative advantage on both sides. In essence, however, it has been a result of a reallocation of resources across the border, made possible by China's open policy. It has not yet led to a benign form of developmental upgrading which embodies the strengthening of the long-term foundation for productivity and competitiveness enhancement. Indeed, the tremendous "windfall profits" obtained so far could be regarded as a disincentive for R & D investments as well as beneficial decisions that may incur painful side effects in the short run.

Problems which are structural and developmental in nature, including bias and duplication in production patterns, inflationary pressure, widening income inequality, and the loss of competitiveness, have emerged in both Hong Kong and Guangdong. These problems could be traced to the lack of countervailing forces that promote far-sighted strategies, vis-a-vis "short-termism" driven by market supplies and demands and yearly profit maximization.

In this chapter, we argue that while better coordination should be pursued to ensure mutually beneficial developments and to avoid duplication in efforts and undesirable convergence in industrial structures, the future trajectories of the two economies will not and cannot be identical. Hong Kong and Guangdong are different in size and endowments, and face dissimilar political and economic frameworks. Independent policies and measures to nurture specific advantages and to solve internal problems have to be made. Indeed, a certain distancing in economic relations between the two economies will be healthy.

II. CHINA'S OPEN POLICY AND STRUCTURAL CHANGE IN HONG KONG

A decade or so after 1978, the Pearl River Delta of the Guangdong province became an important hinterland of Hong Kong's manufacturing industries. This form of economic linkage between the two places has totally altered the development path of Hong Kong. In the 1960s and the 1970s, Hong Kong experienced a process of rapid export-led industrialization. A large labour-intensive manufacturing sector was established. In the second half of the 1970s, however, Hong Kong was troubled by the problems of rising costs, external market constraints, and the pressure of technological upgrading. The Hong Kong government, which had been proud of its commitment to economic *laissie faire*, realized that something had to be done. The Committee on Industrial Diversification was set up in 1977 with an objective to study what strategies Hong Kong should adopt to tackle the escalating problems.

Two years later, in 1979, the Committee submitted a report to the Hong Kong government. The timing was indeed ironical. As soon as China opened its door in the same year, the whole thinking about climbing the technological ladder and diversifying products and markets was de-railed. Literally unlimited supply of labour, asking wages at less than 10% of the on-going rates in Hong Kong, became available in southern China. Similar bargains existed in land, energy and other charges. Even without technological upgrading and industrial diversification, this new found advantage was sufficient to propel the Hong Kong economy forwards for many years to come.

In retrospect, if China had not implemented the "open door" policy, Hong Kong might have been forced to go along the trajectory of technological upgrading of the other three "Asian Tigers" (Singapore, Taiwan, and South Korea). Instead, what has happened is a massive relocation of manufacturing industries to the Pearl River Delta and a further expansion of the labour-intensive industries. Up to now, 3 to 5 million workers in Guangdong are reportedly working directly or indirectly for Hong Kong, compared with the total work force of about 3 million in the territory itself.

The immediate implication of this "transformation" is the release of a great deal of manpower to other sectors. On the other hand, export processing of Guangdong has boosted the demand for Hong Kong's transport and trading services. Since the development of transport and other services of China has been lagging behind the rapid expansion of trading activities, China's reliance on Hong Kong to provide re-export and financial services has grown.

The industrial restructuring, or *de-industrialization*, of Hong Kong has proceeded with full force. In 1980, manufacturing accounted for 23.7% of GDP in 1980, while the service

Table 3.1 Production-based GDP at current prices by economic activity

(unit: %)

	1980	1985	1990	1995
Agriculture and fishing	0.8	0.5	0.3	0.1
Mining and quarrying	0.2	0.1	#	#
Manufacturing	23.7	22.1	17.6	8.8
Electricity, gas and water	1.3	2.6	2.3	2.3
Construction	6.6	5.0	5.4	4.9
Wholesale/retail, import/export trades, restaurants and hotels	21.4	22.8	25.2	27.4
Transport, storage and communications	7.4	8.1	9.5	9.8
Financing, insurance, real estate & business services	23.0	16.0	20.2	24.9
Community, social and personal services	12.1	16.7	14.5	17.1
Ownership of premises	8.9	10.5	10.6	12.7
Adjustment for financial intermediation services indirectly measured	-5.4	-4.6	-5.5	-8.0
	100.0	100.0	100.0	100.0

Source: Hong Kong Government, *Estimates of Gross Domestic Product 1961-1996*, Table 3.11.
Note: # - insignificant share.

sectors took up 67.5%. In 1995, the former's share fell to 8.8% as the latter's rose to 83.8% (see Table 3.1). In terms of employment, Table 3.2 shows the dramatic changes. In 1980, the manufacturing sector employed over 900,000 persons. The number had fallen below 400,000 by 1995. That the manufacturing workforce of an economy could be halved within the horizon of a decade must be one of the records in world economic history.

Table 3.2: Employment by Industry Group

(persons engaged)

	1980	1985	1990	Dec. 1995
Manufacturing	902,521 (46.5)	859,648 (39.6)	741,366 (30.1)	375,766 (14.9)
Wholesale/retail, import/export trades, restaurants and hotels	441,892 (22.8)	588,040 (27.1)	805,411 (32.7)	1,018,198 (40.6)
Transport, storage and communications	74,109 (3.8)	94,560 (4.4)	129,551 (5.3)	172,174 (6.9)
Financing, insurance, real estate and business services	123,883 (6.4)	177,346 (8.2)	270,610 (11.0)	378,244 (15.1)
Other industrial sectors	396,767 (20.5)	453,330 (20.9)	517,107 (21.0)	564,314 (22.5)

Sources: *Quarterly Report of Employment, Vacancies and Payroll Statistics*, various issues.

Note: Figures in parenthesis represent percentage shares of the total.

To critics, however, it also reveals that employment in the territory has largely been non-sector-specific in nature. It reflects rather poorly on the skill level that has been required in the major sectors. To put it dramatically, anyone here can be a textile worker in one month, a salesman in another, and a property agent in yet another. This does not augur well for the long-run prospect of productivity enhancement, which requires specialization, professionalization, and accumulation of expertise in specific areas. It adds weight to the skeptical view that the Hong Kong economy is still ravelling in the bonanza of the China factor for cost reduction and "re-rating" by international investors and speculators. No serious efforts in industrial and technological upgrading have been performed.

III. THE STRENGTHENING OF THE HONG KONG-GUANGDONG LINKAGE

In the opening up of China, it is natural that Hong Kong rapidly increased her linkage with the Guangdong economy, given the latter's geographical and sub-cultural proximity. Table 3.3 shows the relevant trade figures.

Table 3.3: Imports and Exports of Hong Kong and Guangdong

(Unit: US$ 100 million)

		1992	1993	1994
(1)	Total exports of Guangdong	184.40	270.27	469.93
(2)	Exports of Guangdong to Hong Kong	155.58	229.51	391.59
(3)	(2)/(1)	84.4%	84.9%	83.3%
(4)	Total imports of Guangdong	111.79	198.98	342.70
(5)	Imports of Guangdong from Hong Kong	82.68	155.40	254.40
(6)	(5)/(4)	74.0%	78.1%	74.2%
(7)	Total Imports of Hong Kong	1237.07	1386.50	1603.47
(8)	(2)/(7)	12.6%	16.6%	24.4%
(9)	Share of Hong Kong imports from China	37.1%	37.5%	31.0%
(10)	Total Exports of Hong Kong	1194.88	1352.44	1500.02
(11)	(5)/(10)	6.9%	11.5%	17.0%
(12)	Share of Hong Kong exports to China	29.6%	32.3%	32.8%

Source: *Guangdong Statistical Yearbook*, 1994, 1995; *Hong Kong Monthly Digest of Statistics*, various issues.

As can be seen from the table, China's shares in Hong Kong's imports and exports amounted to about one-third in 1992-94. Guangdong's shares, ranging between 7% and one-fourth, increased very fast during those years. Also, the figures indicate that as much as 70%-85% of Guangdong's imports and exports were transacted directly or indirectly through Hong Kong.

Apart from trading, investment across the border from either side also expanded tremendously. Hong Kong has been China's largest "outside" investor, contributing over 60% of the inflow of investment capital. At the end of 1993, a total of 167,500 foreign-invested enterprises (FIEs) were set up in China. Among them, 106,914 or 63.8% were from Hong Kong. Ranked in terms of the total number of foreign-invested enterprises attracted, the best-performing ten provinces in China were, from top down: Guangdong, Jiangsu, Shandong, Fujian, Zhejiang, Shanghai, Hainan, Liaoning, Beijing, and Tianjin. The number of foreign-invested enterprises in Guangdong amounted to 44,705, which represented 26.7% of the national total.[1] During 1990-94, the pledged and the actual

1 See *Jingji yanjiu cankao* (1994).

amounts of utilization of foreign capital of Guangdong totalled US$ 90.12 billion and US$ 30.57 billion respectively. Of the amounts, Hong Kong constituted US$ 71.42 billion (79.2%) US$ 22.41 billion (73.3%) respectively.

On the other hand, mainland China's investment in Hong Kong has also been increasing at an impressive rate. As Table 3.4 shows, by 1994, China's cumulative stock of direct investments in Hong Kong accounted for about 18% of total foreign direct investments in manufacturing and non-manufacturing sectors and ranked third in value after the UK and Japan, followed by the US. The inflow of capital from Guangdong has been very important. In October 1994, the total market value of the shares of Guangdong Enterprises (Holdings) Limited, which was listed in Hong Kong's stock market, amounted to HK$ 8.816 billion (US$ 1.141 billion). On 30 November 1994, it became one of the component shares of the Hang Seng Index, reflecting its rising status.

Table 3.4: Net Assets Attributable to Inward Direct Investments in Manufacturing and Non-manufacturing Sectors in 1994 Value (HK$bn)

Major investor country	Manufacturing	Non-manufacturing	Total	% share
UK	2.97	203.1	206.07	28.2
Japan	14.74	136.4	151.14	20.7
China	4.23	129.8	134.03	18.4
US	11.80	75.9	87.70	12.0
Others	10.23	141.1	151.33	20.7
Total	43.97	686.3	730.27	100.0

Sources: Industry Department, Hong Kong Government, *1994 Survey of External Investments in Hong Kong*; Census and Statistics Department, Hong Kong Government, *External Investments in Hong Kong's Non-manufacturing Sectors.*

The rapid strengthening of the China-Hong Kong or Guangdong-Hong Kong economic ties has profound impact on Hong Kong. According to the estimation of the Economic Research Department of Hang Seng Bank, the contribution of the "China factor" to Hong Kong's GDP rose from 5.3% in 1980 to 25.7% in 1990.[2] Given the trend of increasing linkage in recent years, the share probably has risen to over 30%.

IV. EMERGING PROBLEMS IN HONG KONG

With the big push of the "China factor", Hong Kong has sustained a respectable growth rate and experienced drastic changes in its economic structure. However, some problems

---

2 See Hang Seng Bank (1993).

are noteworthy. First, the growth rate has still been declining. In the 1970s, average annual growth in real terms of Hong Kong's GDP was as high as 9.2%. In the 1980s, it was 7.5%. During 1990-95, it slipped to only 5.5%. One explanation of the declining growth rate often invoked is the slowing down of the growth of the labour force. The average annual growth of the local labour force in the 1970s and the 1980s was 4.2% and 1.7% respectively. During 1990-95, however, it actually revived to a yearly rate of 2.2%, as local demographic factors, returned migrants and increased in-takes from China generated relatively more labour supply.

If we scrutinise the issue more carefully, we can observe some worrying trends. The annual growth of per capita GDP in Hong Kong during 1980-89 averaged 5.5%. It fell to 3.8% in 1990-95. If we further examine the statistics of GDP per worker, we find that the respective growth rates in the two periods were 5.7% and 3.3%. These figures suggest that, *prima facie*, there have been some problems with Hong Kong's productivity. The Hong Kong economy should not have become "mature" so quickly.

The availability of cheap labour from Guangdong has no doubt helped Hong Kong's manufacturing industries to lower production costs. It has also, ironically, alleviated the pressure for Hong Kong to upgrade technology and to improve productivity. As a sudden widening of the hinterland leads to a drastic reduction of labour and related costs, the incentives to invest in R&D and to adopt advanced techniques can hardly become visible. This is particularly true when short-term profits are huge and the authorities are not taking any pro-active measures to induce long-term optimality.

In a way, the Chinese reform has rendered Hong Kong's consideration to upgrade its industry superfluous. To Hong Kong, it is similar to an unexpected discovery of a new gold mine or an oil field. How to make use of the "windfall profit" of such a discovery is crucial. If the "windfall profit", for instance, is not used for reinvestment in productive activities that can raise Hong Kong's long-term advantage, but instead channelled into the pursuit of further short-term profits, asset inflation and consumer inflation will then accelerate. As a result, operation costs in Hong Kong will be pushed up. The sectors that cannot generate "windfall profit" in the short run (e.g. high-tech industries in their formation stages) will encounter heavy pressure and eventually be crowded out. The economy will inevitably suffer from the phenomena of "hollowing out" or the "Dutch Disease".[3]

Whether "hollowing out" or the "Dutch Disease" will occur or has already emerged in Hong Kong is debatable. In any case, there are some noteworthy trends. First, it appears that Hong Kong manufacturers have not used the huge profits that have been earned in Pearl River Delta for investment in technological upgrading. The profits are either used for "extensive expansion", that is, building more factories of the same (or even somewhat lower) technological level in cheaper localities in southern China, or repatriated to Hong Kong for investment in non-manufacturing or even non-productive, speculative, activities.

---

3 For a survey on the literature of the "Dutch disease", see Corden, W.M., (1984).

Conventional wisdom has it that the Hong Kong economy has undergone a "structural transformation" towards higher status: namely from a manufacture-based to a service-based economy, presumably with larger value-added. Such a characterization is in our view misleading. In the textbook case of development economics, such a transformation is a result of technological enhancement and a rise in productivity. In the process, human as well as other resources in the traditional sector are released and allocated to the growing sector. The development of the latter in turn further facilitates the productivity growth of the traditional sector. A virtuous circle will thus be formed, with falling employment in the traditional sector and rising employment in the leading sector.

The so-called structural transformation of the Hong Kong economy is quite different from this kind of upgrading. What has happened is more a change in the regional division of labour and some of its derived consequences. Originally, the mobility of resources (particularly labour and capital) between China and Hong Kong was very low. Once China adopted the open-door policy, most of the barriers to resource flows were lifted. The new mode of division of labour, often called *qian dian hou chang* (the shop at the front, the factory at the back), thus emerged. Obviously, Hong Kong is the *dian* (shop), and southern China is the *chang* (factory). Since production costs differ a lot across the border, a large amount of benefits can be reaped from the simple relocation of industries by both sides. This simply reflects the operation of the law of static comparative advantage.[4]

The side-effect is however a significant *reduction* in the pressure on technological upgrading. The technological sophistication of Hong Kong's manufacturing industries (including their off-springs in the Pearl River Delta) has been lagging behind their competitors in South Korea, Taiwan, and Singapore. What Hong Kong is still relying on is low production costs in its hinterland.

Moreover, Hong Kong has been faced with the problem of "relatively low growth and relatively high inflation" in recent years. Real economic growth has been about 5%, but the consumer inflation rate has been double-digit or close to double-digit for quite some time. As for asset inflation, the situation has been worse. During 1991-93, the prices of residential property rose more than one time. It did not fall until the government introduced a series of measures to cool down the market in early 1994. In any case, the prices and the rental rates of real estates in Hong Kong are among the highest in the world. Certainly, with the upward trend in China's economic power and international status, Hong Kong as a stepping stone is still an attractive site to invest. Even Chinese capital has been flowing into Hong Kong in huge amounts. All these phenomena have contributed to Hong Kong's high inflation; and the ways that Hong Kong businessmen have utilized their "windfall profit" have also added to the price pressure. The rising price level then serves to push up production costs and crowd out unprofitable industries

4 For an earlier analysis of the lack of long-term productivity enhancement in the so called "structural transformation" in the Hong Kong economy, see Tsang Shu-ki (1992).

in the short term. Even the profits of the service sector have been eroded. Some of the services have been moving northwards or outwards.

Third, Hong Kong has witnessed a worsening distribution of incomes. Table 3.5 shows some relevant figures.

Table 3.5: Changes in household income distribution in Hong Kong

Income group	Income share (%)					
	1971	1976	1981	1986	1991	1996
Lowest quintile	6.2	5.4	4.6	5.0	4.3	3.7
2nd quintile	10.2	10.1	9.8	9.8	9.0	8.2
3rd quintile	14.3	14.9	14.3	14.0	13.5	12.7
4th quintile	20.0	20.1	20.9	20.5	20.4	19.1
Highest quintile	49.3	49.5	50.4	50.7	52.8	56.3
Total	100.0	100.0	100.0	100.0	100.0	100.0
Gini coefficient	0.43	0.43	0.451	0.453	0.476	0.518

Seen from changes in the quintile distribution of income and the Gini coefficient, there has been a secular trend of increasing inequality. The situation worsened notably during 1986-96. Indeed, Hong Kong's distribution of income is the most unequal among the countries/areas of similar development levels.[5] The reasons are manifold. First, as the income distribution in the service sector is more dispersed, an increase in Hong Kong's inequality is in a way "natural" in its move towards a "service economy". On the other hand, although the economic ties between Hong Kong and China have benefitted both sides, the distribution of the benefits among recipients is highly uneven. The major beneficiaries have been the Hong Kong enterprises which have invested in China, followed by local authorities, enterprises and workers in Guangdong. As to employees in Hong Kong who work in sectors that do not have close ties to China, they have not benefitted much from the process of economic link-up. Moreover, many in the affected sectors (e.g. mid-aged skilled manufacturing workers who have been replaced by their much cheaper counterparts further north) have been disadvantaged and have suffered from a fall in real incomes, or outright unemployment.

5 See Tsang Shu-ki (1993).

V. ECONOMIC DEVELOPMENT AND RESOURCE FLOW IN GUANGDONG

Guangdong's economic performance since the launch of the open policy has been very impressive. During 1979-93, Guangdong's GDP registered an annual average growth of 13.9% in real terms, much higher than the national average of 9.3%. Apart from the efforts of Guangdong itself, the central policy of letting Guangdong "go one step ahead of other provinces" as well as the geographical proximity factor (lying along the coast and neighbouring Hong Kong) have also helped.

Similar to the case of Hong Kong, China's open policy has facilitated resource mobility and regional division of labour between Guangdong and other places in the country. The only difference is that while Hong Kong has moved factories to Guangdong to make use of its cheap labour, Guangdong has instead absorbed a large amount of labourers from other provinces. In the early 1990s, according to estimates, the labourers coming from other provinces to work in Dongguan and Baoan totalled 1.4 million.[6] Some other reports say that there are already over 10 million "outside" workers in Guangdong, although more official sources put the figure at 7-8 million. Thus, Hong Kong has exported factories, capital, technologies and outside connections to Guangdong. At the same time, Guangdong has imported labourers from other provinces, many of which are working in Hong Kong-invested plants.

As far as labour is concerned, Hong Kong is more reliant on Guangdong than Guangdong is on other provinces. A popular estimation of labourers working in Hong Kong-invested factories in Guangdong is about 3 million, which is already larger than the total labour force in Hong Kong. From another angle, total employed labour in Guangdong amounted to 34.3391 million in 1993.[7] If the report of 10 million "outside" workers in Guangdong is accurate, the share of "outside" worker in total employment is significant, but not to the extent of Hong Kong's external reliance.

Besides, taking "first mover" advantage and making use of its special status, Guangdong has absorbed quite a significant amount of capital and investment from other provinces, which has contributed to its economic growth. One key piece of evidence is the change in the deposit-loan gap in Guangdong's banking system. At the end of 1985, bank loans exceeded deposits by Rmb 19.482 billion, equivalent to 64.1% of total deposits. In end-1990, the gap fell to Rmb 12.602 billion, or 11.0% of total deposits. More notably, outstanding loans became less than deposits in Guangdong's banking system since April 1991 onwards. For the whole financial system in Guangdong (including all non-bank financial institutions) as a whole, total loans have been less than total deposits since June 1991. At the end of 1992, deposits in the banking system exceeded loans by Rmb 56.304 billion, the gap representing 23.7% of total deposits. This

---

6 See Yang Ming (1992).

7 See *Guangdong Tongji Nianjian* (1994).

change reflects not only the increase in the available capital in Guangdong itself, but also the inflow of capital from other provinces.

Nevertheless, the supply of outside capital to Guangdong does not seem to have been very stable. After China had adopted the macro-control measures in mid 1993, large amounts of the "hot money" in real estates, stock and futures markets were withdrawn. Tens of billions yuan were repatriated back to their home provinces. The financial situation of Guangdong deteriorated dramatically. Deposits declined sharply, giving rise to some liquidity problems. At the end of 1993, the positive deposit-loan gap in Guangdong's banking system fell to Rmb 24.839 billion, which was only 10.0% of total deposits (compared with 23.7% a year ago). The situation did not stabilize until the second quarter of 1994.

On the whole, the rapid economic development of Guangdong after 1979 has been a result of a large increase in factor mobility. A huge amount of short-term profits has been generated by this kind of factor mobility. How to consolidate the development and to derive reliable long-term advantage will be a big challenge to Guangdong in the future.

VI. CHARACTERISTICS AND PROBLEMS OF GUANGDONG'S ECONOMIC STRUCTURE

Similar to Hong Kong, the impressive economic growth record in Guangdong has arisen from a regional relocation of resources, more than genuine technological upgrading. Short-term benefits, therefore, coexist with potential long-term difficulties. The problems, moreover, are largely structural in nature.

First, on the whole, the external linkage of Guangdong is much stronger than its internal linkage. In other words, the industrial sectors inside Guangdong have rather weak inter-connections among themselves. There has been little coordination of production amongst various sectors inside the province. Production in various sectors in fact is predominantly dictated by the external market. On the basis of the input-output table of Guangdong in 1987, it has been estimated that the multipliers of the industries (the increase in the output of the whole economy resulting from one dollar's increase in the output of a particular industry) in Guangdong only ranged from 2.3 to 3.2, which implies a rather loose linkage between the industries.[8]

Second, there has been a convergence in the output structure of various production centres in Guangdong. The implication is that cities and townships in the province are increasingly engaged in similar production activities (in particular labour-intensive export processing), with little division of labour and coordination. Table 3.6 lists the results of a comparative study of the functional structures of cities in some major provinces in China conducted by Dai Hezhi, a geographer from Shandong. Eleven

8 See Zhou Jianhua (1992).

Table 3.6: A comparison of the economic functions of cities in major provinces in China

Economic functions	Shandong		Liaoning		Jiangsu		Zhejiang		Hebei		Guangdong		Henan		Sichuan	
	N	P	N	P	N	P	N	P	N	P	N	P	N	P	N	P
Mining	2	5.9	3	15.0	2	7.7	1	4.0	3	13.0	1	5.3	4	15.4	2	8.7
Electricity	2	5.9	1	5.0	2	7.7	1	4.0	2	8.7	1	5.3	1	3.8	2	8.7
Metallurgy	1	2.9	2	10.0	1	3.8	2	8.0	2	8.7	0	0.0	3	11.5	1	4.3
Petro-chemical	2	5.9	4	20.0	2	7.7	2	8.0	2	8.7	1	5.3	1	3.8	2	8.7
Construction material	0	0.0	1	5.0	3	11.5	1	4.0	1	4.3	1	5.3	2	7.7	3	13.0
Machinery and electronics	4	11.8	1	5.0	2	7.7	3	12.0	1	4.3	1	5.3	2	7.7	5	21.7
Textiles	4	11.8	2	10.0	5	19.2	4	16.0	2	8.7	2	10.5	3	11.5	2	8.7
Paper-making	1	2.9	1	5.0	0	0.0	0	0.0	0	0.0	1	5.3	1	3.8	1	4.3
Foods	2	5.9	0	0.0	1	3.8	2	8.0	2	8.7	2	10.5	4	15.4	4	17.4
Transport, postage and telecommunications	1	2.9	0	0.0	1	3.8	0	0.0	0	0.0	0	0.0	0	0.0	0	0.0
Commerce and catering	0	0.0	1	5.0	0	0.0	0	0.0	0	0.0	1	5.3	1	3.8	1	4.3
General cities	15	44.1	4	20.0	7	26.9	9	36.0	8	34.8	8	42.1	4	15.4	0	0.0

Notes: N represents the number of cities and P the percentage share in the total number of cities.

Source: Dai Hezhi, "A study of the structure of the city system in Shandong," *Jingji dili* (Economic Geography), Vol.14, No.2, 1994, p.29. The results are computed with figures published in *Zhongguo chengshi tongji nianjian 1991* (China Statistical Yearbook of Cities 1991).

economic functions, measured in terms of per capita output values of specific sectors, are examined. A city is said to be specializing in one function if its per capita output value of that function is higher than the provincial average. If a city is found to be specializing in more than one functions, the function with the highest above-average output value will be chosen. Moreover, the designated specialized function must rank in absolute output terms among the top four in the city. If a city does not have any specialized function, it is then classified as a "general city".

As shown in Table 3.6, among the 19 cities in Guangdong, eight or 42.1% are "general cities". The share is the second highest among the eight provinces under examination. It is just below the 44.1% of Shandong, the province with the least specialized functions.

Another simple indicator that can show the convergence in the output structure of various Guangdong cities is the index of regional divergence used by Paul Krugman, which is defined as:

$$\Sigma_i |s_i - s_i^*|$$

where s_i is the share of industry i in the total manufacturing output of a city and s_i^* is the share of industry i in the total manufacturing output of the whole Guangdong province.[9] The index ranges from 0 to 2 and a higher value indicates a bigger difference between the average (provincial) output structure and that of the the city under investigation. If, on average, the manufacturing structure of the cities has become closer to the average (provincial) structure, we can say that there is a convergence in the structure. Here we utilise the data of 40 manufacturing industries in 18 Guangdong cities (prefectures) to determine whether there had been a convergence or a divergence of the manufacturing structure between 1988 and 1994.[10] As shown in Table 3.7, out of the 18 cities, nine registered a decrease in the index of regional divergence. The average of the index for the 18 cities decreased from 0.713 to 0.663, implying an increase in the convergence of the output structure.

The problem of the convergence in the output structure probably has not been fully reflected in the above index, as it is based on aggregate data of forty industries. Anecdotal reports show that the duplication of the investments in some specific industrial products has been very serious in the Pearl River Delta. For instance, most cities have their own production factories for air-conditioners and there are a total of 30 such factories in the Pear River Delta. On the other hand, there are 250 cement factories in the Delta, 86% of which have small production capacity of less than 200,000 tons. As for the automobile

9 See Paul Krugman (1991). Note that Paul Krugman uses share of employment while we use share of output in computing the index.

10 The data are available in the *Guangdong tongji nianjian* (1989 and 1995).

Table 3.7: Index of regional divergence

		1988	1994
1	Guangzhou	0.391	0.385
2	Shenzhen	0.751	0.754
3	Zhuhai	0.686	0.484
4	Shantou	0.522	0.613
5	Shaoguan	0.923	1.007
6	Heyuan	1.000	0.751
7	Meizhou	0.702	0.765
8	Huizhou	0.670	0.700
9	Shanwei	0.978	0.695
10	Dongguan	0.580	0.546
11	Zhongshan	0.540	0.448
12	Jiangmen	0.435	0.469
13	Foshan	0.505	0.587
14	Yangjiang	0.878	0.806
15	Zhanjiang	0.662	0.731
16	Maoming	1.152	0.949
17	Zhaoqing	0.542	0.522
18	Qingyuan	0.908	0.714
	Average	0.713	0.663

industry, as many as 97 enterprises had been established by the end of 1993. There has been little coordination among the cities in the development of these industries.[11]

The weak internal linkage and the low level of specialization in Guangdong are not necessarily a bad thing. This kind of phenomena may merely reflect the openness of Guangdong. With a strong outward linkage, Guangdong needs not worry much about the internal division of labour. By responding promptly to external market signals, huge profits can already be earned. The operational mode of "the shop at the front, the factory at the back" in the Hong Kong-Guangdong linkage has been a major factor leading to this structure of "strong external linkage, weak internal linkage, and low specialisation". Moreover, in the process of export-oriented labour-intensive industrialisation, Guangdong's competitiveness has largely been based on low production costs and preferential policies from the central government. Within a certain period of time, coordination of internal production was therefore not relevant.

Yet, there are doubts whether this kind of external linkage can be relied on as the only momentum of growth for very long. The pertinent questions are: should the mode of external linkage (the shop at the front, the factory at the back) be upgraded? If yes, in this process of upgrading, should internal linkage and coordination of production within

11 See Zhang Nan (1996).

Guangdong be strengthened? Should regional division of labour and cooperation be promoted and improved?

The last question brings us to the third structural characteristic of Guangdong's economic development: regional imbalances. In 1978, the gross value of industrial and agricultural output of the Pearl River Delta constituted 32.7% of the provincial total. The share rose to 57.6% in 1990 and 68.7% in 1994. In contrast, the share of the mountainous areas, which constitutes 60% of total land area and 40% of total population, fell from 16% to 13.4% during 1978-1990. Interestingly, the share increased to 15.6% in 1994. Whether this was the result of a shift in government policy to alleviate inequality has to be scrutinised. The per capita figures, on the other hand, show an unambiguously rising inequality. Per capita GDP of the Pearl River Delta was Rmb 1106.4 higher than that of the mountainous areas in 1985. The gap widened to Rmb 2281.5 in 1990 and further to Rmb 12500 in 1994. During the same period, the difference between the average per capita savings deposits rose from Rmb 548 to Rmb 2254 and then to Rmb 3135. One apparent cause of the imbalances has been the uneven allocation of resources. According to the figures of the regional lending of the five major banks and the rural credit cooperatives in Guangdong provided by Han Houyuan, the share of loans provided to the Pearl River Delta increased from 57.94% in 1978 to 68.67% in 1989, while the share for the mountainous areas declined from 14.27% to 12.52%.[12]

This kind of regional imbalances is related to Guangdong's peculiar development path. As external linkage is the major engine of growth, those areas that have poor endowments and unfavourable geographical locations are not attractive to outside investors. Relatively low economic growth thus results. On the other hand, because of very weak internal linkage, the development of the relatively rich areas could not have benefitted the poorer areas, as both forward and backward linkage effects across different regions within the province have almost been absent.

VII. FUTURE DEVELOPMENT STRATEGIES OF HONG KONG AND GUANGDONG

As regards the future, both Hong Kong and Guangdong face a similar set of questions: How to re-invest the "windfall profits" earned in the past decade in a way that can benefit the most the future development of the economy? How to convert short-term and static advantages into long-term and dynamic advantages? During the process of change, how to contain or alleviate problems and negative side-effects that have arisen from structural imbalances?

There are two mostly likely future trajectories for the Hong Kong economy: (1) Continue the "de-industrialization" process, without caring about the phenomenon of "hollowing out", and allocate more resources in the development of the financial and

12 See Han Houyuan et al. (1991) and Tsang Shu-ki (1994).

service sectors. In this way, Hong Kong will develop into a world-class financial centre similar to New York and London. We have coined the term "Manhattanization" for this process.[13] (2) Follow a development strategy that emphasizes both financial services and manufacturing industries with higher value-added and technological content. This requires the investment of the short-term profits from the China bonanza into the manufacturing sector to upgrade technologies and to develop new industries. Singapore and, to a less extent, Shanghai and Greater Tokyo, are successful examples of metropolises with industries. Obviously, the current trend in Hong Kong is to go along where "quick money" can be earned, i.e. down the first road of "Manhattanization". To switch to the second trajectory, a good deal of efforts, buttressed by long-term vision and courage, on the part of the private sector as well as the government, is needed, which lamentably may be lacking around the 1997 political transition.

Down the path of Manhattanization, the problems that we discussed in section IV above, de-industrialization, lack of technological progress, inflation, worsening inequality etc., would tend to aggravate in Hong Kong. Moreover, as the Chinese economy starts to take off, Hong Kong may have to undergo further "structural transformation" to keep ahead of other competing cities and regions in China, in particular Shanghai. In the end, the territory could be forced into a peculiar mode of specialization, under which only activities of "high-risk, high-returns" find it viable to be based here. The trouble is that a limited proportion of the local population can engage profitably in these activities. Structural unemployment may replace labour shortage as a headache. Ironically, Hong Kong will then be even more "Manhattanized" under such a scenario, as de-industrialization becomes total, financial wizardry dominates, and the ugly reality of poverty in the midst of affluence surfaces. The social consequences could be daunting.[14]

Some would argue that even total de-industrialization of Hong Kong is nothing to worry about. Why is it necessary for Hong Kong to have any manufacturing industries at all, while New York does not have such industries, nor does London or Paris? The answer is simple: because Hong Kong, unlike these metropolises in relation to their home country, is supposed to be a separate economic system from the Chinese one under the Joint Declaration and the Basic Law. After 1997, Hong Kong will continue to issue an independent currency, keep its fiscal autonomy, and determine its own migration policy. So in theory the Hong Kong economy cannot be *fully* integrated with the Chinese counterpart because there will not be totally free flows of monetary, fiscal and human resources across the border. The Hong Kong economy must maintain her own *coherence*.

Hong Kong residents cannot migrate to Guangdong in the same way as US citizens move from New York to California. Hence, any local structural unemployment cannot be

---

13 See for example Tsang Shu-ki (1994a).

14 An earlier warning of this scenario was fired by one of the authors. See Tsang Shu-ki (1994a), *ibid.* 1994 was still a year when labour shortage was a problem. However, the situation changed drastically and in the second half of 1995, Hong Kong saw a 10-year high in its unemployment rate at 3.6%. Behind the problem were both cyclical and long-run factors.

easily solved by an expedient transfer of human resources to the north. In the case of a fiscal or a balance-of-payments crisis, Beijing is not supposed to come to our rescue, at least not directly. We also have to look after our own inflation and distribution problems. In a nutshell, Hong Kong is a very special case of regional economics.

As a service economy, Hong Kong faces possible contraction in the internal and external demands for its services. Due to the rise of a number of service centres in China, including Shanghai, Guangzhou, Shenzhen, Zhuhai etc., Hong Kong is under some pressure, particularly as it has been criticized as being too expensive by Chinese sources (see below). However, and this brings us back to Manhattanization again, Hong Kong in the ultimate analysis still has an edge over these competing cities because of its systemic advantage as a capitalist economy (guaranteed for 50 years) vis-a-vis the "socialist market economy" of Shanghai and the like. There must be some financial and related activities which would be regarded as outright "speculative" or "non-productive" by China, which the latter would not want to engage in and for which Hong Kong would excel. In this sense, socialist China would still have to depend on capitalist Hong Kong. We can already observe that Hong Kong is taking a lead in the so called "derivatives revolution" in finance over China. This reinforces our argument that the territory may in the end be shifting into a peculiar mode of specialization that focuses on activities of a very "high-risk, high-returns" nature, under which structural employment could emerge as a problem.

As to internal demand for services, Hong Kong down the road of Manhattanization is likely to be constrained by the trend of widening income inequality (see Table 3.5 above). It is well established in Marxian as well as Keynesian economics that an expanding income gap would harm average consumption as the rich show a much lower marginal propensity to consume than the poor. A concentration of money in the former's hands inevitably results in weak sales of normal goods; and in the extreme, leads to an "underconsumption crisis". As a small open economy, Hong Kong still would not be exempted from such a crisis, as domestic demands for non-tradables (food, housing, transportation etc.) are key pillars of the economy. Weak retail sales in Hong Kong for the past few years have alerted many to such a possibility, although again both cyclical and long-run factors have been at work.[15]

Hong Kong probably could learn more from the experience of city economies that aspire to maintain a balance between industry and service, such as Singapore and Shanghai. Singapore has even set a lower limit for the share of manufacturing in GDP at 25% (Hong Kong already went down to 8.8% in 1995, as Table 3.1 shows); and Shanghai has unveiled ambitious plans to develop high-tech industries on its outskirts. So perhaps instead of becoming the "Manhattan" of southern China, Hong Kong should serve as its "Singapore" or "Shanghai". A possible mode of operation for Hong Kong's industries is the combination of China's capabilities in technological R & D with the territory's expertise in design, packaging, and commercialization. Genuine efforts need to be made to climb the technological ladder and to maintain a viable industrial base, which will bring long-run benefits. It is foolhardy to abandon short-run comparative advantage. Trading and service

15 See Tsang Shu-ki (1995).

sectors should no doubt be further promoted, but not one-sidedly. In any case, a balanced strategy like this can only be implemented through conscious effort by the authorities with regard to macroeconomic and microeconomic policies, as well as cooperation by the Chinese enterprises and the local private sector.

In the recent past, the Hong Kong government seems to have become aware of the pitfalls of complete de-industrialization and letting short-termism prevail. It has put some money into providing matching grants for private sector R & D; establishing technology centres, and most notably, embarking on the construction of a "science park". Without much fanfare, these moves represent a shift form the hands-off attitude of the past (which was often pronounced, but not strictly followed anyway). Whether these moves will have any significant effect on the development of the Hong Kong economy, we can only wait and see.

As far as Guangdong is concerned, Manhattenization was not and never will be an option. With a population of about 70 million, more than 10 times the size of Hong Kong, Guangdong cannot sweep aside manufacturing industries, or even agriculture (lest huge imports, from other provinces or outside the country, will drain provincial resources heavily). On the other hand, services have no doubt been underdeveloped in Guangdong, in a relative sense at least, because of the traditional socialist bias and the rapid rise in living standards that raises demands. Overall, Guangdong has to maintain a more balanced economic structure among the primary, secondary, and tertiary sectors, compared with Hong Kong.

In 1978, the ratio among the three sectors in Guangdong was 29.9 : 46.4 : 23.7; then it changed to 17.3 : 50.4 : 32.3 in 1993.[16] The surge of manufacturing industries in the province has been remarkable, but these industries have been troubled by two key problems: (1) Their technological level was not high; and (2) There was an acute imbalance in sectoral structure, with the raw material and energy sub-sectors lagging seriously behind, thus constraining the improvement in overall efficiency.

Even under the one-sided outward orientation of the Guangdong economy in the past, some notable difficulties already emerged. One classic example is the province's foreign exchange imbalance in 1993. On the basis of customs statistics, Guangdong's exports in the year totalled US$27.03 billion while imports amounted to US$19.90 billion, hence producing a trade *surplus* of US$7.13 billion. However, according to an article on *Guangdong jinrong*, actual foreign exchange receipt from exports turned out to be only US$7 billion whereas the actual usage of foreign exchange for imports was US$10.4 billion. So a *deficit* of US$3.4 billion resulted, and "had to be solved by going through the swap centres".[17] The deviation of the trade-related foreign exchange balance from the recorded trade balance is well known in China because of various forms of leakages and

---

16 Calculated in current prices from figures in *Guangdong tongji nianjian* (1994), *op.cit.*

17 See Li Dan-er (1994).

statistical discrepancies.[18] Nevertheless, the very low receipt rate from exports (only 26%), compared with the import utilization rate of 52%, was striking even by Chinese standards.

The low receipt of foreign exchange from exports reflects the outward nature of the Guangdong economy as a large number of foreign-invested enterprises uses the province as an outward processing zone, with the result that the ratio of value-added accrued to Guangdong remains small. Imports of agricultural produces, raw and semi-processed materials and other industrial products, on the other hand, continue to drain valuable financial resources from the province.

The cold reality is that Guangdong faces difficulties even in balancing its foreign exchange under the operational mode of "shop at the front, factory at the back". Therefore, Guangdong must apparently do two things: (1) enhance the value-added of its production; and (2) develop a more balanced industrial structure with a higher degree of internal linkage and coordination.

The Guangdong authorities appear to have been aware of these problems. With a series of policy statements and measures announced in the past few years, the province has actually embarked on a course of economic upgrading, that is in marked contrast with the "liberal", "non-interventionist" stance of the Hong Kong government. An industrial policy has emerged in the province, under which strategic industries including petro-chemical, automobile, electronics, metallurgy, construction material, textiles and drugs are targetted for promotion. On the other hand, a plan for regional division of labour with the province has also been nurtured, with the western region specializing in raw material, energy and heavy industries and the eastern region focussing on light and consumer goods industries. The centre, in particular Guangzhou, would spearhead the effort to develop services.[19]

This newly emerging economic strategy is encouraging, but its concrete implementation would certainly require more than just official pronouncements. What is needed is a more rational structuring of both industrial and locational patterns within the province, with a view to promote internal linkage, division of labour and cooperation as well as technological upgrading. Moreover, structural duplication and wastage of resources must be minimized, especially with regard to infrastructural developments, a hot issue in the 1990s.

VIII. THE FUTURE MODE OF ECONOMIC LINKAGE OF HONG KONG AND GUANGDONG

Obviously, the economic linkage between Hong Kong and Guangdong should be upgraded in the future. Instead of continuing the old mode of "the shop at the front, the factory at the back" operating at a more or less stagnant technological level of "the shop", a new mode of multi-sphere and multi-dimensional interfaces and cooperation is needed. Greater effort should be spent on creating long-term competitive advantage.

18 See, for example, Tsang Shu-ki (1994b).

19 The major policy documents are compiled in Wang Dingchang (ed.) (1994).

No matter what development paths Hong Kong and Guangdong will follow and no matter what changes in the economic structure will take place in the two places, improvement in infrastructure will be a crucial factor determining the rate of growth. In the 1980s, Guangdong to a very large extent had made use of Hong Kong's intrastructural facilities to conduct external trade, as shown in Table 3.3 above. Into the 1990s, like other provinces, Guangdong has emphasized the construction of infrastructure so as to relieve the bottleneck sectors and to sustain high economic growth. On the other hand, if Hong Kong is to develop further, infrastructural facilities have also to be strengthened. One problem that has emerged is that in order to be cost effective and efficient, infrastructural constructions in Hong Kong and Guangdong, including airports, ports, highways, railways, energy and environmental protection projects, should be coordinated.

Owing to the lack of vision on the part of Hong Kong government and Sino-British conflicts over 1997, the construction of some important infrastructural facilities (particularly the new airport, additional container terminals and related transport systems) has been delayed in Hong Kong. Hence, Hong Kong is in the danger of failing to satisfy the fast-growing demand from China in general, and from Guangdong in particular. Seen from this angle, Guangdong should no doubt expand its own capacities in airports, ports, railways and even water transport, so as to reduce its reliance on Hong Kong.

Another factor is of course the surging charges of re-exports and voyage services in Hong Kong. According to an analysis of China's General Customs, total profits earned by Hong Kong businesses (including Chinese and foreign companies registered in Hong Kong) from serving re-exports to and from China rose from US$5.4 billion in 1980 to US$14.5 billion in 1993. The average gross profit margin thus rose from 21% to 31%.[20] Other studies also point to some worrying statistics. For example, the handling fee for one container ranges from HK$1200 to HK$1800, which is 5 to 7 times that of the normal fee in Mainland China, one-third to one half higher than that charged by Singapore, and double that of Kaohsung in Taiwan.[21] The underlying cause is not just the imbalance between supply and demand, but also the existence of market power among the small number of operators in Hong Kong. Even if Hong Kong speeds up the construction of infrastructural facilities in the future, re-exporting charges are unlikely to fall, unless China and other places can generate effective competition.

To this, there could be two entirely different kinds of response. The first one is an insensitivity to the situation. The traditional mode of planning and construction of transportation system in the 1980s could still be followed - with major routes all pointing from north to south, converging to Hong Kong. The underlying assumption is that Hong Kong should still be the major port for Chinese imports and exports in the future.

Another kind of response is a large scale of "diversion" of the congested transportation system in Guangdong. In the euphoria after the "Deng whirlwind" of 1992, various

---

20 Reported by *Shanghai jingji bao* (1994).

21 See Zheng Tianxiang (1994).

localities have been striving to build their own airports, railways, ports, highways, voyage and communication facilities, often with minimal coordination among themselves. Taking airports as an example, as pointed out by Professor Zheng Tianxiang of Zhongshan University, the new airports in Hong Kong, Guangzhou, and Shenzhen all have an ultimate annual capacity of 80 million person-times, while the airports of Zhuhai and Macau have a designed annual capacity of 1.2 million and 8 million respectively. Besides, there is the extension or establishment of airports in Foshan, Weizhou, Xiaxing and Jiangmen. Therefore, eventually, nine airports will thrive in the Pearl River Delta, with a total annual capacity of 280 million person-times, which will be about 9 times of the projected population in the region. In contrast, the Kai Tak International Airport of Hong Kong had a total capacity equivalent to only 4 times of the population in the territory in 1993. Whether there is sufficient demand to support all the nine airports in the future is a big question.[22]

Obviously, both types of responses are inappropriate. To be cost-effective, there should be coordination in the construction of infrastructural facilities between Hong Kong and Guangdong and within Guangdong itself, so as to avoid duplication and waste on the one hand, and to make use of economies of scale and to enhance efficiency on the other.

As for the issue of technological upgrading in industries, cooperation between Hong Kong and Guangdong will probably not be at a very high level. As discussed above, the choices facing Hong Kong are either (1) "Manhattanization" or (2) the "combination of financial services and high value-added manufacturing industries". The technological upgrading of Guangdong will, in theory, induce Hong Kong to follow the second path. However, as discussed above, the industries that Guangdong is planning to develop include petrol-chemical, automobile, electronics, metallurgical, construction material, textiles, and pharmaceutical industries etc. Among them, Hong Kong has some advantage only in electronics, textiles and perhaps construction material. Hong Kong's industrialization was traditionally based on light industries. Thus, to promote the industries it has targetted, Guangdong should go beyond just cooperation with Hong Kong. Closer ties to European and other East Asian countries, which have comparative advantage in these fields, should be developed. What Hong Kong can help is probably just to provide capital, information and some connections.

At the end of 1994, an official of Guangdong's Commission for Foreign Economic Relations and Trade was cited by a Hong Kong newspaper as saying, "Guangdong will coordinate its economic development with the industrial transformation of Hong Kong. Development centres for high technologies will be established together. Through Hong Kong, findings of foreign research on high technologies will be absorbed and extension to product development and sales will be made. Production and industrial structures will be adjusted in an optimal way."[23] To us, this viewpoint is too optimistic and the description of the economic relationship between Hong Kong and Guangdong too idealistic. The

22 See Zheng Tianxiang (1994), *ibid.*

23 See *Hong Kong United Daily* (1994).

contribution of Hong Kong to Guangdong's development of high-technology industries should not be over-estimated. Hong Kong does not have notable advantage in this aspect. The development, transfer and absorption of high-technology industries are usually effective only through actual investment and production. Will it not be more effective and efficient for Guangdong to absorb foreign technology by dealing with foreign partners directly than through the intermediation of Hong Kong?

As regards financial services and other tertiary industries, the cooperation between the two places is rather complicated. Hong Kong, as a "first-mover", should be able to contribute more to Guangdong than the development of high technology industries. This is particularly true in financing. Guangdong can raise funds by issuing bonds and stocks in Hong Kong's financial markets. Hong Kong's expertise in this area can also facilitate the development of financial and other services in the province. Yet, there will still be a high degree of competition. As far as high-level financial services are concerned, China has already got Shanghai which will soon be at par with Hong Kong. The roles of financial services among Guangzhou, Shenzhen, and Zhuhai, which all aspire to be "international financial centres", should be planned and coordinated. It will be stretching credibility too far to advocate that southern China can host four "international financial centres" in the true sense.

Competition between Hong Kong and Guangdong also exists in trade-related services. When Guangdong has expanded its capacity in airports, ports and other transportation facilities, accumulated sufficient human resources and experiences, its reliance on Hong Kong will be reduced. Part of Hong Kong's re-exporting business will be "diverted" to other places in Guangdong. The problems of congestion and "over-charging" in Hong Kong will only reinforce the trend.

Nevertheless, Hong Kong and Guangdong are not playing a "zero-sum game". Under virtuous competition, it may become a "variable-sum game" and a "win-win" outcome is possible. Taking trading as an example, there has already been the suggestion that Hong Kong and Guangdong should cooperate in building an efficient transportation network, which can be extended to other provinces in middle China. In this way, some of the foreign trade businesses in the middle regions of the Yangzi River can be channelled southward to the Pearl River Delta, benefitting Guangdong as well as Hong Kong.

IX. CONCLUDING REMARKS

In the ultimate analysis, the developmental path of either Hong Kong or Guangdong is not entirely determined by the mode of economic linkage between the two economies. In Hong Kong, questions such as whether Manhattanization is the choice or whether a more balanced production structure should be nurtured are hard ones that must be answered by local entrepreneurs and the government, although as we analyzed above, it is not easy to transcend beyond the temptations of easy money and short-term profits that have arisen from the opening of China and the regional re-allocation of resources. As to Guangdong, a much larger entity with even more complicated factors affecting economic development, the pursuance of a balanced strategy and regional coordination is a very difficult art. Hong Kong's assistance in this aspect can only be limited.

As to the negative side-effects and problems of the bonanza of the past fifteen years, such as inflation, regional and income disparity, "hollowing out" etc., Hong Kong and Guangdong will have to deal with them independently through suitable policies and remedial measures.

These conclusions are not meant to undermine the importance of the economic linkage between Guangdong and Hong Kong. The short-term benefits that it has brought about have been tremendous to both sides, and we have analyzed them in some details in this chapter. Our message is indeed simple: while the mutually beneficial mechanisms should be maintained and improved, there is a strong need to develop long-term competitiveness and dynamic advantage, a task which is likely to call for more independent efforts on the part of Hong Kong and Guangdong than in the past decade. Hence, a certain distancing in economic relationship is healthy.

REFERENCES

Corden, W.M., "Booming Sector and Dutch Disease Economics, Survey and Consolidation", *Oxford Economic Papers*, Vol. 36, 1984, pp.359-380.

Guangdong Tongji Nianjian (Guangdong Statistical Yearbook), 1989, 1994 and 1995.

Han Houyuan et al., "Guangdong chanye jiegou tiaozheng yu jinrong tizhi gaige" (Production Structural Adjustment and Financial System Reform in Guangdong), *Guangdong jinrong* (Guangdong Finance), No. 1, 1991, pp.8-10.

Hang Seng Bank, Hong Kong, *Hang Seng Economic Monthly*, June 1993.

Hong Kong United Daily, 19 November 1994, p.21.

Jingji yanjiu cankao (Economic Research Reference Material), Beijing China, 12 October 1994.

Krugman, Paul, *Geography and Trade*, The MIT Press 1991, pp.75-76.

Li Dan-er, "Jiusi jingrong gaige dui Guangdong jingji di yingxiang" (The Impact of the 1994 Financial Reform on the Guangdong Economy), *Guangdong jingrong* (Guangdong Finance), No.6, 1994, pp.4-6.

Shanghai jingji bao (Shanghai Economic News), 24 June 1994, p.1.

Tsang Shu-ki, "Income Distribution", *The Other Hong Kong Report 1993*, The Chinese University Press, 1993, pp.361-368.

Tsang Shu-ki, "Inflation", *The Other Hong Kong Report 1992*, The Chinese University Press, 1992, pp.425-445.

Tsang Shu-ki, "Money, Banking and Finance" in Y.M. Yeung and David K.Y. Chu (eds.), *Guangdong: Survey of a Province undergoing Rapid Change*, The Chinese University Press, 1994, pp.159-173.

Tsang Shu-ki, "The Economy", in Donald McMillan and Man Si-wai (eds.), *The Other Hong Kong Report 1994*, The Chinese University Press, 1994a, pp.125-148.

Tsang Shu-ki, "Towards Full Convertibility? China's Foreign Exchange Reforms", *China Information*, Vol. IX, no.1, 1994b, pp.1-41.

Tsang Shu-ki, "Xianggang jingji wang hechu qu?" (Wither the Hong Kong Economy?), *Ming Pao Daily*, Hong Kong, 15 November 1995.

Wang Dingchang (ed.), *Er ling yi ling nian de Guangdong: guihua ji zhanlue yanjiu* (Guangdong in 2010: Planning and Strategic Studies), Guangdong People's Publishing House, 1994.

Yang Ming, "Yaoyou quanxin di silu, zhengce he tizhi" (Completely New Thinking, Policy and System are needed), *Gang-Au jingji* (Hongkong-Macau Economics), No.7, 1992, pp.17-18.

Zhang Nan, "`Zhu San Jiao' gongye chanye jiegou qutong de xianxiang yu duice (The current situation of the convergence of the industrial structure in Pearl River Delta and policy prescriptions)", *Zhujiang sanjiaozhou jingji* (Pearl River Delta Economy), No.1-2, 1996, pp.47-48.

Zheng Tianxiang, "Yue-Gang jichu sheshi jianshe xietiao guanjian" (My Views on the Coordination of Infrastructural Construction between Guangdong and Hong Kong), *Gang-Ao jingji yuebao* (Hong Kong Macao Economic Monthly), October 1994.

Zhou Jianhua, "Zhujiang sanjiaozhou jingji fazhen huigui yu qianjian" (Review and Prospects of the Economic Development of the Pearl River Delta), in Zhongshan University (ed.), "*Zhujiang sanjiaozhou jingji fazhen huigui yu qianjian*" (Review and Prospects of the Economic Development of the Pearl River Delta), Zhongshan University Publishing House, 1992, pp. 22-37.

4. THE ECONOMIC INTEGRATION OF GREATER SOUTH CHINA: THE CASE OF HONG KONG-GUANGDONG PROVINCE TRADE

H. Dale

1. INTRODUCTION

Background

The growing economic interdependence of the three Chinese economies of China, Hong Kong and Taiwan has been very conspicuous since the commencement of China's open-door era in 1978. Within these three economies the development of the increasing economic interdependence of Greater South China, (GSC),[1] over time has been well documented. Sung (1992, 1995) for example notes the rapid economic integration that has occurred between Hong Kong and Taiwan with the coastal provinces of China, particularly Guangdong and Fujian, since the inauguration of China's open-door policy. Sung (1992) considers as the starting point what he calls the 'China Circle' which consists of Hong Kong, Macau, Taiwan, and Mainland China.

1 This region consists of Hong Kong, Macau, Taiwan and the mainland coastal provinces of Guangdong and Fujian. Macau is not considered in this analysis.

Table 4.1: The World's Largest Bilateral Merchandise Trade Flows, ($USm)

Trading Partners	1981		1993	
	Value	Rank	Value	Rank
China-Hong Kong	9138	11	148000	3
China-Japan	10387	10	37594	11
China-United States	5660	12	`42276	9
United States -Canada	82722	1	203000	1
United States-Japan	61162	2	156000	2
United States-Mexico	31302	4	80846	4
United States-United Kingdom	23421	6	42945	10
United States-United Germany	21725	8	47206	8
United States-Korea (Rep)	10461	9	32133	12
France-United Germany	34206	3	71099	5
United Kingdom-United Germany	22921	7	50865	7
Italy-United Germany	25868	5	65045	6

*The China-Hong Kong figures include both domestic and re-export trade.
Source: United Nations international trade statistics, STARS, IEDB, ANU.

Hong Kong-China bilateral trade has grown at an extraordinary rate to become the world's third largest bilateral trading relationship in 1993, as can be seen in Table 4.1.

A significant amount of Hong Kong-China bilateral trade occurs within the Hong Kong-Guangdong province trading relationship. The purpose of this chapter is to outline the nature of the growing trade link between the GSC economies; and to examine empirically and to analyse the causes of certain aspects of trade between Hong Kong and Guangdong province for the period 1981 to 1994.

The Economic Integration Process in Greater South China

Drysdale and Garnaut (1993) define economic integration as a:

> '..movement toward one price for any single piece of merchandise, service, or factor of production.'
>
> (Drysdale and Garnaut, 189).

A situation of disintegration will persist where barriers or resistances to trade are present. Such resistances to trade can be defined as phenomena that prevent or retard the immediate movement of commodities in response to price differentials (Drysdale and Garnaut). Sung (1992) notes that economic theory concentrates on tariffs, controls on factor movements, and exchange integration. These barriers can be directly related to an institutional-based approach to economic integration. However the effect geographical and cultural distances exert upon a process of economic integration may be of overriding importance (Sung, 1992).

In the case of the GSC economies there is no formal institutional framework underpinning the integration process. The initiative for integration stems primarily from private enterprise and market forces.[2] This initiative for economic integration closely matches the "market integration" which Drysdale and Garnaut describe as:

> '..the case where the initiative has remained primarily with enterprises acting separately from state decisions, and where official encouragement of regional integration does not include major elements of trade discrimination.'
>
> (Drysdale and Garnaut, 189).

The form of integration taking place with respect to GSC differs from the economic integration associated with the European Community, the North American Free Trade Area or the Australia-New Zealand Closer Economic Relations Trade Agreement. This latter form of economic integration can be defined as:

> 'The discriminatory removal of all trade impediments between the participating nations and the establishment of certain elements of cooperation and coordination between them'.
>
> (El-Agraa, 1988, 1)

---

2 Unilateral institutional initiatives were important in providing the opportunities for market forces to play the integrative roles they did. These initiatives are examined shortly.

The divergences from the law of one price across bilateral relationships are generally very large. The economic integration of GSC exemplifies reductions in resistances attributable to a process of market and non discriminatory integration as opposed to reductions in resistances through a process of official discrimination. The GSC economic integration example, particularly the Hong Kong-Guangdong link, is representative of a relatively small divergence from the law of one price in terms of non-official resistances to trade.

In the case of the Hong Kong-Guangdong province link these two economies are joined together by land. People in Hong Kong have their ancestral roots in Guangdong province, (and this province has received the bulk of Hong Kong's investment in China). A large comparative cost differential exists, (in terms of wages and land rents relative to the cost of capital), relative to the costs of overcoming resistances to trade. Relatively low trade resistances affected by geographical and cultural factors are considered to be very important in this example of economic integration. The implication is large net gains from trade.

Drysdale and Garnaut note that the reduction of resistances to trade takes investment and time and is affected by the whole range of cultural, linguistic, legal and other factors that affect the costs involved in trade transactions. They note that much of the dynamism of Asia-Pacific trade expansion stems from the progressive reduction of subjective and objective but unofficial resistances to trade;[3] and that this process has been driven largely by the search for more profitable patterns of trade by independent enterprises. The GSC region represents one of the best examples of this process in the Asia-Pacific region.

The market integration of the GSC region has been manifested to a large extent in high growth over time in the level of trade and investment flows between Hong Kong and Taiwan on the one hand and Guangdong and Fujian provinces on the other. A large comparative cost differential and a relatively low (and in some instances falling) level of a number of resistances to trade exists. This combination is driving a market-oriented form of integration that is reflected largely in outward processing-oriented activity. For the Hong Kong-Guangdong province link this activity reflects the exports of raw materials or semi-manufactures from or through Hong Kong with a contractual arrangement for subsequent reimportation of the processed goods into Hong Kong (Hong Kong Census and Statistics Department, 1995). This outward processing activity was initiated by Hong Kong investment in factory operations in coastal China. This investment led to large levels of outward processing trade destined primarily for third

---

3 The objective resistance to trade category has two components: costs related to distance such as transport and communication costs; and official barriers to trade which in the main is protection. Subjective resistances to trade can be defined as: '...a range of social, psychological, and institutional factors that cause prices to vary across geographic space by larger margins than can be explained by the necessary costs of overcoming objective resistances to trade' (Drysdale and Garnaut, 1982, 181).

markets. A large proportion of this outward processing trade would conceivably be of the intra-industry trade type, (this point is developed shortly).

The market integration of GSC includes deep commodity market integration. It is useful to distinguish between different commodity markets in China, namely export processing industries and import-competing industries. In Guangdong province for example the former industry type developed rapidly relative to import-competing industries largely because the exported products were not hampered by foreign exchange controls (Sung et al., 1995). Export-oriented production in the form of outward processing activity is dominant in the Hong Kong-Guangdong province link. Outward processing activity commences with a production process in the original country, (Hong Kong). Semi-manufactures are then exported to a foreign country, (China), prior to re-importation into the original country for final completion and/or packaging and distribution. Outward processing production uses largely labour-intensive processes.

The process of commodity market integration in both the Hong Kong-Guangdong province link and in the Taiwan-Fujian province link reflects differences between these economies in political, legal and economic systems. These differences dictate that the overall process of economic integration for GSC will be an uneven one. In the case of the Hong Kong-Guangdong link the integration process has been manifested to a large extent in the development of extremely intense trade and investment flows between the two economies. These flows reflect the relatively liberal control of export processing goods trade relative to the controls on capital and foreign exchange, and on labour migration in particular.

Unilateral Institutional Initiatives

There is no institutional economic integration arrangement for GSC. However broader institutional factors have had a significant role to play. The GSC region provides a very good example of the importance of unilateral institutional factors without a coordinated institutional integration scheme existing to augment the unilateral initiatives.

China's open-door policy began in 1978 and provided the starting point for the integration process. The reform process led to China's resource allocation mechanism moving from one of central planning to a market driven mechanism. During the post-1978 period China's foreign trade has been actively promoted and has grown at an unprecedented rate (Lardy, 1992). A big part of this development stemmed from the increased autonomy the provinces of Guangdong and Fujian were given which allowed them to independently manage their foreign trade and investment and which allowed them to operate special economic zones. An integral part of China's open-door policy was the tailoring of closer links with Hong Kong and Taiwan.

The large labour cost differential between Hong Kong and southern coastal China prompted the former economy to relocate a large amount of its labour-intensive manufacturing activity. The manufacturing sector and the whole of the Hong Kong economy has become increasingly service-oriented. There are two main aspects to the restructuring of Hong Kong's economy. Firstly Hong Kong now concentrates on more skilled processes such as product design and production management, allowing for very high productivity growth in Hong Kong manufacturing in recent years. Secondly the increase in outward processing operations in Guangdong province increased the demand for services such as entrepot trade and shipping. Hong Kong can be regarded as the economic capital of industrialised Guangdong (Sung et al.). In reflection of the restructuring re-exports have come increasingly to dominate Hong Kong's total exports.

The decentralisation of China's foreign trade in the open-door era generated renewed demand for Hong Kong to act as a middleman for China, as the latter economy opened up to and became increasingly integrated with the outside world, and with Taiwan. A continuation of the internationally-oriented growth of China will allow Hong Kong to specialise to an increasingly fine extent in the high value services in which it has such a large comparative advantage.

The development of links between Hong Kong and China was strengthened by the signing of the Sino-British agreement and the second round of Chinese reforms in 1984. An increase in the level of political confidence in future Chinese reforms followed the signing of the agreement.[4] This in turn provided a platform for the development of an increasing level of interdependence among the economies of GSC.

Taiwan followed Hong Kong at a later stage in restructuring its economy to take advantage of a comparative cost differential. Significant barriers to trade exist between China and Taiwan, both in terms of official protection and political barriers. Both these types of barriers make it difficult for this bilateral trade relationship to develop. Certain measures taken in recent years have however led to trade relations improving markedly.

Taiwan liberalised import controls on mainland products from 1987 and by the end of 1993 the indirect import of 1654 items was permitted, (up from 29 items in 1987), including all agricultural and raw materials. Taiwan eased its foreign exchange controls in July 1987 and indirect investment to the mainland grew rapidly as a result. In October 1989 Taiwan promulgated regulations sanctioning indirect trade, investment and technical cooperation with China. Taiwan's promulgation of a policy on national reunification in early 1991 supported the expansion of unofficial exchanges with the mainland. In January 1995 the Taiwanese government announced that from May of 1995 direct shipping links with the mainland would be established through an 'offshore shipping centre' in Kaoshiung. With these developments in relation to the mainland

---

4 Recognising the increase in political confidence is not to ignore the fact that a political constraint still exists with regard to the Hong Kong-China relationship. This constraint increases in size as the handover date in 1997 gets closer. However the economic integration process, having been encouraged by the signing of the Sino-British agreement, has developed to a large extent independently of political problems between China, Great Britain and Hong Kong resulting from the approaching handover of Hong Kong to China.

Taiwan also became keen to expand its presence in Hong Kong in order to handle its thriving business with the mainland.[5]

2. HONG KONG-CHINA AND HONG KONG-GUANGDONG PROVINCE TRADE

Hypotheses and Propositions

In the more open economic environment created initially by the Chinese reforms Hong Kong relocated a significant and increasing amount of labour-intensive operations to Guangdong province. This was in reflection of the liberalisation of the Chinese economy coinciding with an increasingly high labour cost, (and land cost), constraint being faced by Hong Kong. In the liberalised environment a situation existed where a difference in the relative scarcity of a factor of production, (labour), between one country, (Hong Kong), and another, (Guangdong province in China), and the associated difference in comparative costs, could be reflected in expanded trade.

The Hecksher-Ohlin theory of international trade assumes two factors of production and makes international differences in factor endowments the critical and single factor determining comparative advantage (Bhagwati, 1964). The Hecksher-Ohlin[6] theorem states that a country's exports use intensively the relatively abundant factor possessed by that country. The two concepts of relative factor intensity and relative factor abundance are generally defined in the narrow context of a two country two commodity world. Each country is producing the same set of commodities in a competitive setting. This production is supported by constant returns to scale technology that is shared by both countries. Each of the two commodities is produced separately via the use of the two factors of production. Both factors of production are supplied perfectly inelastically. The commodities are traded freely but the factors of production are internationally immobile.

The central empirical prediction of the Hecksher-Ohlin model of international trade is that patterns of international trade can be largely explained by differences in the relative capital and labour endowments of countries. This theory is applicable to Hong Kong-China trade. In terms of autarky relative factor prices the Hecksher-Ohlin theory defines the 'home country', (China), as being relatively labour abundant if its wage rate is lower before trade than the wage rate of the 'foreign country', (Hong Kong).

The proof of the Hecksher-Ohlin theorem itself is made under a set of very strict assumptions, (as in the discussion above). Nevertheless the model can be modified to

---

5 Taiwan's liberalisation of its import and foreign exchange controls, the sharp appreciation of its currency, and the willingness itself to use Hong Kong in an entrepot role all contributed to a rapid development of economic ties between Hong Kong and Taiwan from the late 1980's.

6 Bhagwati notes that this theorem owes much of its work to Samuelson.

incorporate market imperfections such as the presence of resistances to trade. Such resistances include transport costs, official trade barriers and transaction costs,[7] all operating to maintain price differentials between countries. There is a negative relationship between the level of resistances to trade and the level of international trade flows. In the case of the Hong Kong-Guangdong province trading relationship resistances are lower for Chinese export-oriented industries than for import-competing industries.

In the Hong Kong-Guangdong province link a large comparative cost differential together with declining trade resistances, (falling transport costs for example), for a commodity group would generate increased international trade. This situation leads to hypothesis 1:

> **Hypothesis 1:** An increasing relocation of outward processing production from Hong Kong to Guangdong province occurred over time. A large comparative cost differential together with declining costs in overcoming resistances to trade led to an increasing level of outward processing trade in the 1980s and early 1990s, stemming from the relocation process.

The relocation process consisted, (until very recently), of the commencement of a factory operation in Guangdong province to engage in the partial production of a labour-intensive product. Part of the production process, together with the control and distribution aspects of the overall process, were retained in Hong Kong. The trade underlying this process reflects the comparative cost differential between Hong Kong and Guangdong province and increasingly low resistances to trade. This framework is compatible with the foreign processing-based model of intra-industry trade.

Intra-industry trade is defined as the simultaneous exports and imports of goods within the same industry (Grubel and Lloyd, 1975). With regard to the types of products in which intra-industry trade takes place, Grubel and Lloyd highlighted three types of commodities:

- homogeneous products included in border trade and seasonal trade.
- heterogeneous products which are close substitutes in consumption, production or both.
- heterogeneous products of vertically adjacent or complementary stages of production in the same industrial sector.

---

7 Transaction costs in this context can be defined as 'The costs of capturing the gains from Specialisation and the division of labour' (North, 1987).

Foreign processing-based trade falls within the third category above. This type of trade occurs when a product is exported, processed in a foreign country, and then re-imported by the original country.

Foreign processing-based trade represents the embodiment into commodities of the tradeability of services, via the assembly and finishing processes that occur. Foreign processing-based trade is consistent with the Hecksher-Ohlin model because this trade represents the exploitation of comparative advantage in the production of certain services. This form of trade is also consistent with outward processing trade to the extent that the definitions of foreign processing trade and outward processing trade match closely; and both forms of trade are Hecksher-Ohlin based.

The assumption of the Hecksher-Ohlin theory of zero resistances to trade is relaxed for the foreign processing-based model of intra-industry trade, for transport costs and information costs:

- not all services are tradeable via their embodiment into commodities. In order for it to be unprofitable to use domestic substitute services the cost of transporting the goods overseas needs to be sufficiently small; and the cost of services performed overseas must be sufficiently low. Goods that are of a high value but of only small bulk, such as electronics equipment, fit these requirements well.

- in order to guarantee the success of the entire operation, quality and production schedules in the processing field must be maintained. Hence an efficient flow of information and personnel is necessary. Consequently the cost of information with respect to markets for goods and factor supplies needs to be taken into account.

A model of intra-firm trade fits into this framework neatly. The starting point for such trade is locational production and marketing cost differences leading to a cost minimisation strategy for a 'multinational' company. The company will geographically split the production of different varieties to supply the international market, with intra-industry trade being the result (Tharakan, 1989).

A number of factors suggest the outward processing activity occurring in the Hong Kong-Guangdong province relationship closely matches the above intra-industry trade outline. Firstly, both outward processing trade and foreign processing-based intra-industry trade reflect factor endowment differences. Secondly, both types of trade can be reflected in component-based production where labour-intensive processes are likely to be significant. Thirdly, Hong Kong firms relocating production to Guangdong province generally have complete or majority control of the Chinese factory operation. Hence intra-firm trade is likely to occur. Finally, relatively low transport costs and high cultural and language similarity are present in the Hong Kong-Guangdong province link and favour export processing-type trade. Consequently the following hypothesis is advanced:

> **Hypothesis 2:** a significant proportion of total outward processing trade between Hong Kong and Guangdong province in the open-door era consists of intra-industry trade.

The general description of the economic integration of Hong Kong-Guangdong province, (and the GSC region), can be summarised in the following manner. A large comparative cost differential together with relatively low resistances to trade have acted to generate an on-going process of market-oriented integration. This integration process has primarily been represented by large and increasing levels of outward processing trade, a large proportion of which is intra-industry trade.

The economic integration of GSC is being examined here within the context of market integration and a definition of economic integration based on the law of one price. The economic integration of GSC exemplifies reductions in trade resistances attributable to a process of market and non discriminatory integration, as has been outlined previously. The economic integration is to a large extent commodity trade-based. A relatively small and narrowing gap exists between the actual and potential level of trade for outward processing activity in the Hong Kong-Guangdong province trading relationship. This situation is attributable to a comparatively small and decreasing divergence from the law of one price for export processing-type activity due to the relatively low and declining level of certain resistances to trade for this type of commodity trade.

To the extent that various resistances to trade differ across bilateral trading relationships the Hong Kong-Guangdong province bilateral trading link is considered to exhibit a relatively low level of trade resistances, particularly in the area of export processing-type activity. This situation should be reflected in a relatively intense relationship for Hong Kong-Guangdong province outward processing trade compared to other bilateral trade relationships.

This expected reflection is based on the combination of comparative cost differentials and relatively low trade resistances, discussed previously. This combination will generate a relatively intense trading relationship for Hong Kong-Guangdong province. Increasing relative trade intensity is indicative of a process of economic integration and leads to proposition 1:

> **Proposition 1:** empirical evidence should be found of a relatively intense outward processing trading relationship developing between Hong Kong and Guangdong province over time that is reflective of an on-going process of economic integration.

For the case of both developed countries and developing countries the empirical observation has been made that regional economic integration, through membership of a customs union or regional grouping, does appear to exert a significant positive influence on intra-industry trade relative to inter-industry trade.[8]

The theoretical basis for this link is the existence of similar preference structures and the production of similar commodities, (see Drabek and Greenaway, 1984). The likelihood of intra-industry trade levels rising following economic integration depends on pre-integration market structures. Competitive rather than complementary production structures will encourage intra-industry trade relative to inter-industry trade. Similarity in income levels and the stage of industrialisation will encourage intra-industry trade. Such a framework is not relevant for the case of Hong Kong-Guangdong province, (and Taiwan-Fujian province), trade where intra-industry trade would be expected to be driven by factor endowment differences not by product differentiation and economies of scale conditions.

Nevertheless, empirical evidence has been found for the prevalence of intra-industry trade in manufacturing industries between countries with clearly different factor endowment patterns; and for economic integration influencing intra-industry trade positively, (see, for example, Tharakan). It has been concluded that economic integration may contribute to vertical specialisation (Balassa). Culem and Lundberg (1983) concluded that intra-industry trade between developed countries and developing countries appears to consist of primarily an exchange of 'same' types of semi-fabricated products. This resulted in intra-industry trade based on supply side factors that differed from developed country intra-industry trade that was based on demand side factors.

Hecksher-Ohlin based intra-industry trade is driven by factor endowment differences. As such the determinant of this form of intra-industry trade is the same as the determinant of inter-industry trade flows. There is no a priori reason why intra-industry trade levels should increase relative to inter-industry trade levels, within an economic integration process. To this end empirical findings of a positive link between economic integration and Hecksher-Ohlin-based intra-industry trade do not provide strong support for the generalised existence of such a link. Within total trade, inter-industry trade flows rising relative to intra-industry trade flows is just as likely to occur as the reverse case.

It is proposed that the Hong Kong-Guangdong province bilateral relationship represents an on-going process of economic integration; and that this trading relationship consists primarily of outward processing trade, a form of trade conducive to a significant amount of intra-industry trade. Despite empirical support for a process of economic integration positively influencing intra-industry trade relative to inter industry trade, no theoretical rationale for such an influence exists. Proposition 2 states:

8 See for example Balassa (1979).

Proposition 2: with a process of economic integration for the Hong Kong-Guangdong province relationship, no evidence need necessarily be forthcoming of this process exerting a positive influence on Hong Kong-Guangdong province intra-industry trade relative to inter-industry trade.

It is the purpose of the remainder of the chapter to empirically examine these hypotheses and propositions.

3. METHODOLOGY

The data sources employed can be found in Appendix 1. The empirical analysis of the Hong Kong-Guangdong province trading relationship is concerned with outward processing trade, intra-industry trade and the process of economic integration.

Outward Processing Trade

Estimates of the value of outward processing trade are made for the years 1985 to 1988 inclusive. The use of 1985 as the starting date for these estimates reflects two points. Firstly the large growth in manufacturing activity that stimulated outward processing trade is generally believed to have commenced in the mid 1980's following the second round of Chinese reforms in 1984. Secondly, the estimated values for the 1985-88 period are based on the outward processing data for 1989-94. Using this data set to estimate values as far back as 1981 would not be feasible.

The average proportion of total trade accounted for by outward processing during the 1989-94 period is used to find approximate values for the 1985-88 period. These averages are calculated for total trade, domestic trade and re-export trade and appear in Table 4.2 below. Following Sung the assumption is made that for all these trade flows 93% of total Hong Kong-China outward processing trade is accounted for by Hong Kong-Guangdong province outward processing trade.

Table 4.2: Hong Kong-China Trade. The Average Proportion of Outward Processing Trade in Total Trade, 1989-94

	Average
Total exports	0.53
Domestic exports	0.75
Re-exports	0.46
Total imports	0.76
Domestic imports	0.68
Re-exports of China origin	0.79

Source: Estimates based on Hong Kong Census and Statistics Department data.

Intra-industry Trade

Two measures of intra-industry trade are used in the empirical analysis: the unadjusted Grubel-Lloyd index and the Aquino adjusted index. The Grubel-Lloyd unadjusted index is:

$$Bj = \left[\sum_i (X_{ij} + M_{ij}) - \sum_i |X_{ij} - M_{ij}|\right] / \sum_i (X_{ij} + M_{ij}), \qquad (1)$$

where j refers to country j and i refers to individual industries. This index is employed in a bilateral setting in this chapter to represent country j's (Hong Kong) intra-industry trade with one country, China.

The Grubel-Lloyd index is measured as total trade in an industry (or industry group) minus the difference between exports and imports, with the assumption being made that such a difference represents inter-industry trade. However if there is an overall trade imbalance then this difference will incorporate the net trading imbalance in addition to inter-industry trade. Consequently the size of the numerator will fall and the measure of intra-industry trade will be biased downward.

Aquino (1981) provided an 'adjusted' index. He considered the indices advanced by Grubel and Lloyd, (both the unadjusted and the adjusted measures), to be unreliable if a country's trade is substantially unbalanced. Under the assumption that the trade imbalance effect of the total trade surplus or deficit is equiproportional in all industries, Aquino suggested estimating what the values of exports and imports of industry i would have been if total exports had been equal to total imports, and then using these 'corrected' values to estimate intra-industry trade:

$$Q_j = \left[\left[\sum_i (X_{ij} + M_{ij}) - \sum_i |X_{ij^*} - M_{ij^*}|\right] / \sum_i (X_{ij} + M_{ij})\right] \times 100, \qquad (2)$$

where j refers to country j and i refers to individual industries. This index is employed in a bilateral setting in this chapter to represent country j's (Hong Kong) intra-industry trade with one country, China; and where:

$$X_{ij^*} = \left[X_{ij} \times 0.5 \sum_i (X_{ij} + M_{ij})\right] / \sum_i X_{ij} \qquad (3)$$

and,

$$M_{ij^*} = \left[M_{ij} \times 0.5 \sum_i (X_{ij} + M_{ij})\right] / \sum_i M_{ij} \qquad (4)$$

A large and increasing trade imbalance is apparent on the Hong Kong-Guangdong bilateral trade link which is why both an unadjusted and an adjusted measure of intra-industry trade is employed in this chapter.[9]

The Intensity of Trade Approach to Measuring Economic Integration

The measurement of economic integration through observation of changes in price differentials across international borders is difficult to achieve. Data constraints mean that statistics of trade flows are the most commonly used quantitative indicator of the extent and progress of economic integration (El-Agraa, 1989). The examination of economic integration of Hong Kong and Guangdong province is being conducted within the context of examining the *progress* of economic integration for these economies since 1981. A trade-based measure of economic integration is adopted here. In assessing the

---

9 The Grubel-Lloyd adjusted index was not applied in this paper. The trade imbalance for Hong Kong-China trade is reflected in import values exceeding export values across all HKCSD industry categories in a majority of years. This results in the numerator and the denominator of the Grubel-Lloyd adjusted measure being equal in a majority of cases.

progress of economic integration use of the term 'indication' rather than 'measure' is perhaps more appropriate.

The intensity of trade analysis is employed here to provide an indication of the economic integration of Hong Kong-Guangdong province in the open-door era. The intensity of trade approach represents one method of examining resistances to trade. The intensity approach takes export and import values as given. It then measures and seeks to explain any deviations from the level of bilateral trade flows that would exist if resistances to trade were equal on all bilateral routes (Drysdale and Garnaut, 1982). The analysis was pioneered by Brown (1949) but was further developed and popularised by Kojima (1964) and subsequently extended by Drysdale (1969).[10]

Within the intensity of trade analysis two countries are seen to trade more or less intensively compared to trade with the rest of the world for two reasons (Drysdale). Firstly because of the particular commodity composition of their trade in relation to world trade, i.e. the level of complementarity in bilateral trade. The second component takes account of the geographical proximity and special institutional and historical ties of the countries in question-the degree of special country bias in a bilateral trading relationship.

The intensity of trade index is defined as the share of a source country or country group's export (import) trade with a particular focus country or country group, relative to that focus destination's share of imports from (exports to) the rest of the world (Anderson and Garnaut, 1987). The index is written as:

$$I_{ij} = (X_{ij}/X_i)/(M_j/T), \tag{5}$$

where X_{ij}/X_i measures the share of country i's exports directed to country j; and M_j/T is the share of country j's imports in world imports (T). T is equal to world imports, Mw, minus M_j.

The complementarity index measures the extent to which country i's exports (imports) matches that of country j's imports (exports) more or less intensively than it matches the commodity composition of world trade (Drysdale):

$$C_{ij} = \sum_{k=1}^{n} \left[(X_i^{\,k}/X_j) \times (T/T^{\,k}) \times (M_i^{\,k}/M_j)\right], \tag{6}$$

where k refers to individual commodities.

10 For a brief discussion of the inadequacies of Kojima's development prior to Drysdale's extension, see Drysdale and Garnaut (1982, 68).

The relative resistance to trade, or country bias index, is defined as the residual index of the trade bias (Anderson and Garnaut). This index indicates the degree of resistance in the other bilateral relationships country i is involved in, i.e. this concept measures the extent to which country i's exports have a higher or lower level of favourable access to country j's import markets than might be expected from both of these countries' shares of world trade in each commodity k (Drysdale):

$$B_{ij}^{k} = [X_{ij}^{k}/X_{i}^{k}]/[M_{j}^{k}/T^{k}] \qquad (7)$$

Hence the intensity of trade index is the product of the complementarity and country bias indices. A value exceeding unity for either of the two components is a reflection of a positive influence on trade intensity.

Data Constraints

Due to data constraints the empirical situation with regard to Hong Kong-Guangdong province trade must be analysed with reference to Hong Kong-China trade flows. The importance of outward processing trade in overall trade and the dominance of Guangdong province in this outward processing trade will consequently be demonstrated given the focus placed on Hong Kong-Guangdong province outward processing trade in this chapter.

4. OUTWARD PROCESSING TRADE, INTRA-INDUSTRY TRADE AND ECONOMIC INTEGRATION FOR THE HONG KONG-GUANGDONG PROVINCE TRADING RELATIONSHIP

Outward Processing Trade

The proportion of total trade between Hong Kong and China estimated to be accounted for by outward processing trade is very large, as can be determined from Table 4.3 below. Considering the estimate that over 90% of all outward processing trade for Hong Kong-China occurs within the Hong Kong-Guangdong bilateral relationship, the role this bilateral trading relationship plays in overall Hong Kong-China trade is obviously very large. This situation clearly indicates the important role of outward processing trade in the increasing comparative importance of the Hong Kong-China bilateral trading relationship evident in Table 4.1.

Figure 4.1 below shows the trend in the value of outward processing trade compared to total trade, for total exports and for total imports. Several key findings can be observed based on the trend apparent in this Figure.[11]

Firstly, in the second half of the 1980's the trend in outward processing trade closely followed the trend in total trade, on both the export side and the import side. The consistency of these trends in the level of trade largely continued in the 1990's for import trade, but the growth in the level of export outward processing trade declined relative to total export trade. The similarity in trend for outward processing trade with total trade during the 1980's period in question indicates that outward processing trade significantly influenced the increase in overall trade during this period of time.

Table 4.3: Hong Kong-China Trade. The Estimated Proportion of Outward Processing Trade in Total Trade, 1989-94

	1989	1990	1991	1992	1993	1994
Total exports	0.53	0.59	0.55	0.53	0.47	0.48
Domestic exports	0.76	0.79	0.77	0.74	0.74	0.72
Re-exports	0.44	0.50	0.48	0.46	0.42	0.43
Total imports	N/A	N/A	0.71	0.75	0.77	0.79
Domestic imports	0.58	0.62	0.68	0.72	0.74	0.76
Re-exports of China origin	N/A	N/A	0.74	0.78	0.81	0.82

Source: Hong Kong Census and Statistics Department.

The trend on the export side in the 1990's supports the point that during this period Hong Kong manufacturers sought to develop a complete production process as opposed to a partial production process in Guangdong province. This increased relocation would be reflected in the downward movement in the level of outward processing export trade relative to the movement in the level of total export trade, as is apparent in Figure 4.1.

11 When interpreting the trend apparent in this figure it is important to remember that the trade values for 1985 to 1988 are estimated from HKCSD data for the 1989-94 period.

Figure 4.1: A Comparison of Total Trade Values with Outward Processing Trade Values for Hong Kong-China Trade

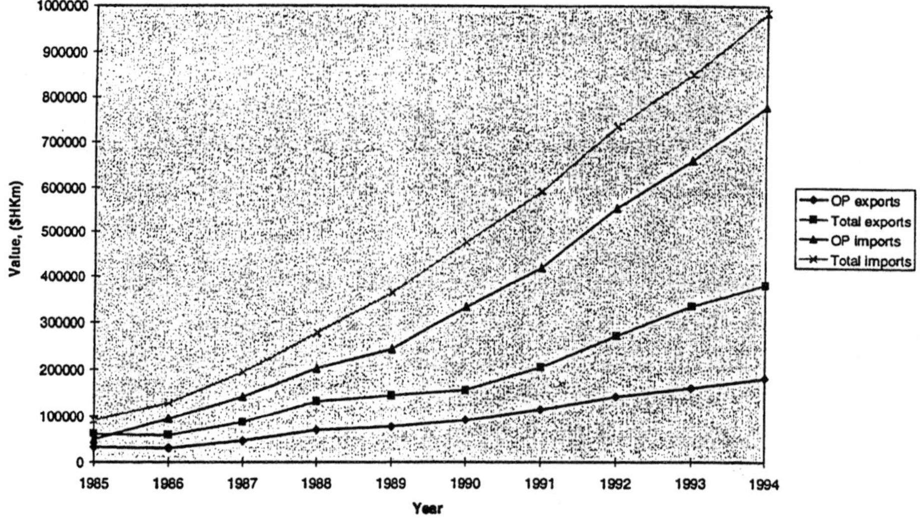

Note:'OP' represents outward processing. Source: Hong Kong Census and Statistics Department.

The general increase in outward processing trade has been maintained as the export of finished products from Guangdong province to Hong Kong and more importantly third markets continues to develop strongly. In light of this continued growth, a closely matching path for outward processing import trade and total import trade, observable in Figure 4.1, is to be expected. The growing disparity over time between the value of outward processing export trade and the value of outward processing import trade further reinforces the changing composition of outward processing trade. Within this changing composition the increase in the value of outward processing trade provides a basis of support for hypothesis 1.

5. INTRA-INDUSTRY TRADE

The level of outward processing trade taking place has been associated with a high proportion of intra-industry trade. This is a reflection of the type of trade occurring in the Hong Kong-Guangdong province bilateral link. Labour-intensive processes for industries such as electronics, textiles and clothing, and toys were transferred to the mainland, while maintaining elements of the production base, plus the control and distribution centre, in Hong Kong. This arrangement led to the exports and imports of various components of a labour-intensive product between Hong Kong and China. The existence of this form of export and import trade underlies the hypothesis that a large proportion of total outward processing trade is intra-industry trade.

Figure 4.2: Unadjusted and Adjusted Intra-Industry Trade Indices for Hong Kong-China Domestic Outward Processing Trade

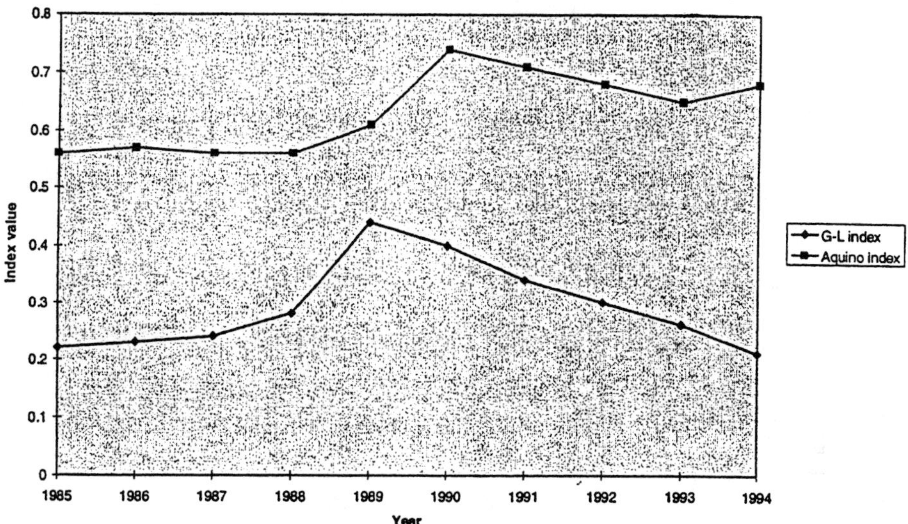

Source: Hong Kong Census and Statistics Department.

In examining outward processing intra-industry trade flows it is important to recognise the large and increasing differential between Hong Kong exports and Hong Kong imports that is observable from the mid 1980's. This differential is common to both total trade and outward processing trade and is readily apparent in Figure 4.1 above. Accounting for this trade imbalance in the calculation of intra-industry trade indices for outward processing trade generated indices that were significantly higher but that displayed largely the same trend over time as those pertaining to unadjusted intra-industry trade. This can be seen in Figure 4.2.

The decline in the level of domestic intra-industry trade, observable for both measures, begins earlier for the unadjusted index. The actual level of intra-industry trade is consistently higher for the Aquino index. While the difference in value between the respective measures narrows noticeably in the middle of the period investigated, the trend in intra-industry trade between the two measures is generally very similar. Empirical evidence exists for the necessity to adjust for trade imbalances in order to avoid a downward biased effect on the level of intra-industry trade indices.

This conclusion is reinforced by the findings for re-export trade, presented in Figure 4.3. The adjusted indices are consistently higher than the unadjusted indices. The trend between the two sets of indices is very similar, with the exception of 1992 when the Aquino index increased noticeably compared to the previous year.

Alternatively it could be assumed that the existence of a trade imbalance was an acceptable finding in any given year between 1985 and 1994, given that such an imbalance did exist in every year. Nevertheless, selecting an unadjusted index for a

Figure 4.3: Unadjusted and Adjusted Intra-Industry Trade Indices for Hong Kong-China Re-Export Outward Processing Trade

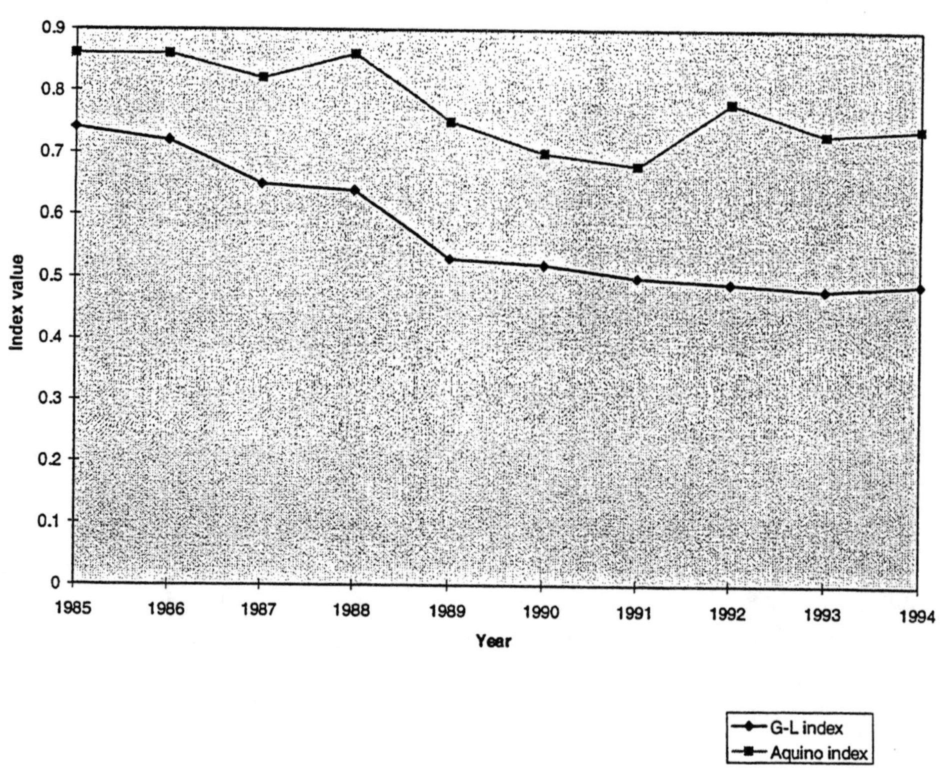

Source: Hong Kong Census and Statistics Department.

particular year, or taking an average of a sub-group of years within the 1985-94 period, would still yield a value for intra-industry trade that was substantially lower than the Aquino indices; (and that was lower than the intra-industry trade index expected to be found for the Hong Kong-Guangdong outward processing trading relationship).

The intra-industry trade indices presented in Figure 4.2 and Figure 4.3 support the proposition that the index of intra-industry trade between Hong Kong and China is biased downward prior to accounting for the existence of trade imbalances. The adjusted indices also suggest that for outward processing trade, the proportion of intra-industry trade in total trade is relatively high, a finding that lends support to Hypothesis 2.[12] There is no evidence to suggest that a failure to adjust for the trade imbalance leads to an apparent trend in the pattern of intra-industry trade over time that differs significantly from the trend observable when the existence of a trade imbalance is accounted for.

With the Aquino intra-industry trade indices, a clear distinction can be made between the respective trends for domestic trade versus re-export trade. A downward trend is apparent for both sets of indices in the 1990's although this trend is more marked for domestic trade given the recovery in the level of re-export intra-industry trade in 1992. Both 1994 indices were higher than the value for the previous year. A slight declining trend from 1988 for re-export trade and from 1990 for domestic trade supports to a certain extent the expectation that the intra-industry trade index would have declined in the 1990's as the number of full production processes in Guangdong province increased.

It can be concluded that a significant proportion of domestic outward processing trade and a substantial proportion of re-export outward processing trade was of the intra-industry trade categorisation between 1985 and 1994. Locational production cost differences led to a cost minimisation strategy on the part of Hong Kong light manufacturing firms reflected in the relocation process previously outlined. Many of these firms have a controlling interest in or complete ownership of the Guangdong province factory operation. The intra-industry trade flows are therefore consistent with a high level of intra-firm trade.

It is important to note that all of the above intra-industry trade indices have been calculated using merchandise trade flows, in line with standard intra-industry trade methodology. This approach does not recognise the value of the Hong Kong support role, over and above the actual level of merchandise trade flows, that continues to add value to the products responsible for the intra-industry trade evident above. The services component of the intra-industry trade taking place, from the Hong Kong end, would be substantial. If it was possible to measure this additional aspect of the intra-industry trade flows then it is conceivable that the apparent decline in intra-industry trade indices during the second half of the period in question would be reversed.

12 Care should be taken when interpreting the intra industry trade indices above as providing evidence of a significant or substantial proportion of total trade being accounted for by intra-industry trade. The intra-industry trade indices have been calculated from HKSCD industry data at a high level of aggregation as this is the only data available. If it were possible to measure intra-industry trade at a more disaggregated level then lower intra-industry trade indices would more than likely be found. Calculations of intra-industry trade indices at a 3 digit level of disaggregation using an SITC equivalent categorisation to the HKCSD industry categories does result in relatively high intra-industry trade indices nevertheless.

6. ECONOMIC INTEGRATION

The importance of relatively low trade resistances in Hong Kong-Guangdong province trade has previously been outlined. Through the use of intensity of trade analysis it is immediately apparent from the results in Table 4.4 that an extremely intense trading relationship exists in the Hong Kong-China bilateral trade link.

A substantial increase in the intensity of trade index is observable in Table 4.4, driven by a consistent increase in the complementarity index over time. The trend in the complementarity index provides evidence of the development of a more complementary trade relationship between Hong Kong and China over time. From 1988 onwards Hong Kong's exports match China's imports more intensively than these exports matched the commodity composition of world trade. Hence from 1988 onwards the commodity composition of Hong Kong-China trade exerted a positive influence on the relative intensity of trade in this bilateral link.

The large values for the country bias index indicate a much higher level of favourable access for Hong Kong's exports to China's import market relative to Hong Kong and China's shares of world trade. The country bias index did fall over time. This observation suggests extremely low relative resistances to trade exist in the Hong Kong-Guangdong province trading relationship.

Table 4.4: An Intensity of Trade Analysis for Hong Kong-China Trade

	I	C	B
1981	9.28	0.70	13.26
1982	10.01	0.75	13.35
1983	10.87	0.69	15.75
1984	11.44	0.76	15.05
1985	12.58	0.89	14.13
1986	12,65	0.91	13.90
1987	12.43	0.98	12.68
1988	12.16	1.10	11.05
1989	13.48	1.12	12.04
1990	13.09	1.19	11.00
1991	12.02	1.22	9.85
1992	11.49	1.24	9.27
1993	13.06	1.30	10.05
1994	12.59	1.28	9.84

Note: I is the intensity of trade index; C is the complementarity of trade index; B is the country bias index.

Source: United Nations comtrade data, STARS, International Economic Data Bank, The Australian National University.

However over the 1981-94 period relative trade resistances were falling faster in other trading relationships.

The results above, in terms of total Hong Kong-China trade, provide evidence of the importance of economic complementarity and relatively low trade resistances in this bilateral relationship. These factors are representative of an environment conducive to a process of market integration, defined at the start of the chapter. The Hong Kong-China trading relationship is clearly an extremely intense trading relationship, relatively speaking. The intensity of trade has increased over time, suggesting a declining gap between potential and actual trade. The outward processing trade on the Hong Kong-Guangdong province link forms a very significant proportion of total Hong Kong-China trade as has previously been demonstrated. The above analysis therefore provides some indication of the increasing economic integration of the sub-region of Hong Kong-Guangdong province and as such provides support for proposition 1.[13]

7. ECONOMIC INTEGRATION AND INTRA-INDUSTRY TRADE

Indication was found of the increasing economic integration of Hong Kong and Guangdong province from 1981 onwards. Outward processing intra-industry trade indices were calculated from 1985 onwards in this chapter. An increasing trend is apparent for domestic trade in the second half of the 1980's but no such trend is apparent for re-export trade. There is no evidence to suggest a positive economic integration effect on the proportion of intra-industry trade in total trade. This result supports proposition 2. Several points related to empirical evidence elsewhere of a positive economic integration/intra-industry trade link are worth noting.

Firstly. The changing composition of outward processing trade between Hong Kong and Guangdong province, previously outlined, is consistent with a declining intra-industry trade index in the 1990's. This trend is also consistent with an on-going economic integration process. Any positive link between economic integration and intra-industry trade will be dependent upon the composition of trade flows. The composition of trade flows between Hong Kong and Guangdong province did not remain constant over time.

Secondly. Intra-industry trade based on product differentiation and economies of scale will, under the right conditions, be encouraged by economic integration, relative to inter-industry trade flows. Such trade will also be internal to a large extent. Hecksher-

---

13 Application of the trade share approach to measuring economic integration, (see Staubhaar, 1987), to Hong Kong-China outward processing trade also provided an indication of increased integration over time. The proportion of internal Hong Kong-China outward processing trade in total Hong Kong-China exports increased consistently between 1985 and 1993. The growth in the level of internal outward processing trade for Hong Kong-China was much larger than the growth in total Hong Kong-China exports over the same period of time.

Ohlin based intra-industry trade flows on the other hand will, by definition, be driven by the same factor endowment differences as inter-industry trade, (and such flows will often be focused on third markets). Therefore intra-industry trade will not necessarily increase relative to inter-industry trade in response to a deepening integration process.

8. CONCLUSION

The general description of the economic integration of GSC, as is best represented by the Hong Kong-Guangdong bilateral link, can be summarised as follows. A large comparative cost differential together with relatively low trade resistances have acted to generate an on-going process of market-oriented integration. This integration process has primarily been represented by large and increasing levels of outward processing trade, a significant proportion of which is intra-industry trade.

Empirical support has been found for outward processing trade on the Hong Kong-Guangdong link being of a large and increasing size; and representing a large component of overall Hong Kong-China trade. A dominant amount of this total trade was accounted for by intra-industry trade. These empirical findings are consistent with trade based on the Hecksher-Ohlin theory of international trade.

Indication was found for an on-going process of economic integration based on evidence of an increasingly intense bilateral trading relationship. No support was found for a positive link between this economic integration process and intra-industry trade as a proportion of total trade. Given the Hecksher-Ohlin-based nature of the intra-industry trade such a result is wholly consistent with an on-going process of economic integration that is accompanied by a high proportion of intra-industry trade in total trade.

REFERENCES

Anderson, K. and Garnaut, R. (1987) *Australian Protectionism: Extent, Causes and Effects*, Allen and Unwin, Sydney.

Aquino, A. (1981) "Intra-industry Trade and Inter-industry Specialisation as Concurrent Sources of International Trade in Manufactures", *Weltwirtschaftliches Archiv*, 275-95.

Balassa, B. (1979) "Intra-industry Trade and the Integration of Developing Countries in the World Economy", *Staff Working Papers 312*, The World Bank.

Bhagwati, J. (1964) "The Pure Theory of International Trade. A Survey", *Economic Journal*, 293: 1-84.

Brown, A.J. (1949) *Applied Economics. Aspects of the World Economy in War and Peace*, George Allen and Unwin, London.

Culem, C. and Lundberg, L. (1983) "The Product Pattern of Intra-industry Trade: Stability Among Countries and Over Time", *Weltwirtschaftliches Archiv*, 77: 113-129.

Drabek, Z. and Greenaway, D. (1984) "Economic Integration and Intra-industry Trade: The EEC and CMEA Compared", *Kyklos*, 37: 444-469.

Drysdale, P. (1969) "Japan, Australia, and New Zealand: Prospects for Western Pacific Economic Integration", *Economic Record*, 45: 321-42 (September).

Drysdale, P. and Garnaut, R. (1982) *Trade Intensities and the Analysis of Bilateral Trade Flows in a Many Country World: A Survey*, reprinted from Hitosobashi Journal of Economics, Tokyo, Hitosubashi University, 22(2): 62-84 (February).

Drysdale, P. and Garnaut, R. (1993) "The Pacific: An Application of the General Theory of Economic Integration", Bergsten, F. and Noland, M. (ed.) *Pacific Dynamism and the International Economic System*, Institute for International Economics, Washington D.C., 183-223.

El-Agraa, A.M. (1988) *International Economic Integration*, Macmillan, Hong Kong.

El-Agraa, A.M. (1989) *The Theory and Measurement of International Economic Integration*, Macmillan, Hong Kong.

Greenaway, D. and Milner, C.R. (1986) *The Economics of Intra-Industry Trade,* Basil Blackwell, New York.

Grubel, H.G. and Lloyd, P.J. (1975) *Intra-Industry Trade. The Theory and Measurement of International Trade in Differentiated Products*, Macmillan Press Ltd, London.

Hong Kong Census and Statistics Department (1995) *Trade Involving Outward Processing in China. 1989-1994.*

Kojima, K. (1964) "The Pattern of International Trade Among Advanced Countries", *Hitosubashi Journal of Economics*, June, 16-36.

Lardy, N. (1992) *Foreign Trade and Economic Reform in China. 1978-1990*, Cambridge University Press, New York.

North, D.C. (1987) "Institutions, Transaction Costs and Economic Growth", *Economic Inquiry*, 25(3): 419-28.

Staubhaar, T. (1987) "South-South Trade: Is Integration a Solution?, *Intereconomics*, January/February.

Sung, Y.W. (1992) "The Economic Integration of Hong Kong, Taiwan and South Korea with the Mainland of China", in Garnaut, R. and Liu Guoguang, *International Reform and Internationalisation: China and the Pacific Region,* Allen and Unwin, Sydney, 149-181.

Sung, Y.W. (1995) "Subregional Economic Integration: Hong Kong, Taiwan, South China and Beyond", in Chen, E.K.Y. and Drysdale, P., *Corporate Links and Foreign Direct Investment,* Harper Educational, NSW, 56-86.

Sung, Y.W., Liu, P.W., Wong, Y.C.R. and Lau, P.K. (1995) *The Fifth Dragon. The Emergence of the Pearl River Delta*, Addison-Wesley Publishing Company, Inc. Singapore.

Tharakan, P.M.K., Chapter 5 in Tharakan, P.M.K. and Kol, J. (1989) *Intra-Industry Trade. Theory, Evidence and Extensions*, Macmillan Press Ltd, Hong Kong.

APPENDIX 1 DATA SOURCES

Data from the Hong Kong Census and Statistics Department, (HKSCD), is available from 1981 to 1994. Separate statistics exist on domestic exports, re-exports, domestic imports and re-exports of China origin. This data source is supplemented by UN Comtrade data from STARS within the International Economic Data Bank at the Australian National University.

Detailed statistics of outward-processing trade and Hong Kong-Guangdong province trade are not available for the entire period. Such statistics are available for the period 1989-1994 inclusive. The outward processing data is based on a quarterly survey conducted by the HKSCD. The HKSCD categorise eight components of manufacturing trade for the purposes of detailing the outward processing aspect of total manufacturing trade:

1. Textile Materials, Yarn, Fabrics and Textile Articles other than Textile Garments.
2. Articles of Apparel and Clothing Accessories (Textile Garments).
3. Plastics and Articles.
4. Machinery and Mechanical Appliances; Electrical Equipment.
5. Sound Recorders and Reproducers, Television Image and Sound Recorders and Reproducers.
6. Clocks and Watches.
7. Toys, Games and Sports Requisites; Parts and Accessories.
8. Base Metals and Metal Products.

5. HONG KONG'S OUTWARD PROCESSING INVESTMENT IN CHINA: IMPLICATIONS FOR HONG KONG ECONOMY

Kui-yin Cheung

1. INTRODUCTION

It is generally recognized that foreign direct investment (FDI) not only contributes to economic changes in the host country, but is itself a consequence of structural change in the home country. Changing comparative cost advantages over time have made industries uncompetitive in more advanced economies; as a result, they move their production to less advanced countries where the factor endowment is more appropriate for the production technology. Factor cost oriented FDI thus becomes a catalyst for structural adjustment by moving the production capacity abroad. In this way, FDI and structural change become mutually reinforcing phenomena. This structural change FDI is "comparative advantage augmenting" [Ozawa 1992], and is complementary to domestic human and capital resources which makes it desirable for economic growth. This argument is supported by the experience in Japan. After the World War II, Japan experienced a rapid economic growth that was accompanied by a reallocation of resources from the primary to the secondary and tertiary sectors, from low productivity light manufacturing to high productivity industries in the manufacturing sector. In the 1970's, the Japanese economy further shifted from 'resource consuming' heavy and chemical industries toward 'knowledge intensive' industries. Outward FDI served as a catalyst to restructure the economy.

Since the 1950s, Hong Kong has developed as a typical export-oriented economy. By concentrating on labour intensive light industries, Hong Kong becomes a vital exporter of clothing, textile, watches, toys, electronic and plastic products. Manufacturing output accounts for almost all domestic exports of Hong Kong. Export orientation is generally considered as one of the reasons for the economic success over the 1960s and 1970s. With the advent of 1980s, Hong Kong's comparative advantage in labour-intensive industries has been eroded by increasing wage rates[1] and land prices. The "open door" policy of China in the late 1970's furnished an unprecedented opportunity for Hong Kong businessman to lower production costs and maintain internationally competitiveness. This led to an outward flow of FDI from Hong Kong to China and other countries in South-east Asia as well. The reform in China has not only changed the bilateral merchandise trade between Hong Kong and China but also contributed to structural change of the Hong Kong economy.

From 1979 onwards, Hong Kong has experienced a dramatic change in its industrial structure. A massive relocation of manufacturing plants from Hong Kong to China is taking place. Over 3 million local Chinese workers in the Guangdong province of China are reportedly working directly or indirectly for Hong Kong companies, compared with the total work force of 2.8 million in the territory itself. In the past decade, Hong Kong was China's largest "outside investor"; its share stood over 60% in China's total contracted foreign investment. It was estimated[2] that 25.7% of Hong Kong's GDP in 1990 was attributed to "the China factor",[3] compared with only 5.3% in 1980.

This chapter tries to investigate the implications of Hong Kong's outward processing investment in China, particularly in the Guangdong province, on the deindustrialisation of the Hong Kong economy at both the industry and macro levels in the past fifteen years. Structural changes within the manufacturing sector and total factor productivity among manufacturing industries will be estimated to confirm whether the local industry is heading towards being a high productivity industry. The structure of the paper is as follows: Section 2 looks at the trade relationship, particularly the re-export and outward-processing trade, between Hong Kong and China. Section 3 highlights Hong Kong's outward processing investment in China. The process of deindustralization will then be demonstrated from two macro aspects: the changes in the contribution of manufacturing industries to GDP and the changes in employment size of the manufacturing sector. Section 4 investigates the structural change from the industry level within the manufacturing sector; Section 5 sets up the model specifications for productivity growth. Section 6 presents the empirical results and sensitivity analysis for model specifications. Section 7 offers the conclusion.

---

1 According to Hong Kong Census & Statistics Department, the nominal daily wages of all manufacturing raises from HK$81 in 1983 to HK$248 in 1993, an average increase of 206% over the period.

2 Hang Seng Economic Monthly, Hang Seng Bank, Hong Kong, June 1993.

3 China is Hong Kong's second largest "outside investor" (with an investment estimated to be about US$20 billion), second only to Britain.

2. HONG KONG'S RE-EXPORTS AND OUTWARD-PROCESSING TRADE[4] WITH CHINA

Since the adoption of open-door policy by China in the late 1970s, one of the significant impacts on the Hong Kong economy is the change in trade structure. The obvious evidence is the rise of re-exports in the territory and the increasing economic integration with Southern China, particularly Guangdong province. The export of *sanzi* enterprises' "outward processing" activities[5] in the Pearl River Delta region (PRD), Guangdong,[6] through Hong Kong has indeed become so substantial that it has been the focal point of China-US trade disputes in the last few years.

From 1979 to 1994, Hong Kong's imports from China increased to 20 times of that in 1979 and reached US$ 60.4 billion. The majority of these imports, however, are for re-export and are of outward-processing in nature. So the re-export portion of imports grew rapidly too and exceeded the retained portion in 1986. The share of Chinese imports re-exported via Hong Kong to total imports from China rose from 29.7 percent in 1979 to 85.2 percent in 1994. At the same time, China became the largest source of, as well as the largest market for, Hong Kong's re-exports. In 1988, for the first time, the value of re-exports exceeded the domestic exports. In 1994, China accounted for 57.6 per cent of Hong Kong's re-exports by origin and 34.1 per cent by destination. The re-export trade involving China reached US$ 92,823 million in 1994 and accounted for 76.4 per cent of Hong Kong's total re-exports in that year. Spurred by the robust growth in outward processing activities, as well as the continued trade expansion in China, it is envisioned that the share of re-exports will completely outweigh the domestic exports in the foreseeable future.

Regarding domestic exports, Hong Kong's role as a direct supplier of goods to China has grown dramatically as well. In 1977, the share of domestic exports was only about 0.1 percent of China's total import. By 1994, this figure had stretched 65 times and reached US$ 7.8 billion. In 1989, for the first time ever, the domestic exports surpassed China's exports retained in Hong Kong, and since then Hong Kong's visible trade has had a direct trade surplus with China. However, it is important to note that, although an increasing proportion of Hong Kong's domestic exports to China are of finished goods in nature and for final consumption, the majority of these exports are raw materials, parts, semi-manufactures, machinery and electrical equipment and are related to outward

4 According to Hong Kong Census and Statistics Department, outward processing trade refers to 3 different components: exports to China for outward processing, imports from China related to outward processing and re-exports of China origin produced through outward processing in China.

5 Hong Kong accounts for 68.2 percent of China's direct foreign investment (FDI) and in Guangdong province 82.5 percent of contractual FDI and 76.4 percent of the realized FDI are come from Hong Kong in 1993.

6 Of Hong Kong's total exports to China, 27% were exported to Guangdong in 1985. The figure was increased to 32% in 1993. On the other hand, in Hong Kong's total imports from China, about 28% came from Guangdong in 1985. This figure was raised to 38% in 1993. From Guangdong's perspective, this represents 85% of its total exports in 1993 (compared with 72% in 1985.)

processing activities commissioned by Hong Kong enterprises, amidst the tight labour market and high rent situation in Hong Kong. Analyzed by broad commodity categories, as shown in Table 5.2, watches and clocks, toys and sports equipment, stereo and video equipment have the highest share in both domestic exports to and imports from China during the period from 1989 to 1994.[7] Machinery and electrical appliances have the lowest proportion in both domestic exports to and re-exports from China. The percentages of outward processing trade with respect to most individual commodity groups were close to their import equivalents, except the ratio for machinery and electrical equipment. In a large measure, we might expect that this was due to the strong demand for such Hong Kong products in China. The same was true for re-exports as there was a large market in China for foreign machinery, electrical equipment, consumer electronics such as television sets and sound recorders, as well as metals and metal products. (Ho and Kueh, 1993, p345)

The estimated value and proportion of outward processing trade for imports from and exports to China are shown from Table 5.3 to Table 5.6. Imports from China related to outward processing increased at an average annual growth of 25.6% from $113,581 million in 1989 (58.1% of total imports from China) to $354,912 million (75.4%) in 1994. Total exports to China for outward processing also increased from $76,868 million in 1989 (53.0% of total exports to China) to $181,179 million (47.7%) in 1994 at an average annual growth of 18.7%. Domestic exports to China for outward processing were $31,962 million in 1989 (76% of total domestic exports) and increased to $41,959 million (71.4%) in 1994, an average annual growth of 5.6%. Re-exports to China for outward processing reached $139,221 million (43.1% of total re-exports) in 1994 from $44,906 million (43.4%) in 1989 at an average annual growth of 25.4%. This, more or less, reflects the growing importance of outward-processing activities in Southern China.

3. HONG KONG'S OUTWARD PROCESSING INVESTMENT IN CHINA

During the period from 1979 to 1992, China attracted a total of US $34.28 billion in realized foreign direct investment (FDI). More than 40 per cent of realized FDI was concentrated in the Guangdong area. As the largest source of China's FDI, Hong Kong accumulated a total of U$$20.842 billion during this period, accounting for 60.8 percent of the total amount of capital utilized. Most of the Hong Kong investments (more than 85 percent) are in the PRD/Guangdong area and are of outward processing in nature (see Table 5.7). These Hong Kong subsidiaries employ more than 3 million local workers, compared with a mere 2.8 million total workforce in the territory.

---

7 Because of the rapid expansion of the outward-processing trade with China since 1980s, the Hong Kong Census and Statistics Department began to compile statistics on domestic exports and re-exports to China for outward-processing purposes in the third quarter of 1988; and statistics on imports from China related to outward-processing in the first quarter of 1989.

Table 5.1. Hong Kong and China Trade (US$ million), 1979-1994

	HK Imports from China			HK Exports to China		
	Total	Retained in Hong Kong	Re-exported elsewhere	Total	Hong Kong goods	Hong Kong Re-export
1979	3044	2139	905 (29.7)	383	121	263 (68.7)
1981	5315	3479	1836 (34.5)	1961	523	1438 (73.3)
1983	5890	3725	2165 (36.8)	2531	856	1675 (66.2)
1984	7100	4224	2876 (40.5)	5033	1443	3590 (71.3)
1985	7449	3893	3556 (47.7)	7857	1950	5907 (75.2)
1986	10252	4963	5289 (51.6)	7550	2310	5241 (69.4)
1987	14776	6131	8645 (58.5)	11290	3574	7716 (68.3)
1988	19406	5926	13480 (69.5)	17030	4874	12157 (71.4)
1989	24431	5127	19310 (79.0)	18816	5548	13268 (70.5)
1990	29482	4825	24657 (83.6)	20305	6086	14219 (70.0)
1991	37615	5435	32180 (85.6)	26631	6974	19656 (73.8)
1992	45423	5513	39910 (87.9)	35141	7949	27192 (77.4)
1993	51564	6654	44910 (87.1)	43321	8116	35205 (81.3)
1994	60370	8936	51434 (85.2)	49205	7822	41389 (84.1)

Figures in parenthesis represent percentage of total exports (imports)Sources:Census and Statistics Department, Hong Kong Review of Overseas Trade, various issues.

In addition to the pushing and pulling factors as suggested in most literature, the continued depreciation of Renminbi versus the US dollar and Hong Kong dollar in real terms since the mid-1980s has been a contributory factor prompting many Hong Kong companies to move to the mainland in an attempt to reduce their costs and increase their profit. The recent more stringent government legislation to control pollution in production has further accelerated this trend. A closer economic integration between Hong Kong and Guangdong will be assured in the foreseeable future.

Table 5.2: Percentage Share of Trade of Outward-processing nature to Total Trade with China by Commodity Groups, 1989, 1992 and 1994

	Domestic Exports			Re-exports			Imports		
Commodity Group	1989	1992	1994	1989	1992	1994	1989	1992	1994
Textiles	84.8	87.4	79.4	71.5	81.9	78.3	12.8	23.0	30.3
Clothing	85.1	93.2	96.4	87.3	76.0	69.0	84.5	84.4	83.1
Plastic Products	83.9	77.5	79.8	58.0	64.5	58.5	73.4	89.3	87.1
Machinery and Electrical	56.7	59.7	57.0	24.9	27.3	29.7	77.8	81.0	82.2
Electronic Products	94.6	92.7	90.6	43.1	41.4	46.2	85.2	92.7	94.7
Watches and Clocks	98.5	98.6	98.7	92.5	97.7	97.9	94.6	94.3	96.4
Toys, Games and Sports Goods	96.4	91.9	93.8	60.1	80.1	73.6	94.1	96.9	94.2
Metals and Metal Products	64.2	69.0	54.4	37.8	34.8	40.4	30.2	43.6	51.2
All Commodities	76.0	74.3	71.4	43.6	46.2	43.3	58.1	72.1	75.9

Source: Hong Kong Census and Statistics Department, Hong Kong External Trade, various issues.

Table 5.3: Hong Kong's Imports from China: Estimated Value and Share of Outward Processing Trade (*Sanlai yibu*)

Year	Imports from China (HK$ Million)	Estimated value of outward processing Trade (HK$ Million)	Estimated Proportion of Outward Processing in percentage of total
1989	195,390	113,581	57.7
1990	234,708 (20.12)	145,103 (27.75)	61.5
1991	291,829 (24.34)	197,384 (36.03)	67.3
1992	352,136 (20.66)	254,013 (28.69)	71.7
1993	400,013 (13.60)	295,203 (16.22)	73.4
1994	467,831 (16.95)	354,912 (20.23)	75.4
1989-94 Av. Annual Growth	19.14	25.78	

Notes: Estimated value of Sanlai yibu are not available before 1989.
Figures in brackets denote percentage change

Source: Hong Kong Monthly Digest, 1991-95, Various Issues, Census and Statistics Department, H.K.

Table 5.4: Hong Kong's Total Exports to China: Estimated Value and Share of Outward Processing Trade (*Sanlai yibu*)

Year	Total Exports to China (HK$ Million)	Estimated value of outward processing Trade (HK$ Million)	Estimated Proportion of Outward Processing in percentage of total
1989	145,051	76,868	53.0
1990	156,422 (7.84)	91,914 (19.57)	58.8
1991	205,328 (31.26)	113,931 (23.95)	55.5
1992	270,503 (31.74)	141,639 (24.32)	52.4
1993	334,334 (23.60)	160,178 (13.09)	47.9
1994	380,160 (13.71)	181,179 (13.11)	47.7
1989-94 Av. Annual Growth	21.63	18.81	

Notes: Estimated value of Sanlai yibu are not available before 1989.
Figures in brackets denote percentage change

Source: Hong Kong Monthly Digest, 1991-95, Various Issues, Census and Statistics Department, H.K.

Table 5.5: Hong Kong's Domestic Exports to China: Estimated Value and Share of Outward Processing Trade (*Sanlai yibu*)

Year	Domestic Exports to China (HK$ Million)	Estimated value of Outward Processing Trade (HK$ Million)	Estimated Proportion of Outward Processing in percentage of total
1989	42,080	31,962	76.0
1990	46,103 (9.56)	36,418 (13.04)	79.0
1991	52,751 (14.42)	40,369 (10.85)	76.5
1992	59,557 (12.90)	44,271 (9.67)	74.3
1993	61,023 (2.46)	45,141 (1.97)	74.0
1994	58,774 (-3.69)	41,959 (-7.05)	71.4
1989-94 Av. Annual Growth	7.13	5.70	

Notes: Estimated value of Sanlai yibu are not available before 1989.
Figures in brackets denote percentage change

Source: Hong Kong Monthly Digest, 1991-95, Various Issues, Census and Statistics Department, H.K.

Table 5.6: Hong Kong's Re-exports to China: Estimated Value and Share of Outward Processing Trade (*Sanlai yibu*)

Year	Re-exports to China (HK$ Million)	Estimated value of outward processing Trade (HK$ Million)	Estimated Proportion of Outward Processing in percentage of total
1989	102,971	44,906	43.4
1990	110,319 (7.14)	55,496 (23.58)	50.0
1991	152,576 (38.30)	735,626 (32.55)	48.0
1992	210,946 (38.26)	97,368 (32.36)	45.9
1993	273,311 29.56)	115,037 (18.15)	41.9
1994	321,386 (17.59)	139,221 (21.02)	43.1
1989-94 Av. Annual Growth	26.17	25.53	

Notes: Estimated value of Sanlai yibu are not available before 1989. Figures in brackets denote percentage change

Source: Hong Kong Monthly Digest, 1991-95, Various Issues, Census and Statistics Department, H.K.

According to Tuan & Ng (1994) studies on the behaviour of cross-border operations of Hong Kong manufacturers in Guangdong, electronics, garments/textiles, metal and plastic products, and toys were the major industries in Hong Kong involved in heavy outward investment and cross-border operations in PRD/Gaungdong in recent years. It was estimated that approximately 80 percent of the firms had moved part or all of their manufacturing processes to PRD/Guangdong. Among these firms, 55 percent moved the whole manufacturing operations outward with only trading activities and industrial management business being maintained in their Hong Kong headquarters. Almost all (97.8 percent) of their Chinese subsidiaries were engaged in assembly and fabrication processes; 42.4 percent were in prototype manufacturing and 59.1 percent were in packaging/package design. Most of the upper stream process, such as R&D, market analysis and management, and shipment were handled by their Hong Kong establishments.

Table 5.7: Hong Kong's Foreign Direct Investment (FDI) in Guangdong, China

Year	Realised FDI (US$ Million)	Contractual FDI (US$ Million)	Hong Kong FDI as % of China's Total FDI	
			Realised	Contractual
1986	622.65	590.98	92.5	68.2
1987	502.67	702.19	84.6	56.3
1988	836.54	1,810.46	91.0	80.8
1989	952.72	1,800.11	64.4	69.8
1990	1,258.27	2,353.66	67.5	78.4
1991	1,622.83	4,229.57	62.8	72.9
1992	3,453.64	1,6429.11	70.7	82.7
1993	7,371.59	28,798.81	76.4	82.5
Total	16,621	56,715	-	-
Average	-	-	76.2	74.0

Source: Guangdong Statistical Yearbook 1991-1993

Without doubt, the opening of coastal cities in China in the late 1970's has given Hong Kong businessman an unique opportunity to lower costs, thus prolonging the life cycle of labour intensive products. The process of pondering on technological upgrading or market diversification was temporarily solved but the basic problem of technological upgrading of Hong Kong industry still remains. With the extensive relocation of manufacturing plants to Southern China, the Hong Kong manufacturing sector was able to release its labour resources to other sectors which were likewise faced with labour recruitment problems in a very tight overall labour market situation. Hence a rapid process of "structural transformation" towards a "service economy" was unfolded. Some would of course call it "de-industrialization". The concomitant process of de-industrialization and the growing importance of its tertiary sector can be illustrated from two macro perspectives: the changes in the contribution of economic sectors to GDP and the changes in employment in different sectors.

(i) Changes in contribution of economic sectors to GDP

The structural change phenomena in the Hong Kong economy can be shown first by the contribution of different economic sectors to GDP. Without sufficient land and natural resources, the primary production which included fishing, mining and quarrying only accounted for 1.1 per cent of GDP in 1979 and then declined to 0.2 percent in 1993 as expected (see Table 5.8). At the same time, the manufacturing sector, which was once the most important sector, has contracted as well. Its contribution to the GDP declined steadily from its peak of 31 per cent in 1970 to 22.8 per cent in 1981. After a short uplift, it fell to 11.0 per cent in 1994. With the manufacturing plants relocated to Southern China in the early 1980's, Hong Kong had to concentrate on the expansion of the tertiary sector. The service sector in general, and trading, finance and business services were able to absorb those labour resources released from the manufacturing industries. As a result, their relative contributions to the domestic economy soared. The financial services sector and the wholesale and trades sector increased from 23.9 per cent and 21.4 per cent in 1980 to 26.1 percent and 27.0 percent respectively in 1994.

(ii) Changes in employment in different sectors.

The de-industrialization process can also be reflected in the employment situation among different sectors. Again, from Table 8, it can be seen that there is a significant decline in the proportion of manufacturing employment. In 1984, the manufacturing sector employed 899,947 workers. The total number was halved by 1994 and fell below 400,000 in 1995. There had been a continuous shift in employment from the manufacturing sector to tertiary sectors. The share of manufacturing employment dropped continuously from 50.7 per cent in 1979 to 18.0 per cent in 1994. On the other hand the tertiary sector expanded steadily from 43.8 per cent in 1979 to 78.8 per cent in 1994.

Given the very-low unemployment rates in recent years, the success of switching of employees across sectors has been claimed to be the result of the flexibility of the local economy. On the contrary, it reflects an underlying problem. Hong Kong's major sectors

Table 5.8. Changes in Hong Kong's Industrial Structure: Percentage Contribution by Industrial Sectors to GDP (at factor cost) and Employment Distribution, 1961-1994

Sector	1961	1971	1979	1981	1983	1985	1987	1989	1991	1993	1994
GDP											
Primary sector	**3.7**	**1.9**	**1.1**	**0.9**	**0.8**	**0.6**	**0.5**	**0.3**	**0.2**	**0.2**	**0.1**
Secondary sector	**32.2**	**34.9**	**36.0**	**31.7**	**31.8**	**29.7**	**29.2**	**26.7**	**23.0**	**18.5**	**16.9**
Manufacturing	23.6	28.1	27.6	22.8	23.0	22.1	22.0	19.3	15.4	11.4	11.0
Construction	6.2	4.9	7.3	7.5	6.4	5.0	4.8	5.2	5.5	5.0	5.2
Tertiary sector	**64.2**	**63.2**	**62.8**	**67.4**	**68.3**	**69.7**	**70.3**	**73.0**	**76.8**	**81.3**	**83.0**
Financial services	10.8	17.5	21.4	23.9	17.7	16.1	17.0	19.5	22.7	25.7	26.1
Wholesale & trades	-	-	-	20.3	20.5	22.8	24.3	25.0	25.9	26.5	27.0
Employment											
Primary sector	**8.1**	**4.2**	**0.05**	**0.05**	**0.05**	**0.03**	**0.03**	**0.02**	**0.02**	**0.02**	**0.02**
Secondary sector	**49.0**	**53.0**	**56.1**	**54.4**	**49.6**	**46.7**	**44.4**	**38.5**	**30.9**	**24.3**	**21.2**
Manufacturing	40.0	42.8	50.7	49.3	45.3	42.9	40.5	35.0	27.7	21.3	18.0
Construction	4.9	5.4	5.0	4.5	3.7	3.3	3.4	3.1	2.6	2.5	2.7
Tertiary sector	**42.9**	**42.8**	**43.8**	**45.5**	**50.4**	**53.2**	**55.6**	**61.5**	**69.1**	**75.7**	**78.8**
Financial services	1.6	2.7	6.6	7.3	8.6	8.6	9.9	11.3	13.0	14.9	15.7
Wholesale & trades	11.0	11.5	24.1	24.9	27.2	29.8	30.7	34.2	38.4	41.8	43.4

Notes: A dash indicates that the entry does not exist. Primary sector refers to all agriculture, fishing, mining and quarrying activities. Secondary sector refers to all manufacturing, electricity, gas and water, and construction. Tertiary sector refers to all financial and other services industries, including transport, storage and communication, community, social and personal services, and ownership of premises. The terms "Financial services" includes financing, insurance, real estate and business services, while wholesale and trades" includes wholesale, retail and import/export trades, restaurants and hotels.

Sources: 1961-1979, Estimates of Gross Domestic Product, 1961 to 1994, Census & Statistics Department, Hong Kong , March 1995.

of production remain rather poor at the skilled level. The Hong Kong economy is still reveling in the bonanza of the China factor for cost cutting. No serious efforts in industrial and technological upgrading have been made.

The passive non-intervention industrial policy adopted by the Hong Kong Government obviously rules out any possible public intervention in research and development in the private sector. Hong Kong manufacturing industries are dominated by small to medium size firms (87.6% employing less than 20 persons.) This puts the small firms in a less favourable position in technological upgrading as compared to other

Asian NIEs who adopt more positive industrial policies. To maintain the sector's competitiveness, efforts will be needed to overcome capacity constraints and to devote resources to industrial and technological upgrading

Apart from investing in China, Hong Kong manufacturers also invested in South-east Asia, particularly in Thailand, Malaysia, Indonesia, the Philippines and Singapore, to diversify their investments and spread business risks.[8] However, these countries lack the linguistic and cultural bonds which link Hong Kong with neighouring Guangdong. China would continue to be Hong Kong manufacturers' major investment destination.

4. STRUCTURAL CHANGES WITHIN THE MANUFACTURING INDUSTRIES

In the previous discussion, we have seen that the contribution of the manufacturing sector to GDP and to the size of employment has dropped off in the past decade. The manufacturing sector was overtaken by the financial services sector and the wholesale and trade sector and was no longer the leading sector in the economy. Accompanying with the outward investment to China, most of the local manufacturers used their Hong Kong establishments as a supporting base for their offshore production. As a result, the demand for services from finance and insurance, and the wholesale and trade, sectors has increased drastically. In fact, the growth in the service (tertiary) sector in the past decade was derived from the increase in demand for the intermediation services[9] from these manufacturing firms. Based on the estimate of GDP from expenditure, the demand for intermediate services increased from 27.23% in 1983 to 40.78% in 1993. In 1994, the manufacturing sector only contributed about 11% to GDP and employed 18% of local workforce. As suggested in growth theory, when an economy has developed to a certain extent, it would associate with a process of quality improvement and variety proliferation rather than with the mere quantity increase. Thus this international division of labour between Hong Kong and Guangdong should lead to quality improvement and technology enhancement. Therefore other than the structural change from manufacturing to service sector, we would expect changes within the manufacturing sector.

Table 5.8 presents the indices of industrial production among the manufacturing industries. Using 1986 as the base year (1986=100), the Paper Products and Printing industry showed the fastest growth in production for the period 1984-94. It increased from 86 in 1984 to 272 in 1994, increasing by 286 percent in a decade. The Electrical and Electronic industry increased from 90 to 165 for the same period as well. This

---

8 The annual exercise pertaining to the renewal of China's Most Favoured Nation (MFN) trading status by the United States has been an area of concern to local manufacturers.

9 The finanical intermediate services include services provided by the banks, deposit-taking companies and other firms dealing with personal loans, mortgages, instalment credit, factoring and bill discounting. Other intermediation services include insurance services and business services -- such as: accounting and auditing, legal and architectural design, engineering and other technical consultancy, data processing, advertising and market research, machinery & equipment rental and leasing services.

Table 5.9: Indices of Industrial Production among Manufacturing Industry, 1982-94 (1986=100)

	Wearing apparel	Textile	Paper Product & Printing	Plastic	Chemical, Rubber & Nonmetallic	Basic Metals	Electrical & Electronic	Machinery & Equipment	All Manufacturing
1982	80	63	-	55	-	66	-	-	69
1983	85	69	-	62	-	64	-	-	78
1984	91	77	86	89	88	92	90	94	91
1985	84	80	86	87	88	89	89	94	87
1986	100	100	100	100	100	100	100	100	100
1987	113	114	126	106	107	116	126	132	116
1988	114	111	153	101	104	139	145	158	123
1989	116	117	167	88	95	126	147	166	124
1990	113	115	182	76	90	112	149	164	123
1991	110	120	201	70	85	110	153	178	124
1992	111	125	235	65	81	106	156	205	126
1993	113	116	265	55	73	96	160	231	125
1994	113	115	272	45	66	95	165	239	125

Source: Annual Digest of Statistics, Census and Statistics Department, various issues.

implied that their share of output to the total gross output of manufacturing sector increased substantially. The Wearing apparel industry and the Textile industry maintained quite a stable growth for the entire period. The Plastic industry, however, suffered the most cutback among the industries in question. The production indices of the Plastic industry declined continuously from 106 in 1987 to 45 in 1994. This indicated that there might be changes in the structure of manufacturing sector. Together with the decline in gross output for most of the manufacturing industries since 1989, the gross output of manufacturing sector decreased from HK$348,161 million in 1989 to $311,816 million in 1993 as well, decreasing at an annual rate of 2.67%. This made the measurement of structural changes within the manufacturing sector more confusing.

Following Chen (1994), we construct comparative indices to measure the structural changes among the industries in the manufacturing sector, i.e.

$$C_i = \Sigma \mid S_{i\,t} - S_{i\,t-1} \mid \qquad (1)$$

where $$S_{i\,t} = Y_{i\,t} / Y_t$$

and $S_{i\,t}$ represents the share of gross output of industry i to that of manufacturing output in time t.

C_i equals the sum of changes, in absolute terms, in the share of industry i's gross output to that of manufacturing output between time t and t -1 for a particular period, say a 5-year period. Thus C_i measures the structural changes of industry i for that particular time period (detail see Appendix).

In addition, we constructed another indices:

$$I_i = C_i / \Sigma(GY_t) \qquad (2)$$

where GY_t is the growth rate of manufacturing output in time t.

and I_i is the ratio of structural changes of industry i for a particular period of time to the sum of growth rate of manufacturing output for the same time period. Thus I_i measures the relative change of the structure of industry i to the growth of manufacturing gross output for a particular period.

Table 5.10 displays the indices of structural changes, C_i , in manufacturing sector. When we look at it from industry level for a 5-year period, it is the Paper Products and Printing industry, the Textile industry and the Electrical and Electronic industry that have the most changes among the industries in question for the period 1979-83, 1984-88 and 1989-93 respectively. However, for the period 1979-93, it is the Leather, Wood and Cork industry that has the least changes. It implies that the share of Leather output to the manufacturing output remains rather stable during the entire study period. When measured in terms of I_i -- the ratio of the structural changes of industry i to the cumulated growth of manufacturing output, it is obvious that this ratio has increased drastically during the period 1989-93. This indicates that the structural changes within the manufacturing sector have increased substantially during this period.

5. MODEL SPECIFICATIONS AND DATA SOURCES

5.1 The Gross-Output Model

We follow the conventional methodology to measure factor productivity which is based on a production function. For a three-input model, a general production function can be written as[10]

$$Q(t) = A(t)f[K(t), L(t), M(t)] \qquad (3)$$

where $Q(t)$ $K(t)$, $L(t)$ and $M(t)$ are output, capital, labour and material inputs, and $A(t)$ is an index of Hicks-neutral technical change or total productivity at time t.

10 This methodology is first used by Solow [1957] and later is used in many productivity studies such as in Denison [1967], and Griliches and Jorgenson [1967].

Differentiating (3) with respect to t, and with some algebraic manipulation, we can derive the following basic productivity growth relationship

$$\dot{q}(t) = \dot{a}_q(t) + w_{qk}, \dot{k}(t) + w_{ql}\dot{l}(t) + w_{qm}\dot{m}(t) \quad (4)$$

where $\dot{q}(t)$, $\dot{a}_q(t)$, $\dot{k}(t)$, $\dot{l}(t)$ and $\dot{m}(t)$ are the growth rates of output, total factor productivity, capital, labour and materials at time t, and w_{qk}, w_{ql}, and w_{qm} are output elasticities of capital, labour and materials respectively.

5.2 The Value-Added Model

Other than the gross-output model, the value-added model is commonly used in estimating the aggregate productivity. The value-added model, which allows the estimation of factor productivity growth without the inclusion of the materials input, can be written as:

$$\dot{v}(t) = \dot{a}_v(t) + w_{vk}\dot{k}(t) + w_{vl}\dot{l}(t) \quad (5)$$

where $\dot{v}(t)$, $\dot{k}(t)$, $\dot{l}(t)$ and $\dot{a}_v(t)$, denote the growth rates of value-added, capital, labour and productivity; and w_{vk} and w_{vl} are output elasticities of capital, and labour.

Given the two models, which one is more appropriate for productivity analysis? The gross-output model has the less restrictive formulation of inputs. Consequently, productivity growth rates estimated using the gross-output model should reflect the true factor productivity growth because gross output is likely to approximate theoretical output. In practice, however, the value-added model is often required when the analysis is undertaken at a highly aggregate level such as the whole economy or an entire manufacturing sector. It is argued that double-counting problem is widespread in aggregate gross output measure. Since outputs of an industry can be used as immediate inputs by another industry for assembly into final goods, value added might be a more appropriate measure of output. In this chapter, since individual industries in the manufacturing sector is being analysis, there is no clear basis for using the gross-output over the valued-added approach. Following this line of argument, we apply both the gross-output and valued-added models in our analysis. A comparison of these models will serve as a sensitivity test of the estimated results from the two competing specifications.

Table 5.10: The Indices of Structural Changes for Various Industries within Manufacturing Sector

	1979-83		1984-88		1989-93	
	C_i	I_i	C_i	I_i	C_i	I_i
Electrical & Electronic	3.72	3.59	6.41	8.10	5.28	626.0
Textile	5.58	5.38	9.06	11.44	4.21	499.8
Wearing apparel	2.84	2.74	6.62	8.36	3.15	374.0
Plastic	1.34	1.29	3.07	3.88	3.69	438.0
Metals and Metal Product	4.46	4.30	5.42	6.84	3.53	419.8
Paper Products & Printing	8.72	0.96	1.22	1.54	4.07	483.0
Leather, Wood & Cork	1.55	1.49	0.63	0.80	1.31	155.4
Cumulative Growth (Manufacturing Output)	103.73		79.13		-0.843	

5.3 Estimation and Sensitivity Tests

We first estimate the coefficients of equation (4) and (5) directly for each industry. In order to compare the models with different methodologies, we also estimate the output elasticities based on the Cobb-Douglas production function. Total factor productivity will then be calculated from:

$$\dot{a}_q(t) = \dot{q}(t) - w_{qk}, \dot{k}(t) - w_{ql}\, \dot{l}(t) - w_{qm}\, \dot{m}(t) \qquad (6)$$

for the gross-output model, and

$$\dot{a}_v(t) = \dot{v}(t) - w_{vk}\, \dot{k}(t) - w_{vl}\, \dot{l}(t) \qquad (7)$$

for the value-added model.

Furthermore, we use the Cobb-Douglas production function to estimate the total factor productivity growth directly. i.e.

$$Q(t) = A(t)\, e^{\lambda t + \varepsilon} L^{\beta} K^{\alpha} M^{\phi} \qquad (8)$$

Equation (8), expressed in logarithmic form, becomes

$$In\ Q_t = ln\ A_0 + \lambda t + \alpha ln\ K + \beta ln\ L + \phi ln\ M + \varepsilon \qquad (9)$$

α, β and ϕ will be the output elasticities of capital, labour and materials and λ is the growth rates of total factor productivity.

5.4 Data and Data Sources

The seven industries selected from Manufacturing are Wearing apparel (ISIC 320 & 322), Leather, wood and cork products (ISIC 323, 324 331 & 332), Textile industry (ISIC 325-329), Paper products, printing and publishing (ISIC 341 & 342), Plastic products (ISIC 356), Basic metals, fabricated metal products, machinery and equipment (ISIC 371-372, 380-381, 386-389), and Electrical and electronic products (ISIC 382-385). In 1994, these industry group in total accounted for more than 90% of the total manufacturing output and 74.5% of total manufacturing employment.

The data are taken from the Hong Kong Annual Digest of Statistics, various issues, and the Estimates of Gross Domestic Product 1961-1994. Since the data on capital stock, K(t), for each industry is not available, it was approximated by using the gross addition to fixed assets, I(t), and a constant depreciation rate, δ, which is assumed to be 0.12, as explained in the Appendix B.

To avoid fluctuations in the first few years, we start the estimation of capital stock for each industry from 1976.

6. EMPIRICAL RESULTS AND SENSITIVITY ANALYSIS

When measured in terms of growth rates, labour employment for the 7 industries has been decreasing for the period 1979-1993, with the exception of the Printing industry. The average growth rate is -2.05% for Textile industry, -3.71% for Electrical and Electronic products, -3.80% for Wearing apparel industry, -7.08% for Plastic industry, -0.95% for Metals and Machinery, -6.80% for Leather and Wood products and 3.28% in Printing industry (see Table 5.11).

The labour productivity which is measured by the average output per worker is shown in Table 5.12. For the period of 1979-1993, the Electrical and Electronic industry group has achieved the highest growth rate in labour productivity (average 7.30%), while the Wearing Apparel industry has the lowest with an average of 0.85%. When compared with the labour productivity in the Manufacturing sector (average 4.44%), the Electrical and Electronic products industry, the Plastic industry, the Metals and Machinery industry, and the Paper Product and Printing industry are doing better than industry as a whole.

Table 5.11: Average Annual Growth of Labour, Capital and Material Inputs by Industry: 1979-93

Industry	*Average Annual Growth (%)*				
	Value-Added	Labour	Capital	Material	Output
Electrical and Electronic	13.27	-3.71	14.18	13.28	13.13
Textiles	11.66	-2.05	8.69	9.68	10.31
Wearing Apparel	8.83	-3.80	4.21	9.42	9.48
Plastic	9.04	-7.08	9.52	7.76	7.73
Metals and Metal Products	13.96	-0.95	12.29	13.54	13.76
Paper Product and Printing	18.90	3.28	17.62	17.20	18.06
Leather, Wood and Cork	5.00	-6.80	5.73	6.86	6.32

Table 5.12: Average Productivity of Labour, Capital and Material Inputs by Industry: 1979-93

Industry	*Average Productivity (%)*		
	Labour	Capital	Materials
Electrical and Electronic	7.30	-1.32	0.83
Textiles	2.91	1.41	0.90
Wearing Apparel	0.85	5.19	0.28
Plastic	5.64	-2.10	0.92
Metals and Metal Products	5.90	1.25	0.73
Paper Product and Printing	4.55	0.70	1.23
Leather, Wood and Cork	3.91	0.44	0.47
Average	4.44	0.80	0.77

Regarding capital stock, the Printing industry has the highest average annual growth in capital stock (17.62%). This implies that the Printing industry is using relatively more capital than others. Next is the Electronics industry and the Metal industry with an average annual growth rate of 14.18% and 12.29% respectively. The lowest is the Wearing apparel industry (4.21%) which is far lower than that of the manufacturing sector average.

In terms of average productivity in capital stock, the Wearing apparel industry has the highest average growth rate of 5.19%. The Electrical industry and the Plastic industry however have a negative growth rate of -1.32% and -2.10% respectively. The average capital productivity of capital stock in manufacturing sector is 0.80%. This implies that the capital productivity in manufacturing sector is at a relative low level.

6.1 Sensitivity Analysis

Table 5.13 reports the total factor productivity for the seven industries based on two specifications: the gross-output model and the value-added model for the period 1979-93. Two aspects of Table 5.13 are worth highlighting. First, we find that, in all the seven industries, the value-added models yield higher productivity growth rate than those obtained from the gross-output models. It is evident that the two output specifications lead to substantially different estimates. The value-added models appear to overestimate the growth rate in all cases. Second, we find that the impact of using estimated output elasticities (based on Cobb-Douglas production function) on productivity estimation is minimal. Thus it appears that the use of different estimation methods do not cause any severe biases in the model parameter estimates.

6.2 Total Factor Productivity Growth Estimates

From Table 5.13, based on the gross-output model, the estimated growth rates of total factor productivity for Electrical and Electronic industry, Textile industry, Paper Product and Printing industry, and Leather industry are 2.86%, 1.79%, 4.40%, and 0.54% respectively; while that for Plastic industry, Metal, Machinery and Equipment industry, and Wearing apparel industry are 2.12%, 0.86%, and 0.22%. Therefore, the Paper Product and Printing industry performs best in the manufacturing industry. The Wearing apparel industry suffers the lowest productivity growth with only 0.22% for the study period. On the average, the total factor productivity of manufacturing industries grows at an annual rate of 1.83% for the study period. Similar pattern is observed when the productivity estimates are obtained by using output elasticities (equation 6). The Paper Product and Printing industry showed the most rapid productivity growth averaging 3.29% annually; while the Textile industry, the Electrical and Electronic industry, the Wearing apparel industry and the Plastic industry maintained a small growth of 0.27% to 1.36%. The Metal, Machinery and Equipment industry, and the Leather industry, however, experienced the negative productivity growth (-0.26 and -0.67%) for the period. Our results suggest that outward investment and cross-border production have basically prolonged the life-cycle of labor-intensive production and have contributed little, if anything, to the upgrading of local manufacturing industries into a capital and technology-intensive nature.

Table 5.13: Distribution of Productivity and Output Growth by Industry: 1979-93 (Results obtained from Model 1 and 2)

Industry	*Average Annual Productivity Growth (%)*					Average Annual Output Growth (%)
Eq.	(4)	(5)	(6)	(7)	(9)	
Electrical and Electronic	2.86	5.65	0.27	8.09	1.60	13.13
Textiles	1.79	5.29	1.36	6.76	2.63	10.31
Wearing Apparel	0.22	1.30	0.43	6.22	1.27	9.48
Plastic	2.12	8.64	0.33	4.99	0.98	7.73
Metals and Metal Products	0.86	2.21	-0.26	2.86	1.16	13.76
Paper Product and Printing	4.40	2.65	3.29	6.61	2.42	18.06
Leather, Wood and Cork	0.54	9.37	-0.67	3.18	0.43	6.32
Average Growth	1.83	5.02	0.68	5.53	1.60	11.26

7. CONCLUSION

The outward investment and cross-border processing from Hong Kong to Guangdong in the last decade has resulted in structural change of the local economy. Nowadays, more manufactured goods are produced across the border than in local plants. As the transportation and servicing facilities in China lag behind the development in trading, China depends heavily on Hong Kong for transportation and business services. Hong Kong's container port, one of the busiest container terminal in the world, now handles more than 50% of China's external trade. The relative stagnation in private domestic fixed capital formation may be a consequence of the outward investment to Guangdong. As a result, the contribution from manufacturing to Hong Kong's GDP has shrunk in the past fifteen years. As local manufacturing firms assume the role of a supporting base for its offshore manufacturing plants, the demand for intermediate services has increased correspondingly. With the expansion of the service sector, structural unemployment could be kept to a relatively low level at around 3% in recent years. After a decade of industrial transformation, it is observed that Hong Kong's technological process in manufacturing remains relatively low when compared with other Asian NIEs, which adopt more positive industrial policies. The opening up of Chinese economy, on the one hand, has augmented Hong Kong's comparative advantage. On the other hand, it dampens local business's incentives technological upgrading and market diversification. The local businessmen are not concerned over the need to achieve high technology and put in serious effort to maintain the sector's international competitiveness.

Our result confirms that FDI from Hong Kong to China not only contributes to economic change in Guangdong, but also causes structural change in Hong Kong. Hong Kong is now moving from a manufacturing base towards a service economy. In addition, we show that the manufacturing sector has undergone great changes in the last five years. The productivity of the manufacturing sector is still relatively low. It grows at around 0.22% to 4.40% annually. Thus the favourable impact of FDI on raising productivity of the home economy, at least, is not observed in Hong Kong's case.

REFERENCES

Chen, C.P. (1994) Structural Change in Taiwan Industries, in Kuo-shu Liang (ed), Readings in Economic Development of Taiwan, Taipei, Taiwan, 260-280. (in Chinese).

Estimates of Gross Domestic Product 1961 to 1994, Census and Statistics Department, Hong Kong, March 1995.

Hang Seng Economic Monthly, Hang Seng Bank, Hong Kong , June 1993.

Ho, Y.P. (1992) Trade, Industrial Restructuring and Development in Hong Kong, The Macmillan Press.

Ho, Y.P. and Kueh Y.Y. (1993) Whither Hong Kong in an Open-door, Reforming Chinese Economy?, The Pacific Review, Vol. 6. No 4. Routledge.

1995 Hong Kong's Manufacturing Industries, Hong Kong Government industry Department, Dec. 1995.

Hong Kong Annual Digest of Statistics, Census and Statistics Department, Hong Kong, various issues.

Maruya, T. (1992) Economic Relations between Hong Kong and Guangdong Province, in Edward K.Y. Chen and T Maruya (ed), Guangdong 'Open Door' Economic Development Strategy, Centre of Asian Studies, the University of Hong Kong.

Mcguckin, R.H. and Nguyen S.V. (1993) Post-reform Industrial Productivity Performance of China: New Evidence from the 1985 Industrial Census Data, *Economic Inquiry*, 323-341.

Ozawa, T. (1992) Foreign Direct Investment and Economic Development, Transnational Corporations, vol. 1. no. 1, 27-54.

Riedel, J. (1974) The Industrialization of Hong Kong, Kieler Studien 124 (Tubingen: J.C. B. Mohr).

Tsang, S.K. (1995) The Political Economy of Greater China, Hong Kong Baptist University Working Paper Series.

Tuan, C. and Ng F.Y. (1995) Hong Kong's Outward Investment and Regional Economic integration with Guangdong: Process and Implications, Journal of Asian Economics, Vol. 6, No. 3, 385-405.

APPENDIX A

The growth rate of manufacturing output, G_t, is expressed as:

$$G_t = \Delta Y_t / Y_{i\,t} \quad \text{(A.1)}$$

where Y_t is the real value of manufacturing output at time t. We can expressed it in terms of the share of industry i's output to manufacturing output, S_{it}. Then, equation (A.1) can be written as:

$$\begin{aligned} G_t &= \Sigma(\Delta Y_{it} / Y_{i\,t-1})(Y_{i\,t-1} / Y_{i\,t}) \\ &= \Sigma G_{it} S_{i\,t-1} \quad \text{(A.2)} \end{aligned}$$

where $S_{i\,t} = Y_{i\,t} / Y_t$ and G_{it} is the growth rate of industry i's output at time t. To analysis the effect of structural change on output growth, we break down equation (A.2) further into:

$$\begin{aligned} G_t &= \Sigma G_{it} S_{i\,t-1} + \Sigma(G_{it} - G_t) S_{i\,t-1} \\ &= G_t + \underset{\text{for } (\,) > 0}{\Sigma(G_{it} - G_t) S_{i\,t-1}} + \underset{(\,) < 0}{\Sigma(G_{it} - G_t) S_{i\,t-1}} \quad \text{(A.3)} \end{aligned}$$

This implies that $\underset{\text{for } (\,) > 0}{\Sigma(G_{it} - G_t) S_{i\,t-1}} + \underset{(\,) < 0}{\Sigma(G_{it} - G_t) S_{i\,t-1}} = 0$.

Since the first term (positive/negative) must be equal to the second term (negative/positive) in magnitude in order to have the sum equal to zero, we can infer that they must be equal in absolute value. The larger the discrepancy between (G_{it} - G_t), the greater will be the structural change of industry i and the absolute value of these terms.

$$\Rightarrow \left| \Sigma(G_{it} - G_t)\, S_{i\,t-1} \right|_{\text{for } (\,) > 0} = \left| \Sigma(G_{it} - G_t)\, S_{i\,t-1} \right|_{(\,) < 0}$$

Since

$$\begin{aligned} G_{it} - G_t &= \Delta Y_{it} / Y_{i\,t-1} \\ &\approx (S_{i\,t} - S_{i\,t-1}) / S_{i\,t-1} \end{aligned} \qquad \text{(A.4)}$$

$$\Rightarrow (S_{i\,t} - S_{i\,t-1}) \approx (G_{it} - G_t)\, S_{i\,t-1}$$

By defining $C_i = \Sigma(G_{it} - G_t)\, S_{i\,t-1}$, then equation (3) can be written as:

$$\begin{aligned} 2\,C_i &= 2\,\Sigma(G_{it} - G_t)\, S_{i\,t-1} \\ &= 2 \left| \Sigma\,(G_{it} - G_t)\, S_{i\,t-1} \right| \\ &= 2\,\Sigma \left| S_{i\,t} - S_{i\,t-1} \right| \end{aligned}$$

Therefore $C_i = \Sigma \left| S_{i\,t} - S_{i\,t-1} \right|$ (A.5)

APPENDIX B

Estimation of the Capital stock's time series

In order to estimate the unobserved capital stock 's time series from the documented gross addition to fixed asset, I(t), it is assumed that the capital stock follows the following motion equation:

$$K(t) = (1-\delta)K(t-1) + I(t) \qquad \text{(B.1)}$$

where δ is the annual depreciation rate. Of course, if the initial capital stock K(0), were known, the time series of capital stock could be easily computed for a predetermined value of δ by virtue of equation B.1. In the absence of such information, we used the following procedure to assess K(0), by assuming that

$$K(t) = K(0)g^t \qquad \text{(B.2)}$$

and then substituting B.2 into B.1 for K(t) and K(t-1). We obtain

$$K(0) = \frac{I(t)}{g^{t-1}[g-(1-\delta)]} \quad \text{(B.3)}$$

where g is the accumulation rate of capital stock. As B.3 holds for t as well as for (t-1)

$$\frac{I(t)}{g^{t-1}} = \frac{I(t-1)}{g^{t-2}} \quad \text{(B.4)}$$

and hence $g = \frac{I(t)}{I(t-1)}$ (B.5)

Since different values of g are likely to be obtained for any arbitrary choice of two consecutive values of I, we used the sample average of $\frac{I(t)}{I(t-1)}$, which is an unbiased estimator of g, i.e.

$$g = \frac{1}{T}\sum \frac{I(t)}{I(t-1)} \quad \text{(B.6)}$$

We substituted t=1 into B.3 to obtain

$$K(0) = \frac{I(1)}{g-(1-\delta)} \quad \text{(B.7)}$$

and computed K(0) for each industry with the first observed value of gross addition to fixed asset (assumed to be 1976), the estimated value of g from B.6 and a predetermined value of δ. By subsequent substitutions, the time series of capital stock for each industry was produced.

6. HONG KONG AS A FINANCIAL CENTRE FOR GREATER CHINA

Y. C. Jao

I. INTRODUCTION

During the past three decades, Hong Kong has emerged as one of the leading international financial centres (IFCs) of the world. Since China began its economic reform and open-door policies in 1979, and since cross-strait economic contacts began to improve in the mid-1980s, Hong Kong's role has also become more varied and multi-faceted. The purpose of this chapter is to evaluate Hong Kong as an IFC of Greater China (which comprises Mainland China, Taiwan, Hong Kong and Macau). The territory's prospects as an IFC after its retrocession to China on July 1, 1997 will also be discussed.

II. SOME MISCONCEPTIONS

We may begin by disposing of two common misconceptions about Hong Kong as a financial centre. The first one, surprisingly prevalent in the West, is that Hong Kong is an "offshore financial centre" or "offshore banking centre". Even respected scholars commit this solecism (Dufey and Giddy, 1978; Johns, 1992).

To understand our argument, it would be useful to quote the definitions of "offshore financial centre" and "offshore banking centre" by two authorities. Roberts (1994a) states:

"The term 'offshore financial centre' came into usage in the 1960s to describe a new phenomenon - the operations of financial centres which, though physically located within a country, have little connection with that country's financial system........ Offshore financial centres form a third tier in the hierarchy of international financial centres, performing a narrower and more passive range of financial functions than the global or the regional international financial centres. But unfortunately the distinctions are not clear-cut; for instance, by some yardsticks London and Switzerland are leading offshore financial centres because of their pre-eminent roles in the euromarket. Another possible source of confusion is the inconsistency in the terminology used in the literature on the subject: in this context, 'offshore financial centre' and 'offshore banking' are used interchangeably with 'international banking centre' and 'international banking'."

According to Johns (1992),

"Offshore banking is a qualitative rather than a geographically explicit locational term. It can apply either to: (1) banks that have located purposely in specific foreign jurisdiction, not necessarily island-based, whose legislative and tax frameworks and regulatory authorities are less restrictive in comparison with their home-based operational environment; or, to (2) specifically designated facilities or financial 'free' zones with their own separate customised legislative and tax regimes, available to domestic and/or foreign banks, which are exempted from all or specific regulatory controls and taxes on international banking activities that otherwise apply in the rest of the local economy."

From these definitions, it is clear that Hong Kong is not an offshore financial centre. The Hong Kong Government has never set up an offshore centre or free zone with special regulatory or tax concessions, and which is completely insulated from the domestic economy. In fact, the authorities do not even distinguish between residents and non-resident, or domestic and foreign currency financial activities, on a substantive legal or administrative basis. Hewson (1982) recognizes this when, in an exhaustive study of offshore banking, he acknowledges that "Hong Kong is not really an offshore centre in the sense that we have developed that term" even though "there are important offshore activities conducted in Hong Kong" (p.425). In other words, onshore and offshore activities are completely fused together in Hong Kong without any artificial barriers between them.

The other misconception is that Hong Kong is the third largest IFC of the world. Not surprisingly, this view is largely confined to Hong Kong and China, though some foreign observers also subscribe to it.[1] The exact basis for this ranking has never been clearly

---

1 For example, a French expert writes: "Hong Kong est la troisième place financière du monde. Elle est de plus en plus considérée comme une alternative à Tokyo par les investisseurs étrangers

spelled out, though it has been vaguely suggested that the number of foreign banks and other financial institutions is the third largest, or the intensity of foreign bank activity is the third highest, next only to London and New York.

In my book (Jao, 1997), I have used an extensive set of quantitative data to rank Hong Kong as a financial centre. Obviously the details cannot be reproduced here, but Table 6.1 presents Hong Kong's rankings in Asia-Pacific and the world according to a number of specific criteria.

As may be seen from the table, Hong Kong can be regarded overall as the second largest financial centre in the Asia-Pacific region, being behind Tokyo but ahead of Singapore. At the global level, Hong Kong is also very strong in international banking, and can be regarded as the fourth largest international banking centre (IBC). But IBC is not equivalent to IFC: when financial markets other than banking are taken into account, Hong Kong's world ranking become much less impressive. Overall, Hong Kong's weighted world ranking was 6.47 in 1995, i.e., Hong Kong was between the sixth and seventh largest IFC of the world.[2]

III. WHAT KIND OF A FINANCIAL CENTRE IS HONG KONG?

How do we then characterize Hong Kong as a financial centre? Financial centres may be classified according to their purpose, geographical reach, and historical development. From the teleological standpoint, Hong Kong is a functional centre, i.e., one where financial activities and transactions really take place, which generate substantial income and employment, both direct and indirect. Despite its low tax rates and narrow tax base, Hong Kong is not a tax haven, and therefore is not a paper centre (or brass-plate centre) which is used to book transactions in order to evade taxation, and which generates little or no income or employment. Hong Kong is also an integrated centre, where onshore and offshore markets are completely integrated, as opposed to a segregated centre, where onshore and offshore markets are clearly demarcated. In other words, once a financial institution is admitted into Hong Kong, it can engage freely in any financial transaction or activity, whether onshore or offshore, whether with residents or non-residents, or whether denominated in domestic or foreign currencies.

---

désirant s'installer en Asie orientale. Les banques internationales y sont plus nombreuses qu'à Paris ou à Tokyo (560 banques, dont 360 succursales de banques étrangères" (Cini, 1993, p.117).

2 The weights I used were: banking, 40%; forex market, 20%; equity and debt markets, 25%; derivatives, 10%; and others, 5%.

Table 6.1: Ranking of Hong Kong as an IFC, 1995

Categories	*Asia-Pacific Ranking*	*World Ranking*
Banking:		
No. of foreign banks	1	2
Banks' foreign assets	2	4
Banks' foreign liabilities	2	5
Cross-border interbank claims	2	6
Cross-border interbank liabilities	2	4
Cross-border credit to non-banks	1	2
Syndicated loans and note-issuing facilities (NIFs) (1994)	1	4
Forex Market:		
Net daily turnover	3	5
Derivatives Market:		
Net daily forex contract turnover	3	5
Net interest rate contract turnover	4	8
Overall	3	7
Stock Market:		
Market capitalization	2	9
Value traded	4	11
No. of listed domestic companies	7	16
Gold Market	1	4
Insurance:		
No. of authorized insurance companies	1	N.A.
Premium income	5	27
Qualified actuaries	1	N.A.
Fund management	2	N.A.

N.A. = not available

Source: Y.C. Jao, (1997).

From the geographical perspective, IFCs can be further sub-divided into global financial centres (GFCs) and regional financial centres (RFCs).[3] By general agreement, there are only three GFCs in the world, namely, London, New York, and Tokyo (Roberts, 1994b). Hong Kong is not in the same league as the three GFCs. It is only a RFC, or more specifically, the second largest financial centre in the Asia-Pacific region.[4]

From the historical point of view, scholars have distinguished between the traditional centre, the financial entrepôt, and the offshore banking centre (Dufey and Giddy, 1978). The traditional centre is one which serves as a net capital exporter to the world either by bank lending, or by capital-raising on the securities market. The financial entrepôt is a centre that offers the services of its financial institutions and markets to both domestic and foreign residents. The offshore banking centre has already been explained. It can safely be said that Hong Kong's role is that of the financial entrepôt.

As Greater China is a sub-set of the Asia-Pacific region, Hong Kong can be regarded, by logical reasoning, as an IFC of Greater China as well. However, there are other more compelling reasons for doing so, as will be explained in the next section. Moreover, after the transfer of sovereignty in 1997, Hong Kong will also become China's offshore financial centre, for reasons that will also be explained shortly. Note however, that the term "offshore financial centre" is used advisedly here from China's point of view. From Hong Kong's own point of view, the territory remains an integrated IFC.

IV. HONG KONG AS AN IFC OF GREATER CHINA: SOME MAJOR DETERMINANTS

In this section, we will explain the reasons for treating Hong Kong as an IFC of Greater China, apart from the simple logical reasoning mentioned above.

The first factor is obviously Hong Kong's political neutrality. Although China always insists that it will seek reunification by peaceful means, it also steadfastly refuses to renounce the use of force as a means of last resort. Taiwan, on its part, despite the lifting of martial law against "communist rebellion" and liberalization of cross-straits contacts, still refuses to accept Beijing's "one country, two countries" model or its demand for direct economic contacts. Hong Kong, fortunately, is not burdened by the legacy of the Chinese civil war. It is the only Chinese city where economic, cultural, or even political contacts between the two sides of the Taiwan Strait can, and do, take place in a normal atmosphere free from political hostility or interference.

Second, Hong Kong has an unrivalled record for economic freedom. Two US think tanks, Heritage Foundation and the Fraser Institute, have recently ranked Hong Kong as the country (territory) with the highest degree of economic freedom (Johnson and

3 A "region" in this context means a supra-national geographical area (say one or two continents), not a sub-national one.

4 The term "Asia-Pacific region" refers to countries or territories along the western edge of the Pacific Ocean, including China, Japan, Taiwan, Hong Kong, Korea, Brunei, Indonesia, Malaysia, the Philippines, Singapore, Thailand, Australia, and New Zealand.

Sheehy, 1996; Gwartney, Lawson and Block, 1996). Both China and Taiwan, especially the former, lag very considerably behind Hong Kong.[5] As a concrete example in the field of banking and finance, it is universally agreed that the complete freedom of capital movement and the full convertibility of the domestic currency are the most important hallmarks of an IFC. Only Hong Kong satisfies this condition fully. In China, the domestic currency, *Renminbi* (RMB), has been convertible for current account transactions only since December 1, 1996. In Taiwan, exchange control on the current account has long been removed; however, control on capital account still exists for capital movement in excess of US$5 million for individuals and US$20 million for firms.

Third, Hong Kong's record of national treatment and reciprocity is also second to none. The concept of "national treatment" forms part of the principle of "non-discrimination", one of the main pillars of the General Agreement Tariffs and Trade (GATT) codified in 1947. As enshrined in Articles I and III of GATT, the "most favoured nation" (MFN) clause requires that, subject to certain exceptions, imports from all sources should face identical barriers, while "national treatment" requires that, once through the customs, foreign goods are subject to no taxes or regulations more onerous than those on equivalent domestic goods (Winters, 1990). Since then the concept has been extended to direct investment and the financial sector.

A previous study (Jao, 1988, pp. 20-1) shows that Hong Kong had the best record of "national treatment" in the Asia Pacific region in 1986. Recent reports by the U.S. Treasury have reconfirmed this finding (US Department of the Treasury, 1990, 1994). The 1994 report contains complaints against 33 countries or regions, including China and Taiwan, for failing to accord full "national treatment" to foreign banks and financial institutions, but none against Hong Kong. It says that "U.S. institutions generally give authorities high marks for fairness and transparency and generally expressed the view that Hong Kong does not discriminate in terms of competitive opportunities. Activities are conducted on an equal legal and regulatory footing with both local and foreign institutions" (p. 267).

A separate concept is "reciprocity", which essentially means according foreign banks or other financial institutions the same treatment domestic banks or other financial institutions receive abroad. In practice, many countries interpret "reciprocity" in a negative or restrictive sense, or use it as a bargaining device in bilateral negotiations. Hong Kong, however, tends to interpret the principle in a liberal or positive sense. According to the Hong Kong Monetary Authority (HKMA), the "reciprocity" required is "availability of some acceptable form of reciprocity to Hong Kong banks", or in other words, absolute equality in mutual granting of banking licences is not required.[6] This has given rise to a situation whereby Hong Kong is under-represented in some countries or territories which nevertheless have a large banking presence in Hong Kong. China and Taiwan are good examples, which will be detailed in the next section.

---

5 The Heritage report ranks Taiwan 8th and China 121th among 140 countries. The Fraser report ranks Taiwan 16th, but does not include China, among 103 countries.

6 See Annex A "Criteria for Authorisation", Hong Kong Monetary Authority 1994 Annual Report.

Fourth, although China since 1981 has advocated the three direct contacts across the strait (direct commercial, navigational and postal links, or the *santong* policy), Taiwan has so far adamantly refused to lift the embargoes on such contacts. Trade, investment, and financial flows across the strait still have to be routed or arranged through Hong Kong. For example, while Taiwanese banks are forbidden to deal directly with PRC-owned or controlled banks, their branches in Hong Kong are permitted to do business with their PRC counterparts. Hong Kong in other words is the natural intermediary by virtue of geography, language, culture and other ethnic ties, between China and Taiwan, whose economic exchanges have been booming since the mid-eighties. Although there are signs that Taiwan may be moving closer to the *santong* policy, imminent lifting of the embargoes is not in sight, given the political tensions which have dominated cross-strait relations during 1995-96.

For all these reasons, Hong Kong serves as the financial entrepôt of Greater China. China, Taiwan, and Macau, are all eager to make use of Hong Kong's freedoms and excellent facilities to engage in activities or transactions which are either prohibited, or are unavailable, within their respective domestic borders.

V. INDICATORS OF HONG KONG AS IFC OF GREATER CHINA

In this section, we present some quantitative evidence of Hong Kong as an IFC of Greater China. Although in principle the whole gamut of financial variables should be used, we agree with Reed (1981) that banks and banking business remain the core of an IFC. Space constraint also prevents us from treating non-bank intermediaries exhaustively.

China in 1996 had 35 banking institutions in Hong Kong's 3-tier system, namely, 18 licensed banks (full-service banks), 2 restricted licence banks, and 15 deposit-taking companies. These institutions can transact all types of banking business, whether onshore or offshore, or whether in local currency or foreign currency. In addition, China had equity interests in at least four other Hong Kong incorporated banks.

The market shares of China-owned banks in deposits, loans and advances, and total assets are given in Table 6.2. China-owned banks as a group are now the second largest banking group in Hong Kong, next only to the Hong Kong and Shanghai Banking Corporation (HSBC). Moreover, in 1994, the Bank of China became the third note-issuing bank in Hong Kong, and now shares with the two existing British note-issuing banks, the HSBC and the Standard Chartered, the chairmanship of the powerful Hong Kong Association of Banks by rotation.

By contrast, at the end of 1994 only 12 Hong Kong banks had branches in China. Actually, 7 of them are China-owned banks incorporated in Hong Kong. Moreover, none of them is allowed to engage in RMB-denominated business.[7]

---

7 Underlying data in *Almanac of China's Finance and Banking*, 1995, pp. 677-680.

Table 6.2: Market Shares of China-owned Banks in Hong Kong (end-1995)

Category	*Hong Kong Dollar*	*Foreign Currency*
Customers' deposits	28.3%	17.1%
Total Loans and advances	19.5%	2.6%
Total assets	23.4%	5.0%
Loans for use in Hong Kong only	19.2%	10.2%

Source: Hong Kong Monetary Authority Annual Report for 1995

The same lack of reciprocity applies also to Taiwan. Taiwan's banks are late-comers to Hong Kong, but in the past five years, no less than four top Taiwan banks have had their representative offices upgraded to branches. However, so far only two Hong Kong incorporated bank have been allowed to establish branches in Taiwan.[8]

Apart from banking institutions in the 3-tier system, in 1996 China also had 3 representative offices, 18 trustee/nominee companies, 10 investment or brokerage companies, 4 finance companies, and 13 insurance companies in Hong Kong.[9]Taiwan had about 8 investment or brokerage companies in Hong Kong in 1994.[10]

Hong Kong's role as a financial entrepôt manifests itself also in the external claims and liabilities of Hong Kong banks vis-à-vis banks and non-bank customers in China and Taiwan. Table 6.3 gives the position with regard to China in both Hong Kong dollar and foreign currencies.

The table shows that liabilities to and claims on banks and non-banks in China have both been increasing substantially since 1991. Generally, Hong Kong had net liabilities in Hong Kong dollars to banks in China, but net claims in foreign currencies on them. For non-bank customers, Hong Kong had net liabilities to them in Hong Kong dollars, but net claims on them in foreign currencies. Note that the term "Hong Kong banks" includes actually many China-owned or controlled banks based in Hong Kong. To that extent, the table shows that China-owned banks actively use Hong Kong's facilities to transact business which would otherwise be forbidden or unavailable inside China.

8 See "List of Financial Institutions", *Financial Statistics Monthly,* Economic Research Department, The Central Bank of China, Taiwan. Note that the HSBC is no longer a Hong Kong incorporated bank as it changed its legal domicile to the United Kingdom in 1990.

9 Underlying data from "List of Hong Kong companies having Chinese interests", Industry Department, Hong Kong Government.

10 *Hong Kong Economic Journal,* Oct. 23, 1994.

Table 6.3: External Liabilities And Claims of Hong Kong Banks vis-à-vis China (HK$ million)

As at end of	Liabilities to banks in China		Claims on banks in China		Liabilities to non-bank customers in China		Claims on non-bank customers in China	
	HK$	FC	HK$	FC	HK$	FC	HK$	FC
1991	79,716	60,528	29,156	75,097	343	3,979	1,843	45,640
1992	74,570	76,574	32,123	80,849	920	5,591	2,822	53,123
1993	67,228	87,814	37,171	101,471	645	5,923	2,732	53,561
1994	99,408	126,367	47,597	129,012	1,371	6,476	1,895	59,744
1995	110,867	105,553	52,230	171,634	2,822	6,494	2,439	62,575
1996(Nov.)	123,651	162,844	65,826	221,605	3,008	8,624	3,357	67,257

Note: FC = foreign currencies
Source: Hong Kong Monetary Authority *Monthly Statistical Bulletin*

Hong Kong is a leading syndication centre of the world, given that of the top 100 banks of the world, some 85 have established their presence in Hong Kong. As there are also a large number of Chinese banks in Hong Kong, the territory is therefore the natural centre for arranging bank loans to China. According to Chen Yuan, the Executive Deputy Governor of the People's Bank of China, "90% of syndicated loans for use in mainland China are arranged in Hong Kong" (Chen, 1996).

Hong Kong is not just a banking centre, but also a capital-raising centre, for China. By the end of 1995, 17 Chinese state-owned enterprises (the so-called H-shares) had been listed on the Stock Exchange of Hong Kong (SEHK), raising more than HK$20 billion (about US$2.6 billion).[11] In addition, there were 39 "Red Chips" at the end of 1995, i.e., Hong Kong listed companies in which China had acquired controlling interests (Lin, 1995). Moreover, "over 40% of the companies listed in Hong Kong have participated in almost one thousand investment projects in mainland China, with a total investment of about HK$500 billion (about US$64.6 billion). The total market value of Chinese enterprises listed on the Hong Kong stock market is almost HK$100 billion (about US$12.9 billion)" (Chen, 1996).

Hong Kong's banking transactions with Taiwan are not as large as those with China, but as shown in Table 4, they have also been growing steadily since 1991. Generally, Hong Kong had net claims in both Hong Kong dollar and foreign currencies on banks in Taiwan, but had net liabilities in both Hong Kong dollar and foreign currencies to non-banks in Taiwan. This shows that Taiwan banks borrowed heavily from the inter-bank market in Hong Kong, but Taiwan's individuals and firms held net credit balances in the Hong Kong banking system. Taiwan has so far no companies listed on the SEHK.

11 Addendum to *The 1996-97 Budget*, Hong Kong Government, p.28.

Table 6.4: External Liabilities and Claims of Hong Kong Banks vis-à-vis Taiwan (HK$ million)

As at end of	Liabilities to banks in Taiwan		Claims on banks in Taiwan		Liabilities to non-bank customers in Taiwan		Claims on non-bank customers in Taiwan	
	HK$	FC	HK$	FC	HK$	FC	HK$	FC
1991	231	11,179	615	40,676	626	9,877	71	3,650
1992	231	5,501	813	45,403	1,041	10,916	119	4,288
1993	348	6,161	1,092	52,302	1,353	12,584	837	4,961
1994	562	5,983	1,327	58,999	1,676	16,078	598	5,433
1995	570	7,861	1,179	45,283	2,010	18,873	193	8,536
1996	564	15,604	1,346	37,977	2,685	19,789	315	8,465

Note: FC = foreign currencies
Source: Hong Kong Monetary Authority

Hong Kong is also playing the role of a mentor for China's fledgeling stock markets - both the reopened Shanghai market and the brand-new Shenzhen market. It is well known that the regulations, organization, and listing rules etc. of these two markets are largely modelled after those of SEHK. Hong Kong accounting firms also regularly advise Chinese state-owned enterprises on how to bring their accounting practices up to international standards (Cheung, Yeung and Yeung, 1992; Hu, 1993; and Ayling and Jiang, 1994). In 1993, the Securities and Futures Commission (SFC), the regulatory body of the securities industry in Hong Kong, signed a memorandum agreement with its counterpart in China for mutual cooperation and exchange of information and personnel. A similar agreement was also signed by the SFC with its Taiwan counterpart in 1995.

An IFC does not however exist in a vacuum: to be viable, an IFC must be complemented or supplemented by other roles. Thus, *pari passu* with its rise as an IFC, Hong Kong has also emerged as a major regional business centre, the most obvious evidence of which is the fact that hundreds of multinational corporations use Hong Kong as their regional headquarters. According to the Hong Kong Government Industry Department, the term "regional headquarters" is defined as "an organization which has control over the operations of one or more other offices or subsidiaries in the region without the need to make frequent referrals to, or consult with, the overseas parent company or headquarters". Tables 5 and 6 present the number of such companies by source country during 1990-96, and their geographical jurisdictions.

Table 6.5: Hong Kong as Regional Headquarters by Source Country of Ultimate Parent Companies

Source Country	1990	1991	1992	1993	1994	1995	1996
USA	252	258	206	182	178	198	188
Japan	20	44	74	88	91	116	122
UK	77	75	73	81	91	94	90
China	-	-	-	67	62	71	85
Germany	13	30	28	26	35	33	40
France	29	25	25	21	26	28	26
Netherlands	31	31	24	26	22	28	30
Switzerland	34	31	33	25	34	23	27
Taiwan	-	-	-	-	14	22	25
Bermuda	-	-	-	-	-	17	16
South Korea	-	-	-	-	-	16	-
Canada	-	-	10	14	-	-	-
Australia	11	9	9	-	14	-	-
Italy	14	11	10	-	-	-	-
Sweden	16	14	-	11	13	-	16
Denmark	14	8	-	-	-	-	-
Liberia	-	-	8	-	-	-	-
Others	70	70	96	88	137	147	148
	581	606	596	629	717	793	829

Source: Industry Department, *Report on the Survey of Regional Representation by Overseas Companies in Hong Kong*, various years.

Several features of Tables 5 and 6 merit attention. First, the large presence of multinational firms using Hong Kong as regional headquarters can be regarded as a mirror image of the concentration of multinational banks and other financial institutions in Hong Kong. Indeed, the 1996 survey also shows that 129 firms, or 15.8% of the total, are in the fields of banking, finance and insurance. Second, despite the approach of 1997, the number of multinational companies followed a fairly consistent uptrend from 581 to 829. To be sure, there have been changes in the source countries. Thus, US representation fell by 25% from 252 to 188, but the US remained the largest source country. Japan's representation rose dramatically by more than six-fold to 122. Surprisingly, despite the impending transfer of sovereignty, the UK's representation also increased from 77 to 90, or by 17%. Third, since 1993, multinational corporations from

Table 6.6: Area of Responsibility of Regional Headquarters (1996)

Area responsible	No. of companies
(a) Hong Kong and China	314 (38.5%)
(b) South East Asia (excluding China)	45 (5.5%)
(c) South East Asia (including China)	172 (21.1%)
(d) East Asia	94 (11.5%)
(e) Asia Pacific	191 (23.4%)
Total	816 (100%)

Coverages: South East Asia (excluding China) refers to Hong Kong, Taiwan, the Philippines, Indonesia, Thailand, Malaysia, Singapore and Vietnam;
East Asia refers to South East Asia (including China) plus Japan and Korea;
Asia Pacific refers to East Asia plus Australia and New Zealand.

Notes: 1. Percentages in brackets indicate the share of the total number of regional headquarters.
2. Figures may not add up to the total due to rounding.

Source: Industry Department, *Report on the 1996 Survey of Regional Representation by Overseas Companies in Hong Kong.*

China and Taiwan have also appeared on the scene. Fourth, Greater China was the focus of the geographical responsibility. To be more precise, every multinational corporation had at least two members of Greater China (Hong Kong being the host) within its regional purview. In short, the data presented above provide a solid evidence that Hong Kong is both the international financial centre and the business centre of Greater China.

VI. HONG KONG'S PROSPECTS AFTER 1997

As the date of reunification draws nearer, speculations about Hong Kong's future have also intensified. Understandably, there are diverse views, some of them diametrically opposed, about Hong Kong's prospects in the post-colonial era.

As far as Hong Kong's role as an IFC of Greater China is concerned, my own view is that it depends on the validity of the following six major premises: that there will be a smooth transition for Hong Kong from a British Crown Colony to a Special Administrative Region (SAR) of the People's Republic of China; that China will strictly observe its commitments and obligations under the 1984 Joint Declaration and the 1990

Basic Law, and allow Hong Kong to enjoy a high degree of autonomy without interference; that China will continue to pursue its market-oriented economic reform and open-door policies on a permanent basis; that cross-strait relations will not degenerate into military conflict; that China will maintain stable external relations with the major industrial powers, particularly the United States; and that Hong Kong will preserve all the favourable internal factors responsible for its past success (such as the rule of law, good and efficient government, business-friendly tax regime, transparent regulatory framework, use of English etc., quite apart from the comparative advantages already mentioned in Section IV).

My considered opinion is that these six premises, on the whole, will probably hold, though not in the ideal manner as one would hope. Moreover, of the six premises, Hong Kong can control the last one only. China is involved in all the rest. China therefore bears a heavy responsibility for the well-being of Hong Kong after 1997, including its role as an IFC, which China professes to take very seriously.

The fourth premise, about the relations between China and Taiwan, is likely to be the most troublesome. Unfortunately, Hong Kong has no influence whatsoever over it. The territory can only pray that the three parties involved in the triangle, China, Taiwan, and the United States, will all exercise the utmost restraint in order to avoid a war the consequences of which are too horrible even to contemplate. China has its legitimate concerns about what it considers as Taiwan's separatist tendencies. But it must realize that the best way to achieve reunification is by peaceful dialogue and the "demonstration effect" of its impressive economic development. The tactic of intimidation which China employed during Taiwan's 1996 presidential election not only proved utterly futile, but alienated world opinion and damaged its own image. Taiwan, for its part, should realize that any independance movement is not only against the wishes of the Chinese people all over the world, but is also against its own interests. Taiwan should also abandon its provocative attempt to rejoin the United Nations, from which it voluntarily withdrew in 1971. If it is so keen to rejoin it, it should negotiate with China for a mutually acceptable formula (e.g., the "Olympic model") of representation. Last but not least, the United States should adopt a more even-handed approach towards China and Taiwan, and be wary of the powerful pro-Taiwan and pro-independance lobby, whose demands, to say the least, do not coincide with the interests of the United States.[12]

Even when the six major premises generally are valid, Hong Kong still has to face growing competition from other financial centres, both established and emerging. Unfortunately, space does not permit a detailed discussion of this topic. Here we must be

---

12 The Taiwan Strait crisis began in the summer of 1995 after President Lee Teng-hui of Taiwan paid a "personal" visit to the United States. Originally, the Clinton Administration, mindful of China's sensibility, refused to grant a visa to Mr. Lee. However, Congress, in an anti-China and pro-Taiwan mood, passed overwhelmingly a resolution welcoming Mr. Lee. The move was especially gratuitous, since only a few months earlier, China's Chairman Jiang Zemin issued a conciliatory appeal to Taiwan to improve cross-strait relations.

content with some cursory remarks on the potential challenges from Shanghai, Taipei and Singapore.[13]

Our analysis in Section IV already implies that Shanghai and Taipei cannot play the role of IFCs of Greater China because of political hostility and relatively poor records of economic freedom, national treatment and reciprocity. Before World War II, Shanghai was the premier financial centre of the Far East, surpassing even Tokyo. The Sino-Japanese War (1937-45) and the subsequent civil war (1946-49) sank Shanghai's status as the leading regional financial centre. No less unfortunately for Shanghai, for nearly 40 years, the new regime pursued what in effect were policies of "financial repression": expulsion of Western banks and other financial institutions, wholesale nationalization of private banks and other intermediaries, closure of all financial markets, and a crushingly heavy fiscal burden on Shanghai (White, 1989). It was not until 1990 that this "financial repression" was corrected by a series of measures aimed at the restoration of Shanghai's former status as a major financial centre: the announcement of a new economic zone (the New Pudong Area), the reopening of the stock exchange in 1990, and the establishment in Shanghai of two national financial markets, the forex market in 1994, and the inter-bank market in 1996. However, 40 years of neglect and perverse policies have left their marks.

Taipei was much more fortunate in being spared such a long period of "financial repression". In 1993, Taiwan announced with considerable fanfare an ambitious plan to develop itself into an "Asia-Pacific Regional Operations Centre (ROC)". The ROC concept comprises six elements, of which one is financial centre. However, an official feasibility study (Ministry of Economics, 1994) concludes that while Taiwan is ahead of Hong Kong in respect of science and technology, trained manpower, land supply, industrial network, and industrial production, it lags behind Hong Kong in respect of economic hinterland, transportation, telecommunications, financial services, legal system, administrative efficiency, tax incentives, marketing, and regional headquarters, all essential ingredients for an IFC. Another more recent study (Economic Development Commission, 1997) also confirms that Taipei is far behind Hong Kong as a financial centre, maritime centre, air transportation centre, and telecommunication centre.

This is not to belittle the potential of Shanghai and Taipei. Both are already important domestic financial centres (DFCs). However, until they can completely remove all exchange controls, permit full convertibility of the domestic currencies, and adhere fully to the international standards of national treatment, reciprocity and regulatory transparency, neither can be IFC in the true sense of the word. And of course, until China and Taiwan resolve all their political differences, neither Shanghai nor Taipei can serve as an IFC of Greater China.

The only other financial centre that can challenge Hong Kong is Singapore. Indeed, the two have been keen rivals for nearly thirty years. So far Hong Kong still has an edge, but it is so slight that Singapore can surpass Hong Kong easily, particularly if the 1997

13 In my book (Jao, 1997), there is a whole chapter dealing with competition from other financial centres.

transition is not managed well.[14] However, as far as Greater China is concerned, Singapore is more distant, both economically and geographically, than Hong Kong. To be sure, Singapore is the undisputed financial capital of Overseas Chinese in Southeast Asia, and it is also cultivating assiduously the Chinese Connection. The fact remains, however, that Singapore can hardly compete with Hong Kong, in view of the latter's many advantages, as the IFC of Greater China.

VII. CONCLUDING REMARKS

Hong Kong's rise as a leading IFC during the past quarter of a century is one of the two outstanding economic achievements of the territory in the post World War II era, the other being its transformation from a mere entrepôt into a modern industrial economy. As a financial centre, Hong Kong is now wearing several hats: the second largest IFC of the Asia-Pacific region, the 6th or 7th largest IFC of the world, the only IFC or financial entrepôt of Greater China, and an offshore financial centre of China after the transfer of sovereignty in 1997.[15]

Hong Kong's future as an IFC depends crucially on China's goodwill and rational behaviour. Provided that the "one country, two systems" model, and its financial counterpart, the "one country, two currencies" model, which implies Hong Kong's financial independance, can be shown to work, and provided that China devotes its energy and resources to peaceful economic development, Hong Kong's potential could be limitless. Even at the end of 1996, Greater China, with a combined population of 1,231 million, GDP of US$1,086 billion, forex reserves of US$220 billion, and foreign trade of US$867 billion, was already a formidable economic force. In 25 years' time, China alone will probably become the largest economy of the world (in terms of total GDP, not *per capita* GDP). In a peaceful setting of sustained economic growth, Hong Kong, as well as Shanghai, Taipei, and Singapore, cannot fail to prosper together as IFCs or DFCs.

REFERENCES

Items marked with * are in Chinese

Ayling, D.E. and Jiang, Z. (1994) *Chinese and Western Stock Markets: International Influences and Development*. Institute of European Finance research paper 94/16, Bangor.

---

14 In Jao (1997), I use 30 economic and financial variables to compare Hong Kong and Singapore as IFCs. I find that Hong Kong leads on 16 counts, while Singapore leads on 10 counts, with 4 remaining variables more or less neutral. This finding is supported by a respected credit rating agency, Political and Economic Risk Agency Ltd., which recently rated Hong Kong as having the best financial system in Asia, ahead of both Singapore and Japan. See "Asia Financial Landscape", in *Asian Intelligence*, May 15, 1996.

15 Technically, Macau can also be an offshore financial centre after sovereignty reverts to China in 1999. However, Macau is too small to be a centre. In reality, Macau is only an economic appendage of Hong Kong.

Carse, D. (1996) Banking and monetary links between China and Hong Kong, *HKMA Quarterly Bulletin*, Feb., 50-55.

Chen, Y. (1995) Financial relations between Hong Kong and the mainland. Pp. 47-55 in: Hong Kong Monetary Authority, *Money and Banking in Hong Kong*, Press and Publication Section, Hong Kong Monetary Authority, Hong Kong.

_______ (1996) Prospects for the financial relationship between mainland China and Hong Kong after 1997, *HKMA Quarterly Bulletin*, Feb., 38-43.

Cheung, M.T., Yeung, D.W.K., and Yeung, L.Y. (1992) *The Shenzhen Stock Market: Development, Prospects, Analysis*, Asian Research Service, Hong Kong.

Cini, F. (1993) Métropole régionale ou place internationale? Pp. 117-152 in: Jean-Philippe Béja et al *Hong Kong 1997: fin de siècle, fin d'un monde?* Espace International, Bruxelles.

Dufey, G. and Giddy, I.H. (1978) *The International Money Market*, Prentice-Hall Inc., Englewood Cliffs, New Jersey.

*Economic Development Commission (1997). *A Comparison of Taiwan, Hong Kong and Singapore as Asia-Pacific Regional Operations Centre,* Taipei, Taiwan.

Gwartney, J., Lawson, R., and Block, W. (1996) *Economic Freedom of the World 1975-1995*, The Fraser Institute, Canada.

Hewson, J.R. (1982) *Offshore Banking in Australia*, AGPS, Canberra.

Hu, Yebi (1993) *China's Capital Market*, The Chinese University Press, Hong Kong.

Jao, Y.C. (ed.) (1988) *Hong Kong's Banking System in Transition*, Chinese Banks' Association, Hong Kong.

Jao, Y.C. (1994) Hong Kong as an international financial centre. Pp. 491-534 in: Roberts, R. (ed.) *International Financial Centres of Europe, North America and Asia*, Edward Elgar, Hants, England.

________ (1997) *Hong Kong as an International Financial Centre: Evolution, Prospects and Policies*, City University Press of Hong Kong, Hong Kong.

Johns, R.A. (1992) Offshore banking, *The New Palgrave Dictionary of Money and Finance*, 3, 63-67.

Johnson, B.T. and Sheehy, T.P. (1996) *1996 Index of Economic Freedom*, The Heritage Foundation, Washington.

Li, D.K.P. (1995) Hong Kong's growing role in world finance, *The Columbia Journal of World Business*, summer, 35-40.

*Lin, T.B. (ed.) (1995) *China-controlled Enterprises in Hong Kong Before and After 1997*, Mainland Affairs Commission, Executive Yuan, Taipei.

*Ministry of Economics (1994) *Feasibility Study of Establishing a Regional Operations Centre in Taiwan*, Investment Office, MOE, Taipei.

Reed, H.C. (1981) *The Preeminence of International Financial Centers*, Praeger Publishers, New York.

Roberts, R. (1994a) Introduction. Pp. xiii - xxiii in: Roberts, R. (ed.) *International Financial Centres*, 4, *Offshore Financial Centres*, Edward Elgar, Hants, England.

_________ (1994b) *International Financial Centres*, 2, *Global Financial Centres: London, New York, Tokyo*, Edward Elgar, Hants, England.

U.S. Department of Treasury (1990, 1994) *National Treatment Study*, Washington.

White III, L.T. (1989) *Shanghai Shanghaied? Uneven Taxes in Reform China*, Centre of Asian Studies, University of Hong Kong, Hong Kong.

Winters, L.A. (1990) The road to Uruguay, *Economic Journal*, 100 (403), 1288-1303.

Yam, J. (1995) Hong Kong as an international financial centre. Pp. 25-46, in: *Money and Banking in Hong Kong*, Hong Kong Monetary Authority, Hong Kong.

7. OVERSEAS CHINESE AND FOREIGN INVESTMENT IN CHINA: AN APPLICATION OF THE TRANSACTION COST APPROACH

C. Simon Fan

1. INTRODUCTION

For almost the last two decades, we have witnessed a dramatic and persistent economic growth in China. In fact, China had experienced spectacular growth even when the whole industrial world was in recession. A key factor that has promoted China's economic growth is its successful implementation of the "Reform and Open Door" policy initiated in 1978. In particular, this policy has resulted in significant increases in foreign investment in China, which has generated a significant impact on China's economic change (e.g. Kueh, 1992).

The important contribution of foreign investment to China's growth can be best understood from the background in which China's "Open Door" policy was initially adopted.

After the communist victory in 1949, China had isolated itself from the industrial world for about thirty years. Largely due to military conflicts and political reasons, China had pursued the policy of "self-reliance" for that period, which excluded any foreign investment in China and limited the international trade with the industrial world. Meanwhile, for that period, the economic system that China adopted was communist state planning system, which was characterized by serious market distortions, inefficient bureaucratic administration, unmotivated labour force, and many other types of inefficiencies. Consequently, when the economic reform was initiated in 1978, China not only had a serious shortage of capital relative to its abundant labour force but also faced its production technology that in many areas was much more backward than the industrial world.

An obvious strategy for China to overcome the technological gap was to absorb foreign advanced technology through increasing the interaction with the rest of world, particularly by attracting foreign direct investment. Indeed, as widely recognized in the literature, foreign direct investment is the means and vehicle for the dissemination of technological knowledge, the transmission of ideas, for the importation of know-how, skills, managerial talents, and entrepreneurship. Thus, foreign direct investment can not only help a developing country to reduce its shortage of capital and promote its exports, but also accelerate the technological diffusion from the industrial world .

Based on this logic, beginning in 1978, China adopted an "open door" policy that complements and reinforces its strategy of the gradual transition from a centrally planning economy to a market economy. Indeed, it has been pointed out that it is China's external opening-up with its various attributes that has sustained the momentum of China's market reforms (Kueh, 1992).

The purpose of this chapter is to attempt to analyze the patterns of foreign investment in China using the transaction cost approach. In a recent book, Sung (1991) also employs the transaction cost approach to analyze Hong Kong's role of intermediation in China's international trade. The current chapter can therefore be regarded as a complement to Sung (1991) and some other existing literature in the application of the transaction cost approach in the context of China.

2. THE LAW OF DIMINISHING RETURNS AND INTERNATIONAL CAPITAL MOVEMENTS

Before considering the transaction cost approach and its application in explaining foreign investment in China, we will first review the "textbook" version of the basic theory of investment. The neoclassical economic theory argues that in a perfectly competitive economy, the profit rate is determined by the marginal product of capital. Thus, the law of diminishing returns (i.e. diminishing marginal productivity) immediately implies that profit rate is low in capital abundant countries, and is (potentially) high in labour abundant countries. This argument seems to provide an explanation for why the pattern of international capital movements is that capital mostly flows from developed countries to developing countries rather than the other way around.

In an influential article, however, Lucas (1990) points out that the neoclassical model runs into trouble when we turn from qualitative to quantitative predictions about the rate of return to capital. Specifically, based on a standard neoclassical model, Lucas's simulation implies that the profit rate in India is 58 times that in the U.S.! Thus, Lucas entitles his famous paper as "why doesn't capital flow from rich to poor countries?"

Lucas (1990) provides some insightful explanations for the puzzle he posed. He argues that there are other factors that might also affect the rate of return to capital, which include the average educational attainment, the externality effect of human capital, and the political risk.

Lucas's puzzle, however, is only one of the puzzles of the neoclassical theory of international capital flows. For example, let us look at the following table.

Table 7.1: Realized Foreign Direct Investment in China (1983-1994)
(Unit: Billion US Dollars)

Year	China	All Developing Countries
1979-82 (cumulative)	1.77	
1983	0.64	16.29
1984	1.26	16.13
1985	1.66	12.25
1986	1.88	13.24
1987	2.31	18.33
1988	3.19	25.33
1989	3.39	31.13
1990	3.49	28.65
1991	4.37	
1992	11.20	
1993	25.76	
1994	33.79	

Sources: (1) Shang-Jin Wei (1995) (2) Nicholas Lardy (1996)

From Table 7.1, it is clear to see two facts: (1) China had experienced exponential growth of foreign direct investment. (2) The "growth rate" of foreign direct investment in China is much higher than that in the developing countries as a whole. In particular, by the mid-1990s, China had become the largest receipt of foreign direct investment in the world.

Thus, by the same logic as in Lucas (1990), in the "Greater China" context, one may ask the following question: why is China more successful than other developing countries in attracting foreign investment for the past two decades? In other words, what other important factors account for the fact that some developing countries (e.g. China) are so much better able to attract foreign investment than others. In the following, I will argue that the application of the "transaction cost" approach will provide a good answer to this puzzle.

3. TRANSACTION COST AND FOREIGN INVESTMENT IN CHINA

International investment is a complicated business transaction. In fact, many economists attribute the significance of transaction costs as the most important reason for the lack of the capital flows from rich to poor countries. For example, when an investor brings capital to enter an unfamiliar territory, he will have to interact with local industries and government to hire enough workers, obtain necessary intermediate goods, and be supported by adequate public utilities (e.g. water, electricity, etc.) In order to set up a firm.

In the following, I will argue and analyze in detail that the existence of Hong Kong and other overseas Chinese firms is the key to the success of China's attracting foreign investment because the overseas Chinese business firms have much less transaction costs in doing business in China. This argument is consistent with the evidence. For example, the following table clearly illustrates the importance of overseas Chinese investment in China.

Table 7.2: Foreign Direct Investments in China 1979-1993

Country	No. of Firms	Percentage	# of Capital (US$ bn)	Percentage
Hong Kong	108914	63.8	103.94355	72.7
Taiwan	20612	12.3	13.22722	9.3
U.S.A.	11554	6.9	8.16857	5.7
Japan	7096	4.2	5.19846	3.6
Macau	4116	2.5	4.12917	2.9
Singapore	3037	1.8	3.33048	2.3
S. Korea	2321	1.4	1.31762	0.9
Canada	1595	0.9	1.02232	0.7
Thailand	1361	0.8	1.62186	1.1
Australia	1269	0.8	0.96327	0.7
Total	167507	100.0	142.92248	100.0

Source: References to Economic Research (*JinJi YanJiu CanKao*), China, October 1994. Tsang (1995)

From the above table, it is easy to see that Hong Kong had been the dominant supplier of foreign direct investment in China for the almost last two decades. Of the total 142.9 billion U.S. dollars' foreign direct investment in China, Hong Kong contributes 103.9 billion, or about 72.7 percent. This is a consistent pattern. Hong Kong's share in total foreign direct investment in China has been above 50 percent for every single year except one since 1979 (Wei, 1995). A comment that has to be made here is that part of the reported Hong Kong investment is actually Taiwan investment in disguise (to avoid political inconvenience with its home government). Another small part of the reported Hong Kong investments is actually Mainland capital in disguise (to take advantage of preferential treatment accorded to foreign investment by the Chinese government). The above table also reveals that other East Asian economies, particularly those with a large Chinese diaspora such as Macau, Singapore, and Thailand, have also supplied a significant amount of direct investment to China.

Why are the cultural and linguistic affinities so important in reducing the transaction cost of investing in China? Most obviously, the commonality of culture and language reduces the communication cost of business transaction. Besides, there are two other related explanations that we will discuss in detail. First, a significant legacy of the communist economic system is the relationship-based trade system, or *guanxi* system, in coordinating production and specialization. About thirty years' centrally planning system generated the *guanxi* system, where the connections among government officials and firm managers control the distribution of raw materials, intermediate goods, and other resources. Indeed, it is necessary for firm mangers to maintain good relationships with all relevant government officials and firm managers in the *guanxi* system to ensure the provision of enough supporting resources (e.g. electricity, water, etc.) and the timely delivery of necessary intermediate goods.

Although the important motivation for the initiation of economic reform in China was the recognition of the efficiency of market economy and the inefficiency of the planned economy, the gradual approach of economic reform in China did not eliminate the central planning system as a coordination mechanism of production and specialization. Instead, it has adopted the "dual track system" (*shuang gui zhi*), which means the coexistence of the centrally planned system and the market mechanism for the allocation of resources. Thus, the economic reform in China still makes use of the *guanxi* system as a coordination mechanism of production and specialization. In fact, the reformists in the central government have decentralized much local power in the economic reform, partly as a strategy to use the local officials as a counterweight to the conservatives in the central government (Shirk, 1993). Consequently, this decentralization strengthens the role of local sectors and makes the *guanxi* system even more important as a coordination mechanism of production in China. (Oi, 1995). Thus, foreign firms who want to invest in China must be able to make use of the *guanxi* system to get the necessary supply of energy, resources, and other local supports, or even use it as substitute for the rule of law and certainty of contracts. For example, Root (1995) points out that in many real estate transactions in China, contracts are accompanied with photographs taken in a public ceremony in which a ranking party officials shakes hands with the would-be owner. These photographs will serve to remedy the weakness of a contract which is often one or two paragraphs in length and so do not fully anticipate the wide range of contingencies or liabilities that owners may occur.

Next, we will argue that the investors who know best how to use the *guanxi* system in China are the overseas Chinese in general, and Hong Kong investors in particular, because the overseas Chinese also do their business in another *Guanxi* system.

When the discipline of economics was just founded, Adam Smith (1965), in the very first sentence of his study of *the Wealth of Nations*, argues that "The greatest improvement in the productive powers of labour, and the greater part of the skill, dexterity, and judgment with which it is anywhere directed or applied, seem to have been the effects of the division of labour." But what are mechanisms that coordinate the division of labour? In a capitalist economy, the prevalent mechanism of the division of labour is the market. However, as emphasize by some economists, the coordination cost of the market mechanism can be significant in many cases, due to principal-agent conflicts, "free ride" problem, "adverse selection" problem, and other opportunistic behaviours of economic agents. Transaction costs may also include the costs arising from finding someone with whom to do business, of reaching an agreement about the price and other aspects of the exchange, and of ensuring that the terms of the agreement are fulfilled (e.g. Parkin, 1990). Thus, significant transaction costs may exist in some market transactions.

The existence of the costs involved in market transactions implies the possible methods of coordination alternative to the market. In fact, institutions then emerge as mechanisms to reduce the transaction costs. According to Douglas North (1993), "Institutions are the humanly devised constraints imposed on human interaction. They consist of formal rules, informal constraints (norms of behaviour, conventions, and self-imposed codes of conduct), and their enforcement characteristics. In short, they consist of the structure that humans impose in dealing with each other." Recently, there has been an increasing awareness in the economic literature that institutions significantly affect economic performance by determining the types of market transaction and transaction costs.

Meanwhile, it should be noted that transaction costs also exist in institutions. These costs include those of organizing , maintaining, and enforcing the rules of institutional arrangement. Thus, the choice of the extent of market transaction and institutions will depend on which costs less.

Different institutional structures achieve coordination in different ways and with different results. So, specifically, what are the basic institutions in a market economy? The most important institution in reducing the costs of market transaction, as first cost recognized by Coase (1937), is also the most fundamental units of production in our daily observations----the firms. Coase argues that it was the avoidance of the costs of carrying out transactions through the market that can explain the existence of the firm in which the allocation of factors comes about as a result of administrative decisions. In a competitive economy, a firm will be able to exist if it performs its coordination function at a lower cost than would be incurred through market transactions.

More recently, much economic literature also identifies another important type of institutions----the families, in the allocation and distribution of resources. The advantage of the family as an institution for coordinating production and exchange arises from its ability to reduce transaction costs with significant interpersonal relationship. Specifically, Robert Pollak (1985) argues that the advantages of family governance can be grouped into four categories: incentives, monitoring, altruism, and loyalty. First, the incentive advantage of family production arises from family members having direct claims on the output of family production. It can be best illustrated by the drastic increase of productivity resulting from the "household responsibility system" at the beginning of the economic reform in China. Second, the monitoring advantage comes from the interaction of economic and personal relationships. A family member has a clear informational advantage to observe and infer other family members' economic and social behaviour because living together with other family members and/or other frequent social interactions provide him (her) with the knowledge on other family member's work habits, honesty, diligence, and other information that are not available to outsiders. Third, "altruism" or "love", and other affectional relationships, which commonly exist among family members, reduce the incentives of opportunistic behaviour and facilitate cooperation. Fourth, family loyalty another basis for cooperative behaviour among family members. The social basis of loyalty depends on the generally accepted norms regarding the treatment of family members which are enforced through reputation.

The advantages of a family as a institution of coordinating production and exchange can be extended to the close interactions among many families, friends, and business partners. In the economic literature, Yoram Ben-Porath (1980) puts forward the idea that the identity of people engaged in a transaction is a major determinant of the institutional mode of transaction. In particular, he argues that investment in resources specific to a relationship between identified parties can reduce transaction costs and promote trade. More recently, Zvi Griliches (1996) emphasizes the empirical relevance of Ben-Porath's idea and argues that personal human capital created by investments in reputation and personal relationships is one of the most important part of one's human capital in business operation and transactions.

The above theoretical argument has particularly important empirical relevance in South East Asia, when the legal system has not been (at least was not) comprehensive enough to enforce contracts efficiently, or when the Chinese were discriminated against in the society so that they could not seek efficient legal protection of their property rights. The *guanxi* system, which can be interpreted as the relationships within and among families, was developed as an alternative or even a more efficient coordination mechanism of production and exchange, and as a substitute for the legal system as a mechanism to protect private property rights and enforce contracts. In fact, it has been argued that there is a strong similarity between the Jews in Europe (before the holocaust) and the Chinese in South East Asia. In particular, both of them do business through the coordination "family capitalism". And, as with Jewish entrepreneurs, family ties have been strengthened by persecution.[1]

---

1 see *Economist*, March 9, 1996, page 12.

This traditional of "family capitalism" still flourished among the business relationships among the overseas Chinese business interactions. Family, trust, and friends are crucial to the overseas Chinese way of conducting business. One seldom does business with someone that one does not know. Indeed, as quoted in the *Economist*[2], one of a Chinese businessman has said: "You do not negotiate a contract, you negotiate a relationship."

The relationship-based nature of business in the network of overseas Chinese implies that a successful businessman must have a good command of the skills of establishing comprehensive and efficient interpersonal relationships with other businessmen and government officials who regulate the business. Thus, although many western firms are not willing or not able to use the *guanxi* system in China as a substitute for the rule of law and the certainty of contracts, the overseas Chinese investors feel it is much less costly for them to establish the necessary relationship with Chinese government officials in the communist *guanxi* system and other local businessmen given the interpersonal business skills that they have obtained in their capitalist *Guanxi* system.

Indeed, one of the most commonly cited problems in foreign investment in China is the complicated and time-consuming administrative procedures that investors have to go through. There are often as many as 20 to 30 offices that one has to go through before the actual production take place (Thoburn et al, 1990). Thus, the interpersonal skills in the *guanxi* system are essential to get help from local government officials to improve the administrative efficiency to escape the costly complicated bureaucratic procedures.

For the western firms which are less able to use the *Guanxi* system in China, an obvious way to circumvent the problem is to hire some Chinese who have good connections with China's power structure. Indeed, this is exactly the practice of many western firms that have investment in China. This can be interestingly illustrated by the following table which shows that the Chinese "princelings" take important positions in some financial institutions that have investment in China.

Moreover, western firms not only have an obvious disadvantage in interpersonal skills in trying to use the *guanxi* system in China, they are also much more constrained by their institutional arrangement than ethnic Chinese investors. For example, the chief of a western firm that has done its business in China very well explains that the key to his success is "to sit down over a cup of tea with the top guy; there isn't documentation; the deal is done.[3]" While doing business in this way is standard business activities for the ethnic overseas Chinese, who operated their business in "family capitalism", it is difficult for most western firms to mimic, because deals without documentation will make it difficult for a firm when reporting to its shareholders.[4]

---

2 see the *Economist*, March 9, 1996, page 12.

3 See Gideon Rachman, "The Battle for Asia," *The Economist*, November 12, 1994, page SS19-SS25.

4 This point is also made in Hilton (1995).

Table 7.3: "Banking's Darling Princelings"

Princeling	Relationship	Career at Investment Bank
Margaret Ren	Daughter-in-law of *Zhao Ziyang*	Bear Sterns (Managing director)
Ding Yuqing	Son of *Ding Guangen*	Bear Sterns (managing director)
Zhou Yuan	Son of *Zhou Nan*	UBS Securities (chief representative-China)
Huan Guochang	Son of *Huan Xiang* (former state council's vice-premier)	BZW (managing director-China)
Liang Xiaoting	Son of the former Shangdong governor	Bank of China (first deputy general manager)
Huang Bin	Son of *Huang Hua* (a former minister)	Salomon Brothers (formerly Beijing representative of Lehman Brothers)
Ken Lu	Son of *Lu Ping*	Formerly with Morgan Stanley (now director of China-HK Telecom)
Susan Ding	Daughter of *Ding Guangen*	CS First Boston (analyst)
Dennis Zhu	Son of *Zhu Rongji*	CS First Boston (vice-president of equity capital markets)

Source: *Eastern Express*, February 26, 1996

Thus, by applying the transaction cost approach, we have provided an explanation for why the overseas Chinese have played a dominant role in the foreign direct investment in China.

4. TRANSPORTATION COST, PRODUCT CYCLE, AND "GREATER CHINA" ECONOMIC INTEGRATION

In the last section, we have analyzed the important role of transaction cost on investing in China. The analysis provides an attracting explanation for why the overseas Chinese have contributed greatly to Chinese success in attracting foreign investment. However, as shown in Table 7.2, overseas Chinese in different parts of the world do not contribute equally in the capital flows in China. Instead, it is clear to see that Hong Kong, and to a lesser extent Taiwan, have played a particularly important role in the rapid increase of the investment flows into China. In fact, the investment activities between these three regions have been so rapidly expanded that they are often referred to as "Greater China" in the literature. To further illustrate the point of the massive process of relocating manufacturing factories from Hong Kong to China, one only need to consider the fact that over three millions workers in South China are reportedly working for the investors in Hong Kong, comparing that the total labour force in Hong Kong is only 2.8 millions (e.g. Tsang, 1995).

In the following, we will argue that there are two major reasons why Hong Kong, and to a lesser extent Taiwan, have played such an important role in the capital flows into China.

The first factor, which is the most straightforward reason and can be broadly incorporated into the transaction cost approach that this chapter emphasizes, is the concern of transportation cost. Geographically, Hong Kong can be regarded as part of China with GuangDong Province as its immediate hinterland. Also, although it has been under the British rule since 1842, over 98 percent of the population in Hong Kong are Chinese, whose dialect is Cantonese, which is also the dialect in GuangDong province.

Indeed, the firms set up by Hong Kong investors are mainly located along the Pearl River Delta with Baoan being the county and DongGuan being the city (except ShenZhen) nearest to Hong Kong. There are also waterways linking these places to the ports of Hong Kong (Thoburn et al, 1990). The advantage of transportation cost and transaction cost can immediately explain why China's open-door policy has induced Hong Kong investors shift their production facilities from Hong Kong to its nearby Pearl River Delta and ShenZhen Special Economic Zones.

Largely because of the facilitating role of Hong Kong, many of the Taiwanese projects are also located in GuangDong. However, an important distinction between the investment from Hong Kong and that from Taiwan is that while Hong Kong businessmen concentrate their investment in GuangDong, Taiwanese businessmen invest heavily in FuJian province. For example, according to a recent study by Luo and Howe (1993), 65 percent of total Taiwanese investment in China is located in Fujian. In particular, the Xiamen Special Economic Zone (SEZ) in southern Fujian accounts for approximately one fifth of the total projects.

Taiwanese businessmen's heavy investment in Fujian, and particularly in the Xiamen SEZ area, is not so much due to the consideration of transportation cost as to that of the transaction cost we analyzed in the last section. Because of the political conflicts, there is still no direct transportation between Fujian and Taiwan. Also, most of the indirect transportation is through Hong Kong, which implies Fujian is by no means the cheapest location when transportation cost is taken into account. Instead, Taiwan's investment in Fujian is mainly due to the close historical, cultural, and social linkage between these two regions. For example, Taiwanese speak the same dialect and share the customs as the people in Xiamen. In fact, many Taiwanese often combine their private visits to Fujian, where they often have family ties, with a search for business opportunities.

That Hong Kong and Taiwan account for the bulk of foreign direct investment can also be explained by the application of the Product Cycle Theory. In the simplest version of the

Product Cycle Theory that was developed by Vernon (1966), a product goes through a full life cycle from innovation to standardization. The innovation of a product and its initial production is most human capital intensive, because, for example, there must be frequent and close communication between factory managers and sales personnel in order to facilitate critical revisions of the product and the technology for producing it. This stage typically occurs in the most developed countries. However, the production will become less and less human capital intensive as the product goes through its life cycle. In particular, in the standardized stage, the production of a product becomes routine and physical labour intensive. So, the production in this stage typically happens in low income countries.

In the late 1970s, many factories in Hong Kong and Taiwan were producing the products that were at the final stage of their product cycles, partly because the government in these two regions did not spend enough resources to encourage research and development in the industrial sector and partly because the highly educated labour force in these two regions that were available to the manufacturing industry was relatively small. The rising wage rate in Hong Kong and Taiwan reduced their comparative advantage in producing these products, but the opening of China provided the investors of these two regions with the golden opportunity of investing their capital and know-how of the standardized products in a region with much lower wage rates and much cheaper land. In contrast, the production technologies owned by the firms in United States, Japan, and other more advanced countries generally have more stringent skill requirement for worker and also need the support of high quality requirements of infrastructure, for example, to produce high quality products.

The empirical relevance of the Product Cycle Model in explaining Hong Kong's investment in China is confirmed in a study by Chen (1981, 1983), who found that Hong Kong investment in China in the early 1980s differs from Hong Kong investment in other Asian countries in that only the most labour-intensive stages were transferred to China from Hong Kong, rather than the production of the whole process. This can be explained because China lacked the necessary technical infrastructure and skilled labour to produce the complete product. In a more recent study, Sung (1995) shows that China's trade with Hong Kong and Taiwan is largely intra-industry trade, which implies that these regions may operate at different stages of product cycles. In other words, the investors tend to relocate the production processes that are routine and labour-intensive to mainland China (i.e. the production process at the last stage of the product cycle), while retaining the skill-intensive production processes.

5. GOVERNMENT POLICY AND FOREIGN INVESTMENT IN CHINA

In order to foster foreign investment, the Chinese government has made a considerable amount of effort to provide various investment incentives. Over the past two decades, the Chinese government has constantly readjusted its policies to improve its investment environment attract foreign investment in terms of both quantity and quality. Three of its most successful policies can be identified: (1) preferential treatment of tax towards foreign investors, (2) flexible contractual forms that are available to foreign investors, both of which reduce the transaction cost of investing in China, and (3) the establishment of special economic zones.

As the following table shows, relatively low tax rates are one of the attractive features to foreign investors. In particular, China's corporate rate for joint ventures is fifteen percent in most areas, compared with an average tax rate of thirty percent or more in most neighbouring developing countries.

Table 7.4: Income Tax on FDI

Country	Income Taxation
China	Corporate income: 15% in SEZs and opened cities and 10% withholding tax on remitted dividends; in other areas, corporate income tax is 30%
Hong Kong	Corporate income tax : 18.5% Other entities: 17% Taxes are levied on profits and interest arising in or derived in Hong Kong
Malaysia	Corporate income tax: 35% Development tax: 5% Excess profit tax: 3%
Singapore	Corporate income tax: 31% Withholding tax: 33% on dividends earned in Singapore
South Korea	Corporate income tax: 0-30%
Thailand	Corporate income tax: 35% Business tax: 1.5-40% Remittance tax: 20%

Source: Phillip Grub and Jian-Hai Lin (1991), *Foreign Direct Investment in China,* Quorum Books: New York.

Another policy that contributes to attracting foreign investment is the flexible contractual forms that the Chinese government offers to foreign investors. These wide range of contractual arrangements include (Thoburn, 1990):

(1) 100% foreign owned ventures (*duzi qiye*)
(2) Equity joint ventures (where some contributions are allowed from the Chinese side in kind) (*hezi qiye*).
(3) Cooperative (or "contractual") joint ventures (where the Chinese contribution is mainly in kind, typically land and buildings) (h*ezuo qiye*).
(4) Processing and assembly arrangements (for which fees are charged)
(5) Compensation trade (where the foreign side supplies machinery and equipment, and is repaid in instalments of the products) (*buchang maoyi*).

The joint ventures play a particularly important role in reducing transaction cost, which can be illustrated by the following surveys on the advantages of the Hong Kong partners and the Chinese partners in joint ventures conducted in a recent article (Lin, 1995),

Table 7.5: The advantages of Chinese partners

Advantages	Average score
the connection with relevant administrations	2.952
the experience in the management in China	2.714
the information channel in China	2.595
the market channel in China	2.548
the currently available facilities	2.524

(Remark: 1=not important, 2=not very important, 3=fairly important, 4=very important).

Table 7.6: The advantages of Hong Kong partners

Advantages	Average score
the channel to international market	3.262
flexibility	3.024
management skills	3.857
capital	2.786
technology and know-how	2.548
economies of scale	2.500

(Remark: 1=not important, 2=not very important, 3=fairly important, 4=very important).

From the above two tables, it is easy to see that the most important reason for the Hong Kong investors and the Chinese partners forming joint ventures is to reduce the transaction cost of production and exchange (in both China and the international market). In particular, Chinese partners have the advantage in establishing the necessary relationship with relevant government officials, while the Hong Kong partners have the cost advantage in searching for the most profitable international markets for their product. In other words, the formation of joint ventures between foreign investors and Chinese partners allows them to pursue their comparative advantage to minimize the transaction cost of production and marketing.

A further comment here is that despite the efficiency gained by the formation of joint ventures, the interest conflicts of different parties within joint ventures also generate transaction costs within the joint ventures, resulting from moral hazard problem, adverse selection problem, or other opportunistic behaviours. Thus, again, overseas Chinese will have an advantage in resolving all kinds of agency problems and reducing the transaction costs within joint ventures.

Finally, the establishment of the special economic zones also contributes significantly to attracting foreign investment to China. When the "Open Door" was just initiated, China faced a severe shortage of energy, transportation and communication facilities. If these scarce resources were equally distributed in all places in China, foreign investors would face a poor infrastructure that would significantly limit the profit that they can make. So, they would have much less incentive in investing in China.

The establishment of a few special economic zones (SEZs) allowed the Chinese government to concentrate resources to strengthen the infrastructure construction in the SEZs. The reduction of the "bottlenecks" of energy, transportation, and communication, etc. attract foreign investments in these SEZs. In fact, as a result, foreign-funded energy, transportation and telecommunications also increased greatly.

Another important function of the SEZs is that they have been granted independent legislative rights by the Chinese National Peoples Congress, which allowed the SEZ government reduce bureaucratic procedures and increase the efficiency of the government. This increase in the bureaucratic efficiency has reduced the transaction cost of foreign investors' interaction with the local government, and hence increases foreign investment in the SEZs.

6. FUTURE PERSPECTIVES

In the final section, we will briefly discuss some future perspectives on foreign investment in China. There are two special features of foreign investment in China. First, as shown earlier, Hong Kong, and to a lesser extent, Taiwan account for the bulk of foreign direct investment in China. Second, most of the foreign investment in China concentrates on the coastal areas, particularly the special economic zones in China.

With the further economic reforms, market will play a more and more important role, eventually dominating in coordinating the production and exchange in China, which implies that the *guanxi* system will be less and less important to foreign investors. Meanwhile, with the increase of Chinese workers` production skills and educational attainment, it is reasonable to expect that more sophisticated production processes will be relocated from advanced economies to China in order to take advantage of the cheap high-quality labour in China.

Meanwhile, the relatively large foreign investment in the coastal areas significantly and continuously increases factor prices in these areas. For example, as the following table shows, the gap in the labour costs between Guangdong and other provinces in China has increased significantly since the beginning of the economic reform in China.

Table 7.7: Average Monthly Wage in Guangdong and in other provinces in China

Year	Average wage in Guangdong (yuan)	Average wage in other provinces (yuan)
1978	30.6	31.1
1985	202	120
1986	204	124
1987	223	136
1988	282	145
1989	322	161
1990	359	186
1991	419	206
1992	456	223
1993	497	239
1994	587	269
1995	674	294

Sources: China Statistics Yearbook (*Zhongguo Tonji Nianjian*) 1996; Guangdong Statistics Yearbook (*Guangdong Tonji Nianjian*), 1996.

So, clearly, the cost advantage in less developed provinces in China will induce foreign investors to relocate their production facilities in Guangdong and other more developed areas to these areas. Moreover, China's economic development will provide the central government with more and more resources to invest in energy, transportation, and communications in these poor areas to strengthen the infrastructure in these areas, which will provide investors with further incentives to invest in the poorer areas.

REFERENCES

Ben-Porath, Yoram (1980) "The F-Connection: Families, Friends, and Firms and the Organization of Exchange," *Population and Development Review* 6(1): 1-30.

Chen, Edward K. Y. (1981),"Hong Kong Multinationals in Asia: Characteristics and Objectives," in K. Kumar and M. G. Mcleod, eds. *Multinationals from Developing Countries*, Lexington Books: Lexington, M.A;

Chen, Edward K. Y. (1983) "Multinationals from Hong Kong," in S. Lall, eds. *The New Multinationals: The Spread of Third World Enterprises*, Wiley, London.

Coase, Ronald (1937), "The Nature of the Firm," *Economica*: 386-405.

Griliches, Zvi (1996) "Education, Human Capital, and Growth: A Personal Perspective," NBER Working Paper, No. 5426.

Phillip Grub and Jian-Hai Lin (1991*), Foreign Direct Investment in China,* Quorum Books: New York.

Kueh, Y. Y. (1992) "Foreign Investment and Economic Change in China," *China Quarterly*, 131: 637-690.

Lardy, Nicholas (1995) "The Role of Foreign Trade and Investment in China's Economic Transformation," China Quarterly, 144: 1065-1082.

Lin, Danming (1995) "Several Strategic Issues in HongKong-GuangDong joint ventures," mimeo, University of Hong Kong.

Lucas, Robert E. Jr. (1990) "Why doesn't Capital Flow from Rich to Poor Countries?" American Economic Review, 80 (May):92-96.

Luo, Qi and Christopher Howe (1993) "Direct Investment and Economic Integration in the Asia Pacific: The Case of Taiwanese Investment in Xiamen," *the China Quarterly*, pp 746-769.

North, Douglass (1993) "Toward a Theory of Institutional Change," in *Political Economy: Institutions, Competition, and Representation*, eds. by William Barnett, Melvin Hinich, and Norman Schofield, Cambridge University Press.

Oi, Jean C. (1995) "The Role of the Local State in China's Transitional Economy," *The China Quarterly*, 1132-1149.

Parkin, Michael (1990) *Economics*, New York: Addison-Wesley Publishing Company.

Pollak, Robert (1985) "A Transaction Cost Approach to Families and Households," *Journal of Economic Literature*, XXIII(2): 581-608.

Root, Hilton (1995) "Has China Lost Its Way? Getting Stuck in Transition." Hoover Institution, Stanford University.

Shirk, Susan (1993) *The Political Logic of Economic Reform in China*, Berkeley: University of Carlifornia Press.

Smith, Adam (1965) *The Wealth of Nations*, New York: Modern Library.

Sung, Yun-wing (1991) *The China-Hong Kong Connection: The Key to China's Open Door Policy*, Cambridge University Press: Cambridge.

Sun, Yun-wing (1995) "Economic Integration of Hong Kong and Guangdong in the 1990s," in R. Kwok and A. So eds., *The Hong Kong-Guangdong link: Parternership in Flux*, M.E. Sharp: New York.

Thoburn, John T., H. M. Leung, Esther Chau, and S. H. Tang (1990) *Foreign Investment in China Under the Open Policy*, Avebury: Hong Kong.

Tsang, Shu-ki (1995) "The Political Economy of Greater China," Hong Kong Baptist University Working Paper Series, No. CP 95010.

Vernon, Raymond (1966) "International Investment and International Trade in the Product Cycle," *Quarterly Journal of Economics* 80: 190-207.

Wei, Shang-Jin (1995) "Attracting Foreign Direct Investment: Has China Reached Its Potential?" *China Economic Review*, 6(2): 187-199.

8. TAIWAN'S TRADE AND INVESTMENT RELATIONS WITH CHINA: IMPACT ON TAIWAN'S INCOME DISTRIBUTION

Kai-cheong Lei

INTRODUCTION

The open door policy of mainland China, which has been enthusiastically implemented ever since 1979, has generated rapid increases both in China's inward direct foreign investment and in China's external trade. China's establishment of the four Special Economic Zones in the early 1980s and the subsequent opening-up of her coastal areas are especially growth-oriented measures. These measures broadly coincided in time with the cost-induced economic restructuring in the Asian NIEs. Among the 'four little dragons' in Asia, Hong Kong and Taiwan are perhaps the most successful ones in taking China as their partner in production and growth. To many scholars and specialists, the rapidly growing economic ties among Taiwan, Hong Kong and China have become so significant that it is hard to deny that a new superpower in the form of 'Greater China' is emerging in the world economy (Shambaugh, 1995).

For the part of Taiwan, the economy has been suffering from both the appreciation of currency and rising labour costs since the mid-1980s. Taiwan's producers have consequently lost the competitive edge which they previously held. Many traditional labour-intensive products became non-competitive in the world market. To regain competitiveness the industrial structure of the economy needs to adjust according to changing comparative advantages. In this regard, the China market not only represents a new market for Taiwan's exports and investment, but also acts as a stabilizer which enables Taiwan's structural adjustments to be both smooth and swift. Without China's provision of cheap land and labour for the migration of Taiwan's labour-intensive industries and without China's growing demand for Taiwan's products the economy may have to go through a painstaking and prolonged adjustment process. The China market is no doubt important for the Taiwanese economy (Lin and Chen, 1996).

Based on this background, the present chapter aims to provide a quantitative assessment of the impact on Taiwan's production and income distribution of Taiwan's increasing investments and exports to China. While the impact on Taiwan's production has been the subjects of several studies (Lin and Huang, 1992; Chiu and Chung, 1993; Kao, Chi and Wu, 1995), the impact on Taiwan's income distribution has been so far overlooked. This chapter represents in a way an attempt to make up the deficiency.

From the functional point of view, the distribution of income changes as the structural distribution of production changes. The structure of production in an open economy such as in Taiwan in turn changes as the pattern of comparative advantages and the pattern of outward investment change. On the other hand, there are two basic functions served by foreign outward investments. The first one is simply an extension of production activities from the home country to the host country. The second function is a substitution of offshore production (in China) for local production (in Taiwan). These two kinds of investments would generate different impacts on domestic employment of resources, both human and non-human. In the case of pure extension, it is not likely that adverse impacts on local employment of labour and capital could be generated. Quite the contrary, the rate of return of capital might become higher as Taiwan's surplus funds/capital could find their ways out in China. In the case with pure substitution, however, adverse impacts on local employment might be highly significant for certain industries. Since from the macro point of view, the reality should be a mixture of extension and substitution, the overall impact on wage income and nonwage income is an subject which really deserves careful study and analysis.

The following study will be first performed by an input-output analysis for the impacts on Taiwan's sectoral productions which were viewed as being generated both by Taiwan's autonomous exports and by Taiwan's investment-induced exports to China. Induced exports by sectors are in turn calculated by using the input-output tables to link sectoral investments in China with the sectoral backward demand in Taiwan. While the autonomous part of exports reflects activities according to the principle of comparative advantages, the induced part represents partly the 'home purchase' policy normally associated with outward foreign direct investments (Dunning, 1995). On the other hand, as investments abroad may lead to a reduction of investments and production at home, there is also a substitution effect to be explained and evaluated. The second major part of the present study focuses on tracing the distributional impacts on wage income and nonwage income due to the changes in sectoral production.

The chapter is organized in four sections below. The first presents the main development of Taiwan's trade with China and Taiwan's investments in China. The next section analyzes the economic consequences of these transactions and activities on Taiwan's domestic production A quantitative assessment for the impact on Taiwan's functional income distribution is then presented and discussed in the subsequent section. The final section is a conclusion section.

CHINA-TAIWAN'S TRADE AND INVESTMENT RELATIONS

(I) Trade Relations

The rapid expansion of China's foreign trade after 1978 is one of the most remarkable features of the impact of the open-door strategy. Between 1980 and 1994 China's merchandise trade grew, on average, by over 14% per annum. The trade with Taiwan, however, does not become significant until 1987 when the government of Taiwan allowed her people to visit their relatives in the mainland. Actually, certain legal export constraints on Taiwan's exporters were already relaxed earlier in 1986, allowing free exports to the mainland as long as the transactions were conducted in an 'indirect' way involving a third party. As these main institutional barriers were being removed, total trade increased rapidly year after year. At the same time, as indicated in Table 8.1, the trade account reveals a serious imbalance between import and export trade in Taiwan's favor. The problem seems to be persistent and real. It certainly reflects the net result of many interacting factors governing the China-Taiwan trade, such as differences in resource endowments, differences in stages of development, as well as differences in production technology.

While the main features associated with the development of the Taiwan-China trade are well documented in the literature (Ash and Kueh, 1995; Chen and Ho, 1994; Kao and Sung, 1994; Lin, 1994), the relative position of the China market in Taiwan's global trading network is a point less discussed. Does the pattern of the Taiwanese trade with China differ significantly from the pattern of the Taiwanese trade with the whole world? The answer seems to be negative as far as exports is concerned. As indicated in Table 8.2, the pattern of exports to China and the pattern of exports to the world is quite similar: both concentrate on items like machinery (SITC 7) and basic manufactures (SITC 6). During 1990 to 1993, these two groups together accounted for more than 60% of total exports in both cases. On the import side, however, the China market seems to have played a different role than the average market has. According to Table 8.3, China has supplied significantly more crude materials (SITC 2), food and beverage (SITC 0 and 1), and miscellaneous manufactured goods (SITC 8) to Taiwan than the average market has.

Table 8.1: Commodity Trade of Taiwan with Mainland China

Unit: US$ million

Year	Total Trade		Imports from Mainland China		Exports to Mainland China		Balance of Trade
	Value	Growth Rate %	Value	Growth Rate %	Value	Growth Rate %	
1981	459	47.6	75	-1.4	384	63.5	309
1982	279	-39.2	84	11.8	195	-49.4	111
1983	248	-11.1	90	6.9	158	-18.8	68
1984	554	123.4	128	42.2	426	169.6	298
1985	1,103	99.1	116	-9.3	987	132.0	871
1986	955	-13.4	144	24.4	811	-17.8	667
1987	1,515	58.6	289	100.4	1,226	51.2	937
1988	2,721	79.5	479	65.7	2,242	82.8	1,763
1989	3,483	28.0	587	22.6	2,896	29.2	2,309
1990	4,043	16.1	765	30.4	3,278	13.2	2,513
1991	5,793	43.3	1,126	47.1	4,667	42.4	3,541
1992	7,407	27.9	1,119	-0.6	6,288	34.7	5,169
1993	8,689	17.3	1,104	-1.4	7,585	20.6	6,481
1994	9,809	12.9	1,292	17.1	8,517	12.3	7,225
1995	11,457	16.8	1,574	21.8	9,883	16.0	8,309

Notes: Value only includes the trade which passed through Hong Kong customs to and from mainland China. Transactions which passed through other harbours to and from mainland China are not included.

Source: *Taiwan Statistical Data Book*, 1996.

Table 8.2: Distribution of Taiwan's Exports to China and to the World

unit: %

SITC Code	1990		1991		1992		1993	
	To China	To World	To China	To World	To China	To World	To China	To World
0	1.08	3.97	0.93	4.14	0.69	3.76	0.57	3.65
1	0.02	0.03	0.16	0.06	0.19	0.06	0.15	0.06
2	1.92	1.75	1.91	1.63	2.12	1.59	1.97	1.49
3	0.02	0.60	0.06	0.58	0.04	0.65	0.05	0.68
4	0.00	0.03	0.01	0.02	0.01	0.02	0.01	0.02
5	12.64	4.15	14.51	4.60	14.33	4.70	14.35	5.08
6	52.40	21.35	51.42	21.51	45.57	21.27	42.61	21.80
7	24.31	39.11	23.25	39.17	27.77	41.02	31.93	44.20
8	7.26	28.87	7.39	28.16	8.82	26.78	7.91	22.90
9	0.35	0.14	0.36	0.13	0.46	0.15	0.45	0.12
Total	100.0	100.0	100.0	100.0	100.0	100.0	100.0	100.0

Note: Commodity Meanings for SITC Code: 0 - Food & Live Animals; 1 - Beverage & Tobacco; 2 - Crude Materials Excl. Fuels; 3 - Mineral Fuels; 4 - Animal, Vegetable Oil & Fats; 5 - Chemicals; 6 - Basic Manufactures; 7 - Machines, Transport Equipment; 8 - Misc. Manufactured Goods; 9 - Unclassified Goods.

Sources: (1) Exports to China: Kao and Sung (1994), p.165.
(2) Exports to World: *Key Indicators of Developing Asian and Pacific Countries*, Asian Development Bank (1995), pp. 306-7.

Table 8.3: Distribution of Taiwan's Imports from China and from the World

unit: %

SITC Code	1990		1991		1992		1993	
	From China	From World	From China	From World	From China	From World	From China	From World
0	11.06	4.62	7.19	4.29	7.48	4.14	4.85	3.90
1	3.18	0.54	5.74	0.54	6.60	0.65	1.42	0.77
2	20.77	8.12	17.82	8.42	18.04	7.09	16.16	6.57
3	0.99	10.88	0.72	9.27	0.63	7.79	0.58	7.38
4	0.22	0.18	0.44	0.18	0.74	0.18	0.28	0.19
5	9.37	12.65	8.71	13.59	8.91	11.95	8.06	11.74
6	22.30	15.44	22.00	17.56	17.10	17.16	19.15	18.72
7	13.33	36.96	14.53	35.73	18.44	39.32	24.57	39.37
8	18.73	5.83	22.72	6.09	21.82	6.42	24.73	7.04
9	0.15	4.78	0.13	4.34	0.24	5.31	0.20	4.32
Total	100.00	100.00	100.00	100.00	100.00	100.00	100.00	100.00

Note: Same as Table 8.2.
Sources: (1) Imports from China: Kao and Sung (1994), p.166.
(2) Imports from World: *Key Indicators of Developing Asian and Pacific Countries*, Asian Development Bank (1995), pp. 306-7.

Another point, which concerns the trade balance, is perhaps even more interesting and striking. Taiwan's trade surplus from the China market has already overtaken the trade surplus from the U.S. market in 1994 (Table 8.4). Historically speaking, the U.S. market has been the single most important market for Taiwan's exports ever since the mid-1960s. While its importance has been continuously declining since 1984, the U.S. market alone still takes up 26% of Taiwan's commodity exports ten years later in 1994. As source of trade surplus, the U.S. market is really indispensable. Even in the recent decade (1985-1995), which has experienced rapid and strong currency appreciation as well as significant tariff reduction in Taiwan, trade surplus from the U.S. market still accounts for 60-95% of Taiwan's total surplus. However, a movement of shifting the major source of surplus from the U.S. market to the China market seems to be already in operation since 1988 when the Taiwan - China trade begins to take-off. As can be seen from Table 8.4, while the combined surplus from the two markets appears to be rather stable throughout the period of 1988 to 1995, the contribution share provided by the China market is increasing rapidly whereas the share by the U.S. market tends to go down. It implies that certain functions which used to be served by the U.S. market are now served instead by the China market.

Table 8.4: Taiwan's Trade Surplus

Unit: US$ million

	with China	with USA	with China and USA	with all markets	China's share in Total (%)	USA share in Total (%)
1981	309	3,397	3,706	1,412	21.9	240.6
1982	111	4,196	4,307	3,316	3.3	126.5
1983	68	6,687	6,755	4,836	1.4	138.3
1984	298	9,826	10,124	8,497	3.5	115.6
1985	871	10,027	10,898	10,624	8.2	94.4
1986	667	13,581	14,248	15,680	4.3	86.6
1987	937	16,037	16,974	18,695	5.0	85.8
1988	1,763	10,460	12,223	10,995	16.0	95.1
1989	2,309	12,033	14,342	14,039	16.4	85.7
1990	2,513	9,134	11,647	12,498	20.1	73.1
1991	3,541	8,207	11,748	13,318	26.6	61.6
1992	5,169	7,801	12,970	9,464	54.6	82.4
1993	6,481	6,865	13,346	8,030	80.7	85.5
1994	7,225	6,294	13,519	7,700	93.8	81.7
1995	8,309	5,636	13,945	8,109	102.5	69.5

Sources: 1. *Taiwan Statistical Data Book, 1996.*
2. *Monthly Statistics of Exports and Imports, Taiwan Area, ROC*

(II) Taiwan's Investments in Mainland China

Like her export and import trade with China, Taiwan's investment in China becomes significant only after 1987 when certain institutional reforms, including the liberalization of capital outflow, were legalized. Yet, exactly how much has been invested is a question with no easy answer. Statistics released by governments on both sides of the Taiwan Strait differ significantly (Table 8.5).

Despite such data discrepancy, it is generally agreed that most of Taiwan's investment projects in China are associated with labour-intensive industries. They are also 'defensive' in nature in the sense that the main purpose for investing in China is to minimize production costs in order to protect and retain certain existing export markets in other countries (Chiu and Chung, 1993; Chiu, 1995; Chung and Lee, 1995; Lin, 1995). Several additional salient features are also well documented. They include the following: (1) projects are typically small-scaled; (2) projects are primarily carried out by small and medium- sized enterprises in Taiwan; (3) strong dependence on home supply for intermediate inputs and machinery equipments, and (4) subsidiaries in China rely heavily on their parent companies in Taiwan to provide technology transfer and financial capital. In short, Taiwan's investment in China is trade-oriented, just like Hong Kong's investment in China is (Zhang, 1995).

Table 8.5: Taiwan's Investment in Mainland China

Unit: US$ million

	Approved in Taiwan		Approved by China		
	Case	Amount	Case	Contracted Amount	Realized Amount
1991	237	174.16	3,815*	3,450*	977*
1992	264	246.99	6,430	5,540	1,053
1993	9,329	3,168.41	10,948	9,970	3,139
1994	934	962.21	6,247	5,397	3,391
1995	490	1,092.71	3,052**	2,783**	2,250**
1991-95	11,254	5,644.48	30,492**	27,140**	10,810**

Note: * representing data up to 1991.
** for the first nine months in 1995 only.

Sources: (1) Taiwan data: Investment Commission, Ministry of Economic Affairs, 1995.
(2) China data: Ministry of Foreign Trade and Economic Co-operation.

For our purpose on hand, namely, to provide a quantitative assessment for the impacts on domestic production and income due to investments in China, the quality of investment data is crucial. In view of the existence of the big discrepancy between the two set of official statistics, we finally decided not to take either one of them for our study.[1] Instead, we take the data released in a research report by several economists associated with the Chung-Hua Institution for Economic Research (CHIER) in Taipei, Taiwan (Kao, Chi and Wu, 1995) as the base for our subsequent computation. Such data are collected on the ground of an extensive field survey in China during 1992-93. The degree of accuracy should be higher. The figures are listed in Table 8.6.

1 Chiu and Chung use the official registered data in Taiwan for their study (1993).

IMPACTS OF EXPORTS AND OUTWARD INVESTMENTS ON PRODUCTION

In order to provide a quantitative assessment of the impacts on production for the whole economy due to exports and outward investments, the input-output analysis is used as the analytical framework. Under this framework, changes in aggregate output are the result of the combined changes of sectoral outputs. Changes in sectoral outputs are conceptualized in turn as the net result of positive effects against negative effects. Positive output effects are generated by changes in sectoral exports. The higher the exports, the higher the outputs both for the originated sectors and for other related sectors. On the negative side, since investments abroad may lead to a reduction of investment and production at home, there is also a substitution effect which could not be overlooked in any proper assessment.

Table 8.6: Investments by Taiwanese Enterprises in China

Unit: US$ 10,000

Industry	By Taiwan Investors	By Local Partners	Total
Processed Food	52474.48	24597.19	77071.67
Beverages	6015.29	5581.77	11597.06
Tobacco	98.00	0.00	98.00
Fabrics	33100.69	23003.49	56104.18
Garments & Accessories	59041.22	28856.12	87897.34
Wood & Wooden Products	27602.62	16222.91	43825.53
Paper, Printing & Publishing	12321.82	8894.06	21215.88
Chemical Materials	17219.17	5799.38	23018.55
Artificial Fibers	4053.34	3635.04	7688.38
Plastics	5399.96	3340.36	8740.32
Plastic Products	51102.34	30434.15	81536.49
Miscellaneous Chemical Products	29903.24	19133.38	49036.62
Petroleum Products	471.04	323.03	794.07
Non-metallic Mineral Products	24129.08	21693.42	45822.50
Steel & Iron	1450.68	2555.99	4006.67
Miscellaneous Metals	1604.65	2110.85	3715.50
Metallic Products	32521.11	21806.58	54327.69
Machinery	35272.12	18284.61	53556.73
Household Elec. Appliances	16460.69	8567.76	25028.45
Electronic Products	34776.15	14995.17	49771.32
Elec. Machinery & Apparatus	19262.73	9561.20	28823.93
Transport Equipments	21235.53	11167.03	32402.56
Miscellaneous Products	59922.45	23991.95	83914.40
Total	545438.40	404555.44	849993.84

Source: Kao, Chi and Wu (1995), p. 271.

(I) Positive Effects

In this study, the export effects are further divided into two groups according to their relations with outward investments: namely, autonomous exports and induced exports. The distinction is important because it helps us to understand how important the role played by outward investments is as a stimulus to domestic production on the one hand, and to make a due assessment for outward investments as a dampening factor to the local economy on the other hand. More analysis on the part of outward investment will be given in later sections below following our discussion on exports and growth.

The basic theoretical linkage from export demand to output supply is outlined in the following equations:

$$\Delta Y = B\,\Delta E \tag{1}$$
$$\Delta Y_d = B\,\Delta E_d \tag{2}$$
$$\Delta Y_a = \Delta Y - \Delta Y_d \tag{3}$$

where ΔY and ΔE stand for changes in output and export, respectively. The subscripts, a and d, mark the distinction between the autonomous part and the induced part of the corresponding activities. Both Y and E are vectors while $B = [I - (I - \hat{M})\,A]^{-1}$ is a matrix, representing the competitive industrial linkage effects (Chiu and Chung, 1993). In essence, the B matrix links together the input-output coefficients matrix, A, and the diagonal matrix $\hat{M}$, which is formed by pooling together the import coefficients vector from each sector.

The framework is simple and straightforward, yet the calculation involves some complications. First of all, export data are normally not available in sectoral form except for those years when the input-output tables are compiled. A conversion scheme has to be provided in order to bridge the gap between trade classifications and input-output classifications. In so doing, certain elements of arbitrariness are hard to avoid. For our present purpose, we are content to use the conversion table prepared by Lin (1988) with some minor modification though.[2]

A second difficulty arises with the effort of making a proper estimation for induced-exports. For this part, we simply follow the work of Kao, Chi and Wu (1995) and accept their estimation which is derived according to the following formula:

$$E_d = D\cdot[K_1\cdot P_k^{*}]\cdot\lambda \tag{4}$$

where D is the domestic input coefficient matrix [3] and K_1 is a vector representing the total paid-in capital in China by both Taiwanese investors and local partners. λ is also a vector, representing the proportion of homeward purchase in total purchase of

2 The main purpose for modification is to reduce the weights originally assigned to the category of 'unclassified goods'.

3 As a proxy,the D matrix is taken from Taiwan's input-output tables rather than from China's tables.

intermediate inputs by Taiwanese enterprises in China. The remaining element, P_K^*, is capital productivity in China for Taiwanese enterprises. In the study by Kao et al (1995), capital productivity in China is assumed to be 1.2 times that of capital productivity in Taiwan, industry by industry. Taiwan's capital productivities are taken from the 1991 Industrial and Commercial Census Report.

Our focus here is on the sizes of the output effects and the whole calculation is performed for the year of 1993 by using the latest available input-output tables of 1991.[4] The time point of 1993 is chosen mainly because we want to take advantage of using the latest data for Taiwan's investment in China, which is compiled on the ground of an extensive field survey in China during 1992-93 (Kao, Chi and Wu, 1995). The main output effects are presented in Table 8.8 and Table 8.9, while the sectoral composition of Taiwan's exports to China in 1993 are given in Table 8.7.

As indicated in Table 8.7, the most important export industry is the fabrics industry. This sector alone takes up about 24% of total exports to China in 1993. Machinery, garments & accessories, chemical products, and household electrical appliances are also important, their combined amount accounts for another 40% of the total. In other words, more than 60% of Taiwan's exports to China in 1993 is supplied by only five sectors. Two of them, fabrics and garments & accessories, belong to nondurable consumer goods (34%), while another two, machinery and household electrical appliances are capital goods and/or durable consumer goods in nature (21%). The remaining industry, miscellaneous chemical products, is mainly an intermediate goods industry (9%).

Table 8.8 summarizes the stimulative effects on output and production due to exports to China. The figures are arranged industry by industry taken directly from our computation according to equations (1) and (3). In order to gain better understanding, the results are further reorganized into a tradable sector versus nontradable sector format, as presented in Table 8.9. For the tradable sector as a whole, the output effects come mainly from autonomous exports. On the contrary, for nontradable sector, the importance of induced exports is just about the same as autonomous exports, each contributing about 50% to total output expansion.

---

4 Chiu and Chung (1993) use the 1986 input-output tables with 29 sectors while Kao et al (1995) also use the 1991 tables with 39 sectors.

Table 8.7: Taiwan's Sectoral Exports to China in 1993

Unit: US$10,000

Industrial Classification	Value
01. Agricultural Products & Livestock	3,131.27
02. Forestry	73.62
03. Fisheries	1,422.53
04. Minerals	205.71
05. Processed Food	1,740.48
06. Beverages	1,151.79
07. Tobacco	0.00
08. Fabrics	183,939.59
09. Garments & Accessories	76,594.65
10. Wood & Wooden Product	2,099.26
11. Paper, Printing & Publishing	14,461.46
12. Chemical materials	6,465.99
13. Artificial Fibers	8,108.49
14. Plastics	15,558.72
15. Plastic Products	22,503.90
16. Miscellaneous Chemical Products	71,478.06
17. Petroleum Products	397.91
18. Non-metallic Mineral Products	3,721.00
19. Steel & Iron	15,317.84
20. Miscellaneous Metals	17,372.92
21. Metallic Products	17,412.69
22. Machinery	98,423.12
23. Household Elec. Appliances	62,166.63
24. Electronic Products	31,899.05
25. Elec. Machinery & Apparatus	24,086.89
26. Transport Equipments	30,919.00
27. Miscellaneous Products	50,422.24
Total	764,422.00

Source: By author's own calculation based on Kao & Sung (1994) and Lin (1988).

Table 8.8: Increases in Outputs due to Exports to China, 1993

Unit: US$10,000

Industrial Classification	Due to Autonomous Exports	Due to Induced Exports	Due to Total Exports
01. Agr.Products & Livestocks	4,752.39	18,598.70	23,351.09
02. Forestry	362.71	137.38	500.09
03. Fisheries	597.82	1,380.31	1,978.13
04. Minerals	3,771.38	2,527.48	6,298.86
05. Processed Food	1,787.21	9,704.73	11,491.94
06. Beverages	1,107.51	98.52	1,206.03
07. Tobacco	0.28	0.18	0.46
08. Fabrics	213,048.16	58,362.49	271,410.75
09. Garments & Accessories	80,188.96	21,203.39	101,392.35
10. Wood & Wooden Products	3,402.48	2,115.83	5,518.31
11. Paper, Printing & Publishing	27,205.20	15,295.79	42,500.99
12. Chemical Materials	35,758.83	14,312.89	50,071.72
13. Artificial Fibers	45,538.98	27,780.52	73,319.50
14. Plastics	26,842.23	13,155.10	39,997.33
15. Plastic Products	30,656.10	16,407.67	47,063.77
16. Misc. Chemical Products	87,526.28	11,162.25	98,688.53
17. Petroleum Products	11,142.89	8,875.30	20,018.19
18. Non-Metallic Mineral Products	8,538.38	2,605.01	11,143.39
19. Steel & Iron	60,329.35	20,900.15	81,229.50
20. Misc. Metals	27,138.41	7,034.55	34,172.96
21. Metallic Products	29,008.89	9,926.71	38,935.60
22. Machinery	106,162.40	3,874.72	110,037.12
23. Household Elec. Appliances	66,857.32	235.97	67,093.29
24. Electronic Products	36,318.81	7,505.23	43,824.04
25. Elec. Machinery & Apparatus	34,582.62	8,527.35	43,109.97
26. Transport Equipment	39,389.72	1,424.99	40,814.71
27. Miscellaneous Products	48,922.82	4,710.32	53,633.14
28. Construction	1,702.61	2,092.15	3,794.76
29. Electricity	21,176.81	17,405.81	38,582.62
30. Gas & City Water	741.12	584.89	1,326.01
31. Trans. Comm. & Warehousing	9,292.81	12,314.02	21,606.83
32. Trade	25,251.29	21,486.51	56,737.80
33. Finance & Insurance Services	21,700.08	23,146.95	44,847.03
34. Real Estate Service	4,357.40	5,270.28	9,627.68
35. Food, Beverage & Hotel Services	747.01	839.27	1,586.28
36. Business Services	10,951.32	10,116.80	21,068.12
37. Public Administrative Services	0.00	0.00	0.00
38. Education & Medical Services	1,077.57	1,045.52	2,123.09
39. Other Services	12,902.07	9,366.89	22,268.96
Total	1,140,838.20	401,532.70	1,542,370.90

Sources: (1) Column 2 from Kao, Chi, and Wu (1995), p. 274.
(2) Other figures based on author's own calculation.

Table 8.9: Output Effect by Tradable and Non-tradable Sectors

Unit: US$ million

	Due to Autonomous Exports	Due to Induced Exports	Due to Total Exports
Whole Economy	11,408.4	4,015.3	15,423.7
(I) Tradable Sector	10,309.4	2,878.5	13,187.9
A. Primary Industry	94.9	226.4	321.3
B. Manufacturing Industry	10,214.5	2,652.1	12,866.6
1. Nondurable Consumer Goods	3,484.6	961.9	4,446.5
2. Intermediate Goods	2,732.1	1,095.9	3,828.0
3. Capital Goods & Durable Consumer Goods	3,997.8	594.3	4,592.1
(II) Non-tradable Sector	1,099.0	1,136.8	2,235.8
A. Infrastructure	329.2	323.9	653.1
1. Construction	17.0	20.9	37.9
2. Public utilities	219.2	179.9	399.1
3. Transportation, Communication, & Storage	93.0	123.1	216.1
B. Services	769.8	812.9	1,582.7

Note: Primary industry includes sectors 1-4. Nondurable consumer goods, intermediate goods, and capital goods and durable consumer goods refer to sectors 5-10, plus 27; sectors 11-18; and sectors 19-26; respectively.

Source: Table 8.8.

(II) Substitution Effects on Domestic Production

As the transplantation of production activities abroad may lead to an increase in overseas production at the expense of domestic output, the substitution effects may be significant for certain industries even if they may be negligible for others. Such output reduction effects could also be estimated through an input-output calculation as in the following way (Kao et al., 1995):

$$\Delta X = B \cdot [(\delta \cdot K_2) \cdot P_k] \quad (5)$$

where ΔX represents the final reduction of output in each sector, K_2 is the paid-in capital by Taiwanese investors only, and P_k is the average capital productivity in Taiwan. The parameter δ is a scalar, representing the proportion of investment reduction at home due to investment abroad.[5] If $\delta=1$, it means complete substitution; if $\delta=0$, it means no substitution at all. In other words, if there is no reduction in domestic investment induced by investment abroad, there is no output reduction. The matrix B has the same meaning as in (4).

Under this framework, the crucial element determining the extent of substitution is δ. In reality the value of δ is not likely to be one or zero. How to determine its proper value is a real challenge. In the present study we choose to determine δ by the following hypothesis. Since the Taiwan economy has been characterized as having prolonged excess savings and huge trade surplus, there is no shortage of funds for domestic investment. Under such circumstancse, it makes sense to think that investment fund will be allocated for domestic production and for offshore production in such a way that aggregate output in the domestic economy is not to be unfavorably affected. To be more specific, we hypothesize that the negative effect on domestic output at the aggregate level is just offset by the stimulative effect on domestic output generated by the investment-induced exports so that the net result is zero. In other words, $\Sigma_i \Delta Y_d = \Sigma_i \Delta X$. Under this scheme, the value of δ will be uniquely determined as the ratio of $\Sigma_i \Delta Y_d$ over $\Sigma_i[B \cdot (K_2 \cdot P_k)]$.[6]

Two points should be made clear before going further. The first is that even though the effects from investment on output at the aggregate level are neutralized by our hypothesis, the effects on sectoral output are subject to no such constraint. At the industry level, while the substitution effect is always positive, the net effect may be positive or negative, depending on the sizes of ΔY_d, ΔX, and δ. The second point is that since our ultimate purpose is to evaluate the impacts on the disbribution of income rather than on the level of income, the idea of constraining the net effect on aggregate output to be zero may be viewed as an effort to set up a benchmark for subsequent anlysis. Looking in this way, the idea may not be as naive as it seems. On the other hand, in the computation of ΔX, we also need to know both K_2 and P_k. K_2 has already been given in the first column of Table 8.6. As for P_k, the latest relevant figures can be taken from the 1991 Industrial and Commercial Census Report for the Taiwan Area. The final results are reported in Table 8.10.

For the manufacturing industry as a whole, Taiwan's investment in China seems to have generated a dampening impact on the domestic economy. Both the consumer goods and capital goods sectors suffer a reduction in production as their substituion effects are too large to be offset. Only the intermediate goods industry has a net surplus even though

5 In reality, this proportion may be different for different industry. For the sake of simplicity it is also assumed to be a single value parameter in this study.

6 The value of that ratio in this study is 0.23825.

the magnitude is comparatively small. The real beneficiary is the nontradable sector, especially the service sector.

The picture is completely different, however, when the stimulative effects from autonomous exports are taken into account. Except for food, beverage, tobacco, and wood & wooden products (not listed in Table 8.10), all other industries enjoy output growth then. Furthermore, output increment in the tradable sector is the largest, about six times as large as in the nontradable sector. Within the manufacturing sector, industries which produce capital goods and/or durable consumer goods receive the highest share of benefit (36.9%), while the intermediate goods industries receive the lowest (29%). For the whole economy, output increases by 11.4 billions of US dollars. It is equivalent to 2.45% of Taiwan's total output in 1993. In other words, about 2.5% of Taiwan's total output could be attributed to Taiwan's investment and export activities toward China.

Table 8.10: Final Effects on Output due to Exports and Outward Investments

Unit: US$10,000

		Substitution Effect*	Net Effect due to outward investment	Final Effect
	$B\cdot(K_2\cdot P_k)$	ΔX	(ΔYd - ΔX)	(ΔY - ΔX)
Whole Economy	16,853.1	4,015.3	0	11,408.4
(I) Tradable Sector	14,398.8	3,430.5	-551.9	9,757.5
A. Primary Industry	603.7	143.8	82.6	177.5
B. Manufacturing Industry	13,795.1	3,286.7	-634.6	9,579.9
1. Nondurable Conusmer Goods	4,977.6	1,185.9	-224.0	3,260.6
2. Intermediate Goods	4,370.2	1,041.2	54.7	2,786.8
3. Capital Goods & Durable Consumer Goods	4,447.3	1,059.6	-465.3	3,532.5
(II) Non-tradable Sector	2,454.3	584.8	551.9	1,650.9
A. Infrastructure	681.6	162.4	161.5	490.7
1. Construction	43.5	10.4	10.5	27.5
2. Public Utilities	382.3	91.1	88.8	308.0
3. Transportation, Communication & Storage	255.8	60.9	62.2	155.2
B. Services	1,772.7	422.4	390.5	1,160.3

Note: * Under the condition of $\delta = 0.23825$.

Source: Input-output computation.

IMPACT ON INCOME AND INCOME DISTRIBUTION

From the increment of output, the increments in GDP (value-added), wage income and gross profits (operating surplus) are derived in this study by using the respective ratios with respect to output in 1993.[7] The calculation is first performed for each industry and then grouped together into sectors. Table 8.11 presents the results from investment alone, while Table 8.12 reports the results from both investments and exports.

Table 8.11: Impacts on Taiwan's Income and Income Distribution from Outward Investment to China, 1993

Unit: US$ 10,000

	GDP	Wage Income	Operating Surplus
Whole Economy	24,573	4,659	17,387
(I) Tradable Sector	-13,746	-11,900	967
A. Primary Industry	4,015	1,062	2,703
B. Manufacturing Industry	-17,761	-12,962	-1,736
1. Nondurable Consumer Goods	-5,330	-5,084	967
2. Intermediate Goods	2,020	959	234
3. Capital & Durable Consumer Goods	-14,451	-8,837	-2,937
(II) Non-tradable Sector	38,319	16,559	16,420
A. Infrastructure	10,076	3,440	3,665
1. Construction	377	274	82
2. Public utilities	5,944	1,272	2,653
3. Transportation, Communication, & Storage	3,755	1,894	930
B. Services	28,243	13,119	12,755

Sources: (1) Table 8.10.
(2) *National Income in Taiwan Area of the Republic of China, 1994.*

7 From the income side, GDP in Taiwan is calculated as the sum of indirect taxes (net of subsidies), consumption of fixed capital, and domestic factor incomes. Domestic factor incomes are the sum of compensation of employees and operating surplus. Prior to 1987, data of operating surplus are given in rent, interest and profit separately. From 1987 on, only the lump sum of operating surplus are given. Chiu and Chung use the official registered data in Taiwan for their study (1993).

Table 8.11 indicates that outward investment to China has led to higher profits and lower wage incomes for the tradable sector. This result is in line with the theory as both the Ricardian model and the Heckscher-Ohlin model predict that a capital movement raises the return to capital but reduces the return to workers in the source country (Kenen, 1994). Within the tradable sector, however, the result varies industry by industry. For the industries producing intermediate goods, for example, both wage incomes and nonwage incomes grow along with outward investments. On the contrary, both wage incomes and profits decline in the industries producing capital goods and durable consumer goods. Turning to the nontradable sector, wage incomes also increase along with profits in each and every subsectors. Finally, for the economy as a whole, both the overall income (GDP) and the major income components benefit from putting investments in China. Notice that as nonwage income outgrows wage income, the owners of capital benefit more than the workers. The ratio of profits to wages in Taiwan would have therefore become smaller if no investment is allowed to move to China.

Table 8.12: Total Impact on Taiwan's Income and Income Distribution,1993

Unit: NT$ million

	GDP		Wage Income		Operating Surplus	
	ΔGDP	ΔGDP/GDP%	ΔW	(ΔW/W)%	ΔS	(ΔS/S)%
Whole Economy	122,578	2.09	64,658	2.07	42,573	2.70
(I) Tradable Sector	91,993	4.62	51,051	5.36	26,775	4.52
A. Primary Industry	2,430	0.99	816	1.04	1,344	0.90
B. Manufacturing Industry	89,563	5.13	50,235	5.74	25,431	5.75
1. Nondurable Consumer Goods	34,042	7.72	19,975	8.30	9,995	12.24
2. Intermediate Goods	25,691	4.80	13,264	6.26	7,477	4.74
3. Capital & Durable Consumer Goods	29,830	3.87	16,996	4.03	7,959	3.92
(II) Nontradable Sector	30,585	0.79	13,607	0.63	15,798	1.60
A. Infrastructure	8,226	0.97	2,632	0.58	3,110	1.36
1. Construction	263	0.08	191	0.08	57	0.08
2. Public Utilities	5,469	3.44	1,183	2.99	2,435	3.57
3. Transportation, Communication & Storage	2,494	0.66	1,258	0.66	618	0.66
B. Services	22,359	0.74	10,975	0.64	12,688	1.68

Sources: (1) Table 8.10.
(2) *National Income in Taiwan Area of the Republic of China, 1994.*

The final impact is even more favorable (Table 8.12). GDP, wage income and nonwage income all become higher in each and every sector and subsector. The increase of overall GDP is equivalent to 2.1% of total GDP in 1993. That means, without resuming the long suspended economic ties with mainland China, Taiwan's GDP might have been 2.1% lower in 1993. That the China market is important for Taiwan is clear and obvious.

As far as income distribution is concerned, the overall picture is also interesting. In terms of values, wage incomes in the whole economy outgrow nonwage incomes by about 50%. Yet, in terms of percentage change with respect to the actual figures in 1993, nonwage incomes grows faster than wage incomes, i.e., 2.7% versus 2.1%. It implies that without investments and exports to China, the ratio of nonwage incomes to wage incomes would have become lower in Taiwan.

SUMMARY AND CONCLUSION

In view of the increasingly close economic relations between Taiwan and mainland China, we have attempted to provide a quantitative assessment for the impact on the former economy in terms of output, income and income distribution. The analysis is based on an input-output framework plus a fixed ratio projection for changes in income components. Due to availability of data, the whole exercise is performed only for 1993 in order to take advantage of using the latest survey concerning Taiwan's investment in China.

As it turns out, the China market is indeed an important market for Taiwan. About 2.1% of Taiwan's GDP in 1993 could be attributed to Taiwan's investment and export activities toward China. The impact on output is even larger, the corresponding figure is 2.5%. When investment activities is considered alone, our calculation indicates a pattern of change in income distribution which is in line with what the theory would predict: namely, an increasing nonwage income versus a decreasing wage income. When both investment and exports are considered together, the final impact is even more favorable. GDP, wage income and nonwage income all become higher in each and every sector of the economy.

To be sure, the present analysis could not be called complete as several factors are absent from the calculation. First of all, in addition to 'indirect' trade, there also exists certain 'direct' trade between the two sides of the Strait, as has been ably argued by Sung in Kao & Sung (1994) and Sung (1995). Our results are thus likely to be underestimated.

Furthermore, as far as trade relations are concerned, what has been emphasized is the export trade to China rather than the import trade from China, which may become increasingly important as Taiwan is going to further open her door for the products made in the China mainland. The third factor concerns the potential competition in the world market between the two sources of exports involving Taiwan: namely, exports made in Taiwan versus exports made in China but owned by Taiwan. This so-called 'export shift' effect is also worth studying. Last but not least, the assigned value for δ is a crucial element for the whole calculation, so perhaps some alternative schemes for the determination of δ may bring us closer to the reality.

REFERENCES

Ash, Robert F. and Kueh, Y.Y. (1995) Economic Integration Within Greater China: Trade and Investment Flows Between China, Hong Kong and Taiwan, Pp. 59-93 in: Shambaugh, David (ed.), *Greater China: The Next Superpower?* Oxford University Press, Oxford.

Chen, Edward K.Y. and Ho, Anna (1994) Southern China Growth Triangle: An Overview, Pp. 29-72 in: Thant, Myo et al (eds.), *Growth Triangles in Asia: A New Approach to Regional Economic Cooperation*, Oxford University Press, Oxford.

Chiu, Lee-in Chen (1995) The Pattern and Impact of Taiwan's Investment in Mainland China, Pp. 143-65 in: La Croix, S.J. et al (eds.), *Emerging Patterns of East Asian Investment in China from Korea, Taiwan, and Hong Kong*, M.E. Sharpe, New York.

Chiu, Lee-in Chen and Chung Chin (1993) An Assessment of Taiwan's Indirect Investment Toward Mainland China, *Asian Economic Journal*, 7(1), 41-70.

Chung, C. and Lee, Joseph S. (1995) Trade and Investment Triangle Between the Chinese Mainland, Taiwan and Hong Kong, paper presented at the International Conference on Sino-American Economic Relations, Hong Kong, 21-23 June.

Dunning, John H. (1995) *Multinational Enterprises and the Global Economy*, Addison-Wesley, New York.

Kao, C., Chi, Peter S.K. and Wu Shin-ying (1995) *A Comparative Study of Foreign Investments in Mainland China* (in Chinese), Chung-Hua Institution for Economic Research, Taipei.

Kao, C. and Sung, Y.W. (1994) *An Empirical Study of Indirect Trade Between Taiwan and Mainland China* (in Chinese), Chung-Hua Institution for Economic Research, Taipei.

Kenen, Peter B. (1994) *The International Economy*, third edition, Cambridge University Press, New York.

Lin, C.C.S. (1995) Production Function, Factor Substitution, and Direct Foreign Investment: A Case Study in Taiwan, *Asian Economic Journal*, 9(2), 193-203.

Lin, T.B. (1994) Economic Nexus Between the Two Sides of the Taiwan Straits - With Special Emphasis on Hong Kong's Role, Pp. 213-31 in: Klein, Lawrence R. and Yu, C.T. (eds.), *Economic Development of ROC and the Pacific Rim in the 1990s and Beyond*, World Scientific, New Jersey.

Lin, Y.J. (1988) A Review of the Indirect Trade Between the Two Sides of the Taiwan Strait and A Study on Potential Impacts (in Chinese), Special Economic Paper No. 114, Chung-Hua Institution for Economic Research, Taipei.

Lin, Y.J. and Huang, C.S. (1992) Development of Trade and Investment Between Two Sides of the Taiwan Strait, paper presented at the Conference on Global Interdependence and Asia - Pacific Cooperation, Hong Kong, 8-10 June.

Lin, J.Y. and Chen C.L. (1996) Dutch Disease, Taiwan's Success and "The China Boom", Pp.53-75 in: Ng, Linda F.Y. and Tuan C. (eds.), *Three Chinese Economies-China, Hong Kong and Taiwan: Challenges and Opportunities*, the Chinese University Press, Hong Kong.

Shambaugh, David (ed.) (1995) *Greater China: The Next Superpower?* Oxford University Press, Oxford.

Sung, Y.W. (1995) The Implications of China's Admission to the WTO for "Greater China", paper presented at the International Conference on Sino-American Economic Relations, Hong Kong, 21-23 June.

Zhang, Z. (1995) International Trade and Foreign Direct Investment: Further Evidence from China, *Asian Economic Journal*, 9(2), 153-67.

PART III TRADE AND INVESTMENT RELATIONS WITH JAPAN AND KOREA

9. JAPANESE FDI, EXPORTS AND TECHNOLOGY TRANSFER TO CHINA*

Elspeth Thomson

INTRODUCTION

A considerable amount has been written since the 1960s about the relationship between foreign direct investment (FDI) and trade. Attention has focused on identifying and distinguishing the particular factors motivating FDI from those of exporting, and on understanding the relative timing of each (Chenery, 1960; Linnemann, 1966; Hymer, 1976; Kojima, 1973; Lipsey and Weiss, 1981 & 1984; etc.). The specific purposes of this chapter are to try to gain a better understanding of the relationship between Japanese FDI and Japanese exports to China since the beginning of China's Open Door Policy, to comment on the extent of technology transfer, and to suggest possible reasons why Chinese expectations for it have not been met.

While a great deal of descriptive material has been written about Japanese economic relations with China in general (Campbell, 1987; Howe, 1990; Taylor, 1993), there seems to have been very little theoretical research on Japanese trade and FDI to China. Kojima (1978) and Ozawa (1979) have carefully surveyed and analysed total Japanese FDI around the world. Yokoi (1990) and Ono (1992) have discussed the relationship between investment and trade in China alone, but have not employed a statistical model. Kinoshita (1995) only makes casual observations about the determinants of Japanese FDI in China. The Sumitomo Life Insurance Research Institute (1989) appears to have published a short theoretical piece,

* I would like to thank Hiroyuki Imai for his suggestions on an earlier draft of this chapter.

but it was not available to the author. A Chinese economist, Zhang Zhaoyang (1995), has employed statistical techniques to test the relationship between trade and investment in China, but his is a general study encompassing all of China's main trade partners.

TRENDS IN JAPANESE EXPORTS TO CHINA

Diplomatic relations between Japan and China were normalised in 1972. Subsequently a number of trade agreements were signed leading up to enormous commitments under the Treaty of Peace and Friendship and Long Term Trade Agreement in 1978. Under this agreement Japan was to export whole plants and the relevant technology, construction materials, and equipment in exchange mainly for oil and coal. At the beginning of the study interval, 1980, China was relying on Japan for the largest share of its imports. At that time Japan accounted for 26.4% of the total, followed by the United States with 19.6%, North Korea with 7.8%, West Germany with 6.8%, Australia with 5.4%, Canada with 4.2%, and Hong Kong and Macau with 2.9%. Over the past decade and a half, China has reduced its dependency on Japan. Out of total imports in 1995, 22.0% came from Japan, 11.2% from Taiwan, 12.2% from the United States and 6.6% from Hong Kong and Macau.

The trade relationship is far from balanced. China depends much more on Japan as an export market than Japan depends on China. Out of all of Japan's exports, 3.9% went to China in 1980 and 4.8% in 1993. In 1980, 20.1% of China's exports went to Japan, and 19.1% in 1995.

The growth rate of Japanese exports to China has not been steady. (See Table 9.1.) By 1984, household income levels were increasing sharply and, concomitantly, the demand for imported consumer goods. Disastrously, at the same time, however, China's supplies of foreign exchange were dwindling at a rapid rate. One cause was the decentralisation of control over foreign exchange which was leading alarmingly to the total depletion of the country's foreign reserves. Secondly, the oil deposits in the northeast of China were producing far short of initial expectations. This was a very serious setback for the country's economic reforms. In the early 1980s oil had been the largest source of foreign exchange and it was hoped that oil sales would pay for most of China's imports for many years to come, much as they had for several Middle Eastern countries.

Thus in 1985 the government had to take drastic measures to curtail the flow of imports. In addition to the shortfall in northeast oil production there were other factors putting downward pressure on imports of Japanese goods. In 1985 anti-Japanese demonstrations staged by Chinese university students called for an end to the Japanese "invasion". They believed that the Japanese were providing only low technology to China and were discriminating against Chinese products, making it impossible to reduce the trade surplus.

Table 9.1: Annual Real Growth Rates of Japanese Manufacturing Exports and FDI to China 1981-1994 (%)

	Growth Rate of Manufacturing Export	Growth Rate of Manufacturing FDI
1981	-3.6	134.8
1982	-25.5	-11.8
1983	42.5	-53.7
1984	45.6	1,189.0
1985	76.3	8.4
1986	-34.5	-13.6
1987	-24.4	177.4
1988	4.6	162.4
1989	-7.5	5.0
1990	-26.9	-19.8
1991	37.6	88.5
1992	34.6	105.4
1993	37.8	102.3
1994	2.3	26.9

Sources: Calculated from (1) data faxed from the Export-Import Bank of Japan, (2) the Japan Statistical Yearbook and (3) Ministry of International Trade and Industry. *White Papers on International Trade*. The export data excludes foodstuffs and raw materials.

Note: To convert the data into real terms, the annual U.S. market exchange rates were obtained from the IMF *International Financial Statistics Yearbook*, making 1980 the base year with value 1. These figures were then divided by the export exchange rates from the *Japan Statistical Yearbooks*. The raw export and FDI data (in current U.S. $1,000) was then multiplied by this index to convert it into constant U.S. $1,000. The raw data is given in Appendix I.

In July 1986 the yuan was depreciated in an attempt to reduce the propensity to import, especially from Japan, with whom China had a very large deficit. The almost concurrent appreciation of the yen after the Plaza Accords was yet another factor as was the June 4th Incident, though the effects of this were short-lived. Total Japanese exports to China in 1990 were about half what they were in 1985, though rose steadily between 1991 and 1993 at an average real growth rate of about 36.7%, but fell sharply to only 2.3% in 1994.

The percentage breakdown of the exports since 1980, given in Table 9.2, shows that they have been consistently dominated by heavy chemical and industrial products. Of this, iron and steel products and general machinery were the largest sub-categories. However, there were notable shifts. Iron and steel products went from accounting for 27.0% of total exports in 1980 to only 10.7% in 1995, while electrical machinery rose from 9.5% to 21.9% in the same period. Transportation equipment went from 8.2% in 1980 up to 17.6% in 1985, and down to 4.3% in 1995. Of the light industrial products, textile products was the largest sub-category and its share fluctuated from 7.9% to 3.8% to 10.8%.

TRENDS IN JAPANESE FOREIGN DIRECT INVESTMENT IN CHINA

Since 1960, the government's insistence on economic independence precluded virtually all FDI to China from Japan, or from any other country. In 1983, by far the largest proportion of China's total actually used FDI, 51.6%, came from Hong Kong and Macau. Japan came next with 20.4% and the United States a distant third with 9.1%. It must be pointed out that, due to tense political relations, at the beginning of the study interval Taiwan was investing in China indirectly through Hong Kong, but in the late 1980s there was direct investment. In 1995, Japan remained in second place with 15.9%, Hong Kong and Macau's increased to 53.4%, Taiwan ranked third with 8.4% and the United States was fourth with 8.2%. Part of the very large proportion from Hong Kong and Macau is actually Mainland money. Though no figures are available, it is well known that many Mainland investors have set up front companies in Hong Kong to make use of the special investment terms granted to foreign investors.

Table 9.2: Percentage Breakdown of Japanese Exports to China

	1980	1985	1995
Foodstuffs	**neg.**	**0.2**	**0.4**
Raw Materials & Fuels	0.5	0.7	2.4
Light Industrial Products	12.2	7.1	16.4
Textile Products	7.9	3.8	10.8
Heavy Chemical & Industrial Products	86.1	91.0	79.3
Chemicals	10.7	5.7	9.3
Metals	33.1	28.3	14.1
Iron & Steel	27.0	25.6	10.7
Nonferrous Metals	1.1	1.3	1.6
Metal Products	5.0	1.4	1.9
Machinery & Equipment	42.3	57.0	55.8
General Machinery	23.1	16.5	27.7
Electrical Machinery	9.5	20.6	21.9
Transportation Equipment	8.2	17.6	4.3
Precision Instruments	1.6	2.2	1.9
Re-Exports, Commodities and Transactions not Classified According to Kind	1.2	1.0	1.5

Source: Japan. Ministry of International Trade and Industry. *White Papers on International Trade.*
Note: Only the main groupings are given.

As a proportion of worldwide Japanese manufacturing FDI, the amount destined for China has been very small. It went from 1.1% in 1983 to 1.0 in 1990, then climbed to 4.5% in 1994. To give perspective, 41.3% went to the United States in 1990, 29.7% to Europe, 5.2% to the NIEs, and 13.1% to the ASEAN countries. The figures for 1994 were 33.2%,

13.5%, 6.1% and 16.3% respectively (JETRO, 1994, 18). Compared to other countries, the proportion of Japan's total FDI devoted to manufacturing in China has been small, while the proportion devoted to service industries such as real estate, commerce and construction, has been large.

Table 9.3 gives the breakdown of Japanese manufacturing FDI in China from 1980 to 1994. During the first four years of the Open Door Policy, investment was limited to only two or three sectors. In 1980, 73% of the investment was devoted to the electrical machinery sector, with the remainder going to the chemical sector. In the following year, 88% went to the chemical sector. In 1982 and 1983 chemicals and wood were the largest sectors. Perhaps, with little in the way of natural resources of its own, Japan was keen to develop these industries in order to maintain its own industrial growth rates. Or, it may have been due to the fact that in the early 1980s, the Chinese had a requirement that 70% of the output produced by foreign firms had to be sold to buyers outside the country.

By 1984 the Japanese had begun to invest in the full range of manufacturing industries, including textiles, non-ferrous metal products, general machinery, transportation equipment, etc. Changes in the dominant sector of investment over the period reflect changing Japanese priorities. In 1984, the largest proportion, almost 50%, was in food products. The main sector was chemicals in 1985 and 1986, electrical machinery in 1987, 1988 and 1989, general machinery in 1990, and electrical machinery again from 1991 to 1994. Obviously there was keen interest in developing China's electrical machinery sector. Not only was it the recipient of the largest investment for much of the period, but its relative proportion was often considerably higher than the second largest category, which for most years was textiles.

Looking at year-on-year trends, it can be seen that after 1984 the relative importance of the foodstuffs sector steadily declined. After an initial spurt, investment in wood products was quite limited after 1983, and investment in chemical products dropped sharply in 1984. Generally speaking, the trend was generally upward for textiles, non-ferrous metal products, transportation machinery, and especially for electrical machinery.

The overall trend in total FDI for the period was upward, but yearly increments were markedly uneven. (See Table 9.1.) Between 1979 and 1981, when the Chinese government was trying to do too much too fast, and oil revenues did not reach anticipated levels, there were alarming investment reversals. In all, about 300 agreements were withdrawn or postponed, including several major projects such as Phase II of the Baoshan Steel Complex. Japanese investors were the most affected. In 1983 a tax treaty was signed between the two countries preventing double taxation. This was a major factor causing the huge influx of investment in 1984. After the sharp appreciation in the yen in the mid-1980s many firms in Japan lost their competitive edge and scrambled to continue production in China where costs were much less. The increase in 1987 was due in part to the Chinese Government's enacting of the "Provision of the State Council of the People's Republic of China for the Encouragement of the Foreign Investment", offering investors a variety of new incentives. In 1988 several events occurred which stimulated investment: more coastal areas were

Table 9.3: Breakdown of Japanese FDI in China 1980-1995 Current (U.S. $1,000 U.S.)

	Food Products		Textile Products		Wood Products		Chemical Products		Non-Ferrous Metal Products	
1980							467	(1)		
1981							3,777	(2)		
1982					1,199	(3)	2,101	(-)		
1983					615	(2)	765	(-)		
1984	10,198	(9)	1,252	(4)			344	(1)	1,480	(3)
1985	4,166	(11)	1,107	(5)	905	(2)	4,552	(6)	2,960	(4)
1986	3,856	(14)	877	(5)	812	(2)	5,202	(4)	2,164	(1)
1987	3,856	(11)	3,751	(8)	602	(2)	4,979	(8)	7,352	(6)
1988	16,327	(20)	16,009	(23)	3,875	(6)	8,570	(8)	10,004	(8)
1989	12,877	(6)	11,118	(23)	1,444	(3)	11,412	(11)	6,044	(5)
1990	8,979	(8)	20,957	(40)	1,341	(3)	11,658	(6)	13,863	(8)
1991	18,921	(11)	70,162	(87)	1,059	(1)	10,708	(6)	11,404	(11)
1992	29,194	(35)	119,753	(187)	3,262	(5)	19,406	(18)	29,012	(13)
1993	66,822	(39)	231,869	(247)	42,971	(20)	95,523	(26)	79,922	(29)
1994	130,121	(30)	331,690	(283)	10,012	(5)	100,391	(18)	158,438	(38)
Apr-Sept 1995	54,049	(13)	238,690	(116)	29,883	(6)	53,875	(15)	173,826	(29)
Total	359,369	(207)	1,047,240	(1,028)	97,985	(60)	333,737	(130)	496,473	(155)

Table 9.3: Breakdown of Japanese FDI in China 1980-1995 Current (U.S. $1,000 U.S.) continued

	General Machinery	Electric/ Electronic Products	Transportation Machinery	Others	Total
1980		1,295 (1)			1,762
1981				528 (1)	4,305
1982				192 (0)	3,492
1983				211 (1)	1,591
1984	1,028 (2)	1,320 (2)	602 (3)	4,440 (6)	20,661
1985	2,210 (6)	2,838 (7)		3,256 (10)	21,994
1986	2,502 (2)	4,554 (3)		2,868 (7)	22,838
1987	2,106 (4)	43,308 (11)		4,179 (8)	70,136
1988	12,024 (11)	101,129 (15)	4,946 (2)	29,792 (24)	202,679
1989	42,052 (6)	80,076 (14)	1,205 (2)	40,037 (15)	206,268
1990	50,098 (6)	22,173 (11)	1,355 (2)	30,549 (29)	160,976
1991	29,074 (5)	123,491 (22)	8,673 (2)	35,276 (33)	308,773
1992	50,393 (19)	189,455 (34)	32,628 (9)	176,617 (61)	649,725
1993	229,181 (46)	332,228 (57)	83,041 (20)	215,544 (95)	1,377,106
1994	130,550 (26)	491,604 (66)	224,062 (29)	275,735 (63)	1,852,598
Apr-Sept 1995	244,266 (25)	272,953 (34)	113,059 (16)	182,918 (27)	1,363,519
Total	795,488 (158)	1,666,429 (277)	469,573 (85)	1,002,147 (380)	6,268,441

Note: The numbers in parentheses are the number of projects.
Source: The Export-Import Bank of Japan.

designated as special zones for investment, the Japanese government extended a third yen credit to China and the two countries signed a treaty protecting Japanese investors. Investment in 1990 fell somewhat due to the June 4th Incident the previous year, as well as to the government's policies to control inflation. However, from 1991 to 1994, there were notable increases and the Japanese were obviously becoming keener on China as a destination for FDI. Amongst factors affecting FDI was the collapse of the former Soviet Union. Japan's fears of weakening its security commitments with the United States by pursuing closer economic ties with China largely disappeared. Although Japan's economic "bubble" burst in 1991 and total FDI worldwide fell sharply, China's share actually increased. The average annual real growth rate of FDI to China was about 99% between 1991 and 1994.

Table 9.4 gives the average value of the Japanese investment projects in China in real terms. The value of the projects (total FDI in a given year divided by the number of projects) between 1984 and 1994 increased by a factor of about 2.5 for food and textile products, but nearly 20 for transportation machinery. This would seem to indicate that as time went on the Japanese were gaining confidence in the Chinese business environment and willing to commit larger and larger sums. However, compared to the investment projects in the United States and other parts of Asia, the projects in China were still very small (Ono, 1992, 25-26).

There are several ways direct investment can take place in China: equity joint ventures, contractual joint ventures, wholly foreign-owned enterprises, joint extraction and joint development (of natural resources), compensation trade, and processing and assembling agreements. The largest amount of Japanese investment has been in the form of equity joint ventures. The next largest has been about equally apportioned between contractual joint ventures and wholly foreign-owned enterprises.

Most Japanese investment in the early 1980s went to the northeast, especially Liaoning, and Shandong, where the Japanese before World War II had held power and to Shanghai which had been the largest commercial centre. In the 1990s, by far the largest amounts were going to Shanghai, followed by Guangdong, Lioaning, Beijing and Jiangsu. Electric and electronic companies chose mainly the provinces of Liaoning, Guangdong, Jiangsu, Zhejiang and Shaanxi, as well as Beijing and Shanghai. Textile enterprises have favoured Jiangsu, Zhejiang, Shandong and Shanghai (Kinoshita, 1995, 15-16).

THE RELATIONSHIP BETWEEN JAPANESE EXPORTS AND FDI IN CHINA

In order to try to gain a better understanding of the relationship between Japanese exports and FDI to China, a series of multiple regressions was run. The dependent variable was exports, while FDI and various other factors were the independent variables. For the sake of consistency, all data was from Japanese sources and it was all converted into real U.S. dollars. (See the notes with Table 9.1 for explanation.)

Table 9.4: Average Value of Japanese FDI Projects in China (Real U.S. $1,000)

	Food Products	Textile Products	Wood Products	Chemical Products	Non-Ferrous Metal Products	General Machinery	Electric/ Electronic Products	Transport-ation Machinery	Others	Yearly Average
1980				295			790			543
1981				2,455					438	1,447
1982			342							342
1983			262						211	237
1984	957	286		248	417	493	469	196	631	462
1985	323	204	387	561	632	356	302		275	380
1986	204	129	301	962	1,604	945	982		350	685
1987	240	315	206	417	839	359	2,362		387	641
1988	521	426	412	632	798	672	3,816	1,534	886	1,077
1989	1,384	306	310	637	780	4,465	3,420	382	1,703	1,487
1990	717	335	286	1,242	1,107	5,336	1,288	433	673	1,269
1991	1,084	477	667	1,157	653	3,530	3,722	2,619	673	1,620
1992	519	373	406	737	1,388	1,525	3,722	2,048	1,801	1,391
1993	1,035	566	1,298	2,550	1,665	2,571	3,841	2,201	1,370	1,900
1994	2,537	693	1,171	3,296	2,439	2,405	4,789	3,740	2,560	2,626
Average of available figures	866	374	504	1,168	1,120	2,060	2,459	1,644	920	1,074

See Table 9.1 for sources.

As the period under study is only fifteen years, and in many sectors there was little or no FDI during the first three years, the available data is not ideal for the employment of time-series statistical techniques. It could be argued that it is apparent just from scanning the figures that FDI from year to year was highly erratic and did not seem to bear any relation to exports. However, it was thought that use of a multiple regression model might reveal the relative influence of FDI and other factors on trends in exports.

Another difficulty with the data (confirmed by fax communications with an official of the Export-Import Bank of Japan in May 1996) was that the FDI categories used by the Ministry of Finance are much less precise than the export categories, e.g., there is an "electrical machinery" category for FDI, while the export data is subdivided into electrical circuit articles, television sets, colour television sets, videotape recorders, communication equipment and other electrical manufactures. This meant that the sectoral regressions were all rather wide. It would have been preferable to measure the relationship of exports and FDI by specific type of manufactured item, such as exports of television sets with FDI in the manufacture of television sets, instead of regressing the electrical machinery data as a whole.

As the FDI data was so limited it was imperative to use only a small number of independent variables. Real GDP was used to represent growth of the economy, and capital construction investment was used to represent general infrastructural development of the economy. The estimation equation was set up in the following form:

$$\log X_t = \alpha_o + \alpha_1 \log FDI_t + \alpha_2 GDP_t + \alpha_3 \log INV_t + \alpha_4 TREND + \in_1$$

where:

X_t	=	Japanese Exports (total or particular sector)
FDI_t	=	Japanese Foreign Direct Investment (total or particular sector)
GDP_t	=	Chinese Gross Domestic Product
INV_t	=	Chinese Capital Construction Investment

The empirical results were as follows:
(Below the coefficient estimates, in parentheses, are their t statistics.)

Total Manufacturing Exports

$$\log X_t = \underset{(1.329)}{15.527} + \underset{(0.635)}{0.136} \log FDI_t - \underset{(-0.817)}{2.385} \log GDP_t$$

$$+ \underset{(3.549)}{1.723} \log INV_t + \underset{(0.040)}{0.0079} TREND$$

R^2 adjusted = 0.653 D.W. = 2.364 F = 5.707 S.E. = 0.192

Textile Products Exports

$$\log X_t = 21.167 + 0.152 \log FDI_t - 3.589 \log GDP_t$$
(2.992) (1.789) (-2.162)

$$+ 1.351 \log INV_t + 0.212\ TREND$$
(4.297) (1.504)

R^2 adjusted = 0.907 D.W.= 2.024 F = 25.284 S.E.= 0.128

Electrical Machinery Exports

$$\log X_t = 1.590 - 0.018 \log FDI_t + 1.117 \log GDP_t$$
(0.080) (-0.110) (0.229)

$$+ 1.026 \log INV_t - 0.115\ TREND$$
(1.308) (-0.359)

R^2 adjusted = 0.581 D.W.= 2.703 F = 4.467 S.E.= 0.251

General Machinery Exports

$$\log X_t = 1.340 - 0.173 \log FDI_t - 0.460 \log GDP_t$$
(0.116) (-1.670) (-0.167)

$$+ 2.156 \log INV_t - 0.201\ TREND$$
(3.865) (-0.924)

R^2 adjusted = 0.763 D.W.= 2.413 F = 9.042 S.E.= 0.211

Food Products Exports

$$\log X_t = 2.408 - 0.001 \log FDI_t + 0.927 \log GDP_t$$
(0.227) (-0.011) (0.370)

$$+ 0.403 \log INV_t - 0.919\ TREND$$
(0.825) (-0.470)

R^2 adjusted = 0.136 D.W.= 2.789 F = 1.395 S.E. = 0.193

Chemical Products Exports

$$\log X_t = \underset{(2.499)}{13.969} - \underset{(-0.617)}{0.0348} \log FDI_t - \underset{(-0.688)}{0.889} \log GDP_t$$

$$+ \underset{(2.537)}{0.581} \log INV_t + \underset{(0.970)}{0.094} \, TREND$$

R^2 adjusted = 0.807 D.W.= 2.852 F = 11.449 S.E.= 0.093

Nonferrous Metals Exports

$$\log X_t = \underset{(0.170)}{2.356} - \underset{(-0.576)}{0.147} \log FDI_t - \underset{(-0.288)}{0.718} \log GDP_t$$

$$+ \underset{(3.278)}{2.114} \log INV_t - \underset{(-0.346)}{0.807} \, TREND$$

R^2 adjusted = 0.649 D.W.= 2.298 F = 5.626 S.E.= 0.229

It is difficult to make any firm conclusions from the limited, unstable data. It can be noted, however, that in every case, the coefficient for the FDI variable was insignificant, meaning Japan's exports to China were not influenced by FDI.

EXPECTATIONS FOR AND ASSESSMENT OF JAPANESE TECHNOLOGY TRANSFER

Soon after the fall of the Gang of Four, China's new leaders began to reverse the self-reliance policies espoused by Mao Zedong. It was realised that if the country was to modernise it had to acquire advanced technology, and that the only way to acquire this was to develop export industries which would earn the foreign exchange needed to pay for it, to invite foreign investors and to obtain as much aid as possible. The government had high expectations that now the door was open foreign countries would quickly come forth with their technologies and China would soon catch up with the rest of the developed world. Many government documents detail the urgency for and faith in the workability of technical cooperation. Included in a small book (Chu Baotai, 1986, 123) aimed at helping foreign investors learn how to become involved in China are Regulations Issued by the State

Council on 20 September 1983 for the Implementation of the Law of the People's Republic of China on Chinese-Foreign Joint Ventures. Article Four says:

> "A joint venture that applies for establishment shall emphasise economic results and satisfy one or more of the following requirements:
>
> (1) It will adopt advanced technology and equipment and scientific managerial techniques, enabling it to increase the variety of its products, improve their quality and raise output, and to conserve energy and materials;
>
> (2) It will benefit the technical renovation (sic) of the venture, and achieve quick results and large profits with a small investment;
>
> (3) It will be able to expand the export of its products and increase foreign exchange earnings; and
>
> (4) It will be able to train technical and managerial personnel."

The same book (Chu Baotai, 1986, 37-38) also includes the following information:

> "The Chinese side expects [investors from overseas] to transfer ... as much advanced technology as possible, using such technology as their investment. If they do not have the know-how, they can contribute cash in foreign exchange as investment, which can be used by the joint venture to pay for the advanced equipment and know-how it needs. Bringing in advanced technology and equipment from abroad enables the joint venture to combine the strong points of the Chinese and foreign participants and gain vantage position in market competition. But the Chinese side does not expect the foreign side to contribute as investment things already available in China. ... From the Chinese point of view, the investment in kind from the foreign side should preferably be specialised equipment."

Potential foreign investors in any country are motivated by a variety of factors relating to the comparative costs of capital, labour and natural resources in the home and host countries, and the comparative size and potential spending power of the markets. Specifically, on the push side, an investor would be interested in investing abroad if resources are not available or are costly in his own country, and/or equipment costs and wages are high, and/or the market is limited in some way. On the pull side, investors would be interested in establishing operations abroad if natural resources were readily available, and/or capital equipment could be procured cheaply, wages were low, and/or if the host market (or a third country's quota, i.e., using the host country to circumvent the trade barriers of another country) were very attractive. The bottom line is that companies decide to invest abroad if they perceive they can make substantial savings in their production costs and/or sell much greater quantities of their products in the host country than they can in their home markets.

However, insofar as China is concerned, Japanese investors have not been motivated solely by business and market forces. Sino-Japanese relations are very complex due to a variety of historical and political factors. Before and during World War II Japanese soldiers destroyed many Chinese cities and tortured and murdered thousands of civilians. Though the atrocities were committed over fifty years ago, on the Japanese side there remains some guilt, and on the Chinese, a strong feeling that Japan has yet to compensate fully for the economic and social damage wrought. Thus it is not surprising that when the door opened, the Chinese held especially high expectations for Japanese investment. Many Chinese complain that the Japanese companies have not brought China their latest production techniques and are continuing to exploit the country.

In commenting on the amount of Japanese FDI in China, and the degree of the sophistication of the technology introduced, various points must be acknowledged. Firstly, Japanese investment in China only really began in 1984. Given the very backward state of China's economy when the door was first opened, this is a relatively short period of time on which to make an meaningful assessment. Secondly, it is unfair to examine Japan's contribution to China's modernisation only in terms of technology. Over half of all official aid to China has come from Japan. In the early 1980s the Japanese Overseas Economic Cooperation Fund began to offer yen credits to China which were to be used for infrastructural development. These were the first loans that China accepted from a foreign country since the loans from the USSR in the 1950s. The Japanese Overseas Economic Cooperation Fund is the largest lender to China, providing more than the World Bank and the Asian Development Bank. The Export-Import Bank of Japan has also extended to China vast sums for producers' goods needed for the development of natural resources. Interestingly, a Chinese economist who examined China's share of the world's investment determined that it was in fact only Japan which seemed to contribute an "adequate" amount, while four other major source countries, the United States, Germany, France and the United Kingdom, did not (Wei, 1995, 187).

Japan's bestowal of such vast amounts of aid are certainly related to the above-mentioned guilt factor, but it is also readily conceded in Japanese publications that such aid is used to prepare the way for investors (Hatch, 1995, 297). As Japan has been involved in several of China's largest infrastructure projects, some would say that Japan has had an effective edge because of all the aid. According to United States government personnel and Japanese Overseas Economic Cooperation Fund officials, however, investors from other countries have had equal opportunity to participate in these projects (Clifford, 1993, 32).

Thirdly, as far as the degree of sophistication of the technology transferred to date is concerned, Japan's transferral of whole industrial plants has given China not only hardware but software. It is virtually impossible to determine whether the technology given by one country to another is modern, for "modern" is relative. Yokoi (1990, 696), who has traced the output growth of several production processes in which the Japanese have invested, believes that China's high world ranking is greatly due to Japanese efforts. "In particular, Japan contributed to the establishment of China's modern industries, including iron and steel, electric-power generation, non-ferrous metals, petrochemicals, fertilisers, synthetic fibres, electric equipment and electronics." Granted, there were other factors at work which would also have contributed to increasing output levels, but without doubt, Japanese money and training were pivotal, especially at enormous projects such as the Baoshan steel complex. According to Campbell (1987, 72), who conducted a survey of 115 foreign companies in Beijing in 1985, Japanese companies had more employees *in situ* than any other country, and these were given the most encouragement to learn Chinese.

In 1986, as a goodwill measure, the Japanese government established the Japan-China Investment Promotion Association, and in 1990 a Chinese counterpart was founded. The author is unable to comment upon their success, although it *is* known without doubt, that in the early 1980s Japan and other investing countries were greatly hampered in transferring modern technology to China by the policies of The North Atlantic Alliance Coordinating Committee for Export Control to Communist Areas (COCOM), whose mandate was to prevent the spread of strategic technology. These policies were relaxed in 1986, but the "Toshiba Case" in May 1987, in which Toshiba Machine Company was barred from selling in China for one year because it exported unauthorised technologies and machines, fuelled anti-Japanese sentiment.

As for quantities of Japanese technology, according to a recent report written by the Japanese Science and Technology Agency, China is by no means the least favoured recipient. Over the 1993/4 fiscal year, Korea had the largest number of technology imports from Japan at 104, followed by the US at 100, China at 80, Taiwan at 52 and Thailand at 32. (*Korea Herald*, 12 June 1996). According to Yokoi (1996, 151), between 1981 and 1988 Japan supplied only 8% of China's technology imports, but in 1992 and 1993 this had increased to 20-30%. It must be pointed out that the term "technology imports" is subjective. The Chinese government would probably not agree with the above figures.

Understandably, Japanese companies have had serious concerns about transferring technology to China. (Chinese suspicions about the low level of technology were given weight by the findings of Campbell (1987, 71), who points out that while, on average, 67% of the foreign companies agreed that "a key success factor is to offer your latest technology," and 72% of the American firms agreed, only 61% of the Japanese firms held this view). However, having few natural resources of her own, Japan was forced to make exports of manufactured goods the foundation of her economic growth strategy. Given the combination of China's low production costs, especially labour costs, and poor record for patent and copyright protection, small Japanese companies in particular, have feared economic collapse should China learn to produce certain export items. Japan is not alone in her cautious approach. According to one survey, 5.8 years elapse before multinational companies make their first transfer of technology to subsidiaries in developed countries, 9.8 years to subsidiaries in developing countries and 13.1 years for outside licensing agreements and joint ventures (Mansfield and Romeo, 1980).

Finally, Japanese companies may well have wanted to transfer higher technology, but were hampered by the many factors frustrating all foreign investors in China, namely: poor infrastructure, including unreliable energy supply and transport, shortages of good quality materials, prolonged bureaucratic wrangling, Party interference, lack of skilled Chinese labour, lack of good interpreters, lack of a strong legal system, tight availability of foreign exchange, dubious accounting procedures, etc. (Whiting, 1989, 109-111; Macleod, 1988, 14-38; Kleinberg, 1990, 221-245.)

Many writers have found from examining Japan's investment patterns in Asia as a whole that reducing production costs, especially labour costs, has been a primary motive in choosing location and type of production (Yoshihara, 1978; Awanohara, 1989; Tokunaga, 1992 and Healey, 1991). Kueh, in his chapter of this book suggests that it has been due to the difficulties encountered in trying to set up factories in China that Japanese companies have found it more lucrative to supply indirectly, industrial inputs to Hong Kong and Taiwanese factories in China. The advantage to them is that they can keep control over the technologies used to make the inputs. They are produced in Japan, shipped to Hong Kong, and then re-exported into China.

To test this hypothesis, Japanese re-exports through Hong Kong to China were regressed separately with Taiwanese and Hong Kong FDI in China. Table 9.5 gives the annual real growth rates of Japanese re-exports through Hong Kong, and of Hong Kong and Taiwanese FDI in China. As only about ten years of data were available, the results can lead only to the most tentative of conclusions.

Hong Kong FDI

$$\log RX_t = \underset{(1.422)}{19.854} - \underset{(-0.057)}{0.017} \log FDI_t - \underset{(-0.879)}{2.768} \log GDP_t$$

$$+ \underset{(0.299)}{0.275} \log INV_t + \underset{(1.520)}{0.402}\, TREND$$

R^2 adjusted = 0.881 D.W. = 1.375 F = 17.719 S.E. = 0.194

Taiwanese FDI

$$\log RX_t = \underset{(3.225)}{23.314} + \underset{(2.354)}{0.140} \log FDI_t - \underset{(-2.539)}{5.393} \log GDP_t$$

$$+ 1.010 \log INV_t + 0.437\, TREND$$
$$(2.153) \qquad (3.098)$$

R^2 adjusted = 0.943 D.W. = 2.070 F = 38.718 S.E. = 0.134

RX_t = Japanese Re-exports through Hong Kong
FDI_t = Hong Kong or Taiwanese Foreign Direct Investment
GDP_t = Chinese Gross Domestic Product
INV_t = Chinese Capital Construction Investment

In both cases the adjusted R^2 and F's are high, but the statistics for the Taiwanese FDI regression are better. It can be more safely said, therefore, that there is a stronger relationship between Japanese re-exports and Taiwanese FDI than between Japanese re-exports and Hong Kong FDI.

Japanese companies first went to the NIEs, then to four ASEAN countries (Thailand, Malaysia, Indonesia and the Philippines), and most recently to China and Vietnam. The choice of these countries was, of course, influenced strongly by the political stability in the host country, the incentives offered, the availability of some measure of infrastructure, the degree of independence from local politics, and the amount of legal protection. It is very likely that Japan would have begun investing earlier in China had the investment environment been better.

The results of a survey carried out in 1990 suggested that initially Japanese companies were most interested in producing goods for export from China, but later when Chinese citizens had more spending power, the Japanese changed their focus to the host country market (Taylor, 1993, 320. Quoting a JETRO survey). In 1993 an economist from the Nomura Research Institute, discussing the surge of Japanese investment in China in the 1990s, explained it was due to the perception "that the promise of China as a market has finally turned into reality" and companies "aren't investing to export to the United States and Europe anymore, but to take advantage of the local market" (Sender, 1996, 47). A survey of forty Japanese companies investing in China carried out in 1995 found that the third and fourth most important factors affecting their decision to invest in China after "political stability" and "continuation of the open door policy" were the "local potential market" and "expected growth rate of the Chinese economy and market" (Tang, 54-56).

Table 9.5: Annual Real Growth Rates of Hong Kong and Taiwanese FDI to China, and Japanese Re-Exports Through Hong Kong

	Growth Rate of Hong Kong FDI	Growth Rate of Taiwanese FDI	Growth Rate of Japanese Re-Exports
1985			47.9
1986	15.7		-40.2
1987	32.3	19.1	37.4
1988	22.5	1,761.3	67.6
1989	-11.0	719.8	-8.6
1990	-16.2	30.6	-3.4
1991	14.6	164.0	29.9
1992	185.2	75.2	41.6
1993	112.5	175.9	29.9
1994	5.3	0	7.4
1995	-5.9	-14.0	-5.4

Sources: Almanac of China's Foreign Economic Relations and Trade; Hong Kong External Trade, Ash and Kueh.

Note: The FDI data was converted into real terms by obtaining the Hong Kong-U.S. dollar exchange rates from the Hong Kong Monthly Digest of Statistics, and making 1983 the base year, with value 1. These figures were divided by the CPI index found in the same source. This index was then multiplied with the FDI data as given in the Foreign Trade Almanacs. The re-export data was first converted into U.S. dollars using the above exchange rate information, and then the same procedures were followed.

The raw data can be found at Appendix I.

CONCLUSION

The first task of this chapter was to gain a better understanding of the effect of Japanese FDI on Japanese exports to China. The dearth of data made time-series analysis less effective. However, it can be fairly safely said that Japanese FDI in manufacturing was not an influencing factor on Japanese manufacturing exports. A chronological review of the export and FDI data revealed that the trends of both were highly erratic, due mainly to political factors in China, but that generally speaking, the growth rate of exports to China was decreasing, while the annual growth rate of FDI was increasing. This would seem to support the argument that Japanese companies are interested in using relatively cheap Chinese labour to produce Japanese products. It could also indicate that another key motivation for Japanese investors is a growing Chinese market. Also, as China is finally approaching entry into the World Trade Organisation, Japanese investors, as all other investors in China, are undoubtedly looking forward to less risky trade and investment conditions.

The second purpose of this chapter was, in the context of Japanese FDI, to comment on Chinese expectations for and assessment of Japanese technology transfer. Many Chinese believe that Japanese companies have not been providing their most efficient technologies. This is backed up by the Campbell Survey (1987). Most countries do not transfer technology to other countries soon after it has been brought into use in the home country. Japan is not unique in this respect. Furthermore, most investors, no matter where they come from, have been frustrated and discouraged by the lack of infrastructure, the political interference and inadequate legal and accounting systems.

Regression analysis suggests tentatively that there is some relation between Japanese exports through Hong Kong with Taiwanese FDI in China. It is quite plausible that in the 1980s and early 1990s Japanese companies preferred not to invest in China, but rather to supply industrial inputs to Taiwanese and Hong Kong factories in China.

Whatever the precise relationship between Japanese exports and FDI in China, it is certain that Japan is fully aware that Chinese spending power is steadily increasing. Without doubt, Japanese companies will continue to choose what they perceive to be the most rational ways, be they direct, indirect, or both, of maximising profits and minimising losses in their business interaction with China.

Appendix I: Raw Data

	1	2	3	4	5
1983	4,872,119	1,592	3,389.3		
1984	7,144,975	20,666	9,481.4		
1985	12,368,748	21,997	14,544.4	955,680	
1986	9,733,808	22,838	8,916.7	1,132,370	570
1987	8,147,042	70,136	12,926.3	1,587,940	720
1988	9,384,120	202,679	23,165.9	2,067,600	14,250
1989	8,415,562	206,268	23,462.4	2,036,900	129,380
1990	5,991,682	160,976	24,885.8	1,880,000	186,000
1991	8,390,978	308,773	36,002.6	2,405,250	548,000
1992	11,573,384	649,725	55,565.0	7,507,070	1,050,500
1993	16,708,089	1,377,106	78,108.5	17,274,750	3,138,590
1994	18,111,602	1,852,598	90,595.8	19,665,440	3,391,040

Column

1. Japanese Manufacturing Exports to China (U.S.$1,000) from Japan. Ministry of International Trade and Industry. *White Papers in International Trade.*
2. Total Japanese Manufacturing FDI to China (U.S.$1,000) from Export-Import Bank of Japan.
3. Japanese Re-Exports Through Hong Kong to China (HK$1,000,000) from *Hong Kong External Trade.*
4. Hong Kong FDI in China (U.S.$1,000) from *Almanac of China's Foreign Economic Relations and Trade.*
5. Taiwanese FDI in China (U.S.$1,000) from *Almanac of China's Foreign Economic Relations and Trade* and Ash and Kueh.

REFERENCES

Almanac of China's Foreign Economic Relations and Trade, Beijing: China Resources Trade Consultancy Co. Ltd. (various years, 1980-1995)

Awanohara, Susumu (1989) *Japan's Growing External Assets - A Medium for Regional Growth?* Hong Kong: Lingnan College, Centre for Asian Pacific Studies.

Ash, Robert and Y.Y. Kueh (1993) "Economic Integration Within Greater China: Trade and Investment Flows Between China, Hong Kong and Taiwan," *The China Quarterly 136* (December) 711-743.

Campbell, Nigel (1987) "Japanese Business Strategy in China," *Long Range Planning* 20 (5) 69-73.

Chenery, Hollis B. (1960) "Patterns of Industrial Growth," *American Economic Review* 50 (September) 624-654.

Clifford, Bill (1993) "Japan's Lending Program in China," *The China Business Review* (May-June) 30-35.

Chu Baotai (1986) *Foreign Investment in China: Questions and Answers*. Beijing; Foreign Languages Press.

Hatch, Walter (1995) "Vietnam's Place in Japan's Regional High Technology Production Alliance." In Duffield, Barbara, *ed. Japanese Investment and Aid Strategies in Vietnam: Implications for Development Directions*. Victoria, B.C.: Centre for Asia Pacific Initiatives, University of Victoria.

Healey, Derek (1991) *Japanese Capital Exports and Asian Economic Development*. Paris: OECD.

Hong Kong, Census and Statistics Department, *Hong Kong External Trade*. Hong Kong: Statistics Dissemination Section, Census and Statistics Department (various issues, 1980-1995)

Hong Kong, Census and Statistics Department, *Hong Kong Monthly Digest of Statistics*. Hong Kong: Statistics Dissemination Section, Census and Statistics Department (various issues, 1980-1995)

Howe, Christopher (1990) "China, Japan and Economic Interdependence in the Asia Pacific Region," *The China Quarterly* 124 (December) 662-693.

Hymer, S.H. (1976) *The International Operations of National Firms*. Cambridge, MA.: MIT Press.

International Monetary Fund, *International Financial Statistics Yearbook*. Washington, D.C.: IMF (various years, 1980-1995)

Japan. Ministry of International Trade and Industry, *White Papers on International Trade*. Tokyo: The Ministry (various issues, 1980-1995)

Japan External Trade Organisation (JETRO) (1994) "Japan's Direct Foreign Investment Continues to Fall," *Tradescope* (April).

Japan Sorifu Tokeikyoku. Japan Statistical Yearbook, Tokyo: Statistics Bureau Management and Coordination Agency (various years, 1980-1995)

Kinoshita, Toshihiko (1995) *Japan's Direct Investment in China - Current Situation, Prospects and Problems.* Unpublished report. Tokyo: Export-Import Bank of Japan, Research Institute for International Investment and Development.

Kleinberg, Robert (1990) *China's "Opening" to the Outside World.* Boulder: Westview.

Kojima, K. (1973) "A Macroeconomic Approach to Foreign Direct Investment," *Hitotsubashi Journal of Economics* 14, 1-21. Quoted by Healey, Derek. (1991) *Japanese Capital Exports and Asian Economic Development.* Paris: OECD.

---------- (1978) *Direct Foreign Investment: A Japanese Model of Multinational Business Operations.* New York: Praeger.

Korea Herald 12 January 1996, "Korea Emerges as Japan's No.1 Tech Exporting Country. January 12, 1996.

Kueh, Y.Y. (1997) "China and the Prospects for Economic Integration Within APEC." In Chai, J.C.H., Kueh, Y.Y., and Tisdell, Clem (eds.), *China and the Asian Pacific Economy.*

Linnemann, Hans (1966) *An Econometric Study of Trade Flows.* Amsterdam: North-Holland.

Lipsey, R.E. and M.Y. Weiss (1981) "Foreign Production and Exports in Manufacturing Industries," *The Review of Economics and Statistics* 63, 488-494.

----------- (1984) "Foreign Production and Exports of Individual Firms," *The Review of Economics and Statistics* 66, 304-308.

Macleod, Roderick (1988) *China Inc., How to Do Business with the Chinese.* Toronto: Bantam.

Mansfield, E. and A. Romeo (1980) "Technology Transfer to Overseas Subsidiaries by U.S. Based Firms," *Quarterly Journal of Economics* 95, 737-750. Quoted by Byun Hyung-Yoon and Wang Yunjong. (1995) "Technology Transfer and Multinational Corporations: The Case of South Korea," *Journal of Asian Economics* 6 (2) (Summer) 203.

Ono, Shuichi (1992) *Sino-Japanese Economic Relationships: Trade, Direct Investment, and Future Strategy.* World Bank Discussion Papers, China and Mongolia Department Series. Washington, D.C.: World Bank.

Ozawa, T. (1979) *Multinationalism Japanese Style.* Princeton: Princeton University Press.

Sender, Henny (1996) "Japan Inc. Let Me Introduce You," *Far Eastern Economic Review* (1 February) 51.

Sumitomo Life Insurance Research Institute (1989) "*Wagakuni no Kaigaichotusetsutoshi no Shinten to Sono Boekishushi ni Oyobosu Eikyo*" (Development of DFI of our Country and its Impact on Balance of Trade) Cited in Ono (1992).

Tang Chi Hong (1995) "*A Study and Analysis of Japanese Investment in China: the Factors Influencing Japanese Firms' Attitudes and Motivations*," Unpublished Directed Research Project, Department of Economics at Lingnan College, Hong Kong.

Taylor, R.I.D. (1993) "Japanese Investment Strategy and Management Training in China: Lessons for British Investors," *Asian Affairs* 24, 315-326.

Tokunaga, Shojiro ed (1992) *Japan's Foreign Investment and Asian Economic Interdependence.* Tokyo: University of Tokyo Press.

Wei Shang-Jin (1995) "Attracting Foreign Direct Investment: Has China Reached its Potential?," *China Economic Review* 6 (2) 187-199.

Whiting, Allen S. (1989) *China Eyes Japan.* Berkeley: University of California.

Yokoi, Yoichi (1990) "Plant and Technology Contracts and the Changing Pattern of Economic Interdependence between China and Japan," *The China Quarterly* 124 (December) 694-713.

----------- (1996) "Major Developments in Japan-China Economic Interdependence in 1990-1994." In Howe, Christopher, ed. *China and Japan: History, Trends, and Prospects.* Oxford: Clarendon.

Yoshihara, Kunio (1978) *Japanese Investment in Southeast Asia.* Honolulu: The University of Hawaii.

Zhang Zhaoyong (1995) "International Trade and Foreign Direct Investment: Further Evidence from China," *Asian Economic Journal* 9 (21) 153-167.

10. THE POLITICAL ECONOMY OF CHINA-KOREA RELATIONS

Brian Bridges

For the post-1949 leadership in China, the Korean peninsula, divided between the Democratic People's Republic of Korea (North Korea) and the Republic of Korea (South Korea), has proved to be an awkward and contentious neighbouring area. In fact, for decades after their creation in 1948, the two Koreas competed in a zero sum game over relations with not just China, but three other major powers, Japan, the Soviet Union and the United States. China and the Soviet Union supported the North; the United States and Japan supported the South. But since the late 1980s the nature of the game has altered as South Korea has forged ahead of its northern rival in the diplomatic competition. This was reflected in first the Soviet recognition of South Korea in 1990, then, more crucially, in the Chinese recognition of the South in 1992.

The ties between the Chinese and North Korean leadership date back to the 1930s, but were sealed in blood through the massive participation of Chinese 'volunteers' on the side of North Korea when it faced extinction in the Korean War. Thereafter Chinese and North Korean leaders referred consistently to their close political, economic, and military relationship as being like 'lips and teeth'. A bilateral security treaty, expanding economic arrangements and regular meetings between leaders confirmed this close relationship through subsequent decades, although there were some cooler periods when the North tilted closer to the Soviet Union (Chung, C.W., 1987). However, in the early 1980s a limited number of contacts, mainly sporting, began between China and South Korea; these developed into unofficial trade contacts, mostly through Hong Kong. Although the Chinese did send delegations to attend the 1986 Asian Games and the 1988 Olympics , both of which were held in Seoul , and trade grew steadily from the mid-1980s, the Chinese were more cautious than the Soviet Union under Mikhail Gorbachev in moving towards formal diplomatic ties with the South. Not until 1992, under strong pressure from the South Koreans, did China take the final step and recognise South Korea. This marked a significant departure in Chinese policy towards the Korean peninsula.

This chapter examines the nature of China's economic relationship with the two Koreas, discussing the motivations behind China's policy changes in the 1990s and assessing recent trends in trade, investment and economic cooperation. The prospects of the Tumen river development programme, which brings together all three countries in a multilateral cooperative venture, will also be analysed . The chapter ends with some assessments of the future course of China's relations with the two Koreas, especially with the uncertain internal situation in the North making the prospect of reunification loom larger.

NORTH KOREA-CHINA ECONOMIC RELATIONS

Both Koreas managed to transform backward economies ravaged by war into predominantly industrial ones. However, since North Korea ceased publishing comprehensive economic statistics in the mid-1960s, it has become difficult to measure and compare the progress of its economy with the South's. The North Koreans initially patterned their economic system closely on the Soviet model of central planning, but although this played a positive role in the early stages of industrialisation, the economic costs of a heavily 'statist' mode of development have become increasingly apparent. (Chung, J.S. 1983). Industrial growth has been affected by the inability of the energy and mining industries to provide reliable and sufficient supplies of power and raw materials ; transportational infrastructure remains inadequate; grain crop yields have fluctuated; and foreign currency shortages and an inability to repay outstanding debts (now estimated to have reached around $ 8 billion) have restricted the import of Western technology and plant.

Whereas other socialist economies, with China in the lead, began to incorporate market elements into their economies in the 1980s, North Korea, if anything, strengthened the role of central planning. This certainly did not help the economy recover competitiveness. The 1980s opened with 'ten long-range economic goals' for the decade; these were subsequently subsumed into the Third Seven-Year Economic Plan, which was due to end in 1993, and more recently they have been quietly dropped from public mention. The Seven-Year Plan itself has been followed by what North Korean officials call a period of 'adjustment' , another sign that targets have not been met. Although estimates by outside observers differ, there is a general consensus that every year since 1990 North Korea has almost certainly been recording negative GNP growth (JETRO, 1995; Korea Herald, 5 June 1996; Nihon Keizai Shimbun, 18 June 1996). The minimal degree of economic reform in North Korea has only served to increase the divergencies between the North Korean and the Chinese economic systems and philosophies.

Kim Il-sung made his home-grown philosophy of juche (self-reliance) his guiding principle of economic development, but in its practical application, at least in the area of foreign trade, Kim was forced to allow a limited degree of flexibility, notably as the 1980s progressed. Even so North Korea predominantly traded with only three states: the Soviet Union, China and Japan; since 1991 this has been reduced to only two.

China has always been a key economic partner of North Korea and with the collapse of the Soviet Union China's position became pre-eminent. However, North Korea's importance to China as a trading partner has never been significant. Even in the early 1970s trade with North Korea represented barely 5% of total Chinese trade; this share has steadily decreased as China has increased and diversified its trading partners under its open-door policy until now in the 1990s trade with North Korea is less than one-half per cent of total Chinese trade. In fact through the 1980s, while Chinese trade with the rest of the world was growing so rapidly, more than tripling in dollar terms, Sino-North Korean bilateral trade fluctuated around the $ 500 million mark and in 1990 was actually about 25% lower than its peak in 1980. As has been the pattern historically, China ran a trade surplus with the North throughout the decade, although the size of this surplus seems to have varied, often for political reasons (Eberstadt, 1995, 671-2).

Table 10.1: China's trade with North and South Korea (US $ million)

	1989	1990	1991	1992	1993	1994	1995
Exports to N.Korea	377.4	358.2	524.8	541.1	602.3	424.5	486.2
Imports from N.Korea	184.6	124.6	85.7	155.5	297.3	199.2	63.6
Total trade with N.Korea	562.0	482.8	610.5	696.5	899.6	623.7	549.8
Exports to S.Korea	-	-	2178.7	2437.5	2860.5	4402.5	6689.2
Imports from S.Korea	-	-	1066.2	2623.2	5360.1	7318.2	10293.3
Total trade with S.Korea	-	-	3244.9	5060.7	8220.6	11720.7	16982.5

Source: Guojia Tongjiju (State Statistical Bureau), Zhongguo Tongji Nianjian, (Beijing: 1991, 1993, 1995, 1996 editions).

Note: As China did not recognise South Korea until 1992, official trade statistics are not available for pre-1991. South Korean figures, which are consistently higher than Chinese figures throughout the 1990s, put Sino-South Korean trade at already around the $ 3 billion level in 1989 and 1990.

China's exports to the North have been mainly energy (coal and petroleum products), food (mainly rice and sweetcorn), and inputs for the North Korean textile industry. The energy imports have always been significant to the North, which has no oil resources, and food supplies have become increasingly important. North Korea's exports to China have usually been minerals, cement and iron and steel. In the 1980s North Korea did also export some coal to China (apparently soft anthracite coal for less expensive bituminous coal) and food (fish for Chinese grain) (Eberstadt, 1995, 674-5), but in the 1990s, as economic conditions deteriorated within North Korea, these exports have all but ceased. A significant illegal movement in goods (and people) is occurring across the China-North Korean border, but there is no means of quantifying this (Noland, 1995, 10-11).

The collapse of the Soviet Union, and with it Soviet/Russian trade with the North, made the North much more dependent on China in practical terms. As shown in Table 10.1, in 1991-92 China exported more to the North, while the North exported less to China, so that the Chinese trade surplus grew. But China reportedly urged the North to export more to pay for these imports; a huge shipment of steel in 1993 seems to have been part of the North's response (Eberstadt, 1995, 676-7). In 1993 China is said to have tried to switch its trade with the North away from 'friendship prices' for key products to a cash basis at world prices, but it is not clear whether this policy has been fully implemented. However, in 1994 Chinese exports to the North did decline by nearly 30% compared with the previous year; but Chinese imports from the North also decreased, by around the same percentage. 1995 saw a further drop in bilateral trade, by around 12 %, which, according to estimates by South Korean economists, meant that Japan, which took an increased amount of North Korean textiles, replaced China as the North's major trading partner (Korea Herald, 28 May 1996). Full figures for 1996 are not yet available, but Chinese sources suggest that bilateral trade was probably around the same level as in 1995 (Asian Wall Street Journal, 14 February 1997).

In 1996, the Chinese appeared to become increasingly concerned about the economic situation in the North. After widespread flooding in parts of the North in the summer of 1995, the North Korean government reversed its proclaimed policy of juche, or self-reliance, and appealed for international food aid. Although Japan and South Korea gave some rice, few other countries did, and the shortfall on North Korean grain production probably totalled between 1.5 -2 million tons (almost one-third of the North's estimated requirements for human and livestock consumption). In May 1996 North Korean Deputy Prime Minister Hong Song-nam was dispatched urgently to Beijing to seek food aid, but he received only sympathetic words and a promise of 20,000 tons of grain (South China Morning Post, 23 May 1996). The Chinese position was that North Korea should, if at all possible, try to obtain food aid from elsewhere.

For China, which has growing grain needs itself, significant food aid could only be spared if the North Korean situation were to be really critical. The North's continued criticism of both Japan and South Korea after the 1995 shipments and its persistent violations of the armistice restrictions in the spring and summer of 1996 did nothing to encourage international donors. Further flooding which took place in the North in July 1996 reduced the annual harvest again and raised the spectre of widespread starvation. As a result the Chinese leadership felt forced to act and a further 100,000 tons of food aid was promised to the North in July; unconfirmed reports suggest that half of this amount was donated, the other half sold to the North at well below market prices. Rumours that China also offered to provide 500,000 tons of food aid per year for five years have yet to be confirmed (Korea Focus, July-August 1996, 125) . The repeated flooding has only masked what are more fundamental problems in the agricultural sector, and indeed in the North Korean economy as a whole. China has continued to try to persuade the North Koreans that economic reform on the Chinese model is the only real answer to their economic problems. These Chinese representations undoubtedly have some resonance for the technocrats in the North Korean elite, but, with the exception of the limited steps to develop the Najin-Sombong special economic zone (discussed below), near to the Chinese and Russian borders, the North has been resistant to endorsing Chinese-style economic reform, not least because of fears that opening the doors economically might bring unbearable political costs for such a closed society. Policy statements accredited to Kim Jong-il since July 1994 have been few in number and clad in the jargon of socialist self- reliance, but one statement carried in the North Korean media in July 1995 in which he attacked 'openness' and 'pluralism' as bringing ideological confusion was interpreted by the Chinese as being aimed at them (Korea Focus, July-August 1996, 124-5) . By early 1997 it was becoming clear that many of those officials believed to be mostly closely associated with advocating economic reform were actually being removed from their posts in the North Korean leadership. This refusal to seriously consider economic reform has undoubtedly played a role in increasing Chinese frustration with the North.

SOUTH KOREA-CHINA TRADE RELATIONS

While the North Korean economy has been stagnating in the 1980s and 1990s, South Korea, with a only few hiccups en route, has developed strongly, so that it is now one of the leaders of the class of 'Newly Industrialising Economies' (NIEs). China has been unable to ignore the growing economic power of the South. Trade between China and South Korea effectively began in 1979, with South Korean imports of Chinese coal indirectly via Hong Kong and Chinese purchases of South Korean black-and-white televisions through the same route. However, as China's economic reforms developed in the early 1980s, China began importing South Korean electrical goods, steel and machinery, while exporting agricultural products, raw materials and textiles to the South. North Korean complaints kept Chinese rather cautious about too open a trading relationship with the South, but China symbolically switched its approach when it authorised a 1 million tonne contract for anthracite coal to be shipped directly to the South on a foreign flag carrier in 1985. Thereafter, trade, particularly direct trade (though carefully concealed by processing paperwork in a third country), began to develop strongly, reaching nearly US $ 3 billion by 1988, according to South Korean calculations.

Despite the Tiananmen Square massacre and the Chinese economic austerity progammes, bilateral trade remained around this level for 1989 and 1990. Private emissaries quietly began shuttling to and fro (Kim, 1994, 37-40); South Korean conglomerates donated millions of dollars to help China host the Asian Games in Beijing in October 1990. Immediately thereafter the South Koreans were rewarded with an agreement to set up trade offices, which would also be empowered to handle consular affairs; these offices began operation in early 1991. A trade agreement was signed later in 1991 and an investment guarantee pact early the next year. Chinese Foreign Minister Qian Qichen described Chinese policy as one of developing substantial relations 'quietly and gradually' (Korea Times, 4 October 1991). The Chinese statistics shown in Table 10.1 suggest that total bilateral trade grew to $ 3.3 billion in 1991 and over $ 5 million the following year (South Korean statistics raise these amounts to $ 4.5 billion and $ 6 billion respectively). In August 1992 the Chinese agreed to the final step of full diplomatic relations with South Korea. At the end of the following month, South Korean President Roh visited China and signed further trade and technological cooperation agreements.

For China the economic motivation was paramount. The stagnation of the North Korean economy - and of Sino-North Korean trade - in the 1980s meant that South Korea had already overtaken the North in terms of being a trade partner of China by the mid-1980s. The Chinese began to look on South Korea as an important source of the intermediate goods and technology necessary for modernisation, but at prices which were competitive with the Japanese. As Chinese resentment against the burgeoning trade deficit with Japan in the second half of the 1980s mounted, South Korea seemed the perfect foil. Even though the Sino-Japanese trade situation turned around after 1989, the Chinese could see - and indeed continue to see - advantages to playing off South Korean and Japanese businessmen. The Chinese also seem to have been frustrated with the North Koreans, who showed no inclination to follow Chinese advice on economic reform as the road to salvation for their economy. Rather than continuing to give out aid and materials to sustain the North, the Chinese came to feel that it would be better if they instead received economic inputs from the South.

A secondary and political motivation, though nonetheless important, was that China was able to insist as part of the agreement on full diplomatic relations that South Korea would de-recognise Taiwan (whereas China was not required to take any such equivalent step with the North); a significant blow against Taiwan which had been having some diplomatic successes earlier in 1992. In fact, Taiwan, having got wind of the impending China-South Korea rapprochement, pre-empted it by severing relations with South Korea first.

For the South Koreans the rationale was primarily political. The logic of the 'northern diplomacy' adopted by President Roh had been that by developing political and economic contacts with the socialist allies of North Korea, the North could be pushed into a more positive mode. When North Korea failed to respond, good relations with the Soviet Union and China became important in their own right. They certainly helped to ensure that China did not vote against the South Korean membership of the United Nations in 1991. Thus South Korea was able to ensure itself a 'very inexpensive security' (Sanford, 1990, 69). The diplomatic breakthrough with China also helped to boost Roh's image domestically, at a time when he faced considerable popular disillusionment over political in-fighting and economic problems. It was these economic difficulties which provided another subsidiary reason for the move towards China. After being the world's fastest growing economy in 1986-88, South Korea began to slow down. Faced with what they saw as growing protectionism in North America and Europe, the South Koreans were looking for new markets; diplomatic protection could bolster their chances of competing with the Japanese in the Chinese market. Subsequently economic motivations remained important.

As shown in Table 1, Sino-South Korean trade has grown to considerable levels in the 1990s and is certainly far larger than Sino-North Korean trade. South Korea is now the fifth largest trading partner of China, while China is the third largest trading partner of South Korea. Chemicals and heavy-industrial products make up over half of China's imports from South Korea. Light-industrial goods, agricultural and fisheries products make up more than 70% of Chinese exports to South Korea. The upward trend in trade volume and value over the past few years is set to continue. Estimates recently released by the South Koreans suggest that their exports to China in 1996 increased by 24% over 1995 (Korea Herald, 14 January 1997). Although textile shortages in China which led to a lifting of import restrictions contributed, more than three-quarters of Chinese imports from the South were heavy industrial, chemical and electrical products. Chinese sources suggest that total bilateral trade reached $ 19.9. billion (Asian Wall Street Journal, 14 February 1997). Thus the gap between Sino-North Korean and Sino-South Korean trade has continued to widen. Given the efforts that the South Koreans are planning to put this year into boosting trade with China, as one of the few potentially bright spots in an otherwise gloomy export prognosis, and the expected stagnant state of Sino-North Korean trade (as the North Korean economy continues to stagger along), the gap can be expected to widen yet again in 1997.

INVESTMENT FLOWS

Flows of foreign direct investment (FDI) have lagged behind trade, but are undoubtedly becoming important now. The first joint venture, by Daewoo to produce refrigerators in Fuzhou, took four years to negotiate through its Hong Kong subsidiary and even after becoming operational in 1988 went through a rocky period. As shown in Table 10.2, early South Korean investments in China were small-scale, with the average size less than $ 1 million. Mostly these investments were pilot operations by companies specialising in garments, toys, leather goods and other labour-intensive sectors, aimed at taking advantage of low cost Chinese labour, as the late 1980s-early 1990s were a period of significant wage rises within South Korea (Hong, Yim and Park, 1991, 72-73). South Korean investors felt themselves exposed with no official legal or tax arrangements and hampered by Chinese restrictions such as only three-month visas for South Korean nationals. The South Korean government therefore pushed for an investment guarantee pact. The Chinese side too, no doubt, came to realise that conducting agreements through third countries was time consuming, complex , legally ambiguous and ultimately discouraging to those major Korean companies which the Chinese wanted to attract. So China finally agreed to an investment guarantee pact in April 1992. As a result, there has been a significant upsurge in the value of South Korean FDI into China in the past four years.

Table 10.2: South Korean investment in China (on approval basis, US $ million)

	Up to 1990	1991	1992	1993	1994	1995	Total
Cases	52	112	269	629	1065	877	3004
Amount	67	85	222	622	820	1232	3048

Source: Ministry of Finance, Republic of Korea

By 1995 China had become the largest single destination for Korean FDI, taking 17% of all such FDI on a cumulative basis. It is clear from Table 10.2 that much of this FDI, however, has remained small-scale in size. The investments by small- and medium-sized Korean companies have been to produce light industrial goods, with about 40% sold to the Chinese market and 60% going for export (Eastern Express, 11 May 1995). Only in the past year or so can a gradual trend towards large-sized investments be detected. Samsung has set up a $50 million videotape recorder plant in Tianjin and is planning a $425 million consumer electronics plant in Suzhou. Hyundai is now constructing a $ 120 million computer disk drive factory in Dalian. In May this year the LG Group unveiled a $ 10 billion programme of investment in China over the next decade; the first project, a LG Electronics television tube factory in Hunan, has just started construction . The LG Group chairman plans to make China into LG's single largest overseas manufacturing base (Korea Herald, 28 May 1996). The Sunkyong group has also announced a decade-long programme of investment in petrochemicals in China valued at $ 9 billion.

Though Fujian and Guangdong provinces were the prime recipients of South Korean FDI in the early years, the difficulties of competing with Hong Kong, Taiwanese and Japanese companies which were better established there coupled with the growing attractions of those Chinese provinces less well-developed but nonetheless geographically closer to the Korean peninsula have contributed to a shift in emphasis to North-eastern China. As a result South Korean FDI is now primarily concentrated in the Bohai Bay area (especially Shandong province) and the three north-eastern provinces of Liaoning, Jilin, and Heilongjiang. By the end of 1994 47% of Korean FDI on a project basis was concentrated in the Bohai Bay (Shandong, Beijing, Tianjin) area and another 40% in the three north-eastern provinces.

Therefore, mirroring the way trade patterns have changed, South Korean FDI in China, has substantially overtaken North Korean FDI . The North Koreans produce no statistics of their outflows of FDI, but from Chinese provincial statistics some kind of picture can be drawn. For example, Shandong provincial statistics of utilised FDI in 1994 show $ 137.6 million coming from the South, but only $ 1.6 million from the North. For the same year, Liaoning province reports $272.6 million from the South and only $ 843,000 from the South. Heilongjiang reported 14 joint ventures with North Korean entities that year, but 278 with South Korean companies (Shandong Tongji Nianjian, 1994; Liaoning Nianjian, 1994, 1995; Heilongjian Tongji Nianjian, 1995).

Links between these Chinese provinces and South Korea have developed significantly in the 1990s. In 1990 ocean freighter and passenger-liner services began between Weihai and Inchon. Shandong province established a representative office in Seoul and worked out a project programme specifically aimed at Korean companies; there are now said to be six Shandong enterprises with offices in South Korea and over 2,300 Shandong citizens working there (North Korea Report, February 1996). The Roh administration began an infrastructural development programme, carried on by the current Kim Young-sam government, which was specifically targeted on the relatively-underdeveloped west coast of South Korea, directly facing China. Improved port facilities and connecting road and rail links have been the focus of this South Korean programme. The flow of FDI has also been assisted by the presence of nearly 2 million ethnic Koreans in China, with more than half of them concentrated in the three north-eastern provinces. Indeed, in the Yanbian Korean Autonomous Prefecture in Jilin province, Koreans make up around 40% of the population (Cui, 1990, 82-83). Visitors to a typical South Korean factory in the region have reported on handful of Korean expatriates managing an almost exclusively ethnic Korean workforce, working with an efficiency the equal of that found back in South Korea. However, recently signs have begun to emerge that not all of these joint ventures are trouble-free; cases of disputes between Korean managers and their workforces have been reported and one Kia motor company executive was murdered, apparently after insulting his trainee workers. These kinds of cases do relate to broader Chinese concerns that some South Koreans tend to treat Yanbian as a kind of 'Korean territory'. Indeed, during 1996 the Chinese government became disturbed sufficiently to ask South Korea to refrain from providing 'special assistance' to the Korean community in China (Korea Focus, Sept-Oct. 1996, 145).

Nevertheless, over the past year or so there have been signs that China and South Korea are preparing to move their economic relationship into a new phase, which involves significant industrial and technological collaboration. This has derived from a series of high-level exchanges between the two countries. Symbolic of this new mood was the visit to Seoul in November 1995 by Chinese President Jiang Zemin. Taken on a tour of Samsung Electronics' most high-technology factory, Jiang was handed a digital mobile telephone, with which he placed a call to China: he then declared that 'This is better than Silicon Valley' (Eastern Express, 16 November 1995). But despite the rhetoric of that occasion, actually a more significant step had been taken earlier during South Korean Prime Minister Lee

Hong-koo's visit to China in May 1995 when an 'industrial alliance' was mooted. Four industrial fields have been under active consideration: auto parts, aircraft, high-definition television (HDTV), and telephone switching systems (Korea Times, 29 June 1995). China has dampened South Korean hopes (led by Daewoo) for joint ventures in car assembly in China, because of fears of over-production, but has agreed to allow cooperation in auto parts. The HDTV project is intended to develop core technology, parts and components, and will initially mean Chinese scientists being seconded to South Korean companies and research institutes. Joint research on a time-division telephone switching system has already begun. However, the most ambitious project, a $ 1.3 billion deal for the joint development of a 100-seater airliner , has collapsed because of serious disagreements between the two sides over which parts of the plane should be built where (each wanted the bulk of the work to be done in its country) and the most appropriate third partner (Foreign Report, 31 October 1996).

A fifth area of collaboration seems set to be nuclear energy. South Korea is poorly endowed with natural resources, although it does have some coal deposits. Industrialisation from the 1960s inevitably increased energy demands, and after the two oil shocks the South Koreans urgently began to diversify sources. Coal began to be imported from China in 1979 and crude oil in 1988. By 1993, China was exporting $ 206 million of crude oil to South Korea, but only $ 134 million to the North. However, the heavy wax content of China's oil has limited its appeal to the South Koreans even though several Korean chaebol have been involved in importing petroleum products for the petrochemical industry (Lee, 1995, 656-60). Overall, energy imports from China still only provide around 3.5% of South Korea's total energy imports. With China having recently become a net oil importer, however, a gradual change of focus in the energy trade can be expected. Indeed, the Chinese have recently shown signs of trying to move from simply suppliers of energy resources to obtaining South Korean inputs, especially technological inputs, themselves. This is where the South Korean experience in nuclear energy development is having an impact. In marked contrast with North Korea, which throughout its negotiations in 1993-95 with the Americans to settle the 'nuclear weapon' dispute persistently claimed that South Korean models for nuclear power plants were technologically (and, of course, ideologically) unacceptable, China signed an agreement in February 1995 for the South Koreans to supply two nuclear reactor plants (Bridges, 1995,105-7). Therefore, despite the sobering effect of the collapse of the aircraft development deal, the Chinese side remain keen, as do the South Koreans, about developing the economic synergy between the two countries.

THE REGIONAL CONTEXT

A Korean proverb warns that the prawn (Korea) will have its back broken by the convulsions of the whales (the neighbouring great powers). Since 1945 there have been two prawns (or perhaps more accurately one prawn broken into two) and four whales: China, the Soviet Union (now Russia), the United States and Japan. The Korean peninsula is regarded by all these four powers as being of political and strategic importance; it lies at the heart of the East Asian theatre. This means that China's relations with the two Koreas do not exist in a vacuum, for they are influenced by and in turn impact upon the complex inter-relationship of these three states with the other interested major powers.

The United States has been and continues to be a strong ally of South Korea, remains suspicious of North Korea (although occasionally, in South Korean eyes, being a little too prepared to give the North the benefit of the doubt) and looks to China to play a constructive role on the Korean peninsula. This means that even in times of Sino-American tensions, such as during 1995-96 over the Taiwan issue, the United States feels a need to call for Chinese political support in coaxing the North into more acceptable behaviour. Japan too, which fears destabilising actions on the peninsula and has strong economic and political links with South Korea, has tried to encourage China to be a 'persuader' of North Korea (Hughes, 1996, 88). Thus both the United States and Japan, while working closely with South Korea over North Korean policy, have also tried to involve China less formally in their policy approaches. China, while flattered by the attention given it, has been rather reticent to position itself too close to the Americans and the Japanese over North Korea. In part this has been because of its difficulties with these two states in other aspects of their bilateral relationships. Indeed, there have been occasions, most notably over the Japanese failure to apologise for the past, when the Chinese have seen political advantage to cosying up to South Korea as leverage against the Japanese and the Americans.

The Soviet Union used to be a strong ally of the North, but after 1991 the new Russia's political and economic links with the North all but disappeared. However, in the past year or so there have been signs that Russia, which has resented being counted out as a player on the Korean peninsula, has begun to reactivate some of its links with the North. While the situation is still far from reverting to the old Sino-Soviet competition for influence with the North, but with the added component of competition for influence in the South, Chinese officials have become more wary of a revived Russian role.

TUMEN RIVER DEVELOPMENT PLAN

The above discussion of China's economic linkages with the two Koreas has highlighted the differences in the nature of the two relationships and shown how the strong rivalry between the two Koreas is also played out in their economic and political contacts with China. However, there is one multinational scheme which has tried to bring the three countries together: the Tumen River project. The basin of the Tumen River, which borders the Russian Primorskiy (maritime territory), China's Yanbian region and North Korea, is now being advocated as the site for the multilateral development of port and other transport infrastructure and industrial facilities (Valencia, 1991; Sugimoto, 1992; Marton, McGee and Paterson, 1995). Starting from a Chinese proposal in 1990, a preliminary conference involving China, the two Koreas and Mongolia was held under the auspices of the United Nations Development Programme (UNDP) in mid-1991; Japan and the Soviet Union (now

Russia) joined soon after. The original concept was to combine Japanese and South Korean capital and technology with cheap Chinese and North Korean labour to exploit and process Russian and Mongolian natural resources. A UNDP-sponsored survey posited two scales of development zones a smaller one centred on North Korea's Najin port, Hunchun in China and Posyet in Russia and a much larger one stretching from North Korea's Chongjin port to China's Yanji city to the Russian port of Vladivostok. Initially, priority has been given to the smaller triangle plan and North Korea, indeed, took the initiative to declare the Najin-Sombong area to be a special economic zone (SEZ) in December 1991.

However, the record since then has not been very satisfactory. Voluminous feasibility studies have been produced, but even within the Najin-Sombong SEZ progress has been slow in setting up the necessary infrastructure (Far Eastern Economic Review, 10 November 1994). There are clear differences of interest and objective amongst the participants. The North Koreans view the Najin-Sambong SEZ and the broader Tumen River plan as a way of revitalising their economy, but, at the same time, keeping contaminating 'capitalist elements' strictly confined to one small area, well away from the bulk of the North Korean population. Despite extravagant North Korean claims of $ 350 million FDI, UNDP officials think only about $ 35 million of investment has been actually committed to the SEZ. An international investment seminar held at the SEZ in September 1996 did not excite much positive interest from overseas in terms of contrastural commitments. Russia is caught up in its own economic difficulties and mainly concerned that its existing port, road and rail facilities do not get ignored; it has also done poorly in attracting foreign investment. The South Koreans prefer to cast the project as a regional, not a purely inter-Korean, cooperative venture, which could solve some of their emerging labour shortage problems as well as provide another means to access the markets of north-east China, but they are suspicious of whether the North will really provide their companies with fair and feasible working conditions on site. The Chinese see it as away of gaining access to the sea from that land-locked north-eastern part of their country, but naturally want to see Hunchun rather than Najin at the hub of the development. So far, the Chinese have proved more successful than either the North Koreans or the Russians in attracting foreign investment with, according to UNDP calculations, $ 226 million entering in Tumen-related projects (Beijing Review, 11-17 November 1996).

UNDP officials continue to keep faith in the project and in October 1996 they promised another $ 3 million in support over the next three years, but they now accept that even if the project does continue, it will not result in a single international free-trade zone but rather as a meeting point for three separate zones each with its own characteristics (South China Morning Post, 29 May 1996).

CONCLUSIONS

The discussion above has shown how the pattern of China's economic relations with the two Koreas has changed quite markedly since the late 1980s. But, despite the limited, even declining, degree of economic interaction with North Korea, China still has important political and security interests associated with the North. Fully committed to its economic modernisation, China needs to have stability on its borders, including on the Korean peninsula. In the past the Chinese saw this as being achieved through support for their ideological ally, North Korea. But, from the late 1980s it became clear that China began to see stability as being achieved through a more balanced relationship, though one primarily focused on political /ideological support for the North and economic contacts with the South. Even after the diplomatic recognition of the South in 1992, China tried to separate politics from economics in balancing its relations with the two Koreas.

However, the past year or so has seen a subtle shift in the Chinese approach. North Korean brinkmanship over the nuclear weapon issue and the transition from Kim Il-sung to Kim Jong-il , who has far fewer personal links with the Chinese leadership, helped in that process, but erratic North Korean actions during 1996 have undoubtedly contributed. North Korean incursions across the Demilitarized Zone in April 1996, the discovery in September 1996 of a North Korean submarine carrying armed commandos off the South Korean coast, the North's 'on-off' responses to the US-South Korean proposal for four-power peace talks (intended to involve China too), and the North's decision to enter into a contract with Taiwan to store nuclear waste all disturbed China. But, when in mid-February 1997 Hwang Jang-yop, a senior North Korean idealogue, sought political asylum in the South Korean embassy in Beijing, China found itself in a real dilemma over how to achieve a solution (Korea Herald, 15, 19 February 1997). After nearly a month, during which the death of Deng Xiaoping undoubtedly slowed down the decision-making process, China over-ruled North Korean demands for his return and allowed Hwang to fly to the Philippines, from where he went on to South Korea. China had of course acted in accordance with the norms of international law, but South Korean officials could rightly feel that their relationship with China was becoming increasingly 'political' in nature.

Recent political science discourse about the international relations of the Asia Pacific region in general and China in particular has introduced the concept of natural economic territories (NET) whereby economic contacts defy provincial and national frontiers in geographically proximate regions; the strength of the NETs can be measured by the intensity of trade and financial flows (The original coinage of the term is credited to US Asia-watcher Robert Scalapino, but it has been much used by other scholars, notably Goodman and Segal, 1994). However, in the case of North-east China, it is less easy to see the establishment of a true NET between China and the two Koreas. Not only do most of the Chinese provinces with strong economic links to the two Koreas also have strong connections with Japan, but also some, such as Heilongjiang, still have reasonably strong economic connections with the Russian Far East. This is not to deny that China will continue to have important economic connections with the Korean peninsula, especially with South Korea, but rather to suggest that it will not become an exclusive NET.

One other issue needs to be explored: the reunification of the Korean peninsula. The current mood in South Korea has shifted noticeably from the euphoric days of 1989, when it naively seemed possible that the Korean peninsula could follow quickly on the German model, to one of caution about reunification. Here, at least, there is some measure of tacit agreement amongst North and South Koreans. The North fears 'absorption' by the South in the way that East Germany disappeared, but the South, having watched the tremendous economic, social and political costs borne by West Germany and aware of its own economic difficulties, does not want to take on the responsibilities of looking after - or paying for - North Korea yet either. The timing and manner of reunification depends now on the fate of Kim Jong-il's regime in the North. More than two and a half years after his father's death, he has still not been confirmed in the top political posts; in the meantime, the growing numbers of defections (including most dramatically Hwang's) and appeals for food aid suggest that not only is the economic and social structure breaking down but that there are significant differences within the political leadership over how to respond to these problems.

International food relief may bring a temporary alleviation of the crisis, but the fundamental problems of the economy will remain. In order to survive, the North 'must loosen the restrictions it places upon economic activity' (Cotton, 1994). However, unlike the Chinese, who have been able to sustain a gradualist reform programme over nearly 20 years, time is no longer on the side of the North. The South is, therefore, well on the way to achieving reunification by 'absorption'. Conceivably by the end of this century, Chinese policy-makers will have to learn how to deal with a reunified Korea. A reunified Korea will obviously be a powerful economic force, although the initial disruption and adjustment needs will be similar to the transitional difficulties in Germany in 1990-91. However, the unified economy will have over 65 million people, a complementary mix of northern mineral resources and docile labour and southern technology and capital. The combined GNP would not be far off that of India or, indeed, China itself (Foster-Carter, 1992,.114). The Chinese, of course, hope that reunification does not come about by destabilising violent action, but whatever form of reunified Korea emerges - and the odds are heavily stacked in favour of a southern-dominated state - China will continue not only to need Korea as a trading and investment partner but no doubt also to have to tread carefully in developing relations with the peninsula.

The author would like to acknowledge the assistance of Ji Yanxun, David, in helping to locate Chinese provincial statistics.

REFERENCES

Bridges, B. (1995) "North Korea after Kim Il-sung", *The World Today* , June, 103-7.

Chung, C-W. (1987) "North Korea's Relations with China", in Park, J.Y., Koh, B.C., and Kwak, T-H, (eds.), *The Foreign Relations of North Korea: New Perspectives*, Kungham University Press, Seoul, pp.169-99.

Chung, J.S. (1987) "North Korea's Economic Development and Capabilities", in: Park, J.Y., Koh, B.C., and Kwak, T-H,(eds.), *The Foreign Relations of North Korea: New Perspectives*, Kungham University Press, Seoul, pp.107-135

Cotton, J. (1994) "Changes to the State-Society Relationship in North Korea under Kim Jong-il", mimeograph, Seoul National University.

Cui, L. (1990) "The Position and Development of Koreans in China", in Suh, D-S and Shultz, E., *Koreans in China*, University of Hawaii Press, Honolulu, pp.78-92.

Eberstadt, N. (1995) "China's Trade with the DPRK, 1990-1994", *Korea and World Affairs*, 19(4), 665-685.

Foster-Carter, A. (1992) *Korea's Coming Reunification: Another East Asian Superpower?*, Economist Intelligence Unit, London.

Goodman, D.S.G. and Segal, G. (1994) *China Deconstructs: politics, trade and regionalism*, Routledge, London.

Hong, S.W., Yim, C.H. and Park, Y.C. (1991) "The Korean Experience in FDI and Sino-Korean Relations", *Journal of Northeast Asian Studies*, Summer 1991.

Hughes, C. (1996) "The North Korean Nuclear Crisis and Japanese Security", *Survival*, Summer, 38 (2), 79-103.

JETRO (1995) *Kitachosen no Keizai to Boeki no Tenbo: 1994 nenban*, Tokyo.

Kim, H. (1994) "The Establishment of South Korean-Chinese Diplomatic Relations: A South Korean Perspective", *Journal of Northeast Asian Studies*, 13(2), 31-48.

Lee H.P. (1995) "South Korea's Energy Relations with the PRC: Trends and Prospects", *Korea and World Affairs*, 19(4), 646-664.

Marton, A., McGee, C. and Paterson, D. (1995) "Northeast Asian Economic Cooperation and the Tumen River Area Development Project", *Pacific Affairs*, Spring 1995, 9-33.

Noland, M. (1995) "Implications of North Korean Economic Reform", unpublished paper, Institute for International Economics, Washington.

Sanford, D.C. (1990) *South Korea and the Socialist Countries*, Macmillan, London.

Sugimoto, T. (1992) *The Dawning of Development of the Tumen River Area*, International Institute for Global Peace, Tokyo.

Valencia, M. (1991) "Economic Cooperation in Northeast Asia: The proposed Tumen River Scheme", *The Pacific Review*, 4(3), 263-71.

PART IV CHINA AND ASEAN

11. ASEAN-CHINA ECONOMIC RELATIONS: COMPLEMENTING OR COMPETING

Noor Aini Khalifah and Mohammad Haflah Piei

1. INTRODUCTION

ASEAN will be celebrating its 30th anniversary in the near future while China has emerged from the "Cold War" poised to be a major player in the upcoming "Asian Century". The world economy and politics is moving towards a multipolar structure with power and influence in regional organisations as well as individual states increasing significantly although the United States still remain as the only super power left. ASEAN has recently increased her membership from six members to seven with the inclusion of Vietnam in the group. Cambodia, Laos and Myanmar are potential future candidates of ASEAN. China's increased political and economic flexibility has led to serious development cooperation with her Asian neighbours (including ASEAN) on a non-ideological basis. A stable and secure China is an essential element in maintaining ASEAN's own economic growth and stability and thus Sino-ASEAN relations merits further study.

This chapter will primarily address the international trade aspects of Sino-ASEAN relations. Section 2 of the chapter will provide broad socio-economic indicators of both the ASEAN countries and China in order to assess the prevailing socio-economic conditions as well as purchasing power of the countries under study. Section 3 will examine the major trade partners of ASEAN and China in terms of exports and imports and how important the trade partners are to the economic well-being of China and ASEAN. The commodities involved in the trade of ASEAN and China will be examined in Section 4. Revealed comparative advantage indices for exports and imports will be presented. Section 5 will look at complementarity of trade among the ASEAN countries and China and the major commodities being exported by the individual ASEAN countries and China. The conclusion and policy implications of the study will be provided in the final section.

2. BASIC SOCIO-ECONOMIC INDICATORS OF ASEAN AND CHINA

The population, gross national product (GNP), GNP/capita, and annual growth rates of the seven ASEAN members individually and as a group and also China are shown in Table 11.1. It can be gleaned from Table 11.1 that China has a population almost three times that of ASEAN while its output is about 1.3 times that of ASEAN. The sheer "size" of China must not be underestimated and this is precisely why Sino relations with others must be handled carefully with trade and investment relations normally being the most important economic relation among countries. Among the ASEAN countries, Vietnam is the only country which has an annual per capita income lower than that of China. In 1993, the annual per capita income of Vietnam was US$170 while that of China was US$490. The diversity of GNP/capita is obvious among the ASEAN countries with Brunei and Singapore at the upper end while Philippines, Indonesia and Vietnam respectively are at the lower end of the spectrum. China's average annual growth rate of 8.2 per cent for the period 1980-93 surpasses that of any of the ASEAN countries. It is precisely this growth potential that may turn China into an economic "giant" in the near future and other countries have to position themselves so as to gain the most economically from this situation.

3. DIRECTION AND INTENSITY OF TRADE

The destination of exports, origin of imports as well as the merchandise trade balance of the individual ASEAN countries, ASEAN as a group and China are shown in Table 11.2 for the years 1990, 1993 and 1994. In the year 1994, ASEAN's exports amounted to US$255 billion while China's exports was about 47 per cent of that of ASEAN or about US$121 billion. ASEAN's exports to the industrialised countries ranged between 54 per cent to 58 per cent of ASEAN's exports with a declining trend for the period examined. China's exports to the industrialised countries accounted for 35 per cent of her exports in 1990 but this share has increased to 52 and 51 per cent respectively for the years 1993 and 1994. A further breakdown of the industrial countries into U.S., Japan and Europe shows that China's percentage of exports to the U.S. increased by slightly more than twice from 8.45 per cent in 1990 to 17.73 per cent in 1994. China's exports of commodities to Japan and Europe individually increased by 3 percentage points between 1990 and 1994. In the case of ASEAN, the U.S. export market is the largest followed by Europe and Japan but for China's exports, the U.S. and Japanese market are of equal importance followed by Europe. China's exports to Hong Kong fell significantly between 1990 and 1994 with exports in the former year representing 43 per cent of China's exports while exports in the latter year accounted for 27 per cent of exports. This phenomena may be explained by China currently accessing the industrial countries markets directly instead of going through the Hong Kong middlemen as was done previously. In the post Cold War era, China is increasingly gaining confidence in dealing with other countries on its own without having to go through Hong Kong. The percentage of China's exports to Korea and Taiwan increased over the study period while the percentage of exports to Singapore and Thailand fell from the 1990 level. The percentage of overall ASEAN's exports to China increased by less than a single percentage point between 1990 and 1994.

Table 11.1: Basic Economic Indicators of ASEAN and China, 1993

Country	Population (million)	GNP (million US$)	GNP/capita (US$, 1993)	Av. annual growth rate (%) 1980-93	Income group
Brunei	0.274		+		High
Indonesia	187.2	138528	740	4.2	Lower middle
Malaysia	19	59660	3140	3.5	Upper middle
Philippines	64.8	55080	850	-0.6	Lower middle
Singapore	2.8	55580	19850	6.1	High
Thailand	58.1	122591	2110	6.4	Lower middle
Vietnam	71.3	12121	170		Low
ASEAN	403.2	443560	1100*		Lower middle
China	1178.4	577416	490	8.2	Low

Notes: + estimated to be high income.
* refers to the weighted average for ASEAN excluding Brunei.

Source: Adapted from data presented in the World Development Report, World Bank, 1995

China imports US$116 billion from the rest of the world in 1994 and this is about 41 per cent of ASEAN's imports of US$281 billion. Relative to China, ASEAN imports relatively more than it exports in 1994 leading to a surplus of US$5.193 billion in the merchandise trade of the former country compared to a deficit of US$26 billion for the latter group. The major source of imports for both ASEAN and China is Japan and this is followed by Europe. Taiwan is the third most important source of imports for China and this is closely followed by U.S. In the case of ASEAN, the third most important source of imports is the U.S. and this is followed by Malaysia.[1] Where the source of imports of China is concerned, between 1990 and 1994, the importance of Japan as a source of imports increased while the importance of Hong Kong decreased. This again may be attributed to the reduced role of Hong Kong as China opens her doors to the rest of the world.

1 The trade data of Singapore as depicted in the *Direction of Trade Statistic*, IMF, 1995 does not seem to show any trade with Indonesia. We have thus not shown it in our tables and this might have resulted in ASEAN's imports from Malaysia being higher than from Singapore.

Table 11.2: Direction of Trade of ASEAN and China 1990, 1993, 1994

Country	Year	Total (million $)	Indus-trial	U.S.	Japan	Eur-ope	Deve-loping	Bru-nei	China	Hong Kong	Indo-nesia	Korea	Malay-sia	Philip-pines	Singa-pore	Thai-land	Viet-nam	Tai-wan
Exports																		
Indo-nesia	1990	25681	70.25	13.1	42.53	12.20	29.58	0.04	3.25	2.41	-	5.31	0.99	0.63	7.41	0.73	0.11	3.31
	1993	36843	62.45	14.2	30.32	14.84	37.36	0.12	3.39	2.44	-	6.03	1.59	0.77	9.15	1.27	0.47	3.90
	1994	37958	68.38	16.81	30.85	17.50	31.36	0.12	3.81	3.03	-	6.81	2.26	0.95	0	1.07	0.46	5.06
Malay-sia	1990	29420	50.57	16.95	15.32	15.64	49.42	0.29	2.1	3.17	1.16	4.62	-	1.34	22.95	3.51	0.02	2.17
	1993	47128	51.27	20.33	12.97	15.24	48.72	0.40	2.55	4.12	1.15	3.42	-	1.02	21.70	3.60	0.29	3.21
	1994	58748	50.61	21.19	11.93	14.54	49.39	0.44	3.29	4.62	1.22	2.80	-	1.04	20.71	3.78	0.27	2.99
Singa-pore	1990	52753	49.6	21.26	8.75	15.86	50.33	1.03	1.51	6.50	*	2.22	13.03	1.27	-	6.62	0	3.60
	1993	74071	46.55	20.35	7.46	15.52	53.39	0.86	2.57	8.65	*	2.78	14.17	1.85	-	5.69	1.32	3.88
	1994	96419	43.22	18.76	7.02	14.13	56.67	0.85	2.18	8.69	*	2.63	19.74	1.64	-	5.55	1.38	4.04
Thailand	1990	23072	67.1	22.71	17.20	24.07	32.16	0.13	1.17	4.50	0.67	1.71	2.49	0.72	7.35	-	0.08	1.45
	1993	37158	60.31	21.54	16.95	18.87	38.38	0.10	1.16	5.27	0.54	1.24	2.80	0.53	12	-	0.31	1.99
	1994	41757	62.04	23.24	18.02	17.65	36.88	0.11	2.19	5.29	0.66	1.32	2.65	0.51	9.67	-	0.48	2.32
Philip-pines	1990	8194	79.23	37.88	19.79	18.77	20.72	0.01	0.76	4.03	0.74	2.81	1.55	-	2.93	1.90	0.11	2.55
	1993	11271	75.42	38.52	16.07	18.03	24.57	0.02	1.48	4.84	0.43	1.95	1.42	-	3.35	1.48	0.33	3.07
	1994	13433	73.95	38.55	15.04	17.76	26.01	0.02	1.22	4.85	0.54	2.17	1.65	-	5.26	0	3.17	3.36
Viet Nam	1990	2364	22.25	0	14.38	7.36	72.12	0	0.34	10.28	0.63	1.14	0.21	2.41	8.25	2.20	-	1.23
	1993	3752	48.99	0	26.01	17.80	40.80	0	2.96	3.36	0.93	2.19	2.24	0.27	8.53	2.05	-	3.73
	1994	4706	53.42	1.06	26.07	21.19	37.29	0	3.70	2.85	0.79	2.19	2.15	0.32	8.69	0.93	-	4.23
Brunei	1990	2212	63.11	3.44	58.09	0.27	33.50	-	0.14	0	0	12.39	1.22	4.88	7.05	7.73	0	0
	1993	2366	74.85	1.23	54.40	18.05	21.77	-	0	0.04	0.04	0	0.13	1.94	8.28	8.71	0	2.58
	1994	2162	71.6	1.99	49.91	19.61	24.24	-	0	0.09	0.05	0	1.34	1.53	8.74	9.81	0	2.59
ASEAN	1990	143696	57.75	19.48	18.97	16.26	41.93	0.47	1.81	4.59	0.40	3.35	5.47	1.08	7.61	3.54	0.04	2.76
	1993	212589	54.65	19.88	15.61	16.13	44.85	0.43	2.38	5.60	0.39	3.13	5.82	1.13	8.92	3.21	0.68	3.34
	1994	255183	53.79	20.34	14.63	15.67	45.75	0.46	2.64	5.97	0.43	3.02	8.36	1.10	6.86	3.23	0.90	3.62
China	1990	62876	34.95	8.45	14.65	10.33	63.31	0.01	-	43.20	0.64	0.69	0.59	0.33	3.21	1.36	0	0.51
	1993	91611	52.20	18.53	17.23	13.82	46.88	0.01	-	24.09	0.76	3.12	0.77	0.31	2.45	0.82	0.30	1.59
	1994	120822	51.25	17.73	17.79	13.19	48.28	0.01	-	26.79	0.87	3.62	0.93	0.39	2.12	0.96	0.28	1.86

Continued

Country	Year	Total (million $)	Indus-trial	U.S.	Japan	Eu-rope	Deve-loping	Bru-nei	Chin a	Hong Kong	Indo-nesia	Korea	Malay - sia	Philip-pines	Singa-pore	Thai-land	Viet-Nam	Tai-wan
Imports																		
Indo-nesia	1990	22008	65.75	11.45	24.79	21.64	33.64	0	2.97	1.24	-	4.51	1.32	0.25	5.83	0.84	0.19	6.12
	1993	28333	65.42	11.49	22.05	24.92	34.24	0	3.3	0.87	-	7.42	1.82	0.2	6.33	0.83	0.13	4.64
	1994	30589	65.96	10.11	27.59	21.33	33.69	0	3.78	3.31	-	9.13	2.57	0.26	0	1	0.13	5.15
Malay-sia	1990	29170	63.62	16.95	24.19	17.36	36.17	0	1.92	1.91	1.08	2.54	-	0.53	14.77	2.41	0.15	5.58
	1993	45616	62.4	16.93	27.48	14.11	37.07	0.01	2.4	2.02	1.57	3.05	-	0.48	15.25	2.49	0.2	5.36
	1994	59555	63.72	16.62	26.71	16.57	35.39	0.05	2.29	2	1.58	3.19	-	0.54	14.08	2.48	0.19	5.11
Singa-pore	1990	60954	54.27	16.08	20.12	15.31	45.71	0.21	3.44	3.08	*	2.91	13.55	0.51	-	2.74	0	4.25
	1993	85041	54.45	16.41	21.95	13.75	45.55	0.25	2.83	3.16	*	3.23	16.51	0.59	-	4.14	0.41	3.98
	1994	102210	53.79	15.29	22.02	14.35	46.21	0.2	2.82	3.38	*	3.83	16.36	0.76	-	4.78	0.44	3.85
Thailand	1990	33408	62.57	10.78	30.36	18.31	36.55	0.53	3.31	1.25	0.59	3.13	3.37	0.33	7.42	-	0.28	5.17
	1993	46065	63.61	11.68	30.31	18.4	34.6	0.39	1.96	1.16	1.11	4.23	3.63	0.39	6.45	-	0.18	5.07
	1994	54324	62.27	11.3	30.45	17.6	35.88	0.43	2.73	1.7	0.77	3.74	4.84	0.47	4.62	-	0.09	4.71
Philip-pines	1990	12993	55.71	19.53	18.45	12.45	44.21	0.86	1.4	4.44	1.54	3.84	2.22	-	3.91	1.15	0.88	6.43
	1993	17638	58.79	20.02	22.8	11.71	41.2	0.29	1.03	4.98	1.94	5.11	2.03	-	5.55	1.01	0.06	5.85
	1994	22534	58.43	18.47	24.17	11.74	41.52	0.16	1.42	5.09	1.77	5.19	2.16	-	6.61	0.94	0.08	5.64
Viet Nam	1990	2726	17.02	0.04	6.2	10.31	79.42	0	0.18	7.23	0.37	1.94	0.04	0.15	18.23	0.62	-	1.5
	1993	6400	23.78	0.13	11.03	10.94	66.36	0	4.75	8.77	2.95	12.52	2.36	0.64	16.84	1.98	-	8.63
	1994	8607	22.46	2.2	8.23	10.05	69.19	0	4.37	6.69	2.25	13.13	2.03	5.45	16.97	2.56	-	9.49
Brunei	1990	1000	51.1	15.3	14.6	18.5	47.2	-	2.7	1.6	1.9	0.6	10.3	0.2	25.9	3.7		
	1993	2607	56.46	20.18	5.37	28.92	40.28	-	0.46	1.15	1.84	0.27	7.94	0.12	26.77	1.53	0	0.38
	1994	3142	54.07	13.18	4.68	34.5	42.84	-	0.57	0.64	1.56	0	9.13	0.13	28.55	1.56	0	0.54
ASEAN	1990	162259	58.69	14.52	23.19	16.86	40.93	0.26	2.85	2.41	0.46	3.15	6.2	0.39	5.75	1.7	0.18	5.03
	1993	231700	58.68	14.84	24.29	16.05	40.5	0.19	2.52	2.53	0.78	4.27	7.32	0.43	6.25	2.26	0.25	4.78
	1994	280961	58.27	14.07	24.81	16.09	40.85	0.18	2.71	2.96	0.71	4.61	7.51	0.68	5.25	2.54	0.24	4.7
China	1990	53915	49.97	12.22	14.2	18.03	48.4	0.01	-	27.01	1.57	0.44	1.58	0.17	1.57	0.72	0	4.18
	1993	103552	52.53	10.27	22.5	16.3	45.82	0	-	10.14	1.4	5.18	1.05	0.21	2.56	0.58	0.12	12.49
	1994	115629	55.91	12.09	22.76	17.08	42.26	0	-	8.21	1.37	6.33	1.4	0.24	2.15	0.75	0.17	12.18

Notes: Singapore's trade with Indonesia is not shown in the "Direction of Trade Statistics Yearbook",IMF, 1995 but Indonesia's trade with Singapore is shown.
Europe include all the 17 industrial countries in Europe with Belgium and Luxembourg treated as a single entity.

Source: Computed from the "Direction of Trade Statistics Yearbook", IMF, 1995.

Overall, China's trade with Hong Kong has resulted in surpluses of US$12.6 billion, US$11.6 billion and US$22.9 billion respectively for the years 1990, 1993 and 1994. This contrast with China's trade with Taiwan which registered deficits of about US$11.5 billion both in 1994 and 1995. The ASEAN countries trade with China has resulted in deficits of US$2 billion in 1990 and this deficit narrowed to US$773 million and US$874 million respectively in 1993 and 1994.

The trade intensity indices[2] of the ASEAN countries and China with their major trade partners are shown in Table 11.3. The trade intensity index "concentrates attention on variations in bilateral trade level that result from differential resistances, by abstracting from the effects of the size of the exporting and importing countries" (Drysdale & Garnaut, 1982). The trade intensity index is calculated by dividing an importing country's share in an exporting country's total exports by the former's share in world imports. Among the industrial countries, ASEAN's trade intensity index of greater than two with Japan shows that ASEAN's trade with Japan is twice as much as warranted by the latter's share in world imports. The ASEAN countries trade with all of the ASEAN members also show high intensity of trade indices with the exception of Indonesia.[3] China's trade with the industrial countries also show a similar pattern to that of ASEAN where intensity of trade indices are concerned. China's trade with Hong Kong was also intense with indices declining from 18 in 1990 to 6.36 and 6.95 respectively in 1993 and 1994. China's trade with Korea showed an increasing trade intensity index over the period studied. In 1994, China's trade with Indonesia and Vietnam was characterised by trade intensity indices greater than unity while the intensity of trade index was less than unity for China's trade with the remaining ASEAN countries and Taiwan.

---

2 Mathematically, the trade intensity index is computed as follows:

$$I_{ij} = X_{ij}/X_i \quad /(M_j/(M_w - M_i))$$

Where X_{ij} is country i's exports to country j
X_i is i's total exports
M_j is j's total imports
M_i is i's total imports
and M_w is total world imports

3 In the case of Indonesia, the small intensity of trade index may be attributed to the lack of data for Singapore's trade with Indonesia as mentioned in footnote 1 earlier.

Table 11.3: Intensity of trade indices for ASEAN and China with its major trade partners, 1990,1993, 1994.

	Year	Indus-trial	U.S.	Japan	Eur-ope	Deve-loping countries	Brunei	China	Hong Kong	Indo-nesia	Korea	Mala-ysia	Philip-pines	Singa-pore	Thai-land	Viet Nam	Tai-wan
Indo-nesia	1990	0.95	0.88	6.28	0.26	1.11	1.49	2.09	1.01	-	2.64	1.17	1.68	4.22	0.76	1.34	2.14
	1993	0.93	0.88	4.69	0.37	1.12	1.67	1.22	0.66	-	2.69	1.30	1.64	4.02	1.03	2.72	1.89
	1994	1.02	1.05	4.82	0.45	0.93	1.62	1.41	0.80	-	2.85	1.62	1.81	0	0.85	2.31	2.50
Malay-sia	1990	0.68	1.14	2.26	0.33	1.84	10.02	1.35	1.33	1.83	2.29	-	3.57	13.06	3.64	0.26	1.40
	1993	0.76	1.26	2.00	0.38	1.45	5.69	0.92	1.11	1.51	1.52	-	2.15	9.49	2.9	1.69	1.55
	1994	0.75	1.31	1.85	0.37	1.45	6.02	1.21	1.22	1.69	1.16	-	1.96	8.62	2.96	1.34	1.47
Singa-pore	1990	0.66	1.41	1.28	0.33	1.86	35.24	0.97	2.71		1.09	15.35	3.36	-	6.80	0	2.30
	1993	0.68	1.25	1.14	0.39	1.58	12.09	0.91	2.30		1.22	11.42	3.86	-	4.54	7.60	1.85
	1994	0.64	1.15	1.08	0.35	1.65	11.33	0.79	2.26		1.08	13.96	3.06	-	4.31	6.74	1.96
Thai-land	1990	0.91	1.52	2.53	0.51	1.20	4.65	0.75	1.89	1.05	0.85	2.96	1.93	4.18	-	0.99	0.94
	1993	0.89	1.33	2.61	0.47	1.14	1.38	0.42	1.41	0.71	0.55	2.28	1.12	5.24	-	1.81	0.96
	1994	0.92	1.44	2.80	0.45	1.08	1.46	0.81	1.39	0.92	0.55	1.90	0.96	4.03	-	2.37	1.14

Philip-pines	1990	1.07	2.55	2.93	0.40	0.78	0.43	0.49	1.70	1.18	1.40	1.85	-	1.67	1.99	1.40	1.65
	1993	1.12	2.40	2.49	0.46	0.74	0.25	0.54	1.31	0.56	0.87	1.17	-	1.48	1.20	1.92	1.49
	1994	1.11	2.40	2.35	0.45	0.77	0.31	0.45	1.29	0.75	0.91	1.19	-	2.21	0	15.82	1.67
Viet Nam	1990	0.30	0	2.14	0.16	2.71	0	0.22	4.35	1.01	0.57	0.25	6.48	4.73	2.3	-	0.80
	1993	0.73	0	4.04	0.45	1.23	0	1.07	0.91	1.24	0.98	1.84	0.57	3.77	1.67	-	1.82
	1994	0.80	0.07	4.10	0.54	1.11	0	1.38	0.76	1.11	0.92	1.55	0.61	3.66	0.74	-	2.10
Brunei	1990	0.86	0.23	8.63	0.01	1.26	-	0.09	0	0	6.20	1.46	13.14	4.04	8.09	0	0
	1993	1.12	0.08	8.47	0.46	0.66	-	0	0.01	0.06	0	0.10	4.14	3.66	7.11	0	1.26
	1994	1.08	0.12	7.85	0.50	0.72	-	0	0.02	0.07	0	0.97	2.92	3.69	7.78	0	1.29
ASEAN	1990	0.75	1.26	2.69	0.33	1.50	15.52	1.12	1.85	0.60	1.60	6.25	2.78	4.17	3.54	0.51	1.71
	1993	0.77	1.17	2.28	0.38	1.27	5.76	0.81	1.43	0.49	1.32	4.50	2.25	3.70	2.46	3.74	1.53
	1994	0.76	1.19	2.15	0.38	1.27	5.88	0.92	1.49	0.57	1.19	5.67	1.97	2.71	2.40	4.20	1.69
China	1990	0.47	0.56	2.14	0.22	2.35	0.44	-	18.03	1.00	0.34	0.69	0.86	1.81	1.40	0.04	0.33
	1993	0.76	1.13	2.61	0.34	1.38	0.17	-	6.36	0.98	1.36	0.62	0.64	1.05	0.65	1.73	0.76
	1994	0.75	1.08	2.72	0.33	1.40	0.18	-	6.95	1.20	1.49	0.65	0.73	0.87	0.74	1.38	0.90

Source: Intensity of trade analysis

4. COMMODITY STRUCTURE OF ASEAN AND CHINA'S TRADE

In this section, the discussion will be based on broad categories of commodities such as food items, agricultural raw materials, fuels, ores and metals and manufactured goods which consist of chemical products, other manufactured goods and machinery and transport equipment. The composition of these broad categories of commodities based on the Standard International Trade Classification (SITC) is as shown below Table 11.4. In spite of China's relatively low per capita income, her percentage of trade in the manufacturing sector is relatively large compared to that of ASEAN. In 1990, about 75 per cent of China's trade was generated by the manufacturing sector and this percentage increased to 82 per cent for the year 1993. It must be remembered that until recently, China's manufacturing sector tended to give priority to import substitution, the development of heavy industry and the production of investment goods rather than consumer goods. A typical pattern of trade that emerged under this strategy of industrialisation was large imports of machinery and industrial raw materials which was financed by exports of food items and also other manufactured exports (see Chia, 1987).

It can be gleaned from Table 11.4 that China's exports of other manufactured goods was a net revenue earner while the category machinery and transport equipment and to a lesser extent the category manufactured chemicals contributed to deficits in the manufacturing sector's trade as a whole. In the primary sector, China's trade in fuels is relatively smaller than that of ASEAN. Where the individual ASEAN countries are concerned, almost all of the ASEAN countries with the obvious exception of Singapore and Brunei exported more food items than they imported. The share of manufactures in Indonesia and Malaysia's exports increased tremendously between 1990 and 1993 while the share of all the other commodities in the primary sector decreased. The share of imports in the manufacturing sector did not change much between 1990 and 1993 for Malaysia and Indonesia. Overall, ASEAN's share of manufactured exports increased 10 per cent between 1990 and 1993 while the share of imports increased about 4 per cent. In the case of China, the share of manufactured exports increased by 9.2 per cent between 1990 and 1993 while the share of manufactured imports increased by 4 per cent. Therefore, where changes in shares of manufactured exports and imports are concerned, ASEAN and China exhibit a similar pattern.

Table 11.4: Commodity structure (percentage) of trade of ASEAN and China, 1990, 1993

Country		Year	Total value (million US$)	Food Items	Agricul-tural raw material	Fuels	Ores & metals	Manufa c-tured goods	Chemi-cal products	Other manufac-tured goods	Machi-nery & transport equip-ment	Unallo-cated
Brunei	Exports	1990	2212	0.00	0.00	86.40	0.20	12.60	0.00	11.50	1.00	0.80
		1992*	2366	0.60	0.00	96.90	0.10	2.40	0.10	1.00	1.30	0.00
	Imports	1990	1000	19.20	0.40	0.90	1.30	77.90	6.90	36.50	34.50	0.30
		1992*	2607	15.70	0.40	0.60	1.10	81.80	6.30	37.20	38.20	0.50
Indonesia	Exports	1990	25681	11.20	5.00	44.00	4.40	35.50	2.40	31.60	1.40	0.00
		1993	36843	10.80	4.20	28.40	3.50	53.10	2.20	45.90	4.90	0.00
	Imports	1990	22008	5.10	4.70	8.90	4.30	76.90	16.10	18.20	42.50	0.20
		1993	28333	6.50	5.20	7.70	4.00	76.30	14.40	19.60	42.40	0.30
Malaysia	Exports	1990	29420	11.70	13.80	17.80	2.10	54.20	1.70	16.40	36.10	0.40
		1993	47128	9.40	8.70	10.30	1.20	69.70	2.10	23.30	44.20	0.60
	Imports	1990	29170	7.30	1.40	5.30	3.60	82.20	8.80	21.60	51.70	0.20
		1993	45616	6.10	1.20	3.70	3.50	83.90	7.50	21.10	55.40	1.50
Philippines	Exports	1990	8194	24.90	4.80	4.90	6.10	39.00	3.40	22.10	13.50	20.4
		1993	11271	15.60	1.50	2.00	4.50	41.60	2.30	20.70	18.70	34.8
	Imports	1990	12993	10.30	2.40	14.90	3.40	53.20	11.40	15.80	26.00	15.8
		1993	17638	7.80	2.30	11.50	2.90	59.60	9.60	17.50	32.40	16.0
Singapore	Exports	1990	52753	5.20	2.60	17.90	1.60	71.70	6.60	17.60	47.50	1.10
		1993	74071	5.00	1.40	12.20	1.50	78.50	6.40	17.30	54.80	1.50
	Imports	1990	60954	6.10	1.70	15.90	2.10	73.20	7.60	23.30	42.40	1.10
		1993	85041	5.90	0.90	10.90	2.20	79.00	6.90	23.20	49.00	1.10
Thailand	Exports	1990	23072	28.70	5.10	0.80	1.00	63.10	2.00	41.40	19.80	1.20
		1993	37158	21.90	4.00	1.10	0.50	71.10	2.80	40.60	27.70	1.50
	Imports	1990	33408	5.00	4.70	9.30	3.60	75.00	10.40	24.00	40.60	2.40
		1993	46065	4.70	4.20	7.50	3.20	77.90	10.10	23.20	44.50	2.50
ASEAN	Exports	1990	141332	12.54	5.86	20.15	2.35	57.25	3.78	23.94	29.53	1.88
		1993	208837	10.55	3.99	13.06	1.75	67.86	3.76	27.84	36.23	2.81
	Imports	1990	159533	6.38	2.74	11.44	3.09	74.13	9.88	21.90	42.35	2.28
		1993	225300	6.03	2.28	8.27	2.94	77.94	8.82	22.04	47.12	2.53
China	Exports	1990	62876	12.70	3.50	8.40	2.10	71.40	6.00	47.90	17.40	1.90
		1993	91611	10.80	2.00	4.50	1.70	80.60	5.00	59.80	15.80	0.40
	Imports	1990	53915	8.70	6.10	2.40	2.60	79.80	12.90	25.90	40.90	0.50
		1993	103552	2.90	3.10	5.60	3.70	84.00	9.40	32.40	42.20	0.70

Notes: * value refer to 1993 values although the structure is for 1992. Food items refer to SITC 0 + 1 + 22 + 4. Agricultural raw materials refer to SITC 2 less (22 + 27 + 28). Fuels refer to SITC 3. Ores and metals refer to SITC 27 + 28 + 68.

Manufactured goods refer to SITC 5 to 8 less 68 of which: Chemical products refer to SITC 5, Other manufactured goods refer to SITC (6 + 8) less 68, Machinery and transport equipment refer to SITC 7.

Source: Handbook of International Trade and Development Statistics, 1995, United Nations

The above pattern of trade of ASEAN and China is further corroborated by the indices for export specialisation (XSP) and import specialisation (MSP).[4] These indices together with the net-export to total trade ratio, that is, (X - M)/(X + M) are shown in Table 11.5. This ratio is sometimes called the trade balance coefficient. The export and import specialisation indices shows the share of a commodity in the exports (imports) of a particular country compared to the share of the commodity in world exports (imports). A value greater than unity shows that the share of exports (imports) in a country's trade is greater than the share of that commodity in world exports (imports). The negative sign for the net export to total trade ratio show that imports exceed exports (see UNIDO, 1982). This ratio takes on values between -1 to +1 with negative values showing comparative disadvantage and positive values showing comparative advantage. In order to evaluate comparative advantage, both of the export and import specialisation indices and net-export to total trade ratio will be used simultaneously (see Rana, 1988 and Khalifah, 1995).

It can be gleaned from Table 11.5 that ASEAN as a group has comparative advantage primarily in food items, agricultural raw materials and fuels while ASEAN is comparatively disadvantaged in the trade of manufactures and ores and metals. We think that one caveat is in order when using the XSP and MSP measures. These indices were primarily derived in the context of inter-industry trade with many of the Heckscher-Ohlin assumptions holding true at that time and ignores the huge amount of intraindustry trade currently prevalent in both developed and developing countries like that of Malaysia and Singapore. In today's world, multinational corporations are responsible for conducting about two-thirds of the world's trade and it is no small wonder that intraindustry trade will be prevalent in this context (see Khalifah, 1996).

China has comparative advantage in the trade of food items and also other manufactured goods while she is comparatively disadvantaged in the other commodities. ASEAN is comparatively advantaged in the trade of food items, agricultural raw materials, fuels and comparatively disadvantaged in ores and metals and manufactured goods as a whole. In the year 1993, ASEAN did have a slight

---

4 The export and import specialisation indices are as follows:

$XSP = X^k_i/X_i \div X^k_w/X_w$

$MSP = M^k_i/M_i \div M^k_w/M_w$

where	X^k_i	=	country *i*'s exports of good *k*
	X_i	=	total exports of country *i*
	X^k_w	=	world exports of good *k*
	X_w	=	total world exports
	M^k_i	=	country *i*'s imports of good *k*
	M_i	=	total imports of country *i*
	M^k_w	=	world imports of good *k*
and	M_w	=	total world imports.

comparative advantage in the production of other manufactured goods. Where individual ASEAN countries are concerned, Indonesia also has a comparative advantage in the other manufactured goods and this is similar to that of China. In fact, Indonesia also has a comparative advantage in all the broad categories of commodities with the exception of chemical products and machinery and transport equipment. Malaysia has a strong comparative advantage in the trade of agricultural raw materials, fuels and food items. Although Malaysia's trade in the machinery and transport equipment sector has high XSP indices, the trade of this category of commodities is in a deficit and thus not comparatively advantaged. Again, the caveat about intraindustry trade mentioned earlier applies here. Philippines in 1993, has a comparative advantage only in food items and a comparative disadvantage in all other categories. It is also interesting to note that Singapore does not possess a comparative advantage in all the categories shown in Table 11.5. Again here, Singapore's entrepot trade with significant amounts of intraindustry trade has led to these results. Also, the category of commodities are broad with many offsetting trade flows within the same category. Thailand's comparative advantage structure is similar to that of China although Thailand's comparative disadvantage in fuels is more significant than that of China.

5. COMPLEMENTARITY OF TRADE BETWEEN ASEAN AND CHINA

Complementarity of trade of the inter-industry type can easily be determined by looking at comparative advantage indices. The presence of oil reserves in a country's soils automatically endows it with this resource and thus enables it to export oil over and above that rendered by domestic demand. Similarly, certain weather conditions makes it more suitable for some commodities to be cultivated cheaply in a country relative to other countries bestowing on it a comparative advantage. From the analysis in the previous section it is obvious that the economies of China and Singapore are largely complementary and this is also true for Singapore and other ASEAN members. Indonesia (and to some extent Thailand) and China's commodity structure of trade as shown by the comparative advantage indices in the broad product categories above are competitive. China's relatively large population will enable her to continue having comparative advantage in the other manufactures category which basically refer to labour-intensive manufactures. Vietnam, ASEAN's youngest member, is relatively poor and initially will develop its agricultural sector before moving up the ladder to venture into the manufacture of labour-intensive commodities and will eventually compete with China. In the near future, Singapore (and possibly Malaysia) will have comparative advantage in technology-intensive and human-capital intensive manufactures and thus could help China in her efforts to modernise and upgrade her

Table 11.5: RCAX and RCAM indices and net-export to total trade ratio for ASEAN and China

Country		Year	Food Items	Agric raw materials	Fuels	Ores & metals	Manu-factured goods	Chemical products	Other manu-factured goods	Machinery & transport equipment	Unallocated
Brunei	XSP	1990	0.000	0.000	9.181	0.064	0.172	0.000	0.429	0.027	0.299
		1992*	0.065	0.000	10.297	0.032	0.033	0.011	0.037	0.035	0.000
	MSP	1990	2.087	0.164	0.096	0.418	1.065	0.775	1.361	0.921	0.112
		1992*	1.707	0.164	0.064	0.354	1.118	0.708	1.388	1.020	0.187
	Net X/ (X + M)	1990	-1.000	-1.000	0.991	-0.492	-0.473	-1.000	-0.179	-0.879	0.710
		1992*	-0.933	-1.000	0.986	-0.848	-0.948	-0.972	-0.952	-0.940	-1.000
Indonesia	XSP	1990	1.218	2.050	4.675	1.415	0.485	0.270	1.179	0.037	0.000
		1993	1.174	1.722	3.018	1.125	0.726	0.247	1.712	0.131	0.000
	MSP	1990	0.554	1.927	0.946	1.382	1.051	1.809	0.679	1.135	0.075
		1993	0.707	2.132	0.818	1.286	1.043	1.618	0.731	1.132	0.112
	Net X/ (X + M)	1990	0.439	0.108	0.705	0.088	-0.300	-0.704	0.339	-0.926	-1.000
		1993	0.367	0.025	0.655	0.064	-0.050	-0.669	0.506	-0.739	-1.000
Malaysia	XSP	1990	1.272	5.657	1.891	0.675	0.741	0.191	0.612	0.964	0.150
		1993	1.022	3.566	1.094	0.386	0.953	0.236	0.869	1.180	0.224
	MSP	1990	0.794	0.574	0.563	1.157	1.123	0.989	0.806	1.380	0.075
		1993	0.663	0.492	0.393	1.125	1.147	0.843	0.787	1.479	0.561
	Net X/ (X + M)	1990	0.236	0.817	0.544	-0.259	-0.201	-0.674	-0.133	-0.174	0.337
		1993	0.228	0.764	0.484	-0.477	-0.076	-0.551	0.066	-0.096	-0.415
Philippines	XSP	1990	2.707	1.968	0.521	1.961	0.533	0.382	0.824	0.360	7.631
		1993	1.696	0.615	0.213	1.447	0.569	0.258	0.772	0.499	13.018
	MSP	1990	1.120	0.984	1.583	1.093	0.727	1.281	0.589	0.694	5.910
		1993	0.848	0.943	1.222	0.932	0.815	1.079	0.653	0.865	5.985
	Net X/ (X + M)	1990	0.208	0.116	-0.656	0.062	-0.368	-0.683	-0.063	-0.507	-0.102
		1993	0.122	-0.412	-0.800	-0.004	-0.383	-0.734	-0.139	-0.461	0.163

Singapore	XSP	1990	0.565	1.066	1.902	0.514	0.980	0.742	0.656	1.268	0.411
		1993	0.544	0.574	1.296	0.482	1.073	0.719	0.645	1.463	0.561
	MSP	1990	0.663	0.697	1.690	0.675	1.000	0.854	0.869	1.132	0.411
		1993	0.641	0.369	1.158	0.707	1.080	0.775	0.865	1.308	0.411
	Net X/	1990	-0.151	0.139	-0.013	-0.205	-0.082	-0.142	-0.209	-0.015	-0.072
	(X + M)	1993	-0.151	0.151	-0.013	-0.255	-0.072	-0.106	-0.212	-0.013	0.086
Thailand	XSP	1990	3.120	2.091	0.085	0.321	0.862	0.225	1.544	0.529	0.449
		1993	2.381	1.640	0.117	0.161	0.972	0.315	1.514	0.739	0.561
	MSP	1990	0.544	1.927	0.988	1.157	1.025	1.169	0.895	1.084	0.898
		1993	0.511	1.722	0.797	1.029	1.065	1.135	0.865	1.188	0.935
	Net X/	1990	0.597	-0.143	-0.888	-0.678	-0.265	-0.766	0.087	-0.496	-0.487
	(X + M)	1993	0.580	-0.131	-0.788	-0.776	-0.152	-0.634	0.171	-0.331	-0.348
ASEAN	XSP	1990	1.363	2.402	2.141	0.756	0.782	0.425	0.893	0.788	0.703
		1993	1.147	1.636	1.388	0.563	0.927	0.422	1.038	0.967	1.051
	MSP	1990	0.694	1.123	1.216	0.993	1.013	1.110	0.817	1.131	0.853
		1993	0.656	0.935	0.879	0.945	1.065	0.991	0.822	1.258	0.946
	Net X/	1990	0.271	0.310	0.219	-0.195	-0.188	-0.494	-0.016	-0.236	-0.154
	(X + M)	1993	0.237	0.238	0.188	-0.287	-0.107	-0.434	0.079	-0.168	0.016
China	XSP	1990	1.381	1.435	0.893	0.675	0.976	0.674	1.787	0.465	0.711
		1993	1.174	0.820	0.478	0.547	1.102	0.562	2.231	0.422	0.150
	MSP	1990	0.946	2.500	0.255	0.836	1.091	1.449	0.966	1.092	0.187
		1993	0.315	1.271	0.595	1.190	1.148	1.056	1.209	1.127	0.262
	Net X/	1990	0.260	-0.198	0.606	-0.030	0.021	-0.297	0.366	-0.337	0.632
	(X + M)	1993	0.534	-0.273	-0.169	-0.422	-0.082	-0.360	0.240	-0.502	-0.328

Notes: * value refer to 1993 values although the structure is for 1992.
Source: Computed from data presented in the "Handbook of International Trade and Development Statistics", United Nations, 1995.

Table 11.5: RCAX and RCAM indices and net-export to total trade ratio for ASEAN and China (continued)

Table 11.6: Export structure at the SITC (Rev. 2), 3-digit level ranked by average 1991-92 values

Country	SITC		Value (millions dollars)	As a percentage of	
				Country total	Developing countries
Brunei	All commodities		2491	100	0.31
	333	Crude petroleum	1223	49.08	0.89
	341	Gas, natural and manufactured	1029	41.32	6.93
	334	Petroleum products, refined	95	3.83	0.25
	931	Special transactions	12	0.47	0.19
	845	Outerwear knit nonelastic	10	0.39	0.06
	846	Undergarments knitted	6	0.26	0.08
	667	Pearls, prec., semi-prec stone	5	0.21	0.09
	842	Mens outerwear nonknit	3	0.12	0.03
	843	Womens outerwear nonknit	2	0.08	0.01
	896	Works of art etc.	1	0.06	0.47
	Remainder		104	4.18	
Indonesia	All commodities		31555	100	3.89
	333	Crude petroleum	5547	17.58	4.05
	341	Gas, natural and manufactured	4116	13.04	27.73
	634	Veneers, plywood,etc	3264	10.34	66.51
	851	Footwear	1141	3.61	8.24
	334	Petroleum products	1110	3.52	2.95
	653	Woven man-made fib fabric	1075	3.41	9.83
	232	Natural rubber,gums	1007	3.19	25.41
	287	Base metal ores,conc nes	852	2.7	13.1
	843	Womens outerwear nonknit	800	2.53	5.02
	036	Shellfish fresh,frozen	792	2.51	9.45
	Remainder		11852	37.57	
Malaysia	All commodities		37544	100	4.62
	776	Transistors, valves, etc	5193	13.83	20.7
	333	Crude petroleum	3676	9.79	2.68
	424	Fixed vegetable oil nonsoft	1982	5.28	54.36
	764	Telecom equipment, parts, access. nes	1614	4.3	11.28
	762	Radio broadcast receivers	1603	4.27	21.35
	759	Office, adp machn parts, access	1564	4.17	12.1
	247	Other wood rough, squared	1507	4.01	52.61
	248	Wood shaped, sleepers	1430	3.81	38.55
	341	Gas, natural and manufactured	1180	3.14	7.95
	232	Natural rubber, gums	953	2.54	24.06
	Remainder		16840		
Philippines	All commodities		9332	100	1.15
	931	Special transactions	1550	16.61	24.76
	776	Transistors, valves, etc	984	10.55	3.92
	424	Fixed vegetable oil nonsoft	392	4.2	10.74
	843	Womens outerwear nonknit	340	3.64	2.14
	845	Outerwear knit nonelastic	322	3.45	1.97
	764	Telecom equipment, parts, access. nes	313	3.35	2.19
	846	Undergarments knitted	311	3.34	3.66
	057	fruit, nuts, fresh, dried	305	3.27	3.63
	036	Shellfish fresh, frozen	289	3.1	3.44
	773	Electricity distributing equipment	226	2.42	5.77
	Remainder				

Continued

Country	SITC		Value (millions dollars)	As a percentage of	
				Country total	Develop-ing countries
Singapore	All commodities		61219	100	7.54
	334	Petroleum products, refined	8965	14.64	23.84
	752	Automatic data processing equipment	8643	14.12	47.65
	776	Transistors, valves, etc	5017	8.2	20
	764	Telecom equipment, parts, access. nes	2740	4.48	19.14
	759	Office, adp machn parts, access	2572	4.21	19.93
	762	Radio broadcast receivers	1727	2.82	22.99
	761	Television receivers	1350	2.21	17.19
	763	Sound recorders, phonograph	1251	2.04	25.55
	772	Switchgear etc. parts nes	943	1.54	17.08
	778	Electrical machinery nes	849	1.39	13.53
	Remainder		27160		
Thailand	All commodities		30399	100	3.74
	759	Office, adp machn parts, access	1502	4.94	11.62
	036	Shellfish fresh, frozen	1460	4.8	17.41
	042	Rice	1311	4.31	46.44
	776	Transistors, valves, etc	1227	4.04	4.89
	037	Fish etc prepared, preserved nes	1169	3.85	33.68
	232	Natural rubber, gums	1058	3.48	26.71
	843	Womens outerwear nonknit	981	3.23	6.16
	054	Vegetable etc fresh, simply preserved	972	3.2	17.9
	851	Footwear	919	3.02	6.64
	667	Pearl, precious, semi-precious stone	892	2.93	15.42
	Remainder		18908	62.2	
Viet Nam	All commodities		2185	100	0.27
	333	Crude petroleum	607	27.79	0.44
	036	Shellfish fresh, frozen	298	13.64	3.55
	042	Rice	184	8.43	6.53
	843	Womens outerwear nonknit	108	4.93	0.68
	842	Mens outerwear not knit	108	4.92	0.97
	322	Coal, lignite and peat	104	4.77	5
	248	Wood shaped, sleepers	80	3.68	2.17
	222	Seeds for soft fixed oil	56	2.56	2.06
	071	Coffee and substitutes	56	2.56	0.93
	057	Fruit, nuts, fresh, dried	55	2.51	0.65
	Remainder		529	24.21	
China	All commodities		78391	100	9.65
	843	Womens outerwear nonknit	3766	4.8	23.65
	851	Footwear	3480	4.44	25.15
	845	Outerwear knit nonelastic	2971	4.34	20.9
	894	Toys, sporting goods, etc.	3832	3.79	28.51
	333	Crude petroleum	2616	3.61	2.07
	842	Mens outerwear not knit	2237	3.34	23.54
	784	Motor vehicle parts, access nes	2042	2.85	33.92
	652	Cotton fabrics, woven	1558	2.6	28.79
	658	Textiles articles nes	1526	1.99	31.89
	762	Radio broadcast receivers	51961	1.99	20.33
	Remainder			66.29	

Source : Handbook of International Trade and Development Statistics, United Nations, 1995

industrial and physical infrastructure. In this sense, Singapore and Malaysia could be seen as complementing China. But of course, other newly industrialised countries like Hong Kong, Taiwan and Korea would also look for opportunities to complement their economic activities with that of China not to mention the developed countries whose investment are already located in China

This then automatically leads to the issue of foreign direct investment (FDI) in China. Almost all the countries in the world would like to invest in China to take advantage of its relatively cheap labour and the huge market potential afforded by a population of 1.2 billion. Direct foreign investment from the more advanced countries will inevitably result in the industrial scaling-up of the host economies. Ariff (1994, p. 164) suggests the following sequence: "complementarity of resources attracting FDI, leading to industrial scaling-up in the host countries, which in turn erodes the initial complementarity. This process, however, need not stop here, since increased competition will lead to further changes in the industrial structure with each country finding its own niches so that a new pattern of complementarity will emerge." FDI will tend to seek opportunities and ways of producing goods cheaply while at the same time protecting its own interest such as slowing the rate of technology transfer to others, maintaining "monopoly" elements so that its profits are secured and its ability to influence the global business environment enhanced. The ubiquitous presence of FDI has led to the phenomena of intraindustry trade and the question of complementing or competing economic structures become rather ambiguous. FDI which originate from other ASEAN countries are already moving into Viet Nam and this will lead to a similar upgrading of the economic structure as that of China.

The export structure of all the ASEAN countries and China is shown in Table 11.6. In the case of Malaysia, SITC 776 dominates her exports but this product group is also important where exports of Singapore, Thailand and the Philippines are concerned. In the case of more labour-intensive manufactures like SITC 843 and 851, China's exports in these products are dominant as can be seen by her share in developing country exports of 23.65 per cent and 25.15 per cent respectively. The product group SITC 843 and 851 are also important exports for Indonesia registering a 5.02 and 8.24 per cent share respectively in developing countries exports. China's exports of more sophisticated products like SITC 784 represent one-third of all developing country exports and this may represent competition for Malaysia in the future where the latter is trying to develop her automobile industry. Similarly, radio broadcast receivers (SITC 762) exported by Malaysia which has a share of 21.35 per cent in developing countries' exports may compete with China's exports of the similar product which has a 20.33 per cent share in developing countries' exports. Thailand's exports of shellfish and rice may complement that of China since these products are not major export products of China. The huge market of China can pose both as a threat and opportunity to the ASEAN countries.

6. SUMMARY AND CONCLUSION

China, a relatively poor country but with a huge market can be viewed both as complementing and competing with ASEAN. China's direction of trade lately is roughly similar to that of ASEAN with the developed countries of Japan, U.S. and Europe being important trade partners. The developed countries serve as important markets for both ASEAN and China and this argues well for maintaining a relatively open multilateral trading system for all countries whether rich and poor.

The future inclusion of Laos, Myanmar and Cambodia into ASEAN will generate dynamic effects and impact on economic growth and competitiveness in the Asian region. The ASEAN Free Trade Area proposes to make ASEAN into a production base and induce regional FDI's to participate in the development of the region. The increased cost competitiveness by producing for a regional rather than a national market place and the ensuing scale economies will induce FDI to source for raw materials and intermediate inputs in the ASEAN region itself. Market forces will also induce FDI to venture into China and this will lead to a rapid realisation of the upcoming "Asian Century".

Revealed comparative advantage, a concept more suited to the Heckscher-Ohlin model of international trade shows that ASEAN and China may compete in the trade of other manufactures (SITC 6 + 8 less 68). But these categories are broad categories and we think there is enough room for all countries concerned to find their own niches and trade in a global market. The emerging phenomena of intraindustry trade in the international trading system though not given serious treatment in this chapter, must be alluded to at this point. From the data shown in Table 11.6, it is quite obvious that China and in the export of textile products and footwear and also some of the electronic components sector. The latter sector being dominated by FDI shows that international trade and FDI are complements to a certain extent. If movements of FDI especially in the Asian region persists, the chances are high that intraindustry trade will predominate compared to inter-industry trade. In an environment where intraindustry trade predominate, the economies of ASEAN and China will most probably complement each other. A more liberal international trading regime will improve the welfare of all countries concerned. Economic adjustments will be less painful since moving displaced factors of production within industries is much easier than across industries. Thus, ASEAN and China should view their economies as complementing each other rather than competing.

REFERENCES

Ariff, Mohamed (1994) "APEC and ASEAN: Complementing or Competing", in Chia Siow-Yue (ed.) *APEC: Challenges and Opportunities*, Institute of Southeast Asian Studies, Singapore.

Chia Siow-Yue (1987) "ASEAN-China Trade in Manufactured Goods", in Chia Siow-Yue and Cheng Bifan (ed.) *ASEAN-China Economic Relations: Trends and Patterns*, Institute of Southeast Asian Studies, Singapore.

Drysdale, P. & Garnaut, R. (1982) "Trade Intensities and the Analysis of Bilateral Trade Flows in a Many-Country World: A Survey", *Hitotsubashi Journal of Economics*, 22(2): 62-84.

International Monetary Fund (1995) *Direction of Trade Statistics Yearbook*, Washington D.C.

Khalifah, N.A. (1995) "Dynamic Comparative Advantage of the ASEAN Countries", *Jurnal Ekonomi Malaysia*, 29: 131-159.

Khalifah, N.A. (1996) "AFTA and Intra-Industry Trade", *ASEAN Economic Bulletin*, March, 351-368.

Rana, P.B. (1988) "Shifting Revealed Comparative Advantage: Experiences of Asian and Pacific Developing Countries", *Asian Development Bank Economic Staff Papers*, Report No. 42.

United Nations (1995) *Handbook of International Trade and Development Statistics*, New York and Geneva: UNCTAD.

UNIDO (1982) *Changing Patterns of Trade in World Industry: An Empirical Study on Revealed Comparative Advantage*, New York: UNIDO.

Wisarn Pupphavesa & Maureen Grewe (1994) "AFTA and NAFTA: Complementing or Competing?", in Chia Siow-Yue (ed.) *APEC: Challenges and Opportunities*, Institute of Southeast Asian Studies, Singapore.

World Bank (1995) *World Development Report*, New York.

12. EXPORT COMPETITION AMONG CHINA AND ASEAN IN THE US MARKET: APPLICATION OF MARKET SHARE MODELS

Thomas Voon and Xiangdong Wei

I INTRODUCTION

Market share models are widely used to evaluate export competition for a country's traded commodities[1]. The theory of using market share analysis was first presented by Armington (1969). Specifically, Armington developed a theory for products differentiated by location of production in world markets. Subsequent to Armington's seminal work, many empirical models were extended to apply the market share approach in international trade analysis (e.g. Sirhan and Johnson 1971; Reddy 1980; Durham and Lee 1985; Shalaby et al 1991; Voon 1994).

Among the frameworks used for assessing export market share, the distributed-lag regression model was the most commonly used (e.g. Saghafi 1987; Tellis 1989; Voon

1 In what follows, competitiveness is defined as country i's ability to gain market share in a common export destination (such as the US import market). Competition, however, measures the intensity with which countries compete for market share of similar goods on a common import market (Voon 1996).

1994) [2]. In those models, market share was commonly specified as a function of lagged share and one explanatory variable (i.e. relative prices). In this paper, we extend the previous analysis by incorporating some changes into the model. First, changes in relative prices will be adjusted by movements in exchange rates. A rationale for this is that export prices of internationally-traded goods are normally affected by fluctuations in exchange rates. Second, a quality index (indicated by the ratio of high quality proportion of the products to lower quality one) is incorporated into the model. According to a priori expectation, quality/composition is deemed to be important in determining export market share (Weiss 1968; Cooper and Nakasishi 1988). In addition to the above extensions, the panel-data estimation methods will be used for the empirical analysis. Unlike the conventional single market share equation approach, the problem with the low degree of freedom arising from short time series could be tackled by using the panel data estimation methodology.

In this paper, market share elasticities computed from our extended framework will be compared across the countries exporting to the common import market. Market share elasticities may be used to indicate the degree of rivalry among the competing countries. For example, where the market is relatively competitive, the market shares of the competitors are expected to be sensitive to changes in relative prices/competitiveness[3]. Otherwise, small changes in market share resulting from a change in relative prices indicate a low degree of rivalry.

In the following section, the basic model and the various panel-data estimation methods are presented. In section III, the models are applied for assessing export competition among China and the Association of South East Asian Nations (ASEAN) in the US market. There are many possible factors contributing to the changing level of competition for China and ASEAN. In this paper, we confine our analysis to evaluating how important relative movements in export prices, real exchange rate and product composition are in influencing the export competitiveness of China and ASEAN in the US import market. The conclusions and implications are presented in section IV.

2 The distributed-lag models were normally applied for assessing agricultural commodities which exhibit long production period. Since our analysis involves manufactured goods with relatively short production intervals, the model with a lag of one year (as in previous studies) may no longer be appropriate for our empirical analysis. The results computed from the distributed-lag model are compared with those estimated using a simple regression model.

3 The level of competition could be high or low depending on the number of substitutes, the elasticity of substitution, proximity of the trading nations, the presence of price policies, the existence of any implicit and explicit forms of trading arrangement and relationship between markets, among others. Our models cannot be used to identify the individual sources of competition.

II THE MODEL AND ESTIMATION METHODS

In what follows, two important independent variables having differential impacts on market share are constructed. First, where countries are competing for market share in a common import market, product prices and exchange rates are critical. Nothing can destroy the competitiveness of an exporter more quickly than a rigid exchange-rate policy (Fleissig and Grennes 1994). In our analysis, a relevant price competitiveness index (I=EPI/E where EPI is export price index and E represents real exchange rate) is constructed by adjusting product prices by exchange rates. Relative price competitiveness (P, which denotes the ratio of competitor i's price index (I_i) to the sum of other competitors' (I_n)) constitute the appropriate independent variable. Where competitor i's price index rises faster than that of all others', country i's export share would decrease vis-à-vis its competitors' share.

Second, changes in product quality characteristics or composition constitute the non-price factor affecting market share. In our analysis, we examine if changes in relative product composition ratio ($C = (X_i/Y_i)/(X/Y)$ where X_i/Y_i represents the ratio of higher-quality to lower-quality portion of the production of country i, and X/Y denotes the average ratio for all other exporters) have any effects on country i's competitiveness. Brakman and Jepme (1987) reported that changes in product composition have a significant impact on total exports.

Traditionally, market share models for each individual country are estimated separately by the Ordinary Least Square (OLS) regression. This method will be adopted here as well, among other plausible approaches. Since we have a relatively short time series (15 years) for each individual country, the OLS estimation for each individual country is likely to be limited by the problem of a low degree of freedom. This problem will be more tractable if we apply the panel data estimation technique and estimate the model by using the entire five-country data. Therefore, in addition to doing separate regressions for each individual country, we will also run regressions using the panel data as a whole.

More specifically, we first estimate the following equation for each individual country with the OLS technique.

$$M_{it} = \beta_{i0} + \beta_{i1}P_{it} + \beta_{i2}C_{it} + \mu_{it} \qquad i = 1,2,...,5 \quad t = 1,2,...,15 \qquad (1)$$

where M denotes market share, β_{ik} (k = 1, 2) are individual country coefficients which are normally different for different countries, u is stochastic error, and other terms are explained as before. This is the unrestricted model. But, as we mentioned above, it may suffer from the problem of low degree of freedom.

Next, we will impose various restrictions on the above model, and run regressions with the whole panel data. First, we set both β_{i1} and β_{i2} to be the same for all countries, and allow the intercept β_{i0} to vary across countries: the so-called fixed-effects model. We designate this as model 2. Second, we allow both β_{i0} and β_{i1} to vary across countries, but still keep β_{i2} as a constant (model 3). The F-test as well as other relevant test procedures (see for example Hsiao 1986) will enable us to select the best specification among these alternatives.

Moreover, we will also run a random-effects model (model 4) as below:

$$M_{it} = \beta_0 + \beta_{i1}P_{it} + \beta_2 C_{it} + v_i + \mu_{it} \qquad i = 1,2,...,5 \qquad (2)$$

$$t = 1,2,...,15$$

where v_i is the individual country-specific random variable, and $E[v_i] = 0$, $Var[v_i] = \sigma_v^2$, $Cov[v_i, \mu_{it}] = 0$, $Var[v_i, \mu_{it}] = \sigma_v^2 + \sigma_\mu^2$.

Comparing to the fixed-effects model with one country-specific slope β_{i1} (models 2 and 3), this random-effects model imposes restriction on the mean of the intercept to be the same for all countries, but allows the intercept to have country-specific variances. The estimation will be run by the general least square (GLS) technique. The Hausman test of fixed versus random effects model (Greene, 1993) will be calculated to show which model gives the better fit.

III AN APPLICATION: THE DATA AND RESULTS

The above models are used to assess export competition between China and ASEAN-4[4]. China and ASEAN-4 have been experiencing rapid economic growth over the last two decades or so. Aside from sharing similar rates of growth, there are some other common features between China and the ASEAN-4 countries. For example, in their initial stages of growth, China and ASEAN-4 were predominantly specializing in the production of primary-based and labour-intensive commodities (e.g. textiles, clothing and electrical goods), as in contrast to the NIE's and Japan's production of largely capital- and technology-intensive products. Another similarity is that both China and the ASEAN-4 countries are heavily dependent on the United States (US) and Japan as important destinations of their exports. By exporting similar products (e.g. labour-intensive goods) to the same markets, these economies might have faced a high degree of export competition or rivalry among themselves.

In our empirical analysis, total exports of China and ASEAN-4 to the US are segregated into 4 major product categories: (i) agricultural products (AP), which include food, livestocks and beverages (SITC codes 0-2), (ii) primary products (PP), comprising minerals, crude materials, fuels and oils (SITC codes 3-4), (iii) relatively more-labour-intensive manufactures (MLIM) (SITC codes 6 and 8) and (iv) relatively less labour-

---

4 The ASEAN economic grouping comprises Singapore, Malaysia, Thailand, Indonesia, Philippines, Vietnam and Brunei. In this paper, we confine our analysis to Singapore, Malaysia, Thailand and Indonesia (hereafter ASEAN-4). These four ASEAN countries share similar growth rates.

intensive manufactures (LLIM) (SITC codes 5, 7 and 9)[5]. Following Garnaut and Anderson (1980), LLIM include textile, yarn and fabrics (under SITC 65), glass (SITC 664-666), clothing (SITC 84), footwear (SITC 85), travel goods and handbags (SITC 83), toys and sporting goods (SITC 894), plastic (SITC 893), office supplies (SITC 895), furniture (SITC 82), plumbing, heating and lighting equipment (SITC 81), and other manufactured goods (SITC 899). Notice that most of the LLIM are categorised under SITC single-digit codes 6 and 8. Goods that are grouped under single-digit SITC codes 5, 7 and 9 are considered to be more capital or technology intensive than those grouped under SITC 6 and 8.

Single-digit SITC trade data on US imports from the ASEAN-4 countries were obtained from the US Foreign Trade Highlights (1984, 1986 and 1994 volumes) available at the US consular office in Hong Kong. The exchange rate data were collected from the International Marketing Statistics published by Euromonitor and Statistical Year Book for Asia and the Pacific, United Nations. Consumer price index data for computing the appropriate real exchange rates for China and ASEAN-4 were taken from the World Trade Tables (1995) published by the International Bank for Reconstruction and Development. Our estimation uses annual observations covering the time span of 15 years (1980 -1994).

The empirical results obtained from estimating equations (1) and (2) with the different methods discussed in the last section are presented in Table 11.1. Since both the dependent and independent variables are in logarithm form, the estimated coefficients on the independent variables represent the elasticities. Table 12.1 shows that almost all the coefficients have got the signs as we expected: negative for the relative price and positive for the relative product composition ratio. In general, the panel data estimations have much better goodness-of-fit than the separate country regressions[6].

The F statistics show that the hypothesis of homogeneous slopes and intercept for all countries should be rejected at 1% level. In other words, the simple fixed effects model (2) should be rejected compared with the model showing separated equations for each country (model 1). However, further tests affirmed that model (1) should be rejected in favour of model (3) - panel data model with country-specific intercepts and slopes on relative price. Using the Hausman test, model (3) was then compared with model (4) where the fixed-effects in model (3) was replaced by the random-effects. It was found that model (3) should be rejected in favour of model (4). Hence, in the subsequent discussion of the estimated effects, we will concentrate on model (4)[7].

5 Of the total exports, manufactures constituted more than 80% of China's and ASEAN's exports to the US in 1994. Of the manufactured products, textiles and clothing are a major category, accounting for around half of total manufactured exports in China and ASEAN (especially Indonesia and Thailand).

6 The R^2 for model (4) was not presented here, since it was negative. This could happen as the model was estimated with 2-stage General Least Square method. Consequently, the R^2 for that model does not carry the normal meaning for goodness-of-fit, and cannot not be used to compare with the R^2 of other models.

7 It is of interest to note that the statistical quality of our results was not improved by applying the distributed-lag models (see footnote 2).

Table 12.1 shows that the market share elasticities with respect to the relative price were the largest for China and Malaysia (price elastic) followed by Singapore and Indonesia (price inelastic). The coefficient for Thailand has got the wrong sign but was not significant. The high market share elasticities with respect to the relative price for China, Malaysia and Singapore may be explained by the fact that these countries have the largest market shares in the US market and their wide range of MLIM and LLIM exports to the US caused them to be in competition with one another. The coefficient for the relative product quality (C) was reported in model (4) to be significant at the 10 per cent level. The coefficient C exhibited a low elasticity value, implying that it was a weaker determinant of changes in market share than the relative prices.

IV CONCLUDING COMMENTS

The analysis of export share elasticities with respect to relative prices adjusted by the real exchange rate suggests a reasonably strong competition for export share in the US import market among China, Malaysia and Singapore. In contrast, the level of competition for Indonesia and Thailand within the same market niche was either small in magnitude, as in the case of Indonesia, or insignificant, as in the case of Thailand. The emergence of the Chinese market since 1979 was considered to be the major force contributing to the competition. China was observed to be gaining export share in the US market at the expense of all the other ASEAN-4 competitors. This is attributed not only to its low wage rate vis-a-vis Singapore and Malaysia, but also to the fact that China has succeeded in lowering its artificially high exchange rate since 1979.

Quality or product composition was shown to be a significant determinant of changes in country i's export share. This implies that country i has the potential to raise its competitive edge in terms of gaining export market share if it could increase its product varieties or the capital intensity of its export output. Malaysia, for instance, should be commended in light of the present study for its success in pursuing the policy of increasing the proportion of its exports with high technology and human-capital contents over the last decade or so. Such a structural transformation would be facilitated by the higher per capita income and higher average educational attainment in Malaysia than in China which would render the transition from MLIM exports to human capital-intensive exports sooner in Malaysia than China.

Table 12.1.: The Estimation Results of the Market Share Model with Both the Individual Country and Panel Data Estimation Procedures

	Individual Country Estimation		Panel Data Estimation	
	Model (1)	Model (2)	Model (3)	Model (4)
Variables				
Relative price:		-0.59 (5.89)*		
China	-1.24 (4.58)*		-1.27 (5.68)*	-1.19 (5.48)*
Indonesia	-0.09 (0.61)		-0.17 (1.16)	-0.22 (1.54)****
Malaysia	-1.12 (3.37)*		-1.27 (4.53)*	-1.19 (4.44)*
Singapore	-0.63 (2.93)**		-0.75 (5.07)*	-0.75 (5.13)*
Thailand	0.03 (0.12)		0.34 (1.66)****	0.25 (1.25)
Relative product composition ratio:		0.26 (4.91)*	0.08 (1.47)****	0.10 (1.93)***
China	0.12 (0.83)			
Indonesia	0.03 (0.45)			
Malaysia	0.21 (1.20)			
Singapore	-0.18 (0.62)			
Thailand	0.25 (1.98)***			
Constant/fixed effects:				4.37 (4.07)*
China	7.05 (8.51)*	5.08 (17.62)*	7.17 (10.80)*	
Indonesia	2.00 (4.47)*	3.51 (11.23)*	2.24 (4.96)*	
Malaysia	5.38 (3.77)*	3.68 (13.81)*	6.28 (7.21)*	
Singapore	5.97 (6.59)*	4.12 (14.95)*	5.29 (11.74)*	
Thailand	1.80 (2.75)*	3.61 (13.27)*	1.15 (2.03)**	
R-square:		0.93	0.96	
China	0.71			
Indonesia	0.03			
Malaysia	0.70			
Singapore	0.60			
Thailand	0.56			
F-test of model specification[a]		(2) vs (1) F(8,60)=4.81*	(3) vs (1) F(4,60)=0.77	
Hausman test of Fixed vs Random Effects model[b]				(3) vs (4) $\chi^2(6)=0.0001$

Notes: Numbers in brackets are t-statistics. * denotes significant at 1% level or better; **denotes significant at 5% level; ***denotes significant at 10% level and **** denotes significant at 15% level. a. When the F-test is significant, model (1) should be accepted. b. When the $\chi 2$ is insignificant model (4) should be accepted.

The analytical results above may be improved by incorporating a substitution variable between the exporters and the importer into the model. In previous market share models, changes in market share among exporters on a common import market were assumed to be the result of substitution between exporters only. This may not be reasonable because substitution which occurs between an exporter and the common importer will also change the export shares among the exporters. Where the export price of country i relative to the average of other competitors rose faster than the importer's domestic prices (CPI), we expect exports of country i to be substituted by the importer's own domestic production. The test for such a hypothesis constitutes a topic for more research.

REFERENCES

Ariff, M. (1994), 'ASEAN's Comparative Advantage in a Changing Pacific Division of Labour: Implications for ASEAN-China Economic Relations', in Tan, J.L.H. and Luo, Z. (Eds), *ASEAN-China Economic Relations: Industrial Restructuring in ASEAN and China*, Institute of Southeast Asian Studies, Singapore.

Armington, P.S. (1969), '*A theory of demand for products distinguished by places of production*', IMF Staff Papers, 16, 159-78.

Brakman, S. and Jepma, C.J. (1987), 'The Impact of the Composition of Exports on Export Performance', *De Economist*, 135 (2), 163-81).

Cooper L.G. and Nakanishi M. (1988), *Market share analysis: evaluating competitive marketing effectiveness*, Kluwer Academic, New York, USA.

Durham, S.E. and Lee, D.R. (1985), 'An evaluation of alternative approaches to market share analysis with application to the Kuwaiti poultry market', *Journal of Agricultural Economics*, 38, 85-97.

Fleissig, A. and Grennes, T. (1994), 'The Real Exchange Rate Conundrum: The Case of Central America', *World Development*, 22 (1), 115-28.

Greene, W.H. (1993), *Econometric Analysis*, 2nd Ed, Macmillan.

Hsiao, C. (1986), *Analysis of Panel Data*, Cambridge University Press.

Lloyd, P.J. (1994), 'Intraregional Trade in the Asian and Pacific Region', *Asian Development Review*, 12 (2), 113-43.

Porter, M.E. (1990), *The Competitive Advantage of Nations*, Free Press, New York.

Reddy, N.N. (1980), 'Japanese demand for US coal: a market share model', *Quarterly Review of Economics and Business*, 16, 51-60.

Saghafi, M.M. (1987), 'Market share stability and marketing policy: An axiomatic approach', *Research in Marketing*, 9, 267-84.

Shalaby, S., Yanagida , J.F. and Hassler, J.B. (1991), 'United States market share of Latin American wheat imports: disaggregated analysis and application of the Armington model', *Journal of Economic Studies*, 15, 5, 24-33.

Sirhan, G.A. and Johnson, P.R. (1971), 'A market share approach to the foreign demand for US cotton', *American Journal of Agricultural Economics*, 53, 593-99.

Tellis, G.J. (1989), 'Advertising exposure, loyalty, and brand purchase: a two-stage model of choice', *Journal of Marketing Research* 25, 134-44.

Voon, J.P. (1994), 'Chinese Demand for Australian Wheat: Application of Market Share Models', *Australian Economic Papers*, December, pp. 228-238.

Voon, J.P. (1996), 'Export Competitiveness of China and ASEAN in the US Market', Paper submitted to the *Journal of International Trade and Economic Development* for consideration for publication.

Weiss, D.L. (1968), 'Determinants of market share', *Journal of Marketing Research*, 5, 290-95.

PART V TRADE RELATIONS WITH AMERICA AND AUSTRALIA

13. AUSTRALIAN EXPORTS TO CHINA: CAN WE DO BETTER?

Hans Blomqvist and K.C. Roy

1. INTRODUCTION

For some time now, Australia's official policy has been to forge closer trade and investment relationships with the Asia-Pacific region. In the case of China, its phenomenal growth in the 1980s and 1990s has lured many Australian investors into undertaking investment activities in China. Australia has, in its turn, considerably opened up its domestic market to exports from other countries, including East Asia, although for the latter, a major concern has been the continuation of some protection measures in Australia, particularly in the textile and clothing industries. Australia has also been a proponent of the concept of "open regionalism" in the context of Asia-Pacific Economic Cooperation (APEC), implying a non-discriminatory approach to regional trade liberalisation.

Since China is destined to surpass the United States as the world's largest economy and to play a major role in the international trade arena, as well as in regional politics, Australia has been consciously developing a closer trade relationship with China from the early 1980s. Increasing trade has been the consequence, but China's *share* of exports has remained, somewhat disappointingly, rather stable, at 3-4 per cent of the exports from Australia while its import share has grown considerably. Exports to China has actually not grown by more than about 6 per cent annually in real values since the early 1980s, a modest figure compared to those of many other countries (see *Figure 13.2* below). Since 1991, China has been the ninth most important destination for Australian exports and the seventh most important source of Australian imports. From China's perspective, however, Australia was less important as a trade partner, ranking fifteenth as a market for China's exports and ninth as a source of imports.

The relative pattern of trade between the two countries has changed markedly since the mid-1980s. From 1984 until 1988, Australia had a surplus in its merchandise trade with China, but from 1989, the pattern changed to a deficit. However, according to the Chinese system of calculation, which does not treat entrepôt exports of Australian origin from Hong Kong to China as exports of Hong Kong, but as exports of Australia to China, China has been incurring a substantial deficit in its trade with Australia. No matter how the trade exchange between the two countries is defined, the current growth trend in China alone suggests that this country will continue to gain prominence in Australia's trade relationship with East Asia.

The purpose of this chapter is to find out whether there is unutilised export potential on the Chinese market today and how this market potential may change during the next decade. To do this, we have to give the term, "potential", an operational meaning. In this chapter we use the term to denote exports predicted by a model of trade flows. Two different ways of determining expected trade flows will be used, based on the trade intensity index and a modified gravity model, respectively.

2. STRUCTURE OF AUSTRALIA'S MERCHANDISE TRADE

Figure 13.1 gives a rough overview of Australia's geographical trade structure and its development since the early 1980s. On the export side, the increasing dominance of Asia is obvious, with Japan as the paramount market. The shares of the United States and the European Union, on the other hand, have been falling slightly over time. As noted before, China's export share has been hovering around 3-4 per cent without any clear trend. (Starting from 1990-91 there has been a tendency for the figures to increase, however, even if it is still uncertain whether this may indicate a trend break or not.)

On the import side, the highly developed countries predominate, even if slightly increasing trends can be observed for ASEAN, Korea and China. In fact, the rate of increase is greatest in the case of China, the nominal value of imports having increased four-fold between 1982-83 and 1993-94. Even so, the import share of China was under five per cent at the end of the period.

Table 13.1 looks more closely into the structure of Australia's exports to China.

Figure 13.1: Australia's Merchandise Trade per Main Market Area

Exports

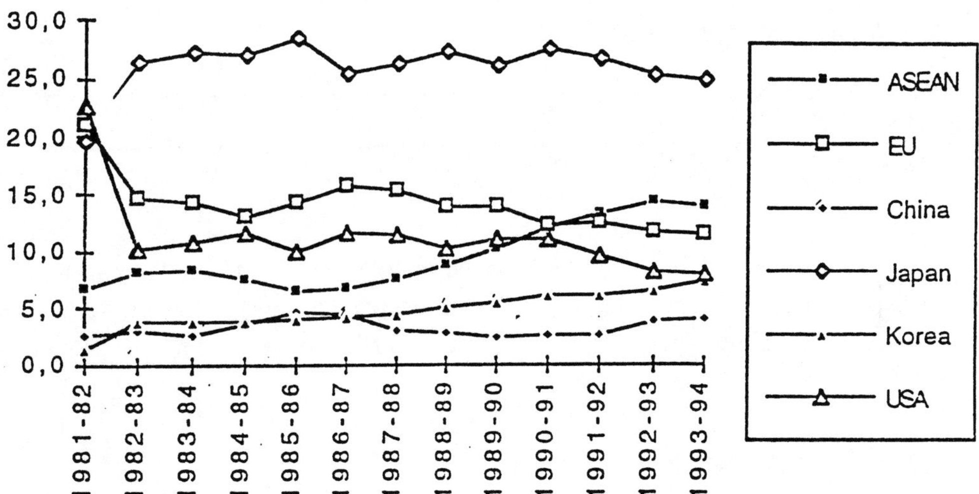

Imports

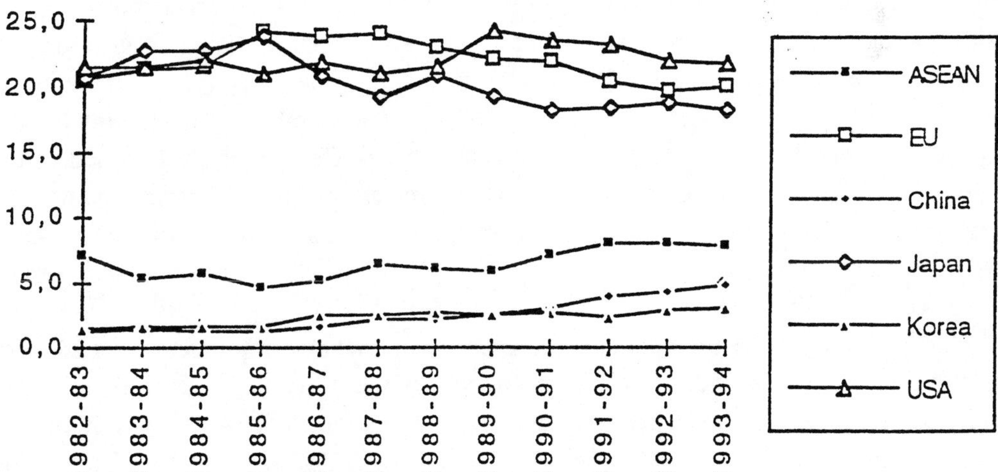

Note: Period goes from 1 July to 30 June.
Source: Compiled from ABS (1994).

Table 13.1: Australia's Exports to China by Main Commodity Groups, per cent, 1993

	Total Exports	Exports to China
Primary Goods	60.4	55.4
Machinery and Transport Equipment	11.2	11.8
Other Manufacturing and Other goods	28.4	32.9
Value (A$ m)	62,772	2,297

Note: Data relates to calendar years.
Source: ABS (1994).

As Australia's exports in general, the exports to China is strongly dominated by primary goods. The category "machinery and transport equipment", which holds most products with high technological or human capital contents comprises only 12 per cent of total exports to China.

2. TRADE BARRIERS IN CHINA

The prospects for increasing trade with a country depend, of course, on existing and expected future trade barriers. China of today is not the extremely inward-looking country it used to be until the late 1970s. Despite economic reforms, however, the trading system in the country is still centralised with official approval required for all exports and imports (Srinivasan 1994). Although trade barriers have been reduced, significant import restrictions still remain. Strong administrative controls which were imposed on imports in mid-1985 have not disappeared. Such controls have led to the imposition of arbitrary and discretionary import restrictions. Such restrictions, in their turn, have created uncertainties in international transactions which have been compounded by China's lack of recourse to GATT-based mechanisms for resolving trade disputes (Elek 1992).

Chai and Sun (1993) attempted to estimate the nominal rate of protection for selected agricultural goods and industrial inputs for which the relevant data were available. Under China's foreign trade regime, domestic prices of agricultural and industrial producer goods are set systematically below international prices as a way of providing protection to these products. Hence, the nominal rate of protection is defined as a percentage by which the domestic price falls below the border price.

Chai's and Sun's estimates suggest that a significant reduction occurred in the magnitude of underpricing of agricultural goods during 1978 and 1984 although the size of such reductions was considerably smaller after 1984. On the other hand, with respect to industrial producer goods, they found that the domestic prices were significantly lower than their international prices in both 9184 and 1990. The extent of divergence measured in terms of absolute difference between the domestic price and border price and expressed as a percentage of border price appeared to have declined from about 81 per cent in 1978 to about 31 per cent in 1984 and 32 per cent in 1990 for agricultural goods, and from about 49 per cent in 1984 to about 41 per cent in 1990 for industrial inputs.

Other studies (USIS 1994) suggest that China still uses an intricate system of tariff and non-tariff administrative controls to implement its industrial and trade policies. Although tariffs on selected products have been reduced, China still uses prohibitively high tariffs in combination with import restrictions and foreign exchange controls to protect its domestic industry and restrict imports. China's import tariffs range from 3 per cent on promoted imports to over 200 per cent on discouraged imports such as automobiles. Many products are subject to quantitative restrictions, to import licensing requirements, and also taxes and value-added taxes.

However, in 1992, tariffs on 225 items were reduced from an average of 45 per cent to 30 per cent and the import regulatory tax was abolished. China pledged with effect from January 1, 1994, to reduce tariffs on 2818 items by an overall average of 8.8 per cent. It also agreed to eliminate 75 per cent of import licensing requirements over a two-year period. At the recent APEC summit in Osaka, the country pledged to reduce its trade barriers again, to a substantial extent. While tariffs have been reduced, and apparently will be reduced more in the future, China continues to use standards and certification requirements as barriers to trade, although it committed itself to eliminate this practice in some areas.

3. ESTIMATES OF UNUTILISED TRADE POTENTIAL

Trade Intensity Index

A simple and widely used indicator of trade bias is the so-called trade intensity index (Drysdale, 1988, p. 86). This index is a market share type of measure, indicating whether the home country's trade with a certain country or region is more or less than the latter country's or region's share of world trade. Formally, we can write

$$I_{ij} = (X_{ij}/X_i)/(M_j/T), \quad (1)$$

where I_{ij} is the index for i's exports to j, X_{ij} is country i's exports to country j; X_i is total exports of country i; M_j is total imports of country j; and T is world exports. Now, if $I_{ij} > 1$, for instance, this means that i's exports to j is greater than what it would be, should it be equal to the share of world exports absorbed by j. Hence, j would be more important as an export market for i than it is for the rest of the world on average. Thus, in our case, if there is unutilised potential as regards Australia's exports to China, we would expect index values smaller than unity. We can also use the index to produce an estimate of the value of untapped export potential, setting $I_{ij} = 1$ and solving equation (1) for X_{ij}.

Table 13.2: Trade Intensity Index for Australia's Exports to China, 1990-1994

Year	Index
1990	1.60
1991	1.57
1992	1.52
1993	1.32
1994	1.61

The trade intensity index has obvious limitations, however. The information whether a country performs better or worse on another country's market for imports is certainly useful as a first approximation, but does not take into account the fact that the economic preconditions for trade are different between any pair of countries, due to different endowments of factors of production and specialisation patterns. Hence, the figures obtained by this method are not based on a model built to capture causal relations.

Table 13.2 shows the values of the trade intensity index pertaining to Australia's exports to China for the period 1990-1994. (The time series is reported to give an idea of the stability of the figure.)

The index values suggest that Australia's exports to China exceed by a wide margin what can be expected from the share of China in world exports. Although there is some variation over the years, t his observation is valid for at least every year during the 1990s. The "expected" exports to China from Australia in 1994 was only US$1271 million, to be compared to an actual value of US$ 2050 million.

A Modified Gravity Approach

To overcome the objection that our estimates of unused trade potential is not based on causal reasoning we also used a model of trade flows known, somewhat misleadingly, as the gravity model. (A prototype of the model, with some theoretical foundations, can be found in Leamer & Stern 1970, pp. 145-170). The gravity model, although based on a general equilibrium approach, does not take discrepancies in comparative advantages into account, however. Hence, we have amended the analytical framework with an element from the Heckscher-Ohlin type of model, according to a technique used by one of the authors in earlier work (Blomqvist 1994, 1995).

The version of the gravity model used in this chapter is a bilateral one, i.e. we study the determinants of export flows from Australia to other countries only. The basic model in this case is then

$$X_{Aj} = f(\underset{+}{Y_j}, \underset{-}{P_j}, \underset{-}{D_{Aj}}) \tag{2}$$

where X_{Aj} stands for Australian exports to country j, Y_j and P_j (j = 1,...,n) denote the absorption capacity of the trade partner and its population, respectively, and D_{Aj} the distance between the home country and the trade partner. (The expected signs of the coefficients are shown beneath the variable symbols.) While the rationale for first variable is obvious, the two other ones require some elaboration. Population is used here as a proxy for potential scale economies, in the sense that the larger the population, *ceteris paribus*, the more industries can reach their minimum efficient scale. Hence, countries with a large population tend to have a diversified industrial structure and be less dependent on foreign trade. The distance is assumed to capture trade resistance due to the combined effect of transport costs, cultural differences and deficient information, all assumed to increase with distance. The model can also be amended in order to take specific factors into account, such as free trade agreements etc.

The model in (2) ignores the obvious possibility that the scope for trade should be greater the larger differences in factor endowments are between two economies. For instance, Leamer (1984) in his classical study used this notion to explain trade flows. Since the size of the economies concerned should matter also in this formulation, we may envisage a model of the type

$$\frac{X_{Aj}}{Y_j} = g(\underset{+}{r_{1j}},...,\underset{+}{r_{mj}}) \tag{3}$$

where r_k (k = 1,...,m) is the relative abundance of factor k.

In the present chapter, we took one step further and amended the factor abundance model not only with Y_j but with all variables included in the gravity model. Combining equations (2) and (3) gives the theoretical starting point for the estimations in a general form:

$$X_{Aj} = X_{Aj}[f(Y_j, P_j, D_{Aj}), g(r_{1j},...,r_{mj})]. \tag{4}$$

Empirical Study

The model was estimated in a log-linear form for the year 1993. The countries included were all OECD countries and, additionally, China, Hong Kong, Korea, Taiwan and all ASEAN countries (i.e. Brunei, Indonesia, Malaysia, the Philippines, Singapore, Thailand and Vietnam). As the number of observations is small (pooling of data for several years adds little to the available information since the explanatory variables change slowly over time), and according to the principle of "Occam's razor", it is necessary to economise on the number of variables included. In addition to the three "gravity variables", we used only two endowment variables, one for relative labour abundance and another one for relative human capital abundance.

The result of a preliminary regression run showed that neither the population or the factor abundance variables contributed to the explanation of the export flows from Australia. (Even the t-values must be interpreted with caution in this case, since the sample is not exactly random, the evidence against an explanatory value of these variables was quite convincing. The adjusted R-squared, for example, actually increased somewhat when the variables were left out). In that respect the result differs strongly from what one of the authors has obtained earlier, for other combinations of countries (see, e.g. Blomqvist 1995). The result can probably be explained by the strong domination of raw materials in the exports of Australia. It is unlikely that the foreign demand for these goods is determined by either labour or human capital abundance, nor should the degree of diversification be of significance in this context. (Including different types of resource abundance may have affected the results, but is difficult because of the large number of possible explanatory variables.)

Because of the result just reported, we re-estimated the model, retaining only the proxy for absorption potential and the distance between the trade partners. The result was

$$\ln X_{Aj} = 26.597 + 0.937 \ln Y_j - 2.749 D_{Aj} \quad (5)$$

$$(9.86) \quad (10.09) \quad (-9.16)$$

$$\bar{R}^2 = 0.809 \qquad F = 70.7$$

(Y_j is proxied by the GDP, t-values are given in parentheses.) This very simple model explains about 80 per cent of the variation in Australia's export flows. As a check for heteroscedasticity indicated a potential problem, we also rerun the regression in a modified form to avoid possibly misleading results. It turned out however, that the coefficient estimates hardly changed at all, so we used the original estimates to assess export potential.

As it happened, the actual export value is somewhat larger than the predicted one. According to this way of reasoning, Australia "overutilised" its export potential by 131.5 million US dollars. This result goes in the same direction as the one suggested by the trade intensity approach, although the latter discrepancy between actual and "expected" exports is rather small. It may also be noted that the overutilisation figure for Hong Kong is over US$ 1200 million, which indicates that the "true" figure for China is substantially larger than the one we obtained. (Despite the fact that Japan is Australia's most important export market, the country still seems to hold great potential for more exports; our model suggests that Japan's market potential is under-utilised by almost US$ 7 billion. Also the markets of New Zealand, interestingly enough, do not appear to be fully exploited.)

4. EXPORT POTENTIAL IN CHINA IN 2003 - SOME ROUGH INDICATORS

Predicting the development of the Chinese market potential for Australian goods is, of course, extremely hazardous. It is by no means certain that the Chinese economy will go on developing at the same rate as has been the case during the last couple of decades. The re-unification of Hong Kong with China will cause a one-time shift in the trade figures, but may have other less easily detected effects on trade as well. Finally, the picture may change if the structure of Australian exports changes substantially during the period. All this notwithstanding, it is useful to try to assess what export values may be reasonably expected ten years from the year evaluated by our model (1993).

For the sake of obtaining a benchmark value, we fitted an exponential trend to the export values between 1981 and 1993 and extrapolated the trend to 2002-3.[1]

The figure, on the next page, shows clearly that the fit of the trend line is not very impressive; for example, a dent apparently caused by the Tiananmen incident in 1989 is clearly detectable. This, and obvious risks for this type of exogenous disturbances also in the future makes extrapolation hazardous. Aware of the heroic nature of the task, we arrived at an export figure for 2002-03 of A$ 3159 million (US$ 2148 million at 1993 exchange rates). Recent developments seem to suggest (see Figure 13.2) that this figure may be too small. On the other hand, new backlashes may occur.

---

1 The trend is calculated from export values in Australian dollars, to avoid the exchange problem in the time series. The export price index has been used to inflate the values to the price level of 1993-4.

Figure 13.2: Trend of Australian Exports to China, 1981-2 - 1992-93

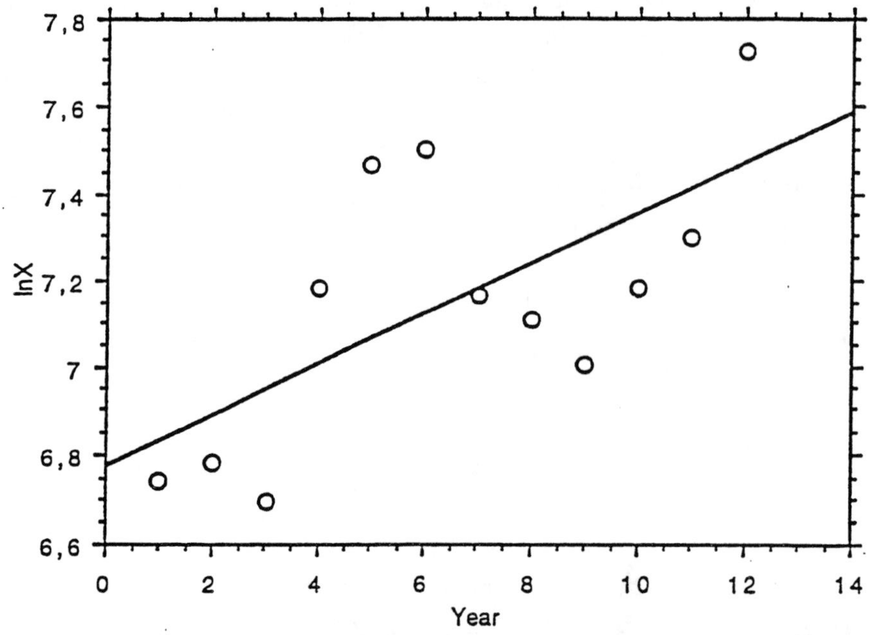

$$\ln X = 6{,}782 + {,}058 * \text{Year};\ R^2 = 0.432$$

Note: Year 1 = 1981-82, and so on.
Source: The relevant data are from ABS (1994) and IMF (1994).

Trend extrapolations are, of course, a naive form of forecasts, since there is no guarantee that exports will develop at the same rate in the future as they have in the past. A more sophisticated way is to use our regression model for generating predictions. There are, however, at least two problems related to this method: Firstly, we cannot know whether the model parameters are stable enough to be useful years from now. Secondly, we need estimates of the independent variables for 2003 to plug into the model.

The first of these problems we can do little about. The second one, although difficult, can partly be overcome by "educated guessing". (Possibly, some kind of sensitivity analysis could be used.) Here, we simply assumed that the rate of growth of China's real GDP will be the same as for the period 1980-1993. (This assumption is likely to lead to erring on the high side as the growth rate of China during the period mentioned is probably overestimated. On the other hand, further trade liberalisation in China should work in the opposite direction.) This gives an export potential of US$ 3340 million (A$ 4911 at 1993 exchange rate) which is almost twice the actual exports in 1993 (but still not more than about the same as the actual exports to Korea during that year). This means that there is room for expansion but also that it may take much longer until China becomes a really important export market for Australia. (The small "income elasticity" (0.94) for Australian exports indicates this already.)

5. CONCLUSIONS

Our results may seem somewhat disappointing at the first glance. There does not seem to exist any unutilised export potential at the moment (which actually suggests that Australian exporters have done quite well already) and the potential increase during the next eight years appears to be rather modest as well. The continuing liberalisation of imports in China may change the outcome in a positive direction, but then again, unexpected backlashes in the development of the country may also occur.

There is no reason for pessimism, however. Apart from the obvious risk that our models are too simplified to give reliable estimates, the aggregate approach taken in this chapter conceals the fact that single products or product groups may have a possibility to do much better than the average. Furthermore, in this chapter we have dealt only with merchandise trade. As a matter of fact, Australia today may have a comparative advantage in many services (education, computer technology etc.) which could be exploited. Traditional Australian exports, dominated by primary goods, do seem to have limited expansion prospects, even if the situation for different commodities may be quite different also in this case.

REFERENCES

ABS (1994) *International Merchandise Trade Australia*, Catalogue No. 5422.0, Canberra.

Blomqvist, H.C. (1994) "Determinants of Intra-Regional Trade Flows in East Asia. A Gravity Approach", in Nguyen, D.T. and Roy, K.C. (eds.) *Economic Reforms, Liberalization and Trade in the Asia Pacific Region*, Wiley Eastern, New Delhi.

Blomqvist, H.C. (1995) Assessing Market Potential: The Case of ASEAN as a Market for Finnish Exporters. Discussion Papers No. 185, Department of Economics, University of Queensland, Brisbane.

Chai, J.C.H. and Sun, H. (1993) Liberalising Foreign Trade: Experience of China. Discussion Paper No. 135, Department of Economics, University of Queensland, Brisbane.

Drysdale, P. (1988) *International Economic Pluralism. Economic Policy in East Asia and the Pacific*, Allen & Unwin, Sydney.

Elek, A. (1992) "Trade Policy Options for the Asia-Pacific Region in the 1990s: the Potential of Open Regionalism", *American Economic Review*, Vol. 82.

IMF (1994), *International Financial Statistics Year Book*, IMF, Washington, D.C.

Leamer, E.E. (1984) *Sources of International Comparative Advantage*, MIT Press, Cambridge, MA.

Leamer, E.E. and Stern, R.M. (1970) *Quantitative International Economics*, Allyn and Bacon, Boston.

Srinivasan, T.N. (ed.) (1994) *Agriculture and Trade in China and India*, ICEG, San Francisco.

USIS (1994) *Economic Backgrounder*, USIS, Hong Kong.

14. AUSTRALIA'S EXPORT PERFORMANCE IN CHINA WITH SPECIAL REFERENCE TO FOOD INDUSTRY

Joseph C.H. Chai and Paul Riethmuller

1. INTRODUCTION

In recent years there has been an euphoria in Australia over the prospects of rapid expansion of Australia's processed food exports to Asia. This euphoria has been fuelled by the following sets of factors (McKinsey 1992, Commonwealth of Australia 1994, EAAU 1994, and Samuel, 1994). First, the Asian market is perceived as huge as three of the world's most populous nations (China, India and Indonesia) are located in Asia. Second, the market has been growing rapidly, with rates of growth well above the 2.9 per cent average for the world between 1980 and 1994. The region as a whole is likely to continue to be the most rapid growing region of the world. Third, the middle class with high consumer spending power in the region is expected to rise rapidly. It is estimated that accompanying the continued rapid growth of its economy, Asian middle class will double or triple in the next decade. By the year 2000, it is predicted that its number not counting Japan will rise to 1 billion (*The Australian*, 13 March 1996). By the turn of this century, Asian affluents with an annual income exceeding US$10,000 will far exceed that of the US and Western Europe combined (McKinsey, 1992, p. 23). Fourth, Asian consumers' taste is changing with increased affluence. They are eating more high protein and fats, and processed foods including Western-style foods. Last, not least, Australia, has the competitive advantage in supplying food for Asia as compared to other Western suppliers such as the US and the EU because of its geographical proximity to Asia and clean environment, high land-man ratio, and expertise in food processing and marketing.

Recently this euphoria is somewhat dampened by the more sober assessment of Heilbron and Larkin (1995) which distinguished between Asian and Western foods. Their study suggests that while the market for Asian food in Asia is growing, the market for Western food is relatively small and its growth is less than certain. Here Australian food processors in order to increase their market share in Asia need to focus on both Asian as well as the Western foods.

This chapter contributes to the current debate by focusing Australia's processed food export performance in China. The purpose of this chapter is to use China as a case study to test some of the important theses as suggested by the above studies. Specifically, it attempts to probe into the following issues: Is the Chinese market for Western processed food growing? How competitive is the Australian suppliers as compared to other Western food suppliers in Chinese markets? What are the major determinants of their varying competitiveness? What policy conclusions can be drawn for the Australian companies to enhance their competitive position in Chinese processed food markets?

There are several reasons why China was chosen for the case study. First, China as the world's most populous country represents the largest potential food market in the world. Second, Chinese economy has been expanding at an annual rate of 10 per cent a year during 1979-1994 (*ZGTJNJ* 1995, p. 21), which makes China the most rapid growing economy in Asia. Third, although, the average Chinese has little to spend currently, those living in the coastal cities already has a per-capita income higher than parts of Southeast Asia (*EIU*, 1994, p. x). It is estimated by the turn of the century Chinese affluents with an annual earning over $US1,000 would reach 300 million (*The Australian*, 2 May 1996). Fourth, there has been a significant change in Chinese consumer tastes in the recent years. According to the Beijing's Austrade report, consumption of processed foods *including* Western style foods has been on the rise in China (*Courier Mail*, 28 September 1994).

The organisation of the chapter is as follows. Section 2 clarifies the distinction between Western and Asian food and examine the myth of Westernisation of Asian taste. Section 3 assesses the performance of Australia and other major Western suppliers to Chinese processed food market and identifies the major determinants of their varying performance. Section 4 evaluates the role of FDI and its impact on Western food suppliers' export performance in China. The chapter concludes with a brief discussion of the implications of the result of the study for trade policy.

Since this study is concerned with the ability of Australia to manufacture and market high value finished goods in competitive Asian market, it focuses mainly on highly processed food (HPF). The definition of HPF in this study is essentially based on that Agri-Food Council (*EAAU*, 1994b p. 331). They include 20 products as listed in Table 14.5.

2. WESTERN VS ASIAN FOOD AND THE MYTH OF WESTERNISATION OF ASIAN TASTE

Most of the analysts in their studies of Asian food market do not have any clear criterion in distinguishing between Western and Asian food. Food are loosely classified as Western and Asian whereas Asian food are simply equated with the traditional Asian food. The grey area of modern Asian food have either been excluded or simply lumped together with the group of Western food. It is true that there has been a change in Asian consumers' taste with a greater emphasis on quality and convenience because of the increased income per capita, the increased female participation in labor forces, the increased value of leisure time due to increased availability of leisure activities and the increased electrification of the kitchen in Asian countries. But this "modernisation" of Asian taste could hardly be considered as "westernisation". Asian food processors in manufacturing modern Asian food to meet this modernisation of Asian taste make use of Western food processing and packaging technology and also Western ingredients, but the finished products ultimately have to be adapted to Asian taste and, hence, could not be simply classified as "Western" food.

Samuel (1994) approached the problem by asking the Chinese urban consumers directly through the consumers' survey what constitutes the distinction between Western and traditional Chinese processed food. The results are shown in the Appendix. China is a large country with a large variety of ethnic and consumer tastes. It is well known that there is a significant taste difference between the Eastern and Western Chinese and within the Eastern region of China between the Northern and Southern Chinese. Even within the Southern Chinese, the tastes of Hunaneses are clearly distinctive from the Cantoneses. Hence it is difficult for the Chinese to agree among themselves what constitutes traditional Chinese food, let alone the more elusive question of what constitutes Western food. The problematic nature of the responses arrived at in this type of consumer survey is obvious from the Appendix. European ham and bacon are clearly traditional Western food but Chinese bacon could hardly be regarded as Western. Similarly one could hardly disagree that tuna and sardine canned fish, chocolate, ice cream, canned oranges, fruit juices, tea bags and ox tail canned soup are Western foods. However, few Westerners would agree that canned fried dace with black bean sauce, red bean paste ice cream, sour prune juice, ginseng tea bags, shark-fin canned soup, etc., could be regarded as Western foods.

This chapter utilizes the revealed preference approach to identify the genuine Western food. It is based on the assumptions that trade data are similar to household expenditure data as it reveals a country's consumers' preference, and that food can be classified according to the countries of origin. Since countries with a predominant European population like the US, Australia, New Zealand, EU and Canada have a comparative advantage in the production of Western processed food, foods imported from these countries are considered as genuine Western food. Processed foods imported from Asian countries are likely to be both traditional and modernised Asian foods adapted to Asian tastes. Hence they are considered as Asian foods. This approach is consistent with the prevalent observation that in most Asian countries consumers tend to identify the product characteristic with country of its origin. The weakness of this classification is that the demand for Western processed foods in Asian countries may be underestimated owing to import substitution.

Between 1988 and 1994, Chinese per capita income expanded at an annual average rate of 8 per cent (*ZGTJNJ*, 1995). Total import demand for the 20 HPFs grew at an annual average rate of approximately 3 per cent and China has become an important market for both the non-Western and Western food exporters. Western processed food suppliers in Chinese markets are mainly confined to EU, US, Australia and New Zealand. Imports from other countries with a predominant European population are relatively small. An analysis of five major processed foods in SITC 022, 023, 0712, 1124 and 091 which accounted for 85 and 79 per cent of China's total Western processed food imports in 1988 and 1992 respectively shows that for four out of the five SITC categories the coverage of the above-mentioned four suppliers is 100 per cent. For the other category - SITC 022 - their coverage is between 91 and 97 per cent. Non Western food suppliers in China are mainly confined to Asian countries as expected.

Table 14.1: The Annual Average Share of 4 Major Suppliers of Western HPFs in Chinese Market, 1988-90 and 1991-94

	1988-90	1991-94	Change
	(%)	(%)	(%)
Australia	11.3	8.0	-3.3
USA	6.7	10.4	3.7
EU	36.1	21.7	-14.4
New Zealand	5.4	4.1	-1.3
"Total"	59.5	45.2	-14.3

Source: UN *Commodity Trade Statistics* and *China Custom Statistics 1993 and 1994.*

Table 14.1 reviews that while China's total import demand for processed food rose during this period, Chinese import demand for Western food actually declined. Its demand for imports of Asian processed food, on the other hand, increased at an annual average of approximately 8 per cent, matching the rate of growth of Chinese income per person during the same period. The divergent growth of Chinese demand for Western and Asian processed food caused the share of Western suppliers in Chinese market to tumble. As is evident in Table 14.1, the annual average market share of Western exporters during the two periods under investigation fell from around 60 per cent in 1988-90 to 45 per cent in 1991-94, a loss in the range of 25 per cent. The heaviest losers in absolute terms were the EU and Australia. These countries had the largest and second largest share of the Chinese market in 1988. Table 14.1 also reveals that, in contrast to the other Western exporters, the US had managed to capture some of the losses of the other Western food exporters and to increase its market share significantly. In the second half of the 1990s the US had displaced Australia as the second largest supplier of Western processed food to China.

The declining market share of "Western" processed food in Chinese markets begs the question whether such loss was confined only to China because of the uniqueness of its market condition. To shed light on this issue, the performance of Western processed food in other Asian markets was also considered. Five neighbouring Asian countries of China were investigated: Hong Kong, Singapore, South Korea, Thailand and Malaysia. The selection of these countries were determined by data availability in *UN Commodity Trade Statistics Series*.

Table 14.2: The Market Share of 4 Major Suppliers of Western HPFs in Hong Kong, Singapore, South Korea, Thailand and Malaysia

Country	1988	1992
	(%)	(%)
Hong Kong	39	42
Singapore	51	58
S. Korea	67	56[a]
Thailand	81[b]	72[c]
Malaysia	73	51[a]

Note: a. 1991
b. 1986
c. 1990
Source: UN, *Commodity Trade Statistics.*

The results, presented in Table 14.2, show that a decreasing market share of Western processed foods was not restricted to China. Only in two out of five countries - Hong Kong and Singapore - were Western processed foods able to gain market share between the late 1980s and the early 1990s. These two countries happened to be very high income countries where almost all of the very westernized population lived in urban areas. Western processed food lost market share in South Korea, Thailand and Malaysia. The extent of the loss was substantial, ranging from 10 to almost 20 percentage points during a period in which all three countries experienced a sharp rise in per person income.

3. AUSTRALIA'S EXPORT PERFORMANCE AS COMPARED TO THAT OF THE US, EU AND NEW ZEALAND

Table 14.3 focuses exclusively on Chinese imports of Western processed foods. It shows that the import shares of the USA and EU changed considerably between 1988-90 and 1991-94. On the other hand, Australia's share fell only slightly while New Zealand's share was almost unchanged. The decline of the Australian and EU share vis-à-vis the US begs the question of what has caused their share to decline.

Table 14.3: The Annual Average Share of 4 Major Exporters in Chinese Western HPFs Market, 1988-90 and 1991-94

	1988-90	1991-94	Change
	(%)	(%)	(%)
Australia	19	18	-1
USA	11	24	+13
EU	60	49	-11
New Zealand	9	9	0

Note: Western HPFs are Chinese total HPF imports from the 4 major suppliers.
Source: See Table 14.1.

A variety of techniques has been developed to explain the changes in market shares of an exporting country over time. Constant market share (CMS) has been one popular approach. Market share of a given country is defined as the ratio between q and Q. q and Q are the total exports of the focus country and the "world" or standard. World exports (Q) are the sum of exports of all competitors of the country in question. Thus, a change in q/Q depends on the relative export growth of the focus country and the "world". The relative export growth of a focus country in turn, depends on (a) its base-year exports and (b) the change in exports of the focus country during the focus period. CMS is essentially a technique to decompose the sources of export change of the focus country, $\dot{q}$:

$$\dot{q} \equiv s\dot{Q} + [\sum_i s_i \dot{Q}_i - s\dot{Q}] + [\sum_i \sum_j s_{ij} \dot{Q}_{ij} - \sum_i s_i \dot{Q}_i] + \sum_i \sum_j Q_{ij} \dot{s}_{ij} \qquad (1)$$

Where i refers to a particular commodity and j to a particular importing region (Richardson, 1971, p. 229). The first term represents the increase of the focus country's exports due to the general increase in the "world" exports. The second term is the commodity effect representing the additional change of the focus country's exports due to the initial commodity composition of its exports. The third term is known as market effect representing the additional change of the focus country's exports due to its initial market distribution. If the focus country's export structure is more concentrated on high-growth commodities and markets than is the "world" export structure, these second and third term will be positive; and vice versa. The last term is a residual which reflects the changes in competitiveness of the focus country's exports.

The application of traditional CMS to analyse the export change of a focus country encountered several problems (Richardson, 1971). One of these is the index problem. The results of the CMS analysis depends on the year chosen to calculate the base year market share and commodity composition. In the following analysis the period of the analysis has been divided into two intervals, 1988-90 and 1991-94, and the decomposition is conducted using the average instead of yearly value within each interval. This has the effect to prevent the year chosen as the base year to dominate the results and, hence, avoid the index problem.

Another problem is the trade value problem according to which, the commodity, market, and competitive effects may be of opposite sign depending on the use of values or quantities. To test the significance of this difference, we have compared the results for a set of selected HPFs (SITC 022, 023, 0712 and 1124) and found that there is no significant difference between the two sets of results based on value and quantity. Hence, we have continued to use the trade value in our following analysis.

Since this chapter focuses only on China, there is only one market and, hence, no market effect. Thus, the modified CMS model for China is as follows:

$$\dot{q} = s\dot{Q} + [\sum_i s_i \dot{Q}_i - s\dot{Q}] + \sum_i Q_i \dot{s}_i \qquad (2)$$

The impact of growth, commodity and competitiveness effect on changes of export value of the four major competitors in the Chinese market, as found from the CMS analysis, is shown in Table 14.4. The last column of the table indicates that all competitors, with the exception of the US, shed their values of exports to China in the first half of the 1990s as compared to late 1980s. The fall was the heaviest for the EU, followed by Australia and New Zealand. The US, on the other hand, has been able to achieve a significant increase of its exports to China inspite of the general decline of Chinese import demand for Western processed food. As the percentage distribution in the parentheses of the Table indicates the heavy fall of the export values of the EU was mainly caused by its negative growth effect or the general decline of Chinese import demand for Western processed food. But as the negative commodity effect and residual suggests, its fall was also aggravated by the loss of competitiveness of their exports and their over-concentration in commodities which suffered the heaviest import cuts by the Chinese authorities.

Table 14.5 shows the types of food which had experienced high and low growth during this period. Only 5 per cent of EU initial export commodities were concentrated in high-growth area compared with 48 and 20 per cent respectively of the US and Australia.

The decline of Australia's export value was mainly caused by the general decline of Chinese demand for Western processed foods and its loss of competitiveness. However its decline in export value was less severe than EU mainly because of its favourable initial export structure.

US exports in value terms, increased significantly during this period because of its gain in competitiveness as well as its favourable initial export composition. In contrast, although, New Zealand had been able to increase its competitiveness during this period, its export values, nevertheless, declined owing both to general decline of Chinese demand as well as its unfavourable initial export composition which almost exclusively consisted of low growth commodities in Chinese markets.

Table 14.4: Results of CMS Analysis (1988-90 to 1991-94) (All 20 Product Groups)

Country	Growth effect	Commodity effect	Residual	Total
	(US$000)	(US$000)	(US$000)	(US$000)
Australia	-3,746 (-88%)	1,340 (31%)	-1,872 (-44%)	-4,278 (-100%)
US	-2,168 (-28%)	4,301 (55%)	5,719 (73%)	7,852 (100%)
EU	-11,828 (-55%)	-3,633 (-17%)	-6,167 (-29%)	-21,628 (-100%)
New Zealand	-1,774 (-107%)	-554 (-33%)	669 (40%)	-1,659 (-100%)

Note: Figures in parentheses are percentage distribution. Due to rounding the individual percentage figures may not add up to 100.
Source: See Table 14.1.

The relative competitiveness of a country's exports is generally assumed to be a function of that country's relative export prices. Other factors such as product quality, the existence of export subsidies, and marketing strategies are also important determinants of a country's relative export competitiveness. As indicated by the negative residual values in Table 14.4, Australia's relative competitiveness as compared to that of

Table 14.5: Percentage Change of Imports of 20 Western HPFs in Chinese Market, 1988-90 and 1991-94

	Change	Remarks
	(%)	
High-Growth Commodities		
Meat, salted, dried, smoked (012)	...	increase from zero to 296 thousand USD
Fish, salted, dried, smoked (035)	...	increase from zero to 817 thousand USD
Chocolate and products (073)	600	
Cheese and curd (024)	348	
Fish, prepared, preserved, NES (037)	211	
Beer, ale, stout, porter (1123)	211	
Vegetables, prepared & preserved	163	
(056)	104	
Wine of fresh grapes (1121)	88	
Bakery products (0484)	87	
Margarine and shortening (091)	76	
Malt including flour (0482)	52	
Sugar candy, non chocolate (062)	20	
Fruit, preserved & prepared (058)		
Low-Growth Commodities		
	-96	
Cocoa powder, unsweetened (0722)	-84	
Butter (023)	-84	
Coffee extracts, essences (0712)	-47	
Meat, prepared, preserved NES (014)	-25	
Distilled alcoholic beverage (1124)	-19	
Non-alcoholic beverage (111)	-16	
Milk and cream (022)		

Source: See Table 14.1.

the US has declined. The following section examines two important factors, i.e. differences in relative prices and in FDI strategy in influencing Australia's relative competitiveness.

To shed light on the relationship between Australia's relative shares and relative prices vis-à-vis the US, Table 14.6 compares the change in Australia's relative share in volume terms with the change in relative prices in five major commodities in which both Australia and the US were major competitors in the Chinese market. This shows that out of the five commodities Australia has lost ground to the US in four commodities. More importantly, out of the five commodities compared, the change of Australia's relative share in four commodities can be explained by its relative price changes. For example, the loss of ground of Australia's exports of milk and cream (022), margarine (091) and chocolate and products (073) to the US can be explained by the increase of the relative prices of Australia's exports.

Table 14.6: Average Annual Relative Share and Prices of Australia's Five HPF Exports to China as Compared with the US, 1988-90 and 1991-94

SITC	Relative Share		Relative Prices	
	1988-90	1991-94	1988-90	1991-94
022	2.88	0.66	1.40	1.46
0712	2.95	2.19	2.43	1.29
091	12.62	8.01	0.71	0.81
058	0.04	0.09	1.58	1.20
073	1.95	0.61	1.11	1.23

Note: Relative shares are Australia's volume share divided by that of the US; and relative prices are ratios of Australia unit value to that of the US.

Source: See Table 14.1.

The conventional market share equation approach considers relative market share of a country as a function of its relative prices and its lagged market share as it is hypothesised that changes in market share do not respond immediately to changes in relative prices. We have attempted to estimate this market share equations for the 5 commodities mentioned above for the period 1988-1994. The result of the estimate indicates that the coefficients of both of the two independent variables (relative prices and lagged market share) are of correct sign. However the R^2 value is poor and none of the coefficient estimates are found to be statistically significant at 0.10 per cent level. This relatively poor statistical quality of the estimates is likely due to the limited number of observations available for each product owing to the relatively short time span considered.

The general decline of Australia's relative price competitiveness as contrast to the US warrants brief discussion. The decline of price competitiveness of a country's exports may be caused by an appreciation of that country's real exchange rate and/or the export price subsidies of that country's competitor. During the period under investigation there has been a significant depreciation of the Australian dollar. The market rate of the Australian dollar has dropped from an average of 80 US cents in 1988-90 to a low of 73 US cents during 1991-94. Similarly, the real effective exchange rate of Australian dollar has depreciated by almost 10 per cent between 1990 and 1994 (IMF). Since the exchange rate does not seem to be the factor behind Australia's loss of relative price competitiveness, the price subsidies of competing exporters come into focus. In fact, there are some analysts in Australia who attribute the increased US share in Asian food market to programs such as the Export Enhancement Programme (EEP) and the Dairy Export Incentive Program (DEIP). Both of these programs were operating during the period of this study and have led to increased US market share in farm products through subsidised sale to this market (Voon, 1994, Ahmadi-Esfahani and Jensen, 1994; Roberts and Andrews, 1994). The United States as part of its World Trade Organisation commitments resulting from the Uruguay Round has established annual export subsidy ceilings by commodity and maximum budgetary expenditure. Besides programs run from Washington, many of the US states also operate programs designed to boost exports (GAO, 1990).

4. FDI AND EXPORT GROWTH

Apart from relative prices, the choice of appropriate marketing strategy is also an important determinant of a country's relative export competitiveness. According to a survey conducted in 1985 in ten Asian countries marketing and distribution costs accounted for 53 per cent of the retail price of the imported non-durable consumers goods in the final market (ESCAP/UNCTC). Thus, the choice of right entry mode to reduce these costs can significantly enhance a country's relative competitiveness in the final market.

According to the entry mode literature, there are basically three types to choose from: (1) indirect or direct exports utilizing the agents in either the home or target country; (2) contractual entry mode based on licensing and franchising of foreign manufacturing companies; and (3) FDI via setting up marketing and distribution or assembly and manufacturing facilities in the target countries.

The optimal choice of whether to use market transaction via entry mode (1) and (2) or setting up branches and subsidiary (entry mode 3) boils down to the issue whether the firm should forward integrate or not. The decision rule according to the transaction cost approach is to minimize the sum of "production" and transaction cost. "Production" cost is the cost of actually performing the marketing-distribution function. According to the channel volume hypothesis, "production" cost is inversely related to the sale volume or the size of foreign market. Due to economies of scale the larger the market size, the higher is the degree of forward integration. Transaction cost is the cost of governing the distribution system. The magnitude of such cost is determined by the cost of monitoring and enforcement of distributor contract and the vulnerability of the firm to opportunistic behaviour by outside agents because of asymmetry of information etc. Transaction cost is high the less competitive the market for distribution services in the target country, the higher the asset specificity or brand knowledge and confidential inside information required from the agents, the greater degree of environmental uncertainty of the target country and the more dissimilar the target country's environment to that of the home country.

In the case of the distribution of high value processed food in China, the cost of relying on agents is likely to be higher as the market for distribution services is not well developed in China and the Chinese market environment is less predictable and very dissimilar to the Western environment. Furthermore, the size of Chinese market is relatively large as compared to other Asian countries, thus forward integration or FDI approach appears to be the most sensible option. Unfortunately, this entry mode has been least utilized by the Australian food processor as compared to its Western counterparts such as the US. Most of the Australian-owned food processors are small and medium firms which are short of financial resources and expertise to integrate forward in China. The twenty largest food processors in Australia, accounting for just under half of the industry's turnover in 1991-92 have a high level of foreign involvement in their operations (BIE 1996). Hence their entry-mode decision in China is likely to be made at the headquarters in Europe and North America.

The lack of long-term commitment of Australian firms in China is evident from its minute FDI in China. The sum of its realized FDI in China stood at US$340.4 million by the end of 1993. This is equivalent to only 1 per cent of Australia's FDI abroad. The bulk of Australia's outward FDI went to the US and UK. Its share in total stock of Chinese FDI intake was also negligible (see Table 14.7). Its share in total stock of Chinese FDI intake in food and beverage sector in particular was also minute despite the fact that some Australian food processors such as Cadbury Schweppes and Fosters Brewing group have become increasingly active in the Chinese investment market. Thus, for example, out of the 2689 foreign invested enterprises approved in 1992 in the food industry, including tobacco and animal feed, the majority were owned by Hong Kong, Taiwan, Thai, Japanese and other Asian firms. Only about 10 per cent originated from the West. Among the Western investors in the food sector, US firms were heavily presented. They accounted for about 8 per cent of total foreign invested enterprises in this sector. Australia and the EU shares were only 1.1 and 1.4 per cent respectively (MOFTEC 1993).

Studies show that FDI and export expansion of the home country are closely linked. FDI enables firms to gain an insider status in target country and to get closer to customers (Market Penetration Task Force 1994). It also enables firms to gain access to relevant government and business leaders in the target country (McKinsey 1992). Investment links also adds substantially to knowledge of trends and opportunities in the target country of the investing firms and strengthen their awareness of export opportunities (EAAU 1994a, p. 15). Lastly, not least FDI contributes strongly to export expansion of the home country by generating additional sales of finished goods, intermediate goods, capital goods and services by the investing or other firms in home country in the target country (EAAU, 1994a, p. 12).

The relatively close link between FDI and export expansion is evident from Table 14.7. The market share of Chinese imports of individual countries is closely corresponding to their share in China's total FDI intake. The most important foreign investors in China happened to be the largest supplier to the Chinese market. The rank correlation coefficient between the investment and import share ranking is 0.78 which is statistically significant at the 1% level.

The positive impact of Australia's investment in China on its export growth is also confirmed by the following regression estimate:

$$X_A = \underset{(3.66)}{518.4} + \underset{(4.34)^{**}}{14.9\,M_c} + \underset{(1.58)^{*}}{3.4\,I_A} - \underset{(-1.29)}{0.2\,I_{US}}$$

$R^2 = 88.1 \quad F = 17.3$

*,** significant at 10 and 5 per cent level respectively.

Table 14.7: Import and Investment Share in China by Country of Origin, 1992

	Import Share[a]	Investment Share[b]
Hong Kong	0.25	0.68
Japan	0.17	0.07
EU	0.12	0.02
USA	0.11	0.05
Taiwan	0.07	0.09
S. Korea	0.03	0.01
Australia	0.02	negl.
Canada	0.02	0.01
Indonesia	0.02	negl.
Singapore	0.01	0.01

Notes: a. Share in Chinese total imports
b. Share in China's total stock of FDI (realized) intake.
Sources: See Table 14.1 and *ZGTJNJ*, various issues.

Where X_A is Australia's total exports to China during 1983-93, M_c China's total imports which is an indicator of Chinese market size, I_A and I_{US} are FDI by Australia and the US in China respectively during the same period. Both the exports and FDI data were drawn from the sources given in Table 14.7. Although the statistical quality of the regression equation is not as strong as expected, owing to the limited number of observations used or to the model misspecification, it does suggest that Australian FDI in China is important in determining its export growth in China. The result also indicates that FDI of competing countries such as the US appears to negatively influence Australian export expansion in China.

5. CONCLUSIONS

This chapter is an exploratory study of the myth of Westernization of Asian taste focusing on the comparative performance of Western food processors in Chinese market. Due to the limited data available, the conclusions reached in this study should be regarded as highly tentative and are to be confirmed when more data are available.

The results of the study indicate that despite the rapid increase of its per capita income in the recent years, Chinese import demand for Western processed food has actually declined. The average annual market share of Western processed food suppliers was reduced from 60 to 45 per cent between 1989-90 and 1991-94. An analysis of the market share of Western food processors in other Asian markets also shows similar results. With the exception of Hong Kong and Singapore, the market share of Western food processors in middle income Asian countries such as South Korea, Malaysia and Thailand also declined during the period under investigation despite the rapid growth of their income per capita. Thus the hypotheses of the Westernization of Asian tastes cannot be confirmed in these countries.

The performance of individual Western food processors in Chinese market was mixed. While Australia's and EU's market share declined, the US has been able to double its share in Chinese market during the investigation period. The CMS results show that the superior performance of US can mainly be explained by its gain in price competitiveness and concentration of its export structure in high-growth products. The increased US export price competitiveness in turn appears to be closely linked to its EEP. The relative decline of Australia's market share, on the other hand, was partly due to the decline of its price competitiveness. There are indications that it was also partly caused by the under-presence of Australia's FDI in China.

The policy implications of the above findings are three fold. First, in a low income country like China, the market for Western processed food is small and its growth potential should not be overrated. However, the growth potential for processed food adapted to Asian taste is much larger. Thus Australian food processors should focus more on Asian rather than Western processed foods. This observation is consistent with those of other studies (Gastin, 1993; Heilbron and Larkin, 1994). Second, in view of the close linkage between FDI and export growth, Australia needs to step up its investment presence in China. Third, the relative strength of Australian food processors lies with its access to raw materials, food processing technology and marketing expertise, whereas the comparative advantage of Asian food processors lies with their inside knowledge of Asian tastes and distribution networks. Thus it is essential that a strategic alliance should be forged between the two in order to capture an increased market share in the rapidly growing Asian economies.

REFERENCES

Ahmadi-Esfahani, F.Z. and Jensen, P.H. (1994) "Impact of the US-EC Price War on Major Wheat Exporters' Shares of the Chinese Market", *Agricultural Economics*, 10: 61-70.

BIE (Bureau of Industry Economics) (1996) *Evaluation of the Agri-Food Strategy*, Report 96/12, AGPS, Canberra.

Commonwealth of Australia (1994), *Food into Asia: The Next Step*, AGPS, Canberra.

EAAU (East Asia Analytical Unit) (1994a) *Changing Track: Australian Investment in Southeast Asia*, AGPS, Canberra.

EAAU (East Asia Analytical Unit) (1994b) *Subsistence to Supermarket: Food and Agricultural Transformation in Southeast Asia*, AGPS, Canberra.

EIU (Economic Intelligence Unit) (1994) *Distribution in China: Getting Down to the Nuts and Bolts*, Hong Kong.

ESCAP/UNCTC (United Nations Economic and Social Commission for Asia and the Pacific/United Nations Centre for Transnational Corporations) (1985) *Multinational Trading Corporations in Selected Asian and Pacific Countries*, Bangkok.

GAO (General Accounting Office) (1990) *International Trade: Foreign Market Development for High Value Agricultural Products*, GAO/NSIAD - 90-47, Washington, January.

Gastin, D. (1993) *Agribusiness and Processed Food Development in Southeast Asia*, RIRDC, Canberra.

Heilbron, S., and Larkin, J.T. (1995) *Corporate Structures and Strategies: Penetrating Asian Markets*, RIRDC, Canberra.

IMF, *International Financial Statistics*, various issues.

McKinsey & Company (1992) *Capturing Opportunities in Asian Food Market*, McKinsey Global Institute.

Market Penetration Task Force (1994) *Inside Asia: Australian Companies Becoming Local Players*, AGPS, Canberra.

MOFTEC (Ministry of Foreign Trade and Economic Co-operation) (1993) *Panorama of Foreign Invested Enterprises*, Beijing.

Richardson, J.D. (1971) "Constant Market Share Analysis of Export Growth", *Journal of International Economics*, 1(27): 227-239.

Roberts, I. and Andrews, N. (1994) "US Agriculture: Perspectives on Support Programmes", *Commodities Forecast and Issues*, 1(2): 217-233.

Samuel, S.N. (1994) *The Market for Processed and Beverage Products in China*, RIRDC, Canberra.

Voon, T. (1995) "Chinese Demand for Australian Wheat: Applications of Market Share Models", *Australian Economic Papers*, 33(63): 228-238.

ZGTJNJ (*Zhongguo Tongji Nianjian*), various issues.

APPENDIX

A Classification of Western and Traditional Processed Food and Beverages in China arrived at by consulting 8 ethnic Chinese

Western Food

Beef canned
Lamb canned
Ham
Bacon
Sardine canned
Tuna canned
Salmon canned
Other canned fish
Cow's milk packed liquid
Cow's milk powder
Butter
Cheese
Ice cream
Yoghurt
Other dairy products (litre)
Other dairy products (kg)
Margarine
Lamb oil
Pears canned
Orange canned
Grape canned
Vegetable canned
Fruit juice canned/bottled
Fruit juice packed
Dried fruit juice
Beer bottled
Beer canned
Grape wine white
Grape Wine red
Grape wine dessert
Wine champagne style
Brandy
Whisky
Tea bags
Instant coffee
Canned soups
Packaged soups
Soup stock
Syrups
Chocolate
Biscuits
Breakfast cereals
Bread

Chinese Traditional Food

Beef dried
Pork canned
Pork dried
Liver cooked
Tongue cooked
Duck canned
Duck fried or cooked
Soybean milk (litre)
Soybean milk (kg)
Peanut oil
Sesame oil
Lard
Lychees canned
Vegetables dried
Noodles

Source: Samuel, 1994, p. 60.

15. OPPORTUNITIES AND CHALLENGES IN SINO-AUSTRALIAN WOOL TRADE

Colin Brown

---

1. OPPORTUNITIES AND CHALLENGES IN SINO-AUSTRALIAN WOOL TRADE

Wool occupies a pre-eminent position in Sino-Australian trade. Although there has been a relative shift away from agricultural exports to manufacturing and mineral exports since the early 1980s, raw and semi-processed wool is still Australia's major export to China (Chai, 1995). In 1994/95, Australian wool exports to China amounted to 154kt greasy equivalent valued at $780 million (Wool International, 1996). With changing regional comparative advantage in wool textiles and growing Chinese domestic consumption of wool, this bilateral wool trade has the potential to grow even further. However the growth will not be automatic, nor without potential pitfalls, nor will it be easily won. For instance, China is currently considering imposing a tariff quota regime on its wool imports as part of its accession arrangements to the World Trade Organisation (WTO).

The opportunities and challenges afforded by the Chinese market for the Australian wool industry are captured at an aggregate level in Figure 15.1. Chinese imports of Australian wool have grown from around 20kt at the end of the 1970s to almost 200kt by the mid 1990s. In the process, China has become Australia's major customer for wool accounting for over one-fifth of its total exports. Part of the growth in Chinese imports has been associated with changing comparative advantage in wool textile production which has seen various stages of wool textile production shift from other Asian countries such as Japan and Hong Kong to China. Of more importance for the Australian wool industry, at least in terms of new markets, is the growth in the domestic demand for wool in China. Chinese domestic per capita consumption of wool of around 2kg/annum remains low by (North) Asian standards. Furthermore, consumption in the urban areas exceeds fivefold that in the relatively poorer areas, and a rise of incomes especially in rural areas may greatly increase demand for this income elastic good (CMAP, 1994).

Figure 15.1 also highlights the main challenge associated with Sino-Australian wool trade, namely its volatility. The major crashes in 1983/84 and, in particular, 1989/90 impacted greatly on the Australian industry. A plethora of factors lie behind this volatility with some, such as the boom-bust cycle of the Chinese economy, beyond the scope of the Australian industry. However, many of the challenges relate to the changing nature of the industry. Brown and Longworth (1995) outline the institutional, agribusiness and other changes occurring in the Chinese wool and wool textile industry. For instance, Australian exporters now deal not with a single monolithic Chinese importer but with a multitude of mills and other importers [see Figures 2(a) and 2(b)]. Furthermore, Chinese mills with little prior experience of wool importing now account for much of the growth in wool imports. Although the Australian wool industry can do little about Chinese economic cycles, except to be much more aware of them in the development of their strategies than they have been in the past, there is much they can do with respect to the changing Chinese industry. Longworth and Brown (1995) highlight the enormous opportunities afforded by the recent developments in the Chinese wool and wool textile industries not only in increased exports of raw and semi-processed wool but also in a wide range of agribusiness opportunities.

The developments that have occurred raise a number of questions for the Australian industry. With China now Australia's major customer for wool, should the recently restructured and re-emerging Australian wool industry gear up on such a volatile customer? And what are the best strategies to adopt in order to maximise the opportunities and effectively meet the challenges? Traditional market surveys or consumer studies tend only to highlight the ongoing potential and market trend and leave many questions unanswered such as how some of the volatility can be addressed and what are some of the underlying factors that impact on developments in the Chinese wool and wool textile industries and which are important in developing trade strategies? A number of these issues have been discussed in other fora (see, for example, Longworth and Brown, 1995; Brown and Longworth, 1995; and Brown and Longworth, 1994). This chapter focuses on a specific current challenge facing Sino-Australian wool trade, namely mooted changes to Chinese wool import arrangements. It draws on an analysis of the political economy of Sino-Australian wool trade and examines some of the nuances of Chinese decision making across different administrative levels to identify some of the underlying factors which have led to the mooted changes and how they may best be addressed.

Figure 15.1: Sino-Australian Wool Trade 1973/74 to 1994/95

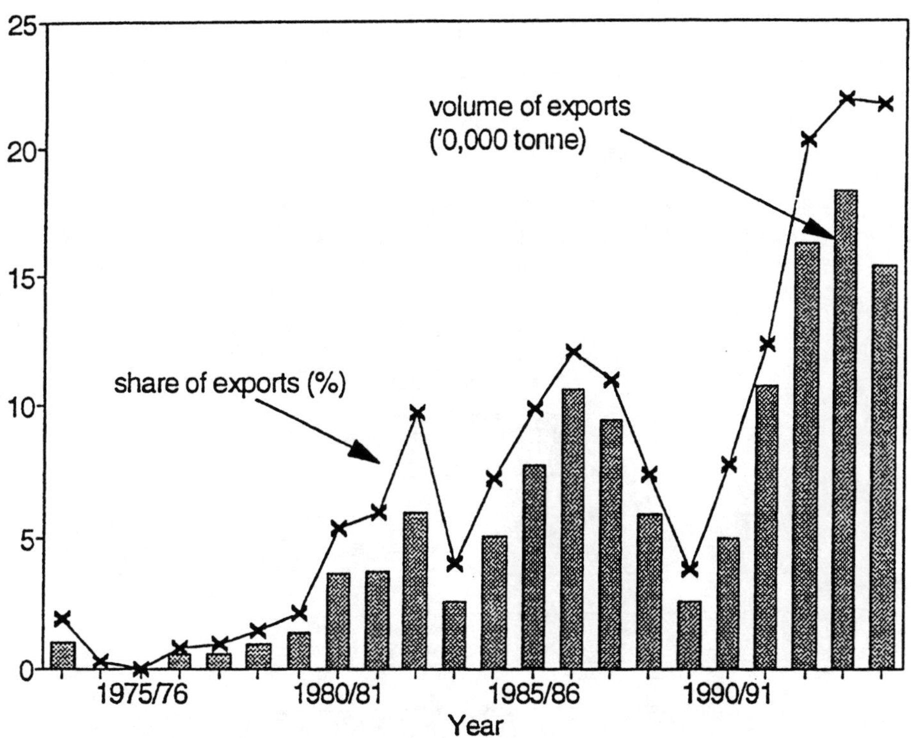

Source: *ABS, IWS, Wool International*

2. TRADE IMPASSE?

One of the more immediate and obvious challenges facing Sino-Australian wool trade are mooted changes to import arrangements. The current import arrangements enable a mix of traditional and non-traditional import channels which are outlined in more detail in Figure 15.2. As part of its attempted accession to the WTO, China is proposing a new quota/tariff regime on wool imports, with higher rates of tariff on above quota levels of import. Although Australia is resisting the general notion of a tariff/quota regime, a lot of the discussion has also centred on how such a regime may be implemented. As with other trade arrangements negotiated in the GATT Uruguay Round, the choice of a base year(s) for the import quotas will determine how binding they will be and their influence on overall imports.[1] Similarly the types of wool to which the quotas are applied will be crucial.

1 China has proposed base year quotas on a three year average of 1991 to 1993 which includes below trend imports in the first two of these years.

Figure 15.2: Wool import channels in China

2(a) Traditional channels

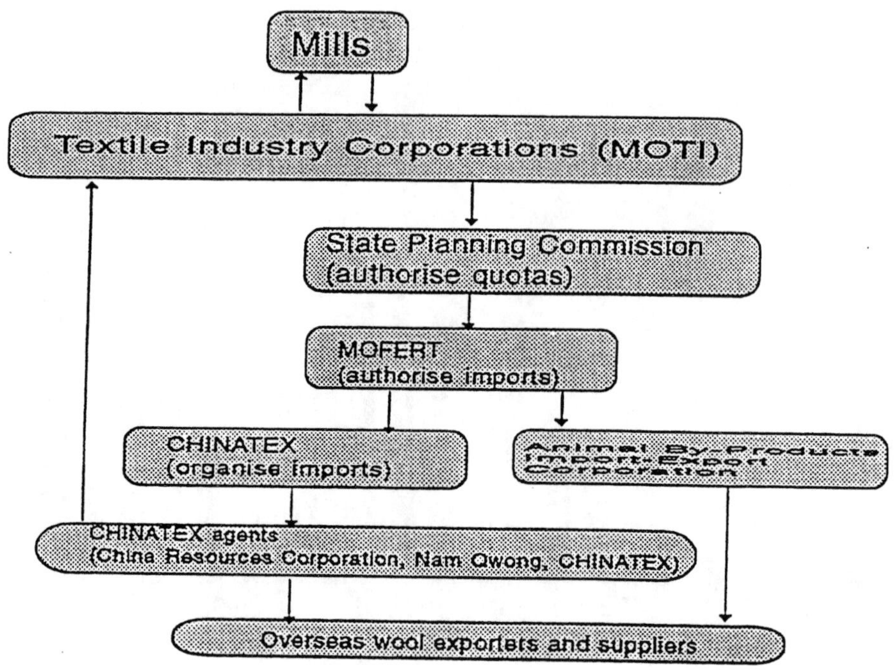

2(b) Non-traditional channels

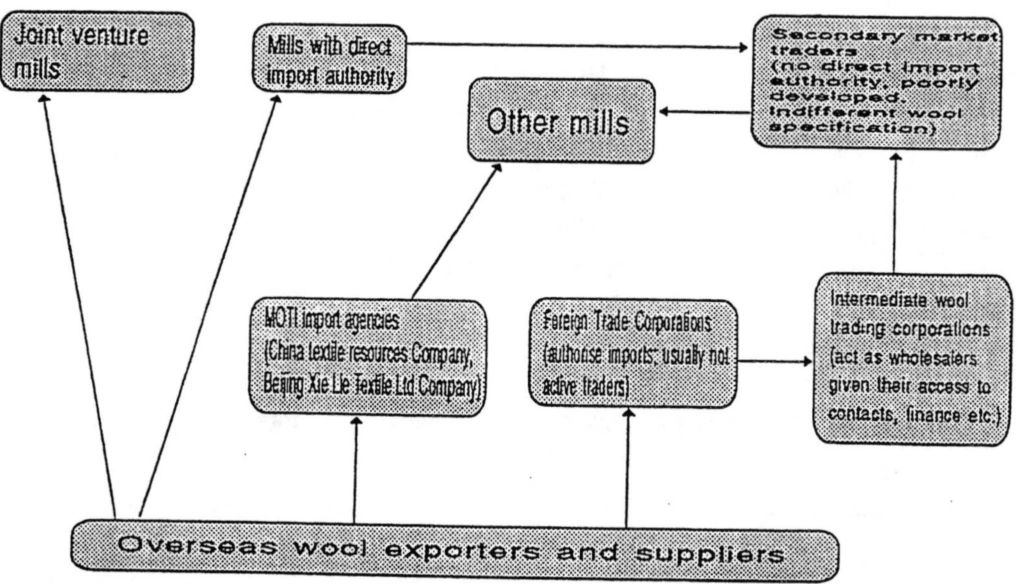

Wool is of importance in a number of bilateral and multilateral trade negotiations with China. Not only is wool important in the bilateral trade between China and Australia, but the two countries dominate world markets for wool and wool textile products. Australia is the world's largest producer and exporter of wool, especially apparel wool. China is the largest consumer and producer of wool textiles, one of the largest importers of raw and semi-processed wool and exporters of wool textiles, and has the third largest sheep flock. Thus policies and market developments in the wool industry of either country will impact on each other and on other wool producing and consuming countries. Thus, for Australia, wool is a major item and source of concern in trade negotiations with China. Other issues dominate China's trade agenda. However, wool is taking on increasing importance as part of China's expanding textile industry and trade.

China has pursued access to the GATT and the WTO for over 9 years with 19 meetings of the GATT working party. In December 1994, the negotiations over Chinese access seemingly broke down. Since then, 3 working parties have been held in 1995, one in 1996, with only one other planned for 1996. Indeed, there seems little urgency from the Chinese side to conclude the negotiations. With political debate intensifying in China over the net benefits of WTO accession, it has become easier for China to pursue its interests at a bilateral rather than multilateral level. China has also offered tariff reductions as part of its downpayment package to APEC but again these have failed to include agricultural products like wool. Australia has been reluctant to conclude a trade deal which will see more formal import quotas imposed on its wool exports.

Despite the stand-off, it is in both countries interests to re-visit the vexed question of wool trade arrangements. For Australia, developments in the Chinese market may determine the fate of its premier rural industry. For China, resolution of WTO access will allow it to enjoy the benefits of trade reform, especially reform of the Multi-Fibre arrangement, and so facilitate China's increasing role in global wool textile production as a result of shifting comparative advantage.

3. COMPLEMENTARY OR COMPETITIVE?

Much of the debate in Sino-Australian wool trade negotiations centres on the competitiveness of Australian and Chinese wool. In its current proposal for a tariff-quota regime, and in the case of previous import restrictions, China has argued that Australian wool imports may compete with domestically grown wool and so impact on the livelihood of herders in its remote pastoral region; a relatively disadvantaged and strategically important minority group in China. The substitutability and competitiveness of Australian and Chinese wool has also arisen in debates within Australia, particularly in relation to the provision of Australian assistance in production and processing to the Chinese wool industry. Young and Moir (1990) reviewed some of this debate and argued that Australian assistance to China's wool processing is in Australia's interests.

Longworth and Brown (1995) went further and argued that Australia's interests may be promoted by assistance to a much broader spectrum of the agribusiness chain including the production level. They argued that the quality of Chinese wool falls well short of Australian wool. The best wool grown in China is shorter, less sound, has lower clean yields and is more heterogeneous than typical Australian wool. For instance, average clean yield rates and staple lengths of 66% and 9cm respectively at Australian auctions in 1991 compared with average clean yields less than 50% and staple lengths of less than 7cm at the corresponding Chinese wool auctions (Longworth and Brown, 1995; Brown, 1996).[2] The difference in physical characteristics combined with the nature of wool processing and wool products has meant there has been little substitution between Australian and Chinese wool. Both are used for different purposes, with the lack of substitution related to quality variations rather than price relativities. Much of the Chinese wool undergoes woollen processing and is used to make products such as blankets and yarns primarily for the domestic market. Conversely Australian wool imports have typically been used to produce worsted fabrics and high quality knitting yarns for export markets.

A lack of substitutability between Australian and Chinese wool is evident in the market developments of the late 1980s/early 1990s when China restricted wool imports in response to escalating stocks of domestic wool. As Lin (1993) pointed out, without access to imported wool, Chinese mills did not turn to the lower quality and relatively highly priced domestic wool but instead turned to chemical fibres. Some of the very best quality Chinese wool does compete with imported wool at the margin and here relative prices and availability are important. However, in general, there needs to be quantum improvements in the quality of Chinese wool if it is to approach the quality of and substitute for imported wool.

Can China improve the quality of its domestic wool to this extent? The better quality wool grown on State farms compared with the wool grown by individual herders suggests that some of the quality problems are management related and so potentially are able to be overcome (Longworth and Williamson, 1993). However, many of the problems relate to the harsh physical conditions in China's pastoral region and have no simple technical or managerial solution. Chinese wool will always be dirtier and shorter due to climatic and physical conditions in the pastoral region. Official policy in China, both at a national and provincial level, has been to promote breed improvement towards fine wool sheep. However, many of the social, cultural and economic incentives for herders are to produce dual-purpose meat and wool sheep. Longworth and Williamson (1993) allude to the reversion in some fine wool sheep breeds throughout the 1980s.

---

2 The Chinese auctions sold the best three per cent of wool grown in China while the Australian auctions represented the bulk of wool grown in Australia. Given that the typical wool grown in China is at least 1cm shorter, has a 10% lower clean yield and is less sound than the wool sold through the Chinese auctions, then Chinese wool is even more differentiated from Australian wool (Brown, 1996).

Even if breeding strategies, management practices and physical conditions did allow Chinese wool to approach the quality of Australian wool then another constraint arises at the aggregate level. The badly degraded state of China's rangeland impose a major limit on sheep numbers and greasy wool output in China. Longworth and Williamson (1993, p.329) showed that, on a clean scoured basis, China produced only one-thirteenth of the amount of wool of 25 microns or less grown in Australia in 1991. These authors provide detailed evidence to support their conclusion that China does not have the resource base to significantly expand its production of this type of wool.

Thus many of the arguments raised in trade negotiations are unfounded. Australian wool is not used for products now made with Chinese wool, and banning imports in China will lead to substitution into other fibres. Similarly, Chinese wool is not likely to develop in quantity or quality to threaten Australian wool markets in China or elsewhere. However, apart from Australian and Chinese wool industries not being competitive, they also exhibit some important complementarities. For socio-political and strategic reasons, Chinese authorities view an integrated wool industry as important in the development of the remote and industrially-backward, pastoral regions. However, the poor quality of domestic wool creates enormous problems for Chinese mills, especially those located "up-country" in the main wool growing areas. The long-term viability of these up-country mills depends on their access to better quality imported wool (Brown and Longworth, 1994). That is, in order to survive in an otherwise competitive and under performing textile sector in China, these mills need to make best use of their processing capacity and marketing opportunities. Although domestic wool can fulfil an important role here (to produce a lower price, lower quality product to local markets), mills also need imported wool to produce a range of higher quality products to meet this segment of the domestic market as well as to supply export markets. As many Chinese mills now importing Australian wool also use domestic wool, then improving the quality of domestic wool and its marketing channels is central to improving the viability of these mills and their ability to pay for imports of Australian wool. Wool competes in China not only in the fibre market but also in the political market. Chinese officials currently support an integrated wool industry as a path for economic development in the pastoral region. But if the costs of such a strategy are too high, then support will switch to other fibres, especially increasing self sufficiency in chemical fibres.

Thus, Australian and Chinese wool are integrally linked and are complementary rather than competitive. These complementary relationships will become even more important in the future as a larger proportion of Australian wool exports to China go to mills servicing the growth in the domestic demand for wool products.

4. POLITICAL ECONOMY OF SINO-AUSTRALIAN WOOL TRADE

If Australian and Chinese wool are complementary, then why are restrictive import arrangements being proposed? Notionally, the wool trade measures mooted are in response to the concern of the Ministry of Agriculture (MOA) concern over the welfare of herders in the pastoral region. However, many different groups in China will be affected in various ways and to a different extent by changes in wool import arrangements. The inability of Australian and other trade representatives to accept Chinese insistence on the protection of particular domestic interests has led to stalled negotiations. Progressing the path of the negotiations and the trade reforms will require a much more detailed understanding of the underlying political economy. Knowing who gains and loses from a particular trade is essential if strategies are to be put in place which relieve some of the adverse impacts while highlighting or enhancing the positive outcomes for the beneficiaries. The following discussion serves to illustrate only some of the important gains and losses from Sino-Australian wool trade. In developing a negotiating position to overcome the current impasse, then a much more detailed and comprehensive study needs to be carried out.

The push for more restrictive wool import arrangements has come primarily from the MOA notionally to protect local sheep herders. The MOA has extensive extension, research and other infrastructure tied to the pastoral areas and any threat, perceived or otherwise, to the growing of local wool would undermine that infrastructure. However, the MOA also controls the wool-growing State farms. (See Longworth and Williamson, 1993, pp.65-67 for a description of the State farms under MOA control.) These State farms grow the best wool in China which was identified earlier as the only Chinese wool which may compete with imported wool under certain price relativities. It is these State farms rather than the numerous individual herders that the MOA is seeking to protect with the import restrictions.

The MOA strategy of seeking to limit wool imports is not without risk. As argued previously, restricting the availability and raising the cost of imported wool may adversely affect the profitability of Chinese mills that also use domestic wool, and raise the profile of competing fibres in China. The MOA has shown an appreciation of the need to improve the quality of domestically grown wool and the domestic marketing of wool if it is to improve the welfare of herders that are dependent on wool. It is also cognisant of the limits imposed by the condition of the rangeland and the need to increase the value rather than the volume of the wool being sold if herder's incomes are to rise. This awareness has manifested itself at the production level through the support of breeding and extension programs. At the marketing level, the MOA formed an alliance with the Ministry of Textile Industries[3] to push for alternative marketing channels such as wool auctions (Brown, 1996). The MOA push for more restrictive import arrangements threatens to undermine its strategic alliance with groups such as the Ministry of Textile Industries that favour the importing of wool.

---

3 The Ministry of Textile Industry was reconstituted as the China National Textile Council in 1993.

Ironically, many of the improvements needed to modernise and commercialise the Chinese wool industry may best be served by Australian entrepreneurs and interests. Assistance could be provided not only in production and processing technology but also in marketing areas such as better commodity grading, testing and inspection procedures, information networks, and selling methods. For instance, one skill well developed in Australia and of particular relevance to the bulk of Chinese wool produced by small, geographically spread herders each with small heterogeneous lots of wool is interlotting. However, Longworth and Brown (1995) highlight many other areas where Australian entrepreneurs could aid the modernisation and commercialisation of the Chinese wool industry.

This raises possibilities for progressing the problematic negotiations. The MOAs concerns may partly be allayed if assistance was provided to improve the quality and marketing of domestic wool in China to allow it to compete more effectively in the long run.[4] Australia could offer this assistance in return for Chinese commitments to maintain open import arrangements with respect to Australian wool.

To the extent that wool imports are perceived as a threat to domestic wool, then there are a range of institutions relying on the domestic industry that may also feel threatened. As Brown and Longworth (1995) and Longworth and Brown (1995) indicate, many of these institutions have recently undergone major structural changes and may feel vulnerable to a surge in wool imports. In particular, a major part of the activities of the Supply and Marketing Cooperatives[5] in the pastoral areas involved the handling of wool. Since the deregulation of wool markets throughout China in 1992, the Supply and Marketing Co-operatives have lost a significant share of wool sales from their previous role as a sole procurement agency. As the Supply and Marketing Co-operatives are unlikely to be involved in the handling or distribution of imported wool, then they may see imports as a further erosion of their domestic wool supply base and so support tighter restrictions. However, if assistance was provided to help the Supply and Marketing Co-operatives say develop interlotting services (given their enormous agribusiness network), then this may serve the dual role of improving domestic wool marketing in China while appeasing groups supporting tighter import arrangements.

---

4 As mentioned previously, the economic incentives for herders in the pastoral region may be to produce sheepmeat rather than grow fine-wool, especially given the dramatic growth in meat demand in China. However, Australia also has expertise to offer assistance in sheep and mutton production, meat processing and distribution channels. Thus, the scope for assistance, or the trade-offs considered in the negotiations should not be confined to the wool market alone.

5 The Supply and Marketing Co-operatives are a quasi-government agency under the Ministry of Domestic Trade which prior to 1993 was known as the Ministry of Commerce. Longworth and Brown (1995, Chapter 7) describe this agribusiness giant, which has over 63,000 product procurement and purchasing agencies and 10,000 warehouse and transport agencies) and how it has reacted to the recent agribusiness reforms in China.

Similar strategic opportunities need to be explored with many other Chinese institutions that primarily service the domestic Chinese wool industry such as commodity inspection agencies, textile research institutes etc. For example, the fibre inspection institutes have inadequate and outdated equipment and poorly trained staff (Longworth and Brown, 1995, Chapter 6). Consequently much of the domestic wool is naively graded and sorted, and must be re-sorted at the mills at additional expense. Once again Australian assistance and expertise in these areas would improve the marketing channels and quality of domestic Chinese wool and gather support from groups who may otherwise oppose Australian wool imports. Another area of strategic assistance is in some early stage processing such as wool scouring. For various reasons outlined in Brown and Longworth (1992), local wool scouring has been particularly problematic, unprofitable and has adversely affected wool quality for later-stage processing. This also applies to scouring imported wool, as Chinese mills often do not have the experience, skills, equipment and detergents to scour and carbonise Australian wool with high burr content.

Opposition to greater wool imports is not confined to elements of the Chinese wool industry. As mentioned, the main beneficiary of restricting wool imports in the late 1980s and early 1990s was not the domestic wool industry but the domestic chemical fibre industry. Thus the greatest threat to increased wool imports may be the Chinese government's desire for self sufficiency in overall fibre production, and its support for chemical fibre production given the resource constraints to increased cotton and wool production. Clearly a full understanding of the political economy of Sino-Australian wool trade needs to extend beyond interests in the wool industry alone.

The primary support for a less restrictive trade policy has come from the wool textile industry. Chinese mills need access to overseas wool if they are to adjust to the changing comparative advantage in the Asia-Pacific region and the expansion in wool textile trade associated with reform of the multi-fibre arrangement. However, not all wool textile mills are the same in China. Brown and Longworth (1994) categorise Chinese mills into three groups, namely the large State-owned mills on the east coast, township enterprise mills and up-country mills.

Traditionally, wool processing was dominated by the large State owned mills on the east coast. These mills had access to the better technology and to the better wool inputs either imported or domestic, and had a disproportionate share of the export and production of the higher quality wool textiles. Nevertheless, as with other State enterprises in China, they have been burdened by an unproductive workforce and work practices. The up-country mills are also typically State-owned. However, they have been the poor cousins of the east coast mills with inferior equipment and restricted access to imported wool.[6] Their information networks both in respect of wool textile exports and imports of raw and semi-processed wool are poor (Brown and Longworth, 1994). Processing capacity at these mills has increased rapidly over the last decade.

The most remarkable growth, however, has been in the township enterprise mills which now account for over 30% of the wool processing capacity, and which have seen a relative shift in wool processing from centres such as Beijing and Shanghai to Jiangsu and Shandong. These mills fuelled much of the increase in Chinese wool processing capacity in the late 1980s which led to the dramatic rise in demand for wool imports. The township mills are not burdened by many of the other constraints facing the older State enterprises, but do not receive the same support from the State and under adverse market conditions most of the industry adjustment occurs in this sector. The township enterprise mills are the source of much of the growth of wool imported through the non-traditional channels shown in Figure 15.2(b).

Thus while freer import arrangements, in general, will favour all mills, some mills will benefit more than others. A tariff/quota arrangement relative to more loosely defined, open ended import arrangements would tend to favour the large State-owned mills on the east coast. These mills have well defined and traditional sources of export contracts and import channels and are likely to receive preferential treatment in the situation where wool imports are restricted. Conversely, in the situation where wool imports are likely to be restricted, namely a fall in domestic demand and rise in domestic wool stocks, up-country mills are unlikely to receive their fair share of any restricted wool imports. This is at odds with the proposed import arrangements which implicitly should support the up-country mills through the notion of an integrated wool system in the pastoral areas. The new township enterprise mills have the most to lose from more constrained import arrangements. They are unlikely to be afforded special access to the restricted imports as their imports come from outside the traditional channels. Not only will restricted wool imports impact on their profitability, but ongoing limits will force them to close or to switch to other fibres.

An appropriate strategy, therefore, may be to encourage the township enterprise and up-country mills to lobby more vigorously to retain and indeed extend more open wool import arrangements. Although the State mills on the east coast will be relatively disadvantaged, their attention will be focussed on other areas that currently afflict State enterprises rather than heightened competition that may arise from other Chinese mills arising from a more level-playing-field in wool imports.

Apart from the mills, any change in the import arrangements will also affect institutions involved with the trading and distribution of imported wool in China. As indicated in Figure 15.2, there are many different institutions now involved in handling

---

6 From 1985 to 1992, a "self-produce, self-process, self-sell" policy was in place in the wool producing provinces which severely restricted imports of wool by the up-country mills (Brown and Longworth, 1994).

wool from the traditional channels such as the Ministry of Foreign Trade and Economic Co-operation and CHINATEX to the non-traditional channels such as intermediate wool trading corporations, secondary market traders and even individual mills. Past wool import arrangements have reflected power struggles among these groups as highlighted in the rapid rise and equally dramatic demise of the China Wool Group[7] in the late 1980s (Longworth and Brown, 1995, Section 11.2.2). The move to a more decentralised and deregulated agribusiness and trade environment has led to restructuring in some of the key institutions that impact on the Chinese wool industry. For instance major changes to the Ministry of Textile Industries and the Ministry of Foreign Economic Relations and Trade in 1993 notionally saw a shift in emphasis from management to services. Whether attempts are made to wind back the clock to a more centralised and controlled trade and agribusiness environment depends on how these institutions perceive and adjust to their new roles.

5. TRADE POLICY MIRAGE

The preceding discussion highlights the dilemma faced by the Chinese government. On the one hand, China's overall interests and those of particular groups are served by freer and increased access to overseas wool. On the other hand, equally strong groups feel threatened by a potential surge in imports and have actively lobbied for tighter arrangements. One way the Chinese government has addressed this type of dilemma in the past is to create a trade policy "mirage". That is, notionally restrictive import arrangements are established while their implementation (whether through loopholes, exemptions, administration, application etc.) allows a higher level of imports. The current proposals are likely to contain elements of this mirage, namely the setting of seemingly restrictive import arrangements to appease particular groups while allowing sufficient flexibility in the administration of them.

The arrangements for importing wool over the last decade illustrate the operation of this mirage. Prior to 1980, imports were tightly controlled at the central level with imports occurring under the traditional import channels outlined in Figure 15.2(a). Mills sought permission from the Ministry of Textile Industries and their local Economic and Planning Commission to import wool. The State Planning Commission, based on information from the Ministry of Textile Industries, set a national quota and authorised agencies under the Ministry of Foreign Economic Relations and Trade to import the

---

7 Set up in 1989 as an attempt by the Ministry of Foreign Economic Relations and Trade and the Central government to re-assert their control over wool imports, the China Wool group consisted of one representative from CHINATEX, China National Animal By-Products Import-Export Corporation, China International Trust Investment Corporation, Tianjin Foreign Trade Corporation, Beijing Foreign Trade Corporation, Shanghai Foreign Trade Corporation and Jiangsu Foreign Trade Corporation and was chaired by the CHINATEX representative. By 1991, the China Wool Group was all but defunct as pressures emerged to import outside of this system.

wool. Specifically, CHINATEX was authorised to organise all fine wool imports and the Animal By-Products Import-Export Corporation was given responsibility for non-apparel wool imports. Since 1984 the China Resources Corporation (based in Hong Kong), Namkwong (Macao) and CHINATEX (Sydney office) have acted as "agents" for CHINATEX.

The growth in the wool textile industry in the 1980s, however, could not be serviced by the traditional import channels and centralised arrangements. Indeed, by the mid- to late-1980s, many different organisations highlighted in Figure 15.2(b) were involved in importing wool with little co-ordination among them or little control over them (Wilcox 1994). The decline in domestic demand and rise in domestic wool stocks in 1989, however, motivated the Central government to re-centralise control over wool imports and to restrict official import quotas to 45kt in 1990.

It became evident, however, that restricting wool imports was not in China's interests. With a rise in domestic demand, increasing pressure arose for an easing of import controls. Although official import quotas were raised, most of the expansion came from imports outside the official quotas. The most important "loopholes" existed for mills producing for the export market. Subject to authorisation, mills could import wool duty free provided that it was used for making products for the export market. The administrative difficulties associated with identifying the precise amount of imported wool used in any particular export product led to considerable abuse of the rules. Numerous anecdotal examples exist of mills diverting imported wool from a single production line destined for export to other product lines oriented to the domestic market. Other exemptions, for example, included joint venture mills which did not require an import permit and which could deal directly with overseas wool suppliers.

Thus even if China imposes a quota import arrangement, it is unclear as to how it will administer it and whether it will use it to restrict actual wool imports. The trade policy mirage seems a convenient and practical means for serving the interests of China as well its suppliers such as Australia. But it does come at a cost. Restrictive quotas and tariffs have well documented distortionary effects and inefficiencies. The trade policy mirage of facilitating loopholes around these official restrictions measures can create additional problems. It can distort import wool flows and processing to where exemptions arise,[8] it encourages abuse and it leads to uncertainty. For example, the Chinese Customs crackdown in 1995 on illegal border trade and import levy exemptions (claimed on much more wool than was actually exported) impacted greatly on Australian wool exporters and Chinese mills which typically keep low stocks of imported wool. More importantly, the operation of the trade policy mirage seems to encourage opportunistic merchants or traders rather than committed exporters and importers who

8 From a second-best perspective, the exemptions may be an attempt to offset the impact of general restrictions. However, often the exemptions will have unforeseen and unintended effects which may lead to even greater distortions.

require a much more certain policy environment to operate in. Thus elements of market development, information networks and a better matching of customer requirements with import supplies have been lacking in recent Sino-Australian wool trade.

Ideally, the arguments raised in the chapter suggest that a first best policy involves removing import restrictions. But the important issue for Australian wool exporters and their Chinese mill customers is whether the trade policy mirage is a second best policy outcome relative to a binding tariff quota regime. In any event, it is essential for Australian exporters operating in China and for Australian trade negotiators to fully understand the operation of this trade policy mirage.

6. OTHER POLICY MIRAGES

A situation in which all parties gain revolves around improving the domestic marketing of wool in China. Chinese interests, including herders in the pastoral region, would gain from a reduction in marketing costs, improved efficiencies, and quality incentives in an environment where there are major constraints of the amount of wool that can be produced. Australian interests are served by improved mill profitability leading to an increased demand for wool imports and ability to pay for these imports. Once again, the Central government in China is well aware of the need to modernise and commercialise the wool industry and to reform its agribusiness sector (Longworth and Brown, 1995). However, often other policy "mirages" arise in a divergence between national strategies and local implementation of these strategies. These divergences arise, among other reasons, because of the autonomy of local governments in China and that local governments often have shorter term objectives and planning horizons than the Central government (Longworth et al., 1996). Longworth and Brown (1995), Longworth and Williamson (1993) and Longworth et al. (1996) discuss a range of these policy mirages in many areas of wool production and wool marketing in China. The following discussion briefly outlines only a few pertinent ones which would need to be overcome before any Sino-Australian joint efforts to modernise the wool sector in China.

In general, the Chinese government has sought to free up the domestic market for wool (and other agricultural commodities) in China. However, despite the rhetoric in Beijing, most segments of the Chinese agribusiness sector, while no longer the exclusive preserve of a single organisation, are still dominated by large State controlled agencies. Thus while the markets for products such as wool are "open" they are far from "free" in the western sense of the word. Local governments in the pastoral areas continue to support intervention purchasing of the lower quality wool through the State input-supply and product-procurement agencies such as the Supply and Marketing Co-operatives (Longworth and Brown, 1995, Chapter 7). Apart from being a means to perform this local form of income redistribution, the Supply and Marketing Co-operatives provide a source of employment for local cadres, provide an effective means for collecting local wool product taxes, and secure supplies for local agricultural processing activities.

Although other buyers can now purchase wool, the way in which the local governments register wool buyers and support the activities of the Supply and Marketing Co-operatives clearly influences the nature of the market. Market deregulation, therefore, has an element of policy mirage associated with it. Thus efforts by the central government, with overseas assistance, to reform and modernise the agribusiness sector may come unstuck at the local level.

Attempts to introduce a new raw wool purchasing standard in China at the end of 1993 illustrate the problem of reconciling national policies with local implementation of them. Despite claims at the Central level of universal application of the new standard throughout the country, there remain many areas throughout the pastoral region which still use the old standard. Although, in some localities the new standard may have been genuinely impractical for technical reasons, often the central government initiatives were ignored for other reasons.

The issue of local autonomy and short-term planning horizons also has implications for overseas assistance. Local officials tend to seek projects which involve the installation of new equipment or some other tangible immediate benefit. Other less tangible forms of foreign assistance needed for the longer term development of the industry, such as improved grading systems and information networks, are viewed with much less enthusiasm.

Understanding the policy mirages is essential if advancing trade negotiations through assistance with the wool agribusiness sector in China is to be made.

7. CONCLUSIONS

Wool is a commodity central to Sino-Australian economic and trade relations. Not only is wool important in terms of its share of Australia's total exports to China, but it also symbolises both the potential and tensions that arise in trade between the two countries. The failure to resolve simmering differences over wool trade arrangements has the potential to adversely impact on these relations. With fundamentally diverging positions, China and Australia perceive the current arrangements, while not ideal, as enabling a continued trade in wool that is so essential to both countries.

Resolution of these differences and arriving at a wool trade agreement suitable to both countries calls for more than a cursory examination and reference to aggregate statistics and macro-developments. This is true for the analysis of other opportunities and challenges associated with Sino-Australian wool trade and indeed for other commodity trade between the two countries. Having a thorough understanding of the political economy behind a particular trade, a full knowledge of the socio-economic and political factors of importance in the Chinese domestic industry and a grasp of the nuances of Chinese decision making is essential for the formulation of strategies that maximise the opportunities of trade between China and Australia.

8. REFERENCES

Brown, C.G. (1996) "Chinese Wool Auctions: Failed Agribusiness Reform or Future Marketing Channel?", *China Economic Review*, 7(2), (forthcoming).

Brown, C.G. and Longworth, J.W. (1992) "Reconciling National Economic Reforms and Local Investment Decisions in China: Fiscal Decentralisation and First Stage Wool Processing", *Development Policy Review,* 10: 389-402.

Brown, C.G. and Longworth, J.W. (1994) "Lifting the Wool Curtain: Recent Reforms and New Opportunities in the Chinese Wool Market with Special Reference to the Up-country Mills", *Review of Marketing and Agricultural Economics*, 62(3): 369-387.

Brown, C.G. and Longworth J.W. (1995) "Wool: China, Change and Trade", *Current Affairs Bulletin*, 72(2): 4-13.

Chai, J.C.H. (1995) *US-China Trade Conflict and its Implication for Australia's Agricultural Trade*, Paper presented to an International Conference on US China Economic Relations, Hong Kong, 20-22 June, 1995.

CMAP (Chinese Members of ACIAR Project No. 8811) (1994) *Economic Aspects of Raw Wool Production and Marketing in China*, Agricultural Scientech Publishing House of China, Beijing.

Longworth, J.W. and Brown, C.G. (1995) *Agribusiness Reform in China: The Case of Wool*, C.A.B. International, Wallingford.

Longworth, J.W. and Williamson, G.J. (1993) *China's Pastoral Region: Sheep and Wool, Minority Nationalities, Rangeland Degradation, and Sustainable Development*, C.A.B. International, Wallingford.

Longworth, J.W., Brown, C.G., and Williamson, G.J. (1996) "`Second Generation' Problems Associated with Economic Reform in the Pastoral Region of China", *International Journal of Social Economics*, (forthcoming).

Lin, X. (1993) "The Outlook for Chinese Wool Production and Marketing: Some Policy Proposals", in Longworth J.W. (ed.) *Economic Aspects of Raw Wool Production and Marketing*, ACIAR Technical Report No. 25, Australian Centre for International Agricultural Research, Canberra.

Wilcox, C. (1994) *Wool Importing System of China*, Paper presented to a workshop on the Wool Industry in China at the 38th Annual conference of the Australian Agricultural Economics Society, Wellington, New Zealand.

Wool International (1996) *Wool Exports: Quarterly Export Review*.

Young, L.M. and Moir, B.G. (1990) "Assessing Assistance to Chinese Wool Production and Processing", *Agriculture and Resources Quarterly*, 2(3): 288-299.

16. AUSTRALIA-CHINA TRADE: LABOUR MARKET AND CONVERGENCE DIMENSIONS

Neil Karunaratne

1. INTRODUCTION

Australia and China are the largest economies in the region occupying land masses of continental dimensions; both cover an area of about 10 million square kilometres. China has more than 66 times the population of Australia. It is the most populous country in the world with more than 1.2 billion inhabitants. But in per capita GDP terms Australians are seven times richer than the average Chinese. Nevertheless, in terms of GDP growth China has been growing at a rate that is five times faster than Australia (See Table 16.1). Since 1978, when China switched from the command economy to a marketised economy both GDP and trade have increased in a spectacular fashion. Currently China exports 25% of its GDP and most of it comprises labour intensive manufactured exports to advanced countries (ACs) like Australia. The rapid growth of the mega economy of China has posed a challenge to the established hegemonic world order and evoked a confrontationist response from some ACs. Populists and academics have become strange bedfellows in supporting neo-protectionist policies to contain the growth and trade expansion of China. Some analysts have argued that pursuing liberal trade policies with developing countries (DCs) like China is like playing poker on the Titanic (Goldsmith, 1994:28) as the penetration of labour intensive imports have contributed to labour immiseration and deindustrialisation in ACs.

Table 16.1: Basic Indicators (latest figures)

Country	Area km^2 mn	Pop. mn.	GDP US$ bn.	GDP pc US$	Exports US$ bn.	K US$ bn.	L mn.	Growth rate
Australia	7.7	17.5	323.4	18500	91.7	645	9.2	1.6
China	9.6	1162.0	2135.0	1837	42.7	323	370.0	8.2

Notes: K, Capital. L, Labour.
Sources: Penn World Table Mark 5.6 (1994); World Development Tables (1993); Asia Year Book (1995).

Conventional factor content measures (FCM) based on labour input-output coefficients from ACs conclude that trade with DCs has not adversely affected unskilled labour (Sachs and Shatz, 1994). But when FCM are recomputed using labour input-output coefficients of DCs the adverse unemployment effects of trade with DCs are more than 20 times the conventional estimates, when account is taken of defensive innovation and spillover effects on the nontradeable sectors (Wood, 1994). However, critics warn that these inflated FCM calculations are measurements devoid of theoretical underpinning and therefore should be viewed with a large dose of scepticism (Leamer, 1994).

This chapter is motivated by the need to analyse the labour market effects of growth of trade between Australia and China using the objective theoretical framework. The neoclassical trade paradigm or the Heckscher-Ohlin trade model provides a logical general equilibrium framework to take a cool look at the politically heated debate on the adverse labour market effects of pursuing open door trade policies with DCs like China. This study will also calculate the speed of convergence or catching up by China of Australia's per capita income using both pooled time-series cross-section techniques and modern unit root and cointegration methods. The trade theoretic perspectives and neoclassical growth empirics confirm that liberal trade with DCs like China is a positive-sum rather than a zero-sum game. As such protectionist policies and support for hegemonic international politics designed to thwart China's economic growth and trade expansion should be given wide berth by Australian policy makers.

The rest of the chapter is organised as follows: Section 2 reviews in terms of the neoclassical trade paradigm and its central theorems the effects on the Australian labour market due to the implementing of liberal trading policies with China. Here, the Stolper Samuelson, Factor Price Equalisation and Rybczynski theorems are reviewed and besides the ravages of labour saving technology or the phenomenon of Marx striking again is investigated. Section 4 reviews the empirical evidence on how the centralised wage-fixing institutionals have activated the Rybczynski adverse unemployment effects due to trade liberalisation instead of the Stolper-Samuelson iron fist. Nevertheless, labour saving technology or 'Marx striking again' appears to have immiserised unskilled labour more than liberal trade. Section 5 uses pooled time-series cross data to measure the speed of convergence of China to Australia's per capita income. Section 5 confirms using unit root and cointegration techniques that China will take an inordinately long time to catch up with Australia's per capita income. Section 6 concludes the chapter with policy perspectives on labour market adjustments and international response to Chinese economic and trade expansion.

2. INSIGHTS FROM THE NEOCLASSICAL TRADE PARADIGM

Contrary to the alarmist prognostications that the pursuit of liberal trading policies with China is like playing poker on the Titanic, the neoclassical trade paradigm or the Heckscher Ohlin (HO) model clearly demonstrates that free trade between Australia and China is first best or Pareto optimal as it would maximise each country's national welfare and therefore global welfare. The HO (2x2x2) model defines comparative advantage in terms of two-countries (Australia and China), two-factors (skilled and unskilled labour) two-goods (skill and unskilled labour intensive each produced using intensively the relatively abundant factor) under a litany of stringent assumptions such as constant returns to scale, identical tastes and technology, non-reversibility of factor intensities, international factor immobility and national factor mobility, no transportation costs, absence of complete specialisation, balanced trade, full employment, and the institutional assumption of perfect competition (Bhagwati and Srinivasan, 1983). The HO model predicts that the maximum gains from trade arise when each country specialises in the production and export of its comparative advantage good. This turns out to be the skill intensive good for Australia and unskilled labour intensive good for China. The benefits from pursuing free trade policies as underscored by the static HO paradigm are exceeded manifold when dynamic comparative advantage is reckoned by considering economies of scale, learning by doing, effects of technology transfer as stylised in imitation gap and product cycle neo-technology theories (Grossman and Helpman, 1991; Baldwin, 1992). Moreover, trade provides access to non-rivalrous public goods with positive externalities in the form of new goods, new ideas, knowledge and blueprints yielding additional welfare effects not captured by the static HO model (Romer, 1994). Therefore, the HO model predicts the bottom line of the welfare gains that could accrue to both economies by the pursuit of free trade policies. The new trade theories aiming to capture the burgeoning intra-industry trade or trade in similar products due to economies of scale, product differentiation, monopolistic competition, world-wide sourcing by multinational corporations leading to the slicing of the value chain in production fail to replace the HO model but rather modifies and complements it (Salvatore, 1995).The spectacular growth performance by Asian economies or the 'Asian Miracle' resulting from the pursuit of liberal trading policies has been cited as evidence supporting the neoclassical paradigms of trade and growth (World Bank, 1993). Nonetheless, the emergence of a supertrading dragon of China has raised hackles and fears giving vent to neo-mercantilist rhetoric and policy posturing in ACs like Australia.

In order to shed light on the labour market effects of implementing open door trading policies with DCs such as China we could use the neoclassical HO trade theory and its three theorems on income, price and growth effects: Stolper Samuelson (SS), Factor Price Equalisation (FPE), Rybczynski. Besides, a fourth factor operating through labour saving technology could immiserise unskilled labour. This phenomenon has been dubbed as Marx striking again phenomenon (Bhagwati and Dehejia, 1994). These trade and technology induced labour market immiseration effects are reviewed next.

First, the Stolper Samuelson (SS) theorem predicts that liberalising trade with China would increase the imports of unskilled labour intensive goods into Australia. This would reduce the wages of relatively scarce unskilled workers and simultaneously raise the wages of skilled workers and thus widen skill differentiated wage inequality. But the SS wage inequality prediction occurs only if reduction of protection causes a reduction in import prices which in turn unleashes downward pressures on unskilled labour wages. However, in Australia the operation of the centralised wage fixing and the Accord institutionals prevented wage flexibility and thus undermined the SS wage inequality predictions. In the United States where trade unions are weak and prices and incomes policies are non existent trade liberalisation has led to the rise of skill differentiated wage inequality following trade liberalisation. While in Europe and Australia the operation of institutional constraints on wage flexibility has prevented the emergence of wage inequality as predicted by the SS theorem (Freeman, 1994; Krugman, 1995).

Second, the Samuelson Factor Price Equalisation (FPE) theorem predicts, given domestic factor mobility and international factor immobility, free trade in goods tend to equalise factor earnings across countries. This implies the wages of unskilled labour in Australia will fall while that of China will rise leading to a convergence of wages in the two countries. Some analysts regard the FPE predictions as Holy Grail but others dismiss it as unrealistic as most of the assumptions required for the operation of the FPE effects are violated in practice. Nevertheless, with increasing globalisation and economic integration of Australia and DCs like China although unskilled labour wages were not determined in Beijing in the past in the future it would be a different story (Freeman, 1994).

Third, the Rybczynski theorem postulates that given centralised wage fixing and the Accord institutionals the trade liberalisation will not cause price changes and therefore reductions in the wages of unskilled workers. In this context labour would be immiserised by increasing the unemployment rate of unskilled labour by effectively increasing the supply of unskilled labour in the form of increased supply of unskilled labour intensive goods from DCs like China. Although, in the past the Rybczynski effect manifested itself in the form of increased unemployment amongst unskilled workers due to the operation of award wages and safety net institutional constraints, in the future with the globalisation and deregulation of the labour market Australian wages will be determined not by the Accord or wage negotiations but may be set in Beijing as predicted by Freeman (1994). The Rybczynski labour immiseration effect under institutionally decreed wage rigidity manifests in the form of increased unemployment as the import of labour intensive goods from DCs like China increases the effective supply of unskilled labour and simultaneously reduces unemployment amongst skilled workers as illustrated in Fig. 1. An alternative geometrical exposition of the Rybczynski effect is given in Krugman (1995).

Figure 16.1: Rybczynski Unemployment Effects

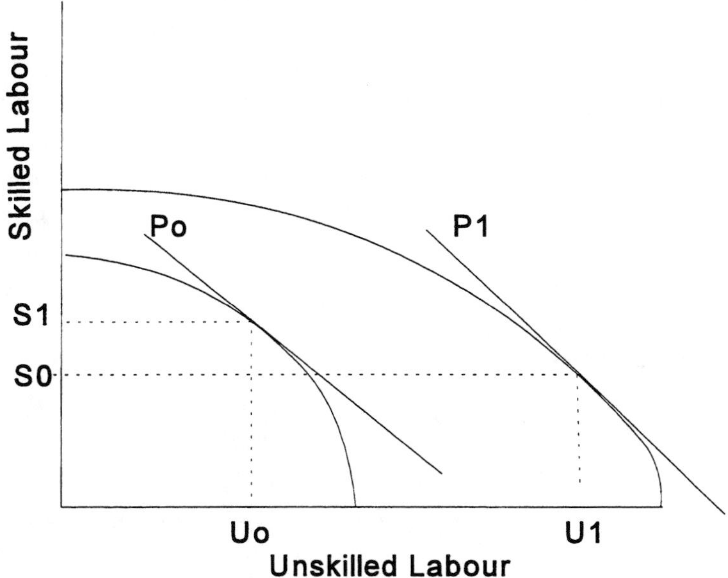

Trade liberalisation increases unemployment/supply of unskilled labour by U0U1 and contracts unemployment/supply of skilled labour by S0S1 given that price and wage ratio of unskilled to skilled labour is constant.

Fourth, autonomous labour saving technical progress could immiserise labour by increasing unemployment amongst the unskilled workers. These technology induced disemployment or Marx striking again effects increased labour productivity whilst throwing unskilled workers into the scrap heap of the reserve army of the unemployed, thus depressing their wages to subsistence levels. Of course the Marx striking effect could also have been triggered by the need to adopt defensive innovations to meet the challenges of competition released by trade liberalisation. The widespread adoption of unskilled labour saving or high skill labour intensive high-tech occurred with Australia's graduation stage-wise to an information economy (Karunaratne, 1991) and parallels widespread adoption of high-tech information technology in other ACs (Brendt et al., 1992). Thus either acting independently or in response to trade liberalisation new technology immiserised unskilled labour in Australia and other ACs in the 1980s.

3. EMPIRICS ON THE TRADE LIBERALISATION EFFECTS ON MANUFACTURING

During the 1980s (i.e. the period 1982-1993 for purposes of this study), Australian protection or the Effective Rate of Assistance (ERA) on manufactured imports fell by nearly 60% (i.e. from 25% to 10%) and it is projected to decline to 5% by the end of the century. Following the reduction of the ERA imports from DCs as a ratio of total imports rose by 53% (i.e. from a ratio of 15% to 23%). The share of China in the total manufactured imports from DCs trebled rising from 1.5% to 4.5%. The unskilled labour intensive Textile, Clothing Footwear (TCF) imports from DCs increased by 23%, while China's share in the TCF imports more than quadrupled. Although the import price of TCF goods fell as a consequence of the scaling down of protection it did not lead to a reduction of wages of unskilled labour in Australia as predicted by the SS theorem. The operation of Accord institutionals nullified the operation of the SS effects. Thus trade liberalisation in the Australian context immiserised labour not through the SS wage reduction effects but rather through the Rybczynski iron fist of employment reduction. During 1980s employment in the manufacturing sector as a whole fell by 25% and employment in the unskilled labour intensive TCF sector dropped by 30%, but the TCF sector accounted for only 6% of total manufacturing employment. But fall in employment in the skill intensive sectors that were not exposed to competitive pressures from trade liberalisation was much larger. For instance, in the skill intensive ETM (Elaborately Transformed Manufacturing) sector encompassing Transport and Basic Metals and Equipment (n.e.s) employment fell by more than 40% during the 1980s, and this despite the increase in exports by 430% (See Table 16.2).

The main force contributing to labour shedding in the skill intensive sectors was technical progress or productivity improvements.

In the manufacturing sector as a whole productivity increased by 40% while wages increased only by 10%. A shift-share analysis estimated that labour saving technology related productivity increases was the major cause of unskilled labour shedding in the manufacturing sector. Almost 100% of unemployment created in manufacturing in the 1980s has been blamed on productivity increases rather than trade liberalisation, which was significant to a small extent only in the TCF sector in the 1980s (Fahrer and Pease, 1993).

Table 16.2: Change in Protection, Trade, Employment and Wages (1982-1993)

(1) Sector	(2) ERA	(3) Trade	(4) Employ	(5) W-ratio	(6) Prod.
Manuf. (China's share)	-60%	+53% (+300%) Imports	-25% (-30%)	-12%	+40% (10%) (Wage)
ETM Skilled	-	+430% Exports	-40%		

Notes: Col.(1) Manuf: Total manufactures.
TCF: Textile, Clothing, Footwear. (ASIC codes 23 & 24)
ETM: Elaborately Transformed Manufactures.
Col.(2) ERA: Effective Rate of Assistance.
Col.(3) Trade: Imports or Exports as specified in the cell.
Col.(4) Employ: Employment. Percentage change.
Col.(4) Wage ratio: Skilled/Unskilled wage ratio.
Col.(5) Productivity.
Sources: Australian Bureau of Statistics, Cat. 5206.0, 6412.0, 6248.0 6306.0; Fahrer and Pease (1994).

The productivity increases associated with the autonomous technical progress or trade induced adoption of defensive innovations played a major role in immiserising unskilled labour in the 1980s than trade liberalisation. Thus Marx striking again rather than trade with Beijing appears to provide the smoking gun for Australia's labour market woes in the 1980s.

4. ß AND σ CONVERGENCE AND CATCHING-UP BY CHINA

The fear that trade liberalisation has opened the floodgates to labour intensive imports from China has been exacerbated by the rapid growth performance of the Chinese economy since it switched from the Soviet style command economy to market oriented capitalist economy in 1978. Premised on the neoclassical growth theory (Solow, 1956; Swan, 1956) using a Cobb-Douglas production function in effective labour units and an intertemporal utility maximising representative consumer, the discrete version of the dynamic equation for estimating the speed of convergence or ß-convergence used in empirical estimation (Cashin and Loyaza, 1995) has been defined by Barro and Sala-i-Martin (1992) as follows:

$$g_{i,r} = 1_i - (1-e^{-\beta r})\ln(y_{i,t-r}) + \epsilon_{i,t-r}$$

Table 16.3: ß-Convergence: China-Australia TSCS data

Dep Var(g_i)	(1)	(2)	(3)	(4)	(5)	(6)
Intercept |t-stat|	0.1233 (3.05)	-	0.0261 (1.75)	-0.1189 (0.66)	0.3432 (1.47)	0.3215 (1.30)
y_{t-r} |t-stat|	-0.0072 (1.47)	-0.0420 (1.66)	-0.0244 (1.35)	-0.0369 (2.56)	-0.0939 (3.83)	-0.0947 (2.06)
i_{t-r} |t-stat|	-	-	-	0.1508 (2.80)	0.1172 (2.72)	0.1096 (2.07)
x_{t-r} |t-stat|	-	-	-	-	0.0353 (2.32)	0.0344 (2.13)
h_{t-r} |t-stat|	-	-	-	-	-	-
ß	0.0003	0.0065	0.0037	0.0057	0.0149	0.0151
LM-test (p-value)	-	-	1.11 (0.2916)	1.10 (0.2932)	1.00 (0.3989)	1.08 (0.2990)
Hausman (p-value)	-	-	0.99 (0.3202)	-0.05 (1.0000)	-0.11 (1.0000)	-0.11 (1.0000)
Autocor(ρ)	-	0.0105	-0.0669	-0.3342	-0.2593	-0.2207
1/2 life yrs.	232	108	188	113	46	43
Method	LS AR1	FE AR1	RE AR1	RE AR1	RE AR1	RE AR1

Notes: All variables are in logarithms.
Sample size: n=14
FE: Fixed Effects. RE: Random Effects.
$g_i = \ln(y_{i,t-r}/y_i)$ = geometric average growth rate.
$ß=-\ln(1+\gamma)/r^*$
Half-life = log(0.5)/log(1-ß) in years. AR1: Autoregressive order one

Here, $g_{i,r}=\ln(y_{it}/y_{i,t-r})$ is geometric average of the growth of real per capita GDP of the i-th country (y_{it}) over the r sub-periods spanning the time period t, α is a country-specific constant, ϵ_{it} is the stochastic error term. The equation has been estimated using pooled time-series cross-section (TSCS) for both countries over the sample period 1960-1992 using the LIMDEP software (Greene, 1995). The ß convergence has been controlled for investment as ratio of GDP (i_t), openness or trade as ratio of GDP (x_t), and human capital proxied by secondary school enrolments (h_t). The data has been collated from the latest Penn World Table 5.1 (Summers and Heston, 1991) and World Bank (1994) sources.

Several alternative methods have been used to estimate ß convergence. The Least Squares (LS) method estimates ß convergence without taking account of country specific effects. The Fixed Effect (FE) method incorporates cross-country heteroscedasticity. The Random Effects (RE) method takes account of cross-country heteroscedasticity and serial correlation over time using generalised least squares (GLS) to calculate efficient estimates. If the Hausman test statistic is less than the Breusch-Pagan LM (Lagrange Multiplier) statistic the RE method is deemed to be superior to the FE method in TSCS estimation. Based on ß convergence, the half-life or the years taken for the economies to reach half-way between initial per capita GDP and eventual steady state GDP has also been calculated. It varies from 232 years with a convergence speed of 0.03% per annum according to the LS method, 108 years with a speed of convergence of 0.65% per annum according to the FE method to 43 years with a convergence speed of 1.51% per annum according to the RE method after controlling for the effects of investment, openness and human capital (See Table 16.3).

The standard deviation (σ_i) of the log of GDP (y_t) and the coefficient of variation (CV) for the six sub-periods indicate a declining trend in the dispersion or σ convergence. The regression coefficient of the standard deviation on a time trend (T_i) shows a significant negative coefficient and confirms the reduction in σ convergence over the sample period.

$$\sigma_i = 1.5475 - 0.0404T_i \quad R^2 = 0.90$$
$$(58.72)\ (6.85) \quad DW = 1.74$$

Table 16.4: σ-Convergence: China-Australia

Period	σ_i	CV
1960-64	1.4815	0.1951
1965-69	1.4697	0.1891
1970-74	1.4452	0.1819
1975-79	1.4290	0.1780
1980-84	1.3344	0.1601
1985-89	1.2643	0.1512
1990-92	1.2787	0.1521

σ_i: standard deviation of log per capita real GDP (y_{it})

5. UNIT ROOT AND COINTEGRATION EMPIRICS ON CONVERGENCE

Some analysts contend that unit root and cointegration methods are logically superior to the TSCS approach to measure convergence as the latter mixes up short-run and long-run dynamics and precludes some plausible hypotheses (Bernard and Durlauf, 1995). If the log per capita GDP difference between Australia and China ($d_t = y_{at} - y_{ct}$) exhibits a unit root it implies non convergence. The Augmented Dickey Fuller (ADF) test, where the lag length (k) is chosen on the basis of the minimum Akaike Information Criterion (AIC) shows that per capita GDP difference is nonstationary (See Table 16.5). However, unit root tests can be easily overturned if the process is subjected to trend segmentation or structural breaks. It is assumed for the study period that Australian per capita GDP is free of structural discontinuities using data from Oxley and Greasley (1995).

Table 16.5: ADF Unit Root Tests on Time-Series

Null H_o	ADF stat	min AIC	lag (k)	CV	Order
d_t no trend	0.17	-5.67	2	-2.57	I(1)
d_t trend	-2.22	-5.82	2	-3.13	I(1)
Coin(y_c,y_a) res	-.61	con	PP	-3.50	I(1)

Furthermore, the Engle-Granger (1987) two-step procedure finds against cointegration of the per capita GDP of Australia and China. This also implies that the error correction mechanism (ecm_{t-1}) capturing the short-run dynamics is non-significant as indicated below:

$$\Delta y_{ct} = 0.0301 + 0.3657\Delta y_{at} + 0.2400ecm_{t-1} \quad n=32$$
$$|t| \quad (2.12) \quad (0.08) \qquad (1.52) \qquad R^2=0.08 \;\; DW=1.86$$

Nonetheless, the absence of bivariate cointegration does not rule out the presence of common stochastic trends in the conditional trade- growth data vector (g_t,y_t,i_t,x_t,h). Johansen (1991) maximum eigen value λ-max and Trace statistic tests reveal that at most three (r=3) cointegration relationships span the Australia-China trade-growth data vector (Table 16.6). Thus, despite the absence of convergence or cointegration common stochastic trends underpin the transitional trade-growth dynamics of the two countries.

Table 16.6: Johansen Multi-cointegration tests (Var=2)

Series	r=coint. vecs.	λ-max	95%CV	Trace	95%CV
[g, ly, li, lx]	r=1	21.97	27.07	33.92	29.68
	r=2	11.36	20.97	11.95	15.41
	r=3	0.59	14.07	0.59	3.76
[g, ly, li, lx, lh]	r=4	5.83	3.76	5.83	3.76

6. CONCLUSIONS AND POLICY PERSPECTIVES

Perspectives from neoclassical trade theory clearly indicate that both Australia and China could maximise their national welfare by specialising in the production or their respective comparative advantage of skilled and unskilled labour intensive goods and thereafter exchanging them freely. Any restrictions to free trade based on comparative advantage in response to the pressures from neo-protectionist lobbies will not only reduce national welfare but also erode global welfare. The empirical evidence from the manufacturing sectors reveals that trade liberalisation immiserised unskilled labour in Australia not through the Stolper-Samuelson but rather through the Rybczynski iron fist, as wage reductions were impounded by the Accord safety net policies. But jackboot of labour saving technology or Marx striking again was more powerful than trade in immiserising labour during the 1980s. The rapid transformation of the Australia to a skill intensive information economy corroborates that technology rather than trade was the 'smoking gun' in the swelling of the ranks of the unskilled unemployed.

As postulated by the neoclassical trade theorems, the comparative advantage skill intensive (ETM and information) sectors became the winners and the inefficient unskill intensive (TCF) sectors became the losers in Australia as effective rates of protection (ERA) were peeled off in the 1980s. Since the winners post-tax were better off after compensating the losers by subsidising labour retraining and other labour market adjustment programs, the nation as whole enhances its national welfare. The neoclassical general equilibrium framework explains that the jobs created in the dynamic and expanding export oriented sectors eventually offsets the jobs destroyed in the inefficient that have contracted due to import pressures. Some proponents of free trade argue that the exposure to the fresh winds of competition and transfer of best practice technology that is facilitated by the adoption of free trade policies results in a 'lifting of all boats' effect on all sectors of the economy. Nonetheless, some advocate interventionist labour market and strategic trade policies to meet the adjustment problems created by trade liberalisation and international competition. But activist labour market policies on the grounds of market failure remains a controversial issue. The contemporary labour market policy stance appears to favour wage flexibility resulting from the forces of the invisible hand rather than awards based on safety net provisions. To infuse further wage flexibility, current policies aim to deregulate the labour market by revamping industrial relations and promoting enterprise bargaining between workers and firms.

Notwithstanding the recent spectacular growth performance of the Chinese economy since the adoption of trade liberalisation policies in the post-Mao era, the ß-convergence estimates reveal that it would take at least 43 years for China to catch-up with Australia's per capita income. The rapid expansion of the mega Chinese economy has sent shock waves throughout the established hegemonic world order. There has been a flurry of allegations against China ranging from unfair trade practices, environmental vandalism, intellectual property piracy, labour convention violations, human rights abuses to other nondescript political misdemeanours. Arguably some of the China bashing is motivated by the threats Chinese expansion poses to the established world hegemonic order.

But regardless China is bound to emerge as economic superpower in the new century. In this context Australia's long-term economic interest would be served by mapping out strategies to harvest the vast export potential offered by the giant Chinese market. In this context, Australia should lend constructive support to international policies that would expedite China's entry to the WTO. Membership of China in international forum will encourage China to become a more responsible partner in the global free trade regime.

REFERENCES

Baldwin, R.E. (1992) "Measurable Dynamic Gains From Trade", *Journal of Political Economy*, 100(1): 162-174.

Barro, R.J. (1991) "Economic Growth in a Cross Section of Countries", *Quarterly Journal of Economics*, 106: 407-43.

Barro, R.J. and Sala-i-Martin, X, (1982) "Convergence", *Journal of Political Economy*, 100: 223-51.

Bernard, A.B. and Durlauf, S.N. (1995) "Convergence in International Output", *Journal of Applied Econometrics*, 10: 97-108.

Bhagwati, J.N. and Dehejia, V. (1994) "Free Trade and Wages of the Unskilled - Is Marx Striking Again?" in Bhagwati, J. and Kosters, M.H. (eds) *Trade and Wages*, American Enterprise Institute Press, Washington, D.C.

Bhagwati, J.N. and Srinivasan, T.N. (1983) *Lectures on International Trade*, MIT Press.

Brendt, E., Morrison, C., Rosenblaum, L. (1992) "High-Tech Capital Formation and Labour Composition in U.S. Manufacturing Industries: An Exploratory Analysis", *Working Paper No. 4010*, NBER.

Cashin, P. and Loayza, N. (1995) "Paradise Lost? Growth, Convergence, and Migration in the South Pacific", *IMF Staff Papers*, 42(3): 608-641.

Engle, R.F. and Granger, C.W.J. (1987) "Co-integration and error correction, representation, estimation and testing", *Econometrica*, 2: 251-276.

Fahrer, J. and Pease, A. (1994) "International Trade and the Australian Labour Market" in *International Integration of the Australian Economy*, Philip Lowe and Jacqueline Dwyer (eds.), Reserve Bank of Australia, Sydney.

Freeman, R.B. (1995) "Are Your Wages Set in Beijing?", *Journal of Economic Perspectives*, 9(7): 15-32.

Goldsmith, J. (1994) *The Trap*, Macmillan, London.

Greene, W.H. (1995) *LIMDEP Version 7.0*, Econometric Software Inc., Castle Hill, NSW, Australia.

Grossman, G.M. and Helpman, E. (1991) "Trade, Knowledge Spillovers and Growth", *European Economic Review*, 35(2/3): 517-526.

Johansen, S. (1991) "Estimation and Hypothesis Testing of Cointegration Vectors in a Gaussian Vector Autoregressive Model", *Econometrica*, 59: 1551-1580.

Karunaratne, N.D. (1991) "A General Equilibrium Analysis of the Australian Information Economy", *Systems Research*, 3(2): 465-479.

Krugman, P. (1995) "Growing World Trade: Causes and Consequences", *Brookings Papers on Economic Activity*, 1: 327-377.

Lawrence, R.Z. and Slaughter, M.J. (1993) "International Trade and the US Wages: Great Sucking Sound or Small Hiccup?", *Brookings Papers on Economic Activity*, 2: 161-226.

Leamer, E.E. (1994) "Trade, Wages and Revolving Door Ideas", *Working Paper* 4716, Cambridge, Mass., National Bureau of Economic Research.

Oxley, L. and Greasley, D. (1995) "A Time-Series Perspective on Convergence: Australia, UK and USA since 1870", *The Economic Record*, 71(214): 259-270.

Romer, P.M. (1994) "New Goods, Old Theory and the Welfare Costs of Trade Restrictions", *Journal of Development Economics*, 43(1): 5-38.

Sachs, J.D. and Shatz, H.J. (1994) "Trade and Jobs in the U.S. Manufacturing", *Brookings Papers on Economic Activity 1*, 1: 1-84.

Salvatore, D. (1995) *International Economics*, Prentice Hall, International Editions, Englewood Cliffs, New Jersey.

Solow, R.M. (1956) "A Contribution to the Theory of Economic Growth", *Quarterly Journal of Economics*, 70: 65-94.

Summers, R. and Heston, A. (1991) "The Penn World Tables (Mark 5): An Expanded Set of International Comparisons. 1950-1988", *Quarterly Journal of Economics*, 106: 327-68.

Swan, T.W. (1956) "Economic Growth and Capital Accumulation", *Economic Record*, 32: 334-361.

Wood (1994) *North-South Trade, Employment and Inequality*, Clarendon Press. Oxford.

World Bank (1993) *East Asian Miracle*, Oxford University Press.

17. AUSTRALIA-CHINA TECHNICAL AND ECONOMIC COOPERATION ON ENVIRONMENTAL IMPROVEMENT PROJECTS

Steve Harrison and Yushan Zhai[1]

---

1. INTRODUCTION

The rapid expansion of export industries in China, and need for equipment and technology, make that country of particular importance for Australia as an expanding trading partner. Australia is a signatory for various international environmental agreements, and is anxious that its overseas trade and cooperation activities be seen as environmentally responsible. With the adoption of the Priority Programme under Agenda 21, China is now placing substantial emphasis on projects to improve the environment.

Australia and China face a number of similar environmental problems. Both countries are well endowed with natural resources, including land, water, coal and minerals, and both face problems of degradation of land, water and vegetation resources problems. Both have mature water economies (heavily committed water resources). Both rely heavily on trade. Australia has traditionally devoted considerable resources to agricultural research, because

---

1 Visiting research fellow, supported by a fellowship program from the International Tropical Timber Organisation (ITTO), in Department of Economics, University of Queensland, Australia.

of the economic importance of our agricultural industries with respect to trade and development. Major research programs are being carried out on land, water and energy problems in Australia, in research organisations, universities and primary industry departments, particularly under funding for Cooperative Research Centres and Research and Development Corporations[2]. A broad skills base has developed, with comparative advantage in areas such as water engineering, coal technology and reforestation. In China, also, professional groups have developed with particular skills in natural resource and environmental management, such as in the Chinese Academy of Sciences.

The above discussion implies that environmental projects offer a growing area of cooperation between Australia and China, and this has in fact been the case in recent years. This chapter reviews some of the forms of cooperation which have taken place, and in particular the DIFF scheme.

2. ENVIRONMENTAL POLICY IN CHINA

China has made the commitment to implement a strategy for sustainable development in accordance with the directions formulated by the United Nations Conference on Environment and Development of 1992 (State Planning Commission, 1994). This has involved more than 500 projects suggested by ministries of the State Council, local governments, industrial sectors, academic institutions and other organisations. Priority is given to projects on environmental pollution control and conservation and sustainable utilisation of natural resources. Special attention is being given to environmentally sound technologies and demonstration projects in agricultural, industrial and energy development.

Nine priority areas are contained in the Priority Program, namely:

1. Capacity building and sustainable development
2. Sustainable agriculture
3. Cleaner production and environmental protection industry
4. Clean energy and transportation
5. Conservation and sustainable utilisation of natural resources
6. Environmental pollution control
7. Combating poverty and regional development
8. Population, health and human settlements
9. Global change and biodiversity conservation.

The State Planning Commission, the State Science and Technology Commission, the State Economic and Trade Commission and the National Environmental Protection Agency

---

2 The Land and Water Resources Research and Development Corporation (LWRRDC) provides major funding for research into sustainable management of land, water and vegetation resources in Australia, and this research has been found to have a large social payoff (McGregor et al., 1994).

guide and coordinate implementation of the priority projects, under the assistance of UNDP. Routine administration is undertaken by the Administrative Centre for China's Agenda 21 (ACCA21). "The Priority Program will be carried out through many varieties of international cooperation, such as multilateral, bilateral, grant, loans, foreign investment, joint-venture, build-operation-transfer (BOT), etc" (State Planning Commission, 1994). Priority projects are divided into three types, viz. assistance, cooperation and investment. About 60% of the total funding is expected to be supplied locally and 40% raised from the international community.

3. TYPES OF TECHNICAL AND ECONOMIC COOPERATION

Australia is involved in various forms of technical and economic cooperation on environmental improvement projects in China, including:

Federal government funded research projects. A number of projects have been conducted in China by Australian researchers under funding from Australian Centre for International Agricultural Research (ACIAR). For example, the ACIAR annual report of 1994/95 provides details of a number of current research projects in China involving environmental benefits components[3] (ACIAR, 1995).

Projects supported under AIDAB (AusAID). The supply of Australian equipment for a variety of development projects in China has been supported by AIDAB (now AusAID) under the Development Import Finance Facility (DIFF) scheme. This federal government program, which was discontinued with the change of federal government in 1996, is discussed in more detail below.

Australian state government initiatives. Australian states have recognised the importance of trade with China. For example, "The Queensland Government through the Queensland-China Council and the China Secretariat, Trade and Investment Development Division, Department of the Premier, Economic and Trade Development is committed to strengthen the trade and commercial relationship with China. Apart from the provision of direct assistance to Queensland companies, the Council and the Secretariat have established Memorandum of Business Cooperation between Queensland and targeted cities and provinces in China" (Ivory et al., 1995, Foreword). These authors draw attention to Australia's expertise in Building, Construction and Environmental Management, as potential trade areas. The

3 These include Project 9044 - Increasing productivity of eucalypt plantations in China by inoculation with ectomycorrhizas and nutrient application; 9127 - Predicting tree growth for general regions and specific sites in China, Thailand and Australia; 9227 - Australian acacias for sustainable development in China, Vietnam and Australia; and 9048 - Efficient use of water for fruit production on the North China Plain.

Queensland government now proposes to set up a trade office in China (Williams, 1996).

Academic communities and exchange visits. A natural follow-up from the more structured research and cooperation projects such as under AIDAB and AusAID is exchange visits by physical and social scientists in the two countries, which is taking place at an increasing rate. As well, contacts and understanding are fostered by a number of students from China studying in Australia, some supported by AIDAB funds.

Chinese communities in Australia and former Chinese students and visitors. Ivory et al. (1995) suggest that these two groups can play an important role in economic cooperation between China and Australia. They note the size and diversity of the Chinese community in Australia, and role of the Australia-China Chamber of Commerce in Western Australia in organising business developments with China. Further, they suggest the formation of a database and network of former students and regular mail contacts, such as takes place in New Zealand. No specific mention is made of environmental projects.

Major resource companies with China experience. The procedure of "corporate mentoring" where large companies provide assistance is establishing export markets to smaller companies in non-competing fields is discussed by Ivory et al. (1995).

4. THE DIFF SCHEME

The Development Import Finance Facility (DIFF), administered by the AusAID, has been part of Australia's Official Development Cooperation Program. It has been designed to promote opportunities for Australian business seeking to undertake sound projects in developing countries. DIFF grants were "combined with loan funds from the Export Finance and Insurance Corporation (EFIC) to provide concessional or soft loans, to enable Australian business to compete with international business offering similar financing terms" (AIDAB, 1994).

University of Queensland economists have been involved with DIFF project appraisal through an agreement between AusAID (earlier AIDAB) and UniQuest (the university's consultancy office). The DIFF process has involved a number of steps, as indicated in Table 17.1. Project appraisal was carried out within strict time and budget limits, which necessitated rapid assessment methods. Data sources included feasibility studies, responses to written questions by suppliers and Chinese project managers, and access to a variety of published literature. When considered justified (of the order of 50% of projects) field missions were carried out, permitting site inspection, briefing sessions and information exchange sessions with local officials.

The total project cost (TPC) for each project was estimated by the appraisal team. AusAID and EFIC established the eligible contract value (ECV), taking into account goods and services provided, freight and insurance, and local costs. The proposed DIFF was 35%

of the ECV. Annual cash flows were estimated, leading to estimates of discounted cash flow performance criteria.

Economic analysis involved drawing up a series of spreadsheets for a project, and estimating the economic internal rate of return (EIRR) and the financial internal rate of return (FIRR). The former includes non-market benefits (economic, environmental and social), and uses shadow prices where appropriate, with the objective of determining whether the project is "developmentally sound", i.e. worthwhile from a social viewpoint. The FIRR was used to indicate whether a project is commercially viable.

Under the Helsinki Agreement of 1992, OECD countries have agreed to restrict the use of tied aid in distorting trade patterns. Australia has been a strong supporter of this agreement, because of its reliance on trade. A consequence of the Helsinki Agreement is that projects which are "commercially viable" are ineligible for concessional financing (and hence for DIFF support)[4]. Australia has an obligation to notify the OECD where concessional finance is involved, and other OECD countries have the right to request detailed information and may make an official challenge[5].

Feasibility studies have been prepared, and Australian concessionary finance provided, for a number of development projects in various countries - perhaps the most important being China - with finance used to purchase Australian equipment. In appraising any project, AusAID sought to ensure that it was "developmentally sound, sustainable, and meets the policy objectives set for development assistance, including social, cultural and gender specific and environmental policies" (AIDAB, 1994). One aspect of DIFF appraisals has been an examination of the potential "risks", including risks to the environment. A number of guidelines have been set for project evaluation, with respect to environment in general (AIDAB, 1991), and to environmental impacts for energy (AIDAB, 1993a), industry (AIDAB, 1993b) and mining (AIDAB, 1993c).

5. EXAMPLES OF DIFF ENVIRONMENTAL IMPROVEMENT PROJECTS

Most if not all development projects have environmental implications, both positive and negative. Our interest here is with projects for which the central feature is more sustainable use of natural resources such as land, water, energy, forestry or wildlife. Several projects are described briefly to illustrate the nature of environmental impacts and the assessment method.

---

4 A project which is commercially viable should be capable of attracting normal commercial funding. Were countries to provide concessional finance for commercially viable projects, this would be tantamount to dumping of exports so as to gain unfair market access.

5 Projects worth more than SDR 50m (about $A 100m) are subject to automatic notification, while projects with a value of less than SDR 2m are not subject to consultation provisions.

Table 17.1: Steps in the DIFF process

- Firms make application for DIFF funds.
- Where applications are accepted in principle, firms are required to submit a feasibility study in support of their project, under guidelines set out in AIDAB (1994). Firms are advised to employ professional consultants to prepare these reports, which address the viability, environmental impact and sustainability of the proposed project.
- A team of independent consultants - with expertise in economics, technical issues, environmental impacts and social and gender impacts - reviews the feasibility study and any other information available about the project. Sets of questions may be forwarded to the suppliers and to the Chinese stakeholders in the project. Where judged necessary, a field mission is carried out involving site inspections and meetings with local officials. Finally, an appraisal report is produced, which is reviewed by a specialist group and after modifications if needed is forwarded to AusAID.
- AusAID notifies the OECD in Paris of the project, and forwards a modified appraisal report. Australian support for the project may face challenge from other OECD countries, requiring further representations by the Australian government.
- Provided there is no OECD challenge, or that challenge is withdrawn or overcome, the Australian firm undertakes direct negotiations and implementation through its China project partner.

Case 1. A project involved supplying water treatment equipment for a new municipal water supply system for a city of over one million people (Jinan). This was necessary because of unsustainable extraction of groundwater. However, the new system would use wetlands as sedimentation areas (with progressive land reclamation). The question thus arose as to whether loss of wetland flora, fauna and functions would be of significance, and whether chemicals used in water treatment could enter the groundwater and cause adverse impacts in downstream wetlands. Obviously, there are important environmental tradeoffs to be considered. Further, these need to be weighted against the social impacts, e.g. inadequate water supply and families having to regularly carry water to upper floor apartments.

This project illustrates how overcoming one environmental problem can potentially place other aspects of environment at risk.

Case 2. A project involved supplying machinery and irrigation equipment for a large irrigation project in the Inner Mongolia Autonomous Region (IMAR). A high proportion of Chinese agriculture on riparian land is already irrigated, and further irrigation to increase food necessarily involves taking water to more marginal land. In traditional grasslands, high stocking pressures combined with a series of drought years can lead to severe rangeland degradation. Irrigation projects have the potential to provide an alternative livelihood for herdsmen, as well as supplementary fodder for livestock. The IMAR project has important social benefits, in terms of increasing food production and reducing the frequency of emergency assistance to the region. However, two environmental problems emerged during the appraisal. First, evidence suggests that introduction of irrigated cropping need not reduce rangeland grazing pressures. In fact, availability of supplementary fodder tends to promote increased livestock numbers (Longworth and Williamson, 1993). Regulatory controls would be needed to reduce rangeland grazing intensity, which would be unpopular and difficult to monitor. Second, where the geological history of newly irrigated land is marine sediments, there can be a high risk of rapid salinisation, particularly when flood irrigation is adopted. In that the Australian suppliers proposed to provide "centre pivot" spray irrigators, which would displace flood irrigation, salinity problems should be reduced. On the other hand, support under the DIFF program could be viewed as encouraging an environmentally unsustainable irrigation project. The Australian government eventually took the latter view and withdrew support for the project.

Case 3. China relies heavily on coal-fired steam boilers for industry and heating. Coal burning is a source of atmospheric pollution, in terms of emissions of CO_2, sulphur and particles. Australian firms have developed advanced travelling grate coal combustion techniques, i.e. more efficient combustion and lower emissions. A DIFF project involved the transfer of coal-fired boiler technology and training from the Sydney-based Maxitherm Australia Pty Ltd to the Tai Yuan No. 2 Boilerworks in Shanxi Province. For this project, it was necessary to determine the economic benefits from reduced coal consumption and reduced greenhouse gas emissions. In an earlier DIFF project (in 1989) Maxitherm had provided steam boiler technology to the Dalian Boiler Works in Liaoning Province. These projects were judged to provide significant economic and environmental benefit, with little environmental or other risk.

Case 4. A major project was carried out in the early 1990s to transfer Australian technology for manufacture of refrigerator plants to Jiangxi Province. This project, with an estimated contract value of over $40 m, was designed to allow production of "one million energy efficient, non CFC refrigeration and freezer compressors annually" (AIDAB, 1992, p. 25).

6. SOME ISSUES ARISING UNDER THE DIFF SCHEME

Compatibility of environmental standards. Although China is a signatory to more than 20 international treaties on the environment, there is limited domestic legislation to implement those treaties. Most of the legislation for sustainable development was promulgated in the 1980s on the basis of a planned economy, and requires adjustment to adapt to the movement towards a market economy. When environmental standards differ between China and

Australia, the question arises as to which country's standards should be imposed in appraisal reports; in general, the Australian standards have been considered the appropriate ones for DIFF appraisals.

Narrow parameters for project approval. As discussed earlier, projects must be developmentally sound (to warrant expenditure), but must not be commercially viable (because OECD challenge would then be likely). The economic internal rate of return and financial internal rate of return will differ in that the former includes estimated values of environmental and social benefits and shadow pricing of inputs and products where possible. Projects have been judged acceptable for DIFF funding only if

$$\text{EIRR} > \text{cost of capital (about 14\%)} > \text{FIRR}$$

and the project risks (technical, economic, environmental, social and gender) are not too great. This greatly restricts the number and types of projects which could be included, although allowing scope for genuine social and environmental projects.

Political acceptability of "tied aid". The DIFF scheme has clearly been a form of tied aid, in that grants and low-interest funds to recipient countries are used to purchase equipment from donor countries. In this context, the scheme should not be thought of as a form of humanitarian aid, but as one of technical and economic cooperation. Further, in judging the scheme, the considerable economic benefits to Australia through both direct equipment sales and future access to major markets need to be kept in mind.

Difficulties in estimating economic values of environmental impacts. Valuation of environmental benefits is usually difficult, and time and budget constraints did not permit application of sophisticated methods such as community surveys. Rather, a "benefit transfer" approach to valuation (OECD, 1994; Pearce and Moran, 1994) was the only workable method. This involves use of standard environmental values tempered by personal judgment. As an example, the benefit from more efficient boilers hence less coal consumption was taken as $10/tonne of carbon[6]. The benefit transfer approach probably has greatest credibility when applied to global pollution problems such as greenhouse gas emissions, for which considerable literature about damage estimates is available and for which carbon taxes of similar magnitudes have been introduced by a number of countries. Standard values have of course been widely used in accounting for loss of life and cost of injury in medical studies, and reduction of travel time in road improvement cost-benefit analyses, but have been more controversial when applied to environmental impacts. The "benefit transfer" approach is supported by the NSW Environmental Protection Authority *Envalue* database of environmental values (NSWEPA, 1995). The objective of this initiative has been to promote greater acceptance of environmental valuations, and greater use of non-market values of natural resources in decision making. Recently, there has been interest by water

---

6 Estimates of the damage costs of carbon dioxide emissions are reviewed by van Kooten et al. (1993) and Pearce and Moran (1994).

resource engineers in benefit transfer methods as a cost-effective alternative to new non-market valuations, with applications to improved water quality and its impact on recreation values and public health (Kask and Shogren, 1994) and to lake recreation (Parsons and Kealy, 1994). The latter study indicated a high degree of reliability in transferring estimated benefits from one site to another; however, it was noted that the sites were in the same state (Milwaukee) and had a high degree of similarity.

Language difficulties. Even with the assistance of competent interpreters, some difficulties were experienced in field missions due to language differences, particularly when investigating specific technical and socio-economic detail.

Resource demands and time delays for suppliers. The DIFF process involved a considerable transaction cost for suppliers, as well as uncertainty where competitive supply proposals were made, and the approval process tended to be lengthy such that some streamlining may have been desirable.

Project scoping. It is often difficult to determine the scope of the development program, e.g. whether it can be viewed as a local project or should be considered within the context of a national infrastructure upgrading effort. This has implications for the commercial viability, and hence for the likelihood of challenge by other OECD countries.

Values changing over time. All calculations for DIFF appraisals were performed in US dollars terms. When high inflation took place in China, changing exchange rates lead to instability in cash flow budgets.

Determining appropriate prices. Serious distortions may take place in markets, so that adjustments to market prices were needed in determining EIRR estimates. Where practicable shadow prices were adopted, for example based on import or export price parities. Valuing labour costs also presented difficulties, because of low wage rates and the fact that wages may be an alternative to income support.

7. THE DEMISE AND POTENTIAL REPLACEMENT OF THE DIFF SCHEME

In spite of the above issues, the DIFF scheme could be judged a clear success. It would not be reasonable to judge the scheme in terms of aid benefits, although there were aid components in the projects, and these projects were sometimes in socio-economically disadvantaged areas. Rather, it was definitely a two-way technical and economic cooperation scheme. The equipment, technology and so on provided was required to be wholly or mainly of Australian origin, taken as an Australian content of over 80%. Australian firms were assisted to gain market access, develop contacts and showcase Australian equipment and technology in China.

An feature of the scheme was the use of a multidisciplinary team to carry out an integrated appraisal of the economic/financial, technical, environmental and social/gender impacts. This, combined with the site inspections and project discussions in China provided an invaluable learning experience for the Australian consultants, and greatly increased their understanding and empathy with development issues in China.

The DIFF scheme was withdrawn by the incoming Liberal-National federal coalition government on taking office in early 1996. The intention to drop the scheme apparently had been announced prior to the federal election. It was reported that 51 Australian companies had spent $70 m on preparation for DIFF projects which were discontinued (ABC, 1996); presumably, substantial amounts had also been spent by foreign countries in seeking DIFF assistance for these projects. While no contracts had been signed, strong expectations had developed, and questions were raised in the media about Australia's trade interests and reliability and commitment to the Asian region.

Various reasons for dropping the DIFF scheme were advanced, including that it was not a humanitarian aid scheme, savings are needed to reduce the budget deficit, the benefits asserted for the scheme have been exaggerated, and funds have not been well targeted. It could be argued that because the DIFF scheme was not primarily a poverty alleviation scheme, it did not fit well within the activities of AusAID. On the other hand, estimates indicated that each dollar spent by the Australian government on the scheme generated $5 in extra trade revenue, although this figure was disputed by the incoming government (ABC, 1996). In discrediting this export income multiplier, government sources argued that if the return from DIFF funding were so high, it would have been advantageous to devote billions of dollars to the program (c.f. the $887m spent over the period 1982-83 to 1995-96), an obviously absurd proposition. However, this logic overlooks the careful project screening process and narrow parameters for approval of DIFF and EFIC funding. With regard to targeting, nearly half of the DIFF funds were provided to Indonesia and one quarter to China, while the Transfield company was a major Australian supplier.

The DIFF scheme was of considerable developmental and environmental assistance to China, and a means of developing trade and fostering understanding between countries. Given the unquestionable benefits, it is to be expected that some similar program will emerge, though perhaps within an industry or trade department. Should this not be the case, individual states would no doubt extend their initiatives, with likely duplication of effort. Because of strong representations by recipient countries, the Australian government has decided to support urgent and high priority projects in China, Indonesia, Vietnam and The Philippines (Shanahan, 1996). Funds are to be provided from the AusAID budget, but not formally under the DIFF scheme, raising concerns that funding for humanitarian aid could be reduced (Sheridan, 1996).

8. CONCLUDING COMMENTS

China is taking active steps to comply with international environmental treaties and manage resources in a sustainable manner. In this endeavour, it is seeking assistance and cooperation with other countries. Environmental improvements in China are important for that country, and also of global importance.

Many development projects are not viable in a strictly financial sense, such that they would not attract commercial loans. However, the environmental and social benefits may be considerable, such that from a wider developmental view they are well worthwhile in economic terms. Evaluation of projects yielding environmental and social benefits not reflected in markets presents particular difficulties. Resort can be made to a number of approaches, including "benefit transfer", to derive approximate benefit estimates for use in a social cost-benefit analysis framework.

From Australia's viewpoint, environmental improvement projects in China create markets for export of equipment and technology. It is clearly in the interests of both Australia and China to develop further the levels of economic and technical cooperation in sustainable development projects, including those designed specifically for environmental improvement. Various forms of research programs and trade enhancement schemes can play an effective role in fostering this cooperation.

REFERENCES

ABC (Australian Broadcasting Commission) (1996) "DIFF Scheme Loans Scrapped", Seven-Thirty Report, 22 May.

ACIAR, Australian Centre for International Agricultural Research (1995), *Annual Report 1994-95*, Canberra.

AIDAB, Australian International Development Assistance Bureau (1991), *Environmental Assessment for International Development Cooperation*, Activity Guideline, Canberra.

AIDAB, Australian International Development Assistance Bureau (1992), *Australian Development Cooperation with China*, AGPS, Canberra.

AIDAB, Australian International Development Assistance Bureau (1993a), *Energy - Environmental Assessment Guidelines for Development Assistance Projects*, Canberra.

AIDAB, Australian International Development Assistance Bureau (1993b), *Industry - Environmental Assessment Guidelines for Development Assistance Projects*, Canberra.

AIDAB, Australian International Development Assistance Bureau (1993c), *Mining - Environmental Assessment Guidelines for Development Assistance Projects*, Canberra.

AIDAB, Australian International Development Assistance Bureau (1994), *Development Import Finance Facility: Feasibility Study Guidelines and Format*, Canberra.

Ivory, P., Nguyen, D.-T. and McEllister, R., *Economic Growth in the Shanghai Region and its Implications for the Queensland Economy*, Report to the Queensland China Council, Griffith University, Brisbane.

Kask, S.B. and Shogren, J.F. (1994) "Benefit Transfer Protocol for Long-term Health Risk Evaluation: A Case of Surface Water Contamination", *Water Resources Research*, 30(10): 2813-2823.

Longworth, J.W. and Williamson, G.J. (1993) *China's Pastoral Region: Sheep and Wool, Minority Nationalities, Rangeland Degradation and Sustainable Development*, CAB International, in Association with the Australian Centre for International Agricultural Research, Wallingford.

McGregor, M.J., Harrison, S.R. and Tisdell, C.A. (1993) *Assessing the Impact of Research Programs Related to Australia's Natural Resources*, LWRRDC Occasional Paper Series No. 08/94, Canberra.

NSWEPA (New South Wales Environmental Protection Authority),1995, *Envalue*, Sydney.

OCD, Organisation of Economic Co-Operation and Development (1994), *Project and Policy Appraisal: Integrating Economics and Environment*, Paris.

Parsons, G.R. and Kealy, M.J. (1994) "Benefit Transfer in a Random Utility Model of Recreation", *Water Resources Research*, 30(8): 2477-2484.

Pearce, D. and Moran, D. (1994), *The Economic Value of Biodiversity*, Earthscan, London.

Shanahan, D. (1996) "Downer Reverses DIFF for Asia", *The Australian*, 23 July, p. 1.

Sheridan, G. (1996) "Downer Perfects the Art of Losing", *The Australian*, 24 July, p. 11.

State Planning Commission (1994) *Priority Programme for China's Agenda 21: First Tranche*, State Science and Technology Commission, Beijing.

van Kooten, G.C., Thompson, W.A. and Vertinsky, I. (1993) Turning Down the Heat: Economics of Reforestation in British Columbia when Benefits of CO_2 Reduction are Taken into Account, Forest Economics and Policy Analysis Research Unit, Working Paper 174, University of British Columbia, Vancouver.

Williams, B. (1996) "State's Future Lies in Power, Ports and Dams", *The Courier Mail*, 15 June 1996, p. 3.

World Bank (1991), *China: Efficiency and Environmental Impact of Coal Use*, Industry and Energy Division, China Department, Washington.

18. CHINA - NAFTA TRADE: WHAT DOES THE FUTURE HOLD?

Shengliang Deng and Katherine Braun

1. BACKGROUND

Two global trends emerged during the 1980s which offer significant opportunities for international trade. The first is the trend to liberalising economies, offering greater scope and facility to market forces. The second is the internationalisation of markets and the resulting expansion of global trade in services. The maximum benefit of these opportunities will only be achieved if there is a functioning open, global trade system. And yet, the trend today is the opposite; global trade opportunities are threatened by rising protectionism and the inclination to regional trade arrangements; the EC, ASEAN and NAFTA are only some examples of this growing trend. Regional economic arrangements are not themselves, bad. But, when they operate to reduce exposure to international markets and thus, reduce competitiveness, opportunities for growth are reduced and global-scale operations are threatened.

Now that NAFTA is two years old, it is natural for all of those interested in the healthy evolution of the international economy, to be concerned about the implications of this trade arrangement. Will NAFTA member countries continue to reflect trade policies which embrace an open, multi-lateral trade system and greater global integration? Or instead, will such arrangements over time, tend to increase trade barriers against non-members, while moving closer to intra-bloc trade alliances? These questions are crucial to the evolution of the world economy into the next century. Yet, there are no clear, immediate answers.

This chapter examines the nature of China-NAFTA trade, to determine the implications of major regional trade agreements like NAFTA, for emerging economies like China. A brief overview of the socio-demographic indicators in the NAFTA and Chinese economies is followed by an analysis of economic developments in China and a synopsis of the NAFTA Agreement. Analysis of recent economic performance in China and NAFTA countries along with progress in global trade, offers the reader some insight into the factors which have contributed to China's success in the international marketplace and the obstacles China continues to face. The growing trend to regionalism is examined to identify the implications for the future of China - NAFTA trade, with address of the more frequent vocal, anti-China sentiment expressed in the US. The chapter concludes by raising some concerns on the future of multi-lateral trade and how global forces may have an impact on the future of Chinese economic development.

Of late, a growing number of authors have addressed issues raised in this chapter. Goodhart and Xu (1996) and Wong (1995) for example, examine the growing competitiveness of China and conclude that dynamic growth in the Asia-Pacific region into the 21st century will continue to be led by China. Anderson (1992, 1993); Elek (1992); Schott (1991) examine the growing trends to regionalism and their implication on trade policies. An excellent compendium on the challenges posed by NAFTA, edited by R.G. Cushing (1993), offers the views of several authors concerning the effects of regional trade blocs on world trade (Krueger), NAFTA and the Asia-Pacific region (Drysdale, Garnaut, Shott/Hufbauer) and NAFTA and Australia-New Zealand (Baker). On the topic of protectionism, economists such as Johnson (1965), Corden (1971) and Bhagwati (1988), have authored seminal views on the costs of such policies and the merits of liberal trade, while other authors, Baldwin (1992), offer evidence on the measurable gains from trade.

2. SOCIO-DEMOGRAPHIC INDICATORS

Examining the social and human development in China and NAFTA economies, it is clear that China poses exceptional opportunities for trade. World Bank data reported in Table 18.1 indicates that China's estimated population is about 1.2 billion, which represents almost 25% of the world's estimated population, and three times the NAFTA region population of 408 million. Moreover, China will continue to represent the largest country on earth, as its population is projected to increase by a further 17% over the period Yr 2000-2025. In addition, that growing population will be increasingly urbanised and better-educated, as China continues to improve overall literacy and life expectancy through investment in education and health care.

Table 18.1: China - NAFTA Economies: Basic Indicators

	Population (millions)			Total Fertility (1993)	Life Expectancy at Birth years (1993)	Adult Illiteracy Rate (1993)	Urban Population av. growth 1990-93
	1993	2000	2025				
China	**1,178**	**1,255**	**1,471**	**2.0%**	**69**	**27%**	**4.3%**
Canada	29	31	38	1.9%	78	<5.0%	1.3%
USA	258	275	331	2.1%	76	<5.0%	1.2%
Mexico	90	102	137	3.1%	71	13%	3.1%

Source: World Bank (1995), Tables 1, 26 and 31.

3. THE DYNAMIC ECONOMY OF CHINA

The remarkable economic vigour of the Chinese economy continues to be evident; for example, Table 18.2 shows that economic growth as measured by GDP has averaged over 13% in 1992 and annual GDP growth has averaged over 8% since 1980. In fact, China continues to outperform every other country not to mention the NAFTA region. Although 1994 economic growth declined to 11.5% and is expected to slip to 9.8% in 1995 and further to 8.9% by 1996,[1] growth of the Chinese economy will remain higher than most of the Asia-Pacific region and the industrialised OECD nations.[2] Chinese exports will continue to boom, as recent economic reforms register stronger growth performance, further expanding interest in China's economy by foreign investors. Moreover, measured on a PPP[3] basis, China's GDP in 1994 was just under US$3 trillion, making it the second largest economy, next to the United States at US$6.7 trillion. By the Year 2020, China is expected to surpass the USA and represent the largest economy on earth.[4]

1 Asian Development Bank, *Outlook 1995/96*, p.80.

2 The Asia-Pacific region, as commonly defined, comprises eleven countries: Japan, China, the ASEAN countries of Brunei, Indonesia, Malaysia, the Philippines, Thailand, South Korea, Taiwan, Hong Kong and Singapore.

3 The size of different country's economies can be compared by converting their GDP into dollars, using purchasing-power parities (PPP), which takes into account what money actually buys in each country. *The Economist*, January 27, 1996, p. 102.

4 "A Survey of the Global Economy", *The Economist*, October 1, 1994.

Table 18.2: China - NAFTA Economies: Economic Indicators

	Total GDP US$ (mil) 1993	GNP per capita		Real GDP Growth: annual % chg				Inflation Rate aver. annual % chg (1994)
		US $ (1993)	aver. annual growth rate (1980-93)	1977-86	1990	1992	1994	
China	**425,611**	**490**	**8.2%**	**9.0%**	**3.8%**	**13.1%**	**11.5%**	**21.7%**
Canada	477,468	19,970	1.4%	3.1%	-0.2%	0.8%	4.6%	0.2%
USA	6,259,899	24,740	1.7%	2.7%	1.2%	2.3%	4.1%	2.6%
Mexico	343,472	3,610	-0.5%	3.8%	4.4%	2.8%	3.5%	7.0%

Source: World Bank (1995) *IMF World Economic Outlook (1995)* and Asian Development Bank, *Outlook (1995/96).*

4. THE NAFTA AGREEMENT

Canada and the US have the largest trade relationship of any two countries in the world. In the mid-1980s, the argument for Canada seeking a Free Trade Agreement (FTA) with the US (effective January 1, 1988), was both defensive and offensive. The best defence against growing American protectionism was to act bilaterally to eliminate tariffs and try to contain non-tariff barriers (NTBs). In fact, small open economies like Canada have much to gain from more liberalised trade and a trade agreement with the US gave Canada further access to American markets. This concept of a bilateral FTA expanded to Mexico in 1991, which broadened trade links to a wider, continental trade agreement, the North American Free Trade Agreement (NAFTA), effective as of January 1, 1994.

Market access is the fundamental aspect of traditional trade agreements. Therefore, the aim of the NAFTA is to create an expanded and secure market for goods and services produced in the three member countries, to provide a predictable framework for business planning and investment opportunities and to promote conditions of fair competition and enhance member competitiveness in global markets. NAFTA establishes a single trade zone, comprising nearly 377 million people (1993), which will significantly liberalise the treatment of services, investment and intellectual property rights across the continent. At over 1,000 pages, the NAFTA text incorporates most of the provisions of the 1988 Canada-US FTA, while also improving on provisions addressing rules of origin, government procurement and customs administration. The NAFTA eliminates tariffs on almost 10,000 products traded between the three countries over 15 years. Since tariffs on most goods traded between Canada and the US were negotiated for phase-out under the existing FTA, the largest impact of the NAFTA agreement is expected to be on Mexico, which has maintained a relatively high tariff rate system averaging 20%.[5]

NAFTA is a milestone development in negotiation of international trade agreements, in that it is the first trade agreement to integrate the economies of developed and developing countries and to adopt a sectoral approach to identifying areas of exclusion. What the NAFTA does, in effect, according to Weintraub (1993), is to deepen the economic relationship within North America, by facilitating the integration of production and marketing, throughout the continent. The NAFTA identifies those areas not covered by the Agreement, assuming that free trade will result in all other areas. As a result, the NAFTA significantly enhances the scope and application of trade in goods and services, by removing the majority of barriers which distort trade among North American countries. In addition, the direct linkage between trade and the environment will likely set a new minimum standard for future international trade agreements. The NAFTA also provides for a dispute settlement mechanism to deal with resolution of disputes on countervailing duties, dumping and enforcement of intellectual property rights. To date, the dispute settlement mechanism process has addressed 25 cases, perhaps the most well known being softwood lumber. More significantly and perhaps controversial, according to Holick and Debusk (1992), the dispute settlement mechanism in NAFTA has, for the first time, opened the administration of American domestic law to binding scrutiny by an international panel.[6]

5. WHAT DO THE CRITICS SAY ABOUT NAFTA?

NAFTA is the latest in a long series of bilateral and regional trade agreements. In North America itself, there has been relatively little analysis of how NAFTA will affect other countries and the global trading system. On the other hand, NAFTA appears to cause a great deal of concern for excluded countries, where the Agreement is being scrutinised for its impact on the global trading system and its implications for American trade policy into the next century. The Asian-Pacific region has been watching the emergence of NAFTA and according to McKinney (1993), some countries such as Japan, have concerns on how it will affect their trade relations. Kreinin and Plummer (1992) estimate the costs of trade diversion from southeast Asia to NAFTA countries and suggest that many Asian manufacturers, particularly in textiles and apparel, will be placed at a distinct disadvantage compared to Mexico, which benefits from country of origin and the eventual elimination of tariffs and duties on intra-NAFTA trade.

---

5 GATT, *Trade Policy Review, Mexico*, Vol.1, 1993.

6 For a detailed analysis of the dispute settlement mechanism, see G.N. Holick and F.A. Debusk (1992) "The Functioning of the FTA Dispute Resolution Panels", in L. Waverman (ed.) (1992) *Negotiating and Implementing a North American Free Trade Agreement*, The Fraser Institute, Vancouver.

Young (1993) and Schott/Hufbauer (1993) sight some major danger points associated with NAFTA's potential for trade diversion. Firstly, there is a strong likelihood that NAFTA trade could extend beyond Mexico to the western hemisphere and include Latin American countries, creating the "NAFTA Fortress". Some critics contend that NAFTA is a large and potentially discriminatory trading arrangement, that has emerged during a period of much uncertainty about the future of multi-lateral trade. For example, Drysdale and Garnaut (1993) sight the potential for more trade regionalism and American re-evaluation of its multi-lateral trade policy, while Baker (1993) suggests that NAFTA will be a further step to a protectionist and uni-lateralist US approach. Anderson (1993) and Krueger (1993) maintain that NAFTA may be another step in the "drift" to a world divided into major trading blocs.

6. ECONOMIC DEVELOPMENTS IN NAFTA COUNTRIES AND CHINA

Canada

As a small, open economy, Canada has benefited from the progressive liberalisation of global trade during the last forty years and has been a constituent supporter of GATT negotiated tariff reductions. Exports have been the driving force stimulating Canadian economic growth, buoyed by strong markets for commodities and weakness of the Canadian dollar. Contrary to pessimistic beliefs, the Canada-US FTA did not cause a disastrous loss of investment in Canada and in fact, Canada has clearly been a "winner" from the FTA. The FTA has played a key role in opening up the US market to Canadian exports. During the five year period 1988-93, the US$-value of Canadian exports into the US market increased by 45%, while Canadian exports to the European market declined by 2.2%, by 3.9% to Japan and by 11% to south east Asia respectively. As a result, Canada has expanded its trade surplus with the US, which has tripled between 1987 and 1994, according to Schwanen (1994).

Not only is Canada exporting more to the US, but a growing proportion of all Canadian exports are shipped to the US; 80.5% in 1994 compared to 73% in 1984. According to GATT, Canada continues to benefit not only from more open American market, but also from the growing trend of intra-industry trade (IIT), which has grown rapidly in manufacturing, particularly the auto sector. American intra-industry trade with Canada as a share of total annual Canada-US merchandise trade, has progressively increased from 40% of total 1970 trade to 46% of 1980 trade to 55% of total 1990 trade.[7]

---

7 Based on GATT calculations using a total of 625 4-digit SITC lines. Reported in GATT, *Trade Policy Review, United States*, vol.1, 1994, p.223. Intra-industry trade refers to trade in products classified in the same industrial category, so the measurement of ITT is sensitive to the way products are aggregated into these categories. The more highly disaggregated the product classifications for example, the lower

Recent analysis on the first two years of the NAFTA indicates that bilateral trade between Canada and the US has surged by 35%, to a record US$371 billion in 1995, 73% of which (US$272 billion) is accounted for by merchandise trade.[8] Real GDP growth is projected to be 4.3% in 1995 and 2.6% in 1996,[9] reflecting continued strength in trade partner import markets and progressive improvement in economic competitiveness.

Mexico

As the newest member of NAFTA, Mexico faces the most extensive obstacles to compete in the liberalising global marketplace. To meet its GATT obligations, Mexico had to effectively eliminate 75% of its import licensing requirements, rationalise and lower tariffs to a historical weighted average of 13.1% (1992),[10] ease restrictions on foreign direct investment and continue to progressively eliminate customs duties on imported industrial goods. Mexico also faces challenges to contain high inflation, which averaged 31% in 1995, following sharp 50% depreciation of the peso in December 1994. The 1994 currency crisis significantly battered real GDP of the Mexican economy, having grown at 3.5% in 1994, real GDP was estimated at -2.0% in 1995 and slow growth is expected for 1996.

Over the last 25 years, Mexico's leading trade partners have been the US and Japan. In fact, Mexico is the third largest trade partner of the US, while the US is the largest market for Mexican exports, taking 80% of Mexico's exports in 1994 (see Table 18.6). The US plays an even more significant role if in-bond processing (maquiladora) production is accounted for. The structure of Mexico's merchandise exports has changed markedly since the 1980s. In 1980 for example, oil represented almost 67% of total exports, but that share dropped to 32% by 1991, while manufacturing exports increased from 12% - 59% over the same period.[11]

---

will be the measurement of IIT. When IIT is substantial, as in the case of Canada-US trade, a country's trade largely involves the exchange of similar goods. For a more explicit analysis of intra-industry trade, see, H. Grubel and P. Lloyd (1975) *Intra-Industry Trade*, MacMillan Press, London.

8 "U.S. gives Canada a qualified "thumbs up"", *The Globe and Mail*, April 2, 1996.

9 IMF, *Outlook 1995/96*, p. 11.

10 Mexico joined the GATT in August 1986. GATT, *Trade Policy Review, Mexico*, vol.1, 1993, p.74. This 1992 low of 13.1% is less than half the 1982 average of 27%.

11 GATT (1993) *Trade Policy Review, Mexico*, 1: 3.

United States

The US continues to be the world's largest trading nation, accounting for 14% of total global trade in 1994. A striking feature of US economic development over the past several years has been the role of external trade; almost half (43%) of total growth in real GDP during 1988-91 arose from increased net exports, which were particularly important in cushioning the impacts of the 1990-91 recession.

The continuing increase in net exports during the most recent five year period 1991-95, has been stimulated by falling unit labour costs and increasing productivity in manufacturing relative to major trade partners, as well as favourable global growth. As reported in Table 18.6, the US economy has been the driving force behind NAFTA trade performance. American exports increased by 134% over the 1984-94 decade, while imports rose by 96%. Preliminary data from the IMF shows that US exports in 1995, increased by a further 14% to an all-time high of US$584 billion, while imports into the US market increased by 12% to US$771 billion. Underpinned by strong domestic demand, the American economy expanded to meet 4% growth in real GDP in 1994, although growth is expected to slip to 3.2% in 1995 and to 1.9% in 1996.[12]

China

China's economic performance has been remarkable during the post war period[13] and its export drive has been a major factor in the last 30-year revolution in global trade. China's growing openness and integration into the global economy, and its efforts to progressively liberalise the trade system, has contributed to increasing its share of total world trade, from one to two per cent during 1975-1994. According to the Asian Development Bank, total trade as a share of China's GNP has increased from 11.6% (1975) to 29.1% (1985) to 40.7% (1994), and by over 251% during the 1975-1994 period. Preliminary data from the IMF shows that the Chinese trade drive continued into 1995; exports from China increased to a record US$149 billion, representing a 23% increase over 1994, while imports rose to US$129 billion, a 12% increase over 1994. The Bank projects that China's GDP will average 9.8% in 1995 and 8.9% in 1996, down from the 13% average growth rate during 1992-94. China's expected growth will continue to be dynamic, benefiting from strong trade performance and domestic economic activity

---

12 IMF, *World Outlook 1995*, p. 11.

13 For a detailed account of economic development in China during the post war period 1949-78, see; Chu-yuan Cheng (1982) *China's Economic Development: Growth and Structural Change*, Westview Press, Boulder; Gregory C. Chow (1985) *The Chinese Economy*, Harper & Row, New York; and Carl Riskin (1987) *China's Political Economy: The Quest for Development Since 1949*, Oxford University Press, New York.

arising from productivity gains, which have made substantial improvement in real incomes and living standards.[14]

China is also becoming a favoured tourist destination and is now ranked as the number five most popular destination for tourists in the world. Earnings from tourism have increased by an average of 30% per year during the 1990s. In 1995 alone, tourism earned China US$8.7 billion from 46.5 million tourist visits. By the Year 2000, earnings from tourism, both domestic and international, are expected to account for 5% of GDP, or US$41 billion per year, while tourism-related investment into China is expected to increase four-fold to US$80 billion.[15] So dynamic is China's march to economic development, China is touted as the "great growth pole of the 21st century."

7. RECENT PROGRESS IN WORLD TRADE

Global trade exploded during the latter part of the 1970s and has continued throughout the 1980s and 1990s. According to the IMF, the volume of total global trade increased at an annual average rate of 3.7% during the 1977-86 decade, averaged 5.5% during the 1987-93 period and jumped to 9.4% in 1994. The World Trade Organization (WTO) reports that world trade volume grew by 8% in 1995 and expects that global trade will expand by 7% in 1996.[16] Not surprisingly, exports have been the driving force in growing global trade volume. The last decade has been particularly active.

Analysis of IMF data confirms the dynamism of global trade. During the 30-year period 1965-1994, the US$-value of total world exports increased by an average of 81% per year, while imports increased by 73.5%. The greatest momentum occurred during the 1965-1974 decade, as global trade expanded by 36% per year on average, slowed to an annual average growth rate of 12% during 1975-1984, and then increased slightly to an annual average 13% growth rate over the latest 1985-1994 decade. The hottest region will continue to be Asia, with expected real GDP growth averaging 7.5% over the 1995-2000 period, while annual growth in per capita GDP is projected to grow by 6% into the new century. China is expected to continue driving this Asian economic growth.[17]

Table 18.3 reports some interesting findings. Firstly, Chinese exports rose by an impressive 31.6% in 1994 over 1993, assisted by effective devaluation of the yuan and

---

14 Asian Development Bank, *Outlook 1995/96.*

15 Quoted by the World Tourism Organization, "China profits from tourism", *Toronto Globe and Mail,* January 8, 1996, and "Tourism soars in China, racing ahead of GDP", *The Financial Post,* May 4, 1996, and "Tourism Receipts", *The Economist,* February 17, 1996, p. 104.

16 IMF, *World Outlook 1995,* p. 149, and the World Trade Organization, as reported in *The Economist,* April 6, 1996, p. 109.

17 IMF, *International Financial Statistics Yearbook 1995.* Calculated percentage changes based on US$-value of annual exports (fob) and imports (cif).

Table 18.3: Direction of China's Trade with NAFTA Countries

Year	Exports Annual Aver. Growth (%)	Exports from China Share (%) of total annual exports to:					Imports Annual Average Growth (%)	Imports to China Share (%) of total annual imports from:				
		USA	Canada	Mexico	NAFTA	Asia		USA	Can-ada	Mex-ico	NAFTA	Asia
1987	---	7.7	1.0	0.02	8.7	43.6	--	11.2	3.2	0.2	14.6	25.3
1988	20.6	7.2	0.8	0.03	8.0	46.9	28.0	12.0	3.4	0.3	15.7	28.4
1989	8.6	8.5	0.8	0.08	9.4	50.7	5.6	13.5	1.8	0.3	15.6	28.5
1990	18.8	8.7	0.7	0.2	9.6	53.4	-10.0	12.5	2.8	0.2	15.6	38.2
1991	15.0	8.8	0.8	0.1	9.7	57.1	19.2	12.8	2.6	0.3	15.7	41.7
1992	14.2	10.7	0.8	0.2	11.7	55.0	22.0	11.7	2.5	0.2	14.3	41.6
1993	13.0	18.7	1.3	0.2	20.2	36.8	35.0	10.3	1.3	0.1	11.8	34.7
1994	31.6	17.9	1.2	0.2	19.2	40.3	11.2	12.2	1.6	0.1	13.9	33.6

The US-Canada Free Trade Agreement was effective January 1, 1989 and the North American Free Trade Agreement (NAFTA) was effective as of January 1, 1994.

Source: IMF, *Direction of Trade Statistics Yearbook (1995)*, Washington. Calculated and rounded percentage changes. Based on US$ value of trade reported as IFS. Exports are (fob) and imports (cif).

Table 18.4: China's Leading Trade Partners, 1985-1994

	Per cent of Total Exports to		Per cent of Total Imports from	
	1985	1994	1985	1994
United States	9.3%	17.9%	14.8%	12.2%
Japan	20.8%	17.8%	31.0%	22.8%
Hong Kong	26.5%	26.8%	10.9%	8.2%
Europe	2.4%	2.6%	3.4%	5.0%
Asia	37.7%	40.3%	16.0%	33.6%

Source: IMF, *Direction of Trade Statistics Yearbook* (1991 and 1995). Data is reported as IFS, US$ millions. Calculated percentages.

stronger demand in main export markets. Imports increased by a modest 11.2% in 1994 compared to 1993, reflecting easing of domestic demand conditions and increase in the local currency cost of imports. As a result, China's trade and current-account balances moved from deficit to surplus in 1994. Secondly, the US is an increasingly popular market for Chinese exports; Chinese exports into the US more than doubled over the last decade, from 7.7% (1987) to 17.9% (1994). The growing penetration by Chinese exports is reflected by the doubling in share of China's exports into the NAFTA market, from 8.7% (1987) to 19.2% (1994).

On the import side, data for the last decade concludes that NAFTA economies have not been as equally successful in penetrating the Chinese domestic market, but rather, appear to have lost some of the momentum established in the last 1980s. In fact, exports from NAFTA countries have lost ground to Asia, particularly Canada, whose import share of the Chinese market continues to deteriorate. On balance, China has clearly succeeded in benefiting from more liberalised global trade and the growing NAFTA market: it is selling more to NAFTA members and is buying less from them.

Recent IMF data shown in Table 18.4, confirms that the largest penetration by Chinese exports was in the US market, which contributed to increasing the US$-value of Chinese exports by 259% during the 1985-94 period, or by an average of 26% per year. Over the same period, imports into China increased by 174%, or by an average of 17% per year, led by Asian exporters.

Table 18.5 reports total world, Chinese and NAFTA export and import trade. Although the average US$-value of China's annual export-import trade is substantially smaller than that of NAFTA, China's emergence as a global trader is evidenced in the exceptional growth of 342% in US$-value of exports over the 1985-94 decade. The US$-value of 1994 exports from NAFTA countries represented 16% of total global exports compared to 18% in 1985 and 1975. On the other hand, Chinese exports accounted for

Table 18.5: Total Export and Import Trade: China and NAFTA Economies (US $-value billions)

	Exports						Imports					
	1965	1975	1985	1990	1994	% chg 1985-94	1965	1975	1985	1990	1994	% chg 1985-94
World	$172.0	816.5	1,832.8	3,334.4	4,367.5	138%	$185.9	855.7	1,907.7	3,455.4	4,285.9	125%
China	$2.6	7.7	27.4	62.1	121.1	342%	$2.3	7.9	42.3	53.4	115.7	174%
NAFTA	$36.3	145.8	331.9	548.4	712.4	115%	$33.4	148.6	447.1	670.2	905.3	104%
USA	$26.7	108.9	218.8	393.6	512.5	134%	$23.2	105.9	352.5	517.0	689.2	96%
Canada	$8.4	34.1	91.0	127.6	165.4	82%	$8.6	36.1	80.6	123.2	155.1	92%
Mexico	$1.2	2.9	22.1	27.1	34.5	56%	$1.6	6.6	14.0	30.0	61.0	336%

Source: IMF, *International Financial Statistics Yearbook* (1995 and April 1996), Washington. Calculated and rounded percentage changes. Based on US$-value of trade, reported as IFS. Exports are (fob) and imports (cif).

3% of 1994 global exports, but in the span of two decades, that represents a threefold increase from just under one per cent in 1975 and a doubling from 1.5% in 1985.

More germane to the issue of China-NAFTA trade, Table 18.6 reports the direction of inter-country trade in 1987 and 1994, which adds further evidence on the growing Chinese trade penetration and the momentum of China's export drive into the NAFTA market. It is clear that major gains have been made by China in the NAFTA region - a doubling of its export share from 8.7% to 19.2% during the seven-year period, while imports from NAFTA economies into China actually declined, from 14.6% to 13.9%. Moreover, while only 1.8% of American exports went into the Chinese economy in 1994, 6% of American imports came from China in that same year. The share of China's exports into the American market over the 1987-94 period increased by eight percentage points, while the share of American imports into China increased by only one percentage point.

A similar trend in gains from trade are reflected in the data for the Canadian market; China has made some inroads in penetrating the Canadian import market, while Canadian exports to China actually declined by over 50%, to only 1.6% of total Chinese imports in 1994. On balance, the growing attractiveness of Chinese exports has placed China in a solid trade surplus position with NAFTA. China closed the deficit with the US and Mexico in 1992 and is now in a comfortable surplus, while it also continues to narrow its deficit with Canada.

8. WHAT HAS CONTRIBUTED TO CHINA'S SUCCESS?

There are a number of factors which will continue to be important in sustaining the future economic growth of China, five of which are of particular interest: investment and development of infrastructure, continuing foreign investment, macro policy to liberalise trade and harmonisation with international standards, the growing interest in entrepreneurship and market economy, and finally, the impact of exchange rates on competitiveness. Gross domestic investment as a per cent of GDP has averaged around 40% over the last few years, reflecting the strong investment trends now ongoing in China, particularly infrastructure development of transportation, electricity and telecommunications. For example, in 1995 alone, three major projects account for an estimated US$50 billion worth of infrastructure investment; the Beijing-Kowloon railway (US$20 bil), the Guangdong expressway (US$15 bil) and the first phase of the Three Gorges Dam on the Yangtze river (US$10 bil).[18]

18 Asian Development Bank, *Outlook 1995/96*, p. 80, and D.L. James (1995) "Can a Socialist Republic find Happiness Trading in a Capitalist World?", *Business Economics*, 30(2): 41-44.

Table 18.6: Inter-Country Trade: China - NAFTA, 1987 and 1994

		Exports (Share of total)					Imports (Share of total)				
		USA	Canada	Mexico	NAFTA	China	USA	Canada	Mexico	NAFTA	China
USA	1987	--	23.5	5.7	29.3	1.4	--	16.9	4.8	21.7	1.6
	1994	--	22.3	9.9	32.3	1.8	--	19.2	7.3	26.5	6.0
Canada	1987	74.3	--	0.4	74.7	1.1	66.0	--	1.1	67.1	0.7
	1994	80.5	--	0.4	80.9	1.0	65.8	--	2.3	68.1	2.0
Mexico	1987	66.4	1.5	--	67.9	0.6	64.7	2.9	--	67.6	0.4
	1994	80.4	5.5	--	85.9	0.2	70.6	1.0	--	71.6	0.3
China	1987	7.7	1.0	0.02	8.7	--	11.2	3.3	0.2	14.6	--
	1994	17.9	1.2	0.2	19.2	--	12.2	1.6	0.1	13.9	--

Source: IMF, *Direction of Trade (1995)*, Washington. Calculated and rounded percentages. Based on US$-values reported as DOTS. Exports are (fob) and imports (cif). Mexico data excludes maquiladora trade.

China's high domestic savings rate, coupled with growing foreign direct investment (FDI), are often cited as major factors in the dynamic economic success of China's economy over the last two decades. In fact, the domestic savings rate in China, averaging around 40% of GDP, is the world's highest and has played an important catalytical role in economic development.[19] Furthermore, China's rapid economic growth during the past few years, its large and lucrative domestic market and growing per capita income, have made it an attractive FDI destination. FDI inflows into China increased by 107% during 1991-92, by 131% over 1992-93 and by 31% in 1993-94, as FDI remained buoyant at US$34 billion.[20] Moreover, the growing trend of inter-regional direct investment will continue to make China the top foreign investment destination in the world into the new century. According to Wong (1995), in 1992, of the US$11.2 billion of FDI into China, 80% or US$8.7 billion, came from Hong Kong and Taiwan alone. FDI is expected to further increase as Hong Kong, South Korea and Japan continue to relocate their manufacturing industry into south China. As well, evidence of China's growing competitive advantage is reflected in the success of free trade zones such as Guangdong Province, where the estimated 1995 GDP growth was 15%[21] and where, according to Wong (1995), the per capita income of the 65 million populace, has doubled every three years. Over the long run, economic integration of China within the Asia-Pacific region will strengthen and serve to promote further inter-country investment and economic growth for all countries of the region.

Thirdly, an important requirement is the maintenance of sound macroeconomic policies to control inflation and chronic fiscal and current-account deficits. Like all emerging economies, China faces a number of obstacles. Rapid growth in recent years has challenged China to sustain growth while minimising the consequences of "overheating". China's high annual growth rates of 13% in 1992/93, impacted domestic prices and inflation rates jumped to 22% in 1994. A strengthening of stabilisation efforts

---

19 An important distinction should be made between domestic and national saving. National saving includes domestic saving, plus remittances from abroad and other net factor income flows, which can constitute a significant proportion of national income. Domestic saving tends to be greater than national saving, in countries with substantial interest payments on external debt. See "The Search for the Asian Manager", *The Economist*, March 9, 1996, survey p. 5.

20 There is significant controversy on the issue of FDI. Large capital FDI inflows may in fact, be a "mixed blessing". FDI can be effectively used to augment domestic investment and to accumulate foreign exchange reserves to accelerate economic growth. FDI inflows also provide an economy with access to contemporary technology. However, large capital inflows may create macroeconomic management problems and generate inflationary pressures. Inflation and a deteriorating current-account position, could send adverse signals to external investors and prices of financial and real estate assets could be subject to volatility. Furthermore, another factor to consider is the nature of external FDI, particularly whether investment is of a long term, enduring nature, or alternatively, whether FDI inflows reflect temporary shifts, taking advantage of short term profit opportunities. Data from the IMF, *World Outlook 1995*.

21 "Guangdong to keep growing", *The Financial Post*, May 4, 1996.

is projected to slow growth over the next few years and inflation is expected to continue its decline to average 13%.[22] China has continued its reform and liberalisation of its trade policy and has undertaken a number of trade and market related reforms to strengthen its bid for WTO membership. Tariffs have been lowered on over 5,000 commodities and China has cut its average import tariff rate from 35% to 23% as of April 1996.[23] Moreover, under an agreement on trade liberalisation reached with the US in October 1992, China agreed to remove the bulk of its import licensing and quota controls over the next five years. Recently, a new phase of economic reforms were introduced in 1994, aimed at tackling the need for more effective infrastructure and an ambitious agenda to develop and conform the legal and accounting practices to international standards. To remain attractive to foreign capital, China continued reforms in the financial market during 1994, notably reform of the Central Bank and the commercial banking sector.

Another factor which has contributed to China's economic growth has been the progressive liberalisation of private ownership and the subsequent blossoming of market economy. This "entrepreneurial" spirit in China is evident in the growing number of dynamic, medium-sized private and semi-private companies, which now account for over one third of China's annual output. In fact, during the 1985-1994 decade, while the share of state-owned enterprise declined from about 62% to 35% by 1994, the semi and private enterprise sector increased its share of total annual industrial production from under 5% to represent more than 15% in 1994. This trend is expected to continue, as more foreign joint ventures and direct FDI are attracted to China.[24]

During the last two decades, the exchange rate has been a powerful mechanism in making countries more attractive in the global marketplace, and China has been a major beneficiary. China has taken a number of steps to reform its exchange rate system. In January 1994 for example, a new managed-floating system was introduced, unifying the dual-rate structure and moving toward full current-account convertibility. Restrictions on purchase of foreign exchange were lifted for trade transactions and foreign exchange bank accounts are now obtainable.

Clearly, China has not been the only beneficiary of currency depreciation, but since the early 1990s, the attractiveness of Chinese export prices has not been lost on the American market. Table 18.7 demonstrates the gradual and progressive depreciation of the Chinese yuan to the US dollar, which has played an important role in China's export drive during the last two decades.

---

22 IMF, *World Outlook 1995*, p. 38.

23 China has been waiting for full GATT/WTO membership since 1987. See, "Industry in China: Under New Laws", *The Economist*, April 13, 1996, p. 62.

24 "The Search for the Asian Manager", *The Economist*, March 9, 1996, survey p. 19.

Table 18.7: International Currency Exchange Rates (end of calender year, annual averages)

	Chinese Yuan/US$	Canadian $/US$	Mexican Peso/US$
1975	1.9663	1.0164	12.500
1980	1.5303	1.1947	23.256
1985	3.2015	1.3975	371.700
1990	5.2221	1.1603	2.9454
1991	5.4342	1.1556	3.0710
1992	5.7518	1.2711	3.1154
1993	5.8000	1.3240	3.1059
1994	8.4462	1.4028	5.3250
1995	8.3174	1.3652	7.6425

Source: IMF, *International Financial Statistics Yearbook* 1995 and April 1996. In January 1986, a new peso was issued in Mexico. Exchange rates are quoted as end of period, average market rates.

9. THE GROWING TREND TO REGIONALISM

All countries have a future stake in a healthy, open-market world trading system and a number of developing and emerging countries in southeast Asia have embarked on programs of economic reform and trade liberalisation in recent years, which depend on the continuation of a liberal, multi-lateral global trading system. Moreover, within the Asian-Pacific region, there has been a deepening of integration and economic cooperation between economies and new trade groups such as ASEAN, APEC and EAEC, promote open regionalism to encourage freer trade and investment.[25] With the development of a substantial consumer base in southeast Asia, the regionalisation of production and consumption is bound to increase.

25 ASEAN was first established in 1967 and is the only formal trade agreement in the Asia-Pacific region. The East Asia Economic Caucus (EAEC) is regarded as a informal council, while the Asia-Pacific Economic Cooperation (APEC) group, which first met in 1989, is more of a political and economic forum advocating open regionalism. APEC is now an 18-member club, including Australia, Brunei, Canada, Chile, China, Hong Kong, Indonesia, Japan, Malaysia, Mexico, New Zealand, Papua New Guinea, the Philippines, Singapore, South Korea, Taiwan, Thailand and the United States.

China has benefited from this growing regional integration in Asia-Pacific; trade within Asia has grown at a much faster rate than has trade with the rest of the world, as shown in Table 3. Moreover, China's economic integration within the Asian-Pacific region has grown remarkably since 1978. According to Wong (1995), the Asia-Pacific region as an export market increased its share of annual Chinese exports, from 49% in 1978, to 65% in 1992, while over the same period, the Asia-Pacific region captured a larger share of the annual Chinese import market, from 32% to 51%. The growing integration of the Chinese economy, with its large population and resource base, into the Asia-Pacific region, promises to further enhance the region's overall economic growth potential.

While China was moving towards closer integration within Asia, the NAFTA economies were following a similar path. In fact, North America increasingly accounts for a growing share of its own exports. Intra-NAFTA trade data reported by GATT in Table 18.8 below, confirms that a growing proportion of exports originating in NAFTA countries is exported to other NAFTA member countries.

Table 18.8: Intra-NAFTA Merchandise Trade by Destination and Origin

	1963	1973	1983	1993
Merchandise Exports (fob) to NAFTA Destination (US$ bil)	$8.7	$36.4	$106.0	$259.5
Intra-NAFTA exports as a % share of total world exports	29.6%	37.3%	38.0%	42.6%
Merchandise Imports (cif) of NAFTA Origin (US$ bil)	$8.6	$36.6	$114.3	$245.3
Intra-NAFTA imports as a % share of total world imports	37.0%	39.1%	34.5%	33.4%

Source: GATT, *International Trade 1994*. Adjusted to include Mexico. Mexican data includes maquiladora exports.

On the import side however, it appears that NAFTA members are buying less from each other, as demonstrated by the declining share of intra-NAFTA imports since 1973. This lends further evidence of China's penetration of NAFTA import markets, particularly in the US. Referring again to Table 18.5, the US$-value of China's exports over the 1975-85 decade increased by 258%, to reach US$27 billion in 1985 and then to increase four-fold to US$121 billion by 1994. Furthermore, China's increasing share of NAFTA imports, from 8.7% to 19.2% (1987-94), as shown in Table 18.3, reconfirms that most of the shift away from intra-NAFTA import trade, is likely owing to Chinese penetration of the NAFTA import market.

10. GROWING ANTI-CHINA SENTIMENT IN THE U.S.

American trade policy with China appears to be incurring some difficulties of late. The most closely watched bilateral trade deficit in the US is with China, but the US and China can not agree on the size of this deficit. Some recent work conducted by the US-China Business Council, reports that the US overestimates its deficit with China by as much as 50%. China contends that not only is American protectionism "deliberately compromising statistical integrity, but that the US is arbitrarily assigning the country of origin to China, as a penalty". According to the trade body, the impact of the added-value margin for Chinese exports through Hong Kong, which has grown from 16% in the late 1980s to 25% in 1995, is typically ignored by the US. The Business Council contends that the 1995 trade gap is around US$23 billion, rather that US$35 billion reported by Washington.[26]

This type of "problem" highlights the growing frustration in the US, concerning the direction of its trade policy. Schott and Hufbauer (1993) suggest that other US "trade policy torpedoes" against China are gaining prominent attention. While the US affords MFN treatment to China,[27] it is subject to annual review, giving some room for the growing and vocal protectionist movement to have influence on the degree of bilateral trade liberalisation. Recent review of MFN status has produced rather virulent warnings from the US concerning Chinese trade policies and threats of significant trade sanctions "as a weapon to bully China into compliance".[28] Schott and Hufbauer also suggest that the US will seek ways to continue to discriminate against China, both in bilateral trade and in foreign policy, until its political regime becomes more democratic and its economy is more market-oriented.

Despite the MFN status conditionally afforded China, and its continued penetration of the American import market, trade with the US has not been without some cost. According to GATT, the total US$-value of import duties levied on China has

---

26 "US trade gap with China Challenged", *The Globe and Mail*, February 19, 1996.

27 China was first granted MFN status by the United States in 1979 by means of an annual waiver of the Jackson-Vanik amendment to the 1974 *Trade Act*, which stipulates that extension and renewal of MFN status is contingent on existence and application of freedom of emigration legislation.

28 See for example, "U.S. set to impose tariffs on China", *The Globe and Mail*, May 15, 1996, and "Beijing warned on trade backlash", *The Globe and Mail*, May 22, 1996.

skyrocketed. In 1986 for example, China paid US$487 million in import duties, or about 3.7% of all import duties collected by the US in that year. By 1992, just six years later, the value of import duties levied on China grew to just under US$2 billion, representing 11.4% of all import duties collected in that year. Overall, China paid 302% more import duties for access to the US market in those six years. China now has the dubious distinction of being the leading contributor of import duties to the US Treasury. Although China is not alone in paying higher import duties, it has faced the largest burden. Mexico paid 48% more import duties between 1986-92, while Canada now pays about 24% less in import duties.[29]

Perhaps little is more controversial however, than the growing application of Section 301 of the *Trade Act*. Popularly referred to as "Super-301", this Section of the *Act* provides authority to introduce trade measures in response to a foreign country's trade practices, if they are perceived to damage US export interests. The US does apply Section 301; between 1991-93 alone, thirteen cases were active. Canada was not excluded from Section 301 sanctions, as sanctions were taken against Canada in June 1990 concerning beer and in October 1991 over softwood lumber. China has also faced Section 301 sanctions; in May 1991 [special] Section 301 negotiations concerning intellectual property rights guided China to overhaul its legal framework on this issue. In October of that same year, US retaliatory actions resulted in multi-lateral commitment by China to remove the majority of active non-tariff barriers by December 1995. More recently, the intellectual property issue has resurfaced, fuelling the bilateral trade dispute and American threats of sanctions and greater import tariffs on Chinese imports.[30] Section 301 is criticised for its potential of uni-lateral American retaliation and for being discriminatory, in that it encourages erosion of the MFN principle in favour of bilateral agreements, which ultimately increase the costs associated with trade. While China is not openly vocal, it is a victim of some negative backlash in the US and although Chinese exports continue to flow into the American market, the growing friction between China and the US places increasing liberalisation of international trade at risk.

---

29 GATT, (1994) *Trade Policy Review: USA*, 2: 113.

30 GATT, *Trade Policy Review: USA*, vol.1, 1994, pp.123-124. China's copyright and patent protection for pharmaceuticals was the object of [special] Sec.301 investigation in May/91. A Memorandum of Understanding, was signed under which China agreed to a major overhaul of its laws on intellectual property rights. China's market access was later investigated in October 1991. A list of US$3.9 billion of Chinese exports were to be made subject to additional tariffs of up to 100%, unless China removed import restrictions before Oct/92. Recent US criticism concerning Chinese policy on intellectual property rights maintains that copyright piracy by China costs American business US$2.3 billion a year. See, "U.S. set to impose tariffs on China", *The Globe and Mail*, May 15, 1996.

11. WHAT DOES THE FUTURE HOLD?

During the post war period, the progressive liberalisation of multi-lateral trade, coupled with declining tariff rates, have resulted in remarkable growth in global trade and real improvements in the standard of living. Yet, are there reasons to worry that the growth of regional trade blocs might contribute to less global expansion and integration in the next 10-20 years? From the viewpoint of global welfare, the key issue is whether this growing interest and participation in regional trade agreements is causing world trade to become more restrictive. The growing strength of regional trade groups certainly raises the possibility of additional acrimony in trade disputes between regions, escalating protectionist pressures and gradually eroding the multi-lateral trading system. And in fact, it is possible that those benefiting from the preferential trading arrangements within regional blocs like NAFTA, may strengthen their opposition to multi-lateral trade and be tempted to divert protectionist sentiment towards developing countries like China.

Will the growing trend to regionalism endanger multi-lateral, liberal global trade, or can trade harmonisation and liberalisation be achieved within the context of regional arrangements?

The answers to this issue are however, not immediately evident. In the one camp, the argument suggests that the dangers posed by trade arrangements like NAFTA, are not that the US will become more insular or regionalist. Rather, the mounting dominance of NAFTA may be used by the US to "bully" other parts of the world, in ways that may generate conflicts and retaliation, as suggested by Snape (1993).

Although the relationship between world trade and economic growth remains strong, the danger is that if trading blocs such as NAFTA or the European Community, continue to expand, Asian economies like China, could be discriminated against, having no preferential arrangements with these major trading regions. Moreover, if new trade barriers are imposed against non-members, using rules of origin, local content, new technology standards or other administered regulations of trade, dynamic economies like China will face greater obstacles to trade.

On the other hand, a more positive interpretation on the impacts of regionalism, is put forth by Lawrence (1991), who suggests that this growing trend to regional trade blocs is, in fact only a temporary state of affairs, which is itself, complimentary to liberalisation of the multi-lateral trading system. Lawrence maintains that the dynamics of regional integration creates a larger market and positively impacts income growth and competitiveness, which in turn, generates greater export opportunities for its members. Moreover, the improving terms of trade will encourage greater liberalisation of multi-lateral trade, to take advantage of members' new competitiveness. At the same time, non-members will try and negotiate lower tariff rates in order to gain access to this larger, prospering regional import market. Lawrence would suggest that on balance, regionalism could in fact, make all parties better off.

The debate on the potential of regionalism as concerns the future of the multi-lateral trading system, reflects the dichotomous nature of today's trade practices; free trade in some areas but protectionism in others. The rise of regional trade blocs, to the extent that they result in trade barriers to non-members, neatly enables a country to exhibit both free trade and protectionist behaviour at the same time. This pertinent insight by Koch (1989), captures what is perhaps the greatest threat posed by the drift away from liberalised, open multi-lateral trade. The combination of exclusionary regional trade blocs and protectionist policy, would indeed, be "poisonous" for countries like China and a threat to its future prosperity. How trade with Asia-Pacific countries evolves during the end of this decade, will demonstrate whether regional blocs can sustain an open, multi-lateral trade system.

As the global economy becomes progressively more regionalised, how will members of different trade arrangements behave within their respective blocs? What will happen to the notion of independent trade policy or to the principle of liberal, multi-lateral trade, as more and more countries join different trade groups? Canada's trade policy has recently faced this dilemma concerning potential American sanctions for not accommodating its policy on Cuba. This issue of potentially incompatible trade policy could lead to significant friction between countries participating in preferential regional trading arrangements. Each new agreement could undermine the value of preferential access granted to other countries under different agreements and lead to growing tension. Schott (1989) notes that this problem has arisen regarding the US-Israel FTA, with Israel critical that Canada obtained better terms in the US-Canada FTA concerning dispute settlement and provisions on trade in services. Moreover, a proliferation of regional preferential trade agreements could give rise to practical problems, resulting from overlapping agreements including mis-matches in phasing of tariff reductions, different rulings in dispute settlement judgements and conflicting enforcement on rules of origin.

How will countries contend with the conflicts and pressures on their domestic trade policy, posed by issues of high unemployment, persistent debt and deficits, or the political preferences of member countries? One danger is a return to the easy solution of protectionism. The US may be especially vulnerable to protectionist pressures, as suggested in a recent 1995 survey of NAFTA business leaders, which found that American executives hold the least favourable attitude towards NAFTA.[31] Any move to protectionist preference in the US, will certainly impact China. The ongoing trade dispute between the US and China, casts a shadow on China's growth prospects and doubts linger over its WTO membership. Increasing pressure on China may be forthcoming from the US, to reduce its trade barriers to American products, in light of recent results that China's trade surplus with the US widened to US$16.7 billion in 1995 from US$5.3 billion in 1994, and that Chinese exports rose by 23% in 1995, from US$121 to US$149 billion during the year.[32]

---

31 Survey conducted in December 1995 for the Canadian Bank of Montreal, "NAFTA popular, survey finds", *The Globe and Mail*, February 23, 1996.

32 In Asia: "China's trade surplus widens", *The Globe and Mail*, January 18, 1996.

Moreover, aside from the increasingly popular escape into protectionism, a growing uneasiness seems to hover over discussions on likely developments after 1997, when Hong Kong reverts to Chinese authority. Some authors, Goodhart and Xu (1996) and Wong (1995), have recently expanded the issue into one of "Greater China Economic Area", encompassing China, Hong Kong and Taiwan, which could soon become the world's largest economy in [absolute] purchasing power terms. A larger and more competitive China may further fuel protectionist flames, as it challenges the growing domination of regional arrangements like NAFTA.

China will continue to be the world's most vibrant economy, offering unmatched opportunities to all its trade partners. China now accounts for 25% of the world's purchasing power, set to increase to 33% by the turn of the century. The emerging middle-class consumer market in China, offers the US a promising US$3 billion market.[33] In fact, the US has every reason to expand trade with rapidly growing China, but according to Bosworth (1996) and Drysdale and Garnaut (1993), existing political issues are compromising the tremendous economic gains from trade between the two nations. The Chinese market is ripe for US technical and industrial expertise as well as for the global export products the US is so well known for. At the same time, the US market, the world's largest, offers China numerous opportunities to expand trade. Both markets need each other and as Bosworth (1996) so aptly points-out, it is in the mutual interest of both China and the US to relax their trade conflicts and work together to promote harmonious trade policies, which aim to expand economic welfare in both North American and in the Asia-Pacific region. The US could begin to ease the path to more harmonious trade relations, by affording China permanent MFN status and by expediting the process of China's entry into the World Trade Organization.

All predictions are inherently, hazardous. But one thing is certain ... China will continue its march to economic development well into the new century. Trade has been the engine of Chinese growth and promises to achieve new heights during the coming years. Indeed, the global pattern of trade has been made better off by the emergence of China and the extraordinary opportunities it presents. There can be no turning back now.

REFERENCES

Anderson, K. (1991) "Is an Asian-Pacific Trade Bloc Next?", *Journal of World Trade*, 25(4): 27-40.

Anderson, K. (1993) "NAFTA, Excluded Pacific Rim Countries and the Multi-lateral Trading System", pp. 33-52 in Cushing, R.G. (ed.) *The Challenge of NAFTA*, University of Texas Press, Austin.

---

33 "Canadian Exporters in for flat '96; study", *The Globe and Mail*, April 30, 1996, and "The Search for the Asian Manager", *The Economist*, March 9, 1996, survey p. 23.

Anderson, K. and Blackhurst, R. (ed.) (1993) *Regional Integration and the Global Trading System*, Harvestor Wheatsheaf, London.

Appleton, B. (1994) *Navigating NAFTA: A Concise User's Guide to the North American Free Trade Agreement*, Carswell Thomson, Ontario.

Asian Development Bank (1995) *Key Indicators 1995*, Oxford University Press, New York.

Asian Development Bank (1995) *Outlook 1995 and 1996*, Oxford University Press, New York.

Baker, R.D. (1993) "NAFTA and US Political Relations with Australia and New Zealand: Where's the Beef?", pp.289-301 in Cushing, R.G. (ed.), *The Challenge of NAFTA*, University of Texas Press, Austin.

Baldwin, R.E. (1992) "Measurable Dynamic Gains from Trade", *Journal of Political Economy*, 100(1): 162-174.

Bhagwati, J.N. (1988) *Protectionism*, MIT Press, Cambridge.

Bosworth, B.P. (1996) "Growing Pains: Trade Frictions Corrode the US-Asian Relationship", *The Brookings Review*, 14(1): 4-9.

Canadian Chamber of Commerce (1991) "The North American Free Trade Agreement and its Implications for Canada's Relationship with the Countries of Asia-Pacific", Pacific Economic Cooperation Conference (PECC), Fifth Trade Policy Forum, Kuala Lumpur, August.

Corden, M. (1971) *Protection*, Claredon Press, Oxford.

Cushing, R.G. (ed.) (1993) *The Challenge of NAFTA: North America, Australia, New Zealand and the World Trade Regime*, University of Texas Press, Austin.

de la Torre, A. and Kelly, M.R. (1992) *Regional Trade Arrangements*, International Monetary Fund, Washington.

Drysdale, P. and Garnaut, R. (1993) "NAFTA and the Asia-Pacific Region: Strategic Responses", pp. 103-122 in Cushing, R.G. (ed.), *The Challenge of NAFTA*, University of Texas Press, Austin.

Elek, A. (1992) "Trade Policy Options for the Asia-Pacific Region in the 1990s: The Potential of Open Regionalism", *American Economic Review*, 82(2): 74-78.

GATT (1994) *Trade Policy Review: USA*, Vols. 1 and 2, Geneva.

GATT (1992) *Trade Policy Review: Canada*, Vols. 1 and 2, Geneva.

GATT (1993) *Trade Policy Review: Mexico*, Vols. 1 and 2, Geneva.

GATT (1994) *International Trade 1994*, Geneva.

Goodhart, C. and Xu, C. (1996) "The Rise of China as an Economic Power", *National Institute Economic Review*, February, pp. 56-80.

Holick, G.N. and Debusk, F.A. (1992) "The Functioning of the Free Trade Agreement Dispute Resolution Panels", in Waverman, L. (ed.), *Negotiating and Implementing a North American Free Trade Agreement*, The Fraser Institute, Vancouver.

International Monetary Fund (1995) *International Financial Statistical Yearbook 1995*, Washington.

International Monetary Fund (1995) *Direction of Trade Statistics Yearbook 1995*, Washington.

International Monetary Fund (1995) *World Economic Outlook 1995*, Washington, May and October.

Johnson, H.G. (1965) "An Economic Theory of Protectionism, Tariff Bargaining and the Formation of Customs Unions", *Journal of Political Economy*, 73(3): 256-282.

Koch, J.V. (1989) "An Economic Profile of the Pacific Rim", *Business Horizons*, March-April, pp. 18-25.

Kreinin, M.E. and Plummer, M.G. (1992) "Effects of Economic Integration on ASEAN and the Asian NIEs", *World Development*, 20(9): 1345-1366.

Krueger, A.O. (1993) "The Effects of Regional Trading Blocs on World Trade", pp. 21-32, in Cushing, R.G. (ed.) *The Challenge of NAFTA*, University of Texas Press, Austin.

Langdon, Frank (1995) "Canada's Goal in the Asia-Pacific", *The Pacific Review*, 8(2): 383-399.

Lawrence, R.Z. (1991) "Emerging Regional Arrangements: Building Blocs or Stumbling Blocs?", in R. O'Brien (ed.) *Finance and the International Economy*, Oxford University Press, London.

McKinney, J.A. (1993) "Implications of NAFTA for Japan's Trade Relations", pp.123-135 in Cushing, R.G. (ed.) *The Challenge of NAFTA*, University of Texas Press, Austin.

Randall, L. (1995) "The Changing Structure of Mexico", *Challenge*, 38(2): 12-29.

Schott, J.J. (ed.) (1989) *Free Trade Areas and US Trade Policy*, Institute for International Economics, Washington.

Schott, J.J. (1991) "Trading Blocs and the World Trading System", *The World Economy*, 14(2): 1-17.

Schott, J.J. and Hufbauer, G.C. (1993) "Implications of NAFTA for US Trade Policy in the Pacific Basin", pp. 145-157 in Cushing, R.G. (ed.) *The Challenge of NAFTA*, University of Texas Press, Austin.

Schwanen, D. (1994) *Trade, Jobs and Investment in the New Economy: What we have learned from the 1988-93 period*, C.D. Howe Institute, Toronto.

Snape, R.H. (1993) "How Should Australia Respond to NAFTA?", pp. 193-224 in Cushing, R.G. (ed.) *The Challenge of NAFTA*, University of Texas Press, Austin.

Tseng, W. (1994) "Economic Reform in China: A New Phase", World Bank Occasional Paper No.114, Washington.

Weintraub, S. (1993) "NAFTA and the Realities of Trade Regimes and Regionalism in the 1990's", pp. 321-327 in Cushing, R.G. (ed.) *The Challenge of NAFTA*, University of Texas Press, Austin.

Wong, J. (1995) "China in the Dynamic Asia-Pacific Region", *The Pacific Review*, 8(4): 617-635.

World Bank (1994) *China: Foreign Trade Reform*, Washington.

World Bank (1995) *World Development Report 1995: Workers in an Integrating World*, Washington.

World Bank (1995a) *China: Macroeconomic Stability in a Decentralized Economy*, Washington.

Young, M. (1993) "NAFTA and the Future of US Trade Policy in the Asia-Pacific Region", pp. 139-144 in Cushing, R.G. (ed.), *The Challenge of NAFTA*, University of Texas Press, Austin.

INDEX

A

B

C

D

E

F

G

H

I

J

K

L